A HISTORY TODAY BOOK

CONFRONTING THE NAZI PAST

New Debates on Modern German History

———

Lc
nc
ᴧ

Edited by

MICHAEL BURLEIGH

COLLINS & BROWN

First published in Great Britain in 1996
by Collins & Brown Limited
London House
Great Eastern Wharf
Parkgate Road
London SW11 4NQ

A CIP catalogue record for this book
is available from the British Library

ISBN 1 85585 183 0

Commissioning Editor: Juliet Gardiner
Typeset by Falcon Oast Graphic Art
Printed and bound in Great Britain

CONTENTS

INTRODUCTION

S TUDIES OF MODERN GERMAN HISTORY have reached not so much a
crossroads, as one of those motorway junctions where the driver circles around aimlessly amidst the bewildering choice of exit routes. In the
1960s and 1970s conventional diplomatic or narrative political history
was challenged by the structural models developed by advocates of
history as social 'science'. In the 1980s these were themselves partially
displaced by a new generation of historians concerned with, for example,
gender or mentalities; with the local, and some would say the trivial,
rather than the general; or with the repressive potentialities of supposedly
'progressive' disciplines such as medicine or psychiatry, with there not
being very much to distinguish doctors from policemen. It is too early to
speak with much certainty concerning how recent events — the collapse
of Communism; the resurgence of ethnic nationalism across Eastern
Europe and the former Soviet Union; the reunification of Germany; or,
to be more parochial, the self-immolation of such gurus of the 1980s as
Althusser, de Man, or Foucault — will influence the future writing of the
subject. Judging from very recent trends, the big picture — as distinct
from the current penchant for the minute, the marginal or the quirky —
is going to be dominated by the revival of forms of 'discourse' akin to the
totalitarian theories that were modish in the 1950s. The writing on the
wall can be seen from a few recent developments. Recently, the German
Volkswagen Foundation invited tenders for a vast research project on
'European Dictatorships in the Twentieth Century'. Among the project's
major concerns will be the 'comparative' study of the 'two German dictatorships', as if there is some intellectually serious comparison to be
made between the regimes of Hitler and Honecker or between the Stasi
and the Gestapo. According to the new director of the authoritative
Institut für Zeitgeschichte in Munich, the Nazi period will gradually lose
its salience in the collective memory of contemporary Europeans, being
supplanted by the 'much longer lasting experience of suffering' under the
Communists. A rather sinister example of this gradual displacement of
emphasis can be seen in the spate of memorials established to remember
those former Nazis imprisoned, and in many cases killed, after the war
in the special camps which the Soviet secret police created in former

concentration camps. At Sachsenhausen a new memorial now commemor-
ates those who 'after 1945 . . . sacrificed their freedom, health and life
in resistance' as well as those who died in the camp during the Nazi
period — a singularly distasteful aggregation of victims and persecutors.

Many of the broad developments described above have been reflected
in the ways in which historians treat the Nazi period which, because of
its unique character, has generated not only an enormous volume of
scholarship, but also a quasi-philosophical literature and, indeed, many
notable artistic products such as films, novels and paintings. Academic
historians do not enjoy a monopoly of this subject in the way they do
with other periods of history. Indeed, even among academic historians it
is far from agreed whether the period of the Third Reich is 'history' in
the sense that, to take an example often used, the religious conflicts of sixteenth-century France are, undoubtedly, 'history'.

During the 1980s, while the *Historikerstreit*, or 'historians' dispute' —
with its explicit attempt to relativise Nazi barbarities — occupied all and
sundry, the eminent German historian Martin Broszat suggested that
after forty years it was time to go beyond what had become a blandly
routine black and white condemnation of the evils of Nazism, and to
begin assembling a more complex picture giving due consideration to the
predominantly grey areas of human behaviour during that period as
revealed by new social history approaches, and to continuities between
the Third Reich and the post-war Federal Republic. Broszat explained his
plea for the 'historisation' of the Nazi period or, in other words, for the
recovery of conventional historical 'distance' in the following passage:

> As I see it, the danger of suppressing this period consists not only in the
> customary practice of forgetting, but rather, in this instance — almost in
> paradoxical fashion — likewise in the fact that one is too overtly 'con-
> cerned' for didactic reasons, about this chapter in history. As a result, what
> happens is that an arsenal of lessons and frozen 'statuary' are pieced
> together from the original, authentic continuum of this era; these increas-
> ingly take on an independent existence. Particularly in the second and third
> generation, they then intrude to place themselves in front of the original
> history — and are finally, in naive fashion, understood and misunderstood
> as being the actual history of the time.

Broszat's 'plea' provoked considerable criticism from a number of
Israeli scholars, not surprisingly alert at the time of the *Historikerstreit* to
any attempts to adjust perceptions of the Nazi period. Sustained criticism

came from Saul Friedländer, one of the most intellectually sophisticated historians of the Nazi period working anywhere. Friedländer drew attention to some unfortunate similarities between Broszat's apparent concern with conceptual 'taboos' and the no-holds-barred approach of Ernst Nolte and Andreas Hillgruber, wondering quite where the line lay between Broszat's desire to restore the grey areas and Hillgruber's 'empathetic' identification with German soldiers allegedly holding back barbaric Bolsheviks from the frontiers of a western civilisation, which included Auschwitz. He was sharply critical too of attempts to discover normal patterns of evolution in Nazi Germany through parallels between, say, the welfare schemes of the German Labour Front and the British Beveridge Report, a subject that we will return to. Most profoundly, Friedländer argues that, given the universal relevance of Nazi Germany, the questions German historians wish to pose in order to come to terms with their own history or present society, should not preclude the very different concerns of others also affected by Nazism. As Friedländer says, 'the same past may mean something else to the victims of Nazism, whoever they may be, and for them, there are other, no less legitimate, modes of historicising the era'.

The remainder of this introduction is devoted to showing how for many people the Nazi period is not 'history', still less a period they remember for its 'modernising' impact, its 'normality', or its similarity to the United States or Bolshevik Russia. Popular perceptions of the period may for once have greater veracity than the increasingly febrile constructions of some academic historians, whose writings have an unreality akin to that of some branches of theology. All of the essays in this book represent original contributions commissioned from leading researchers in the field, working in Britain, Germany, Israel and the United States. None of the contributors belongs to a self-conscious historical 'school', or self-styled 'new' generation of scholars, and some of them would, no doubt respectfully, agree only to differ regarding their interpretations of the subject.

The desire of some historians to treat the Nazi period as 'history' immediately encounters considerable resistance when it cuts across the experiences of people directly affected by Nazi policies. For the latter, Nazism is not a matter of academic contemplation; but rather something which explains why they have no relatives or children; why they are chronically ill or have severe psychological problems; or why they live in Britain, Canada, Israel or the USA rather than Central Europe. The argument that the Nazis were in the business of modernising German society or defending Western civilisation from an 'Asiatic' barbarism whose political system their own paradoxically resembled, cuts little ice among those whose lives were shattered during that period.

One very large category of such people is that of former 'foreign workers', some of the seven million people, for the most part forcibly removed to work in Germany during the war. Almost half of them came from Poland or the Soviet Union, there being about 600,000 survivors alive in Poland alone today. Their collective experience consisted of appalling maltreatment at the bottom of the Nazis racial hierarchy; wages (in so far as they were paid at all), deliberately pegged below the levels paid to Germans; no provision for insurance, health care or pensions; and discrimination by the German population at large. The story of their quest for compensation is complex, and several factors contributed to their neglect. Firstly, the enormity of the Holocaust and the priority given to compensation agreements with Israel and the Jewish Claims Conference, led to the *de facto* marginalisation of other groups of victims. Secondly, wholescale plundering by 'Displaced Persons' in Germany after the war, and the mass exodus of ethnic Germans from the Communist states of Eastern Europe in the late 1940s, were deemed to be either compensation enough or a commensurate crime by many sectors of the German population. Finally, in a calculated move designed to reduce the enormous sums likely to result from individual claims, the West German authorities insisted on purely inter-governmental reparations. Supported by the Western Allies, who feared the economic and political consequences of a defeated Germany drained of its meagre resources, the West German government thus successfully managed to exclude from compensation by far the largest group of persons affected. The Soviet Union's decision — 'in agreement with the government of the People's Republic of Poland' — in August 1953 to waive any further reparations from the German Democratic Republic was interpreted by the government in Bonn as applying to the whole of Germany.

A further legal fiction was introduced to insulate private sector concerns from former 'foreign workers' seeking compensation. Although many firms had clearly actively solicited 'foreign workers', they were now deemed to have been merely 'proxies of the Reich' with the State being the 'quasi employer'. Approximately one third of all those employed in the armaments industry in 1944 were 'foreign workers', and in many private concerns the number of 'foreign workers' was between

50 and 70 per cent of the total workforce. The argument against compensation was that these concerns would pay fewer taxes which, in turn, would diminish the capacity of the Federal Republic to take an active part in the NATO alliance, to pay Israel and the Jewish Claims Conference, to contribute development aid to the Third World, and so on. Pressed to pay by their Western European allies, the Federal government eventually concluded 'voluntary' bilateral compensation agreements with eleven West European states worth DM876 million. The interests of German Ostpolitik and Polish restrictions on ethnic German would-be migrants eventually led to an agreement with Poland. In 1975 a deal was struck by Helmut Schmidt and Edward Gierek which consisted of a loan at favourable rates of interest and a one-off payment to cover pension claims, albeit at Polish rather than West German levels. Schmidt sarcastically noted that claims were addressed solely to the Federal Republic, 'as if the Germans living today in the GDR had absolutely nothing to do with it'. No deals were done with the Soviet Union, partly because the level of repression directed against former prisoners of war and civilian workers deemed 'collaborators' by the Soviet state would have made such claims embarrassing. The Federal Republic continued to refuse compensation to individuals.

Some of Germany's vast industrial concerns also refuse such compensation, despite corporate profits exceeding the budgets of some Third World countries, and an EEC directive recommending that they compensate former 'foreign workers'. Only very recently has Volkswagen (annual turnover DM68,000 million) decided to pay DM12 million to set up cultural and youth exchange facilities in countries that once supplied 'foreign workers'. It refuses to compensate individuals. The manner in which the concern recruited 'foreign workers', prisoners of war and concentration camp inmates and the conditions in which they lived, worked and in some cases died, are discussed in the chapter by the Wolfsburg historian Klaus-Jörg Siegfried. Like many major businesses, Volkswagen also invests in its own corporate history, commissioning the widely regarded contemporary historian Hans Mommsen to write what – when it appears – will clearly be an important social history of a major manufacturing and armaments firm intimately involved with the Nazi regime, rather than just an exercise in corporate vanity publishing.

Unlike many business histories, which tend to be commissioned as part of the firm's public relations, and read perfunctorily for references to oneself or to the founding 'geniuses', Mommsen's book is going to receive a very close reading, at least judging by the public furore that accompanied the recent publication of an interim report on the findings of his team, which was like an action replay of the scandal that in 1986 ensued after the publication of an official 'business history' to mark the centenary of the rival automotive giant Daimler-Benz. Alternative and radical journalists accused Mommsen of whitewashing Ferdinand Porsche, Volkswagen's founder, and suggested that the three million Deutschmarks which the project has so far cost, could have been better spent compensating some of the surviving 'foreign workers'. His attempts to present a balanced interpretation of Porsche's wartime record were oddly at variance with the willingness of Volkswagen executives to damn Porsche as an 'amoral technocrat'. Indeed, one of the more ironic aspects of the affair was the way in which the Porsche family was reduced to citing the firm's official historian to defend Ferdinand Porsche from criticisms being made by members of Volkswagen's present board of directors.

Although the charge of whitewashing the concern's history can be dismissed out of hand, it is not so easy to explain to many outraged former 'foreign workers', and concerned citizens of Wolfsburg, Mommsen's claim that during the war the Volkswagen workforce was 'a multicultural society', or his rejection of compensation to individuals because of (his) anxieties about 'manifestations of secondary corruption'. In an almost classic illustration of the difficulties that 'historicisation' can encounter when it collides with experience and memory, Joseph Rovan, an emeritus professor of German history at the Sorbonne and a former inmate of Dachau observed in a letter to *Die Zeit* regarding Mommsen:

> That a 'respected' historian could still defend his insensitive blunder despite the anger which his use of the words 'multicultural society' to describe the emaciated, starving, demoralised mass of foreign workers, Soviet POWs, and concentration camp inmates occasioned, is further proof of the inability of the historian to grasp what happened.

Volkswagen continues to reimburse those Germans who in the 1930s regularly saved in anticipation of one day owning a 'people's car'.

Sinti and Roma are a further group of victims of the Nazi regime who still experience considerable difficulties obtaining any form of compensation. An estimated five hundred thousand Sinti and Roma (or 'Gypsies', to use the word they keenly resent) perished in the *Porajmos*, the Roma word for the Nazi Holocaust. Persecuted under the Communist regimes of Eastern Europe, they have become one of the principal targets for aggression both in the 'democratic' successor states, and as refugees in Western Europe, most recently in the disgraceful occurrences in Rostock's Lichtenhagen a few years ago where two hundred of them were hounded out by a mob of alienated and murderous working-class bootboys with the encouragement of many of the ordinary inhabitants. They have experienced great difficulties in securing compensation for their suffering under the Nazis. The dice have been loaded against them for several reasons. Compensation claims tend to be acknowledged in cases where there was material loss or deliberate retardation of educational and professional prospects. Such a system clearly does not favour the propertyless; people without conventionally structured careers; or those who learn their 'life-skills' — whether as craftsmen or entertainers — within the family rather than in schools or colleges.

More significantly, compensation was withheld from Sinti and Roma because of the continuation of 'anti-Gypsy' prejudices after the war. In January 1956 the West German Federal Supreme Court decided that 'Gypsies' were fundamentally 'asocial' because of their nomadic way of life and allegedly 'criminal' inclinations. The court based this decision on the observation that Nazi laws against Sinti and Roma were not substantially different from similar legislation in both Imperial and Weimar Germany. Instead of concluding that the legislation from earlier periods was also inherently discriminatory because of its collective character, the Supreme Court used its existence to prove the normality of measures introduced by the Nazis. Following the logic of its decision as to what constituted legitimate police measures, the court also decided that Sinti and Roma had only become victims of racial persecution following the issuing of the so-called 'Auschwitz Decree' on 1 March 1943 which dispatched them to the extermination camp. These were far from being merely academic or jurisprudential matters. In 1957 a 'Gypsy' woman who had emigrated to Belgium in 1939 was denied compensation because the courts could not determine whether her flight had been provoked by Nazi persecution. A year later another 'Gypsy' was refused redress for false arrest by the Nazis, because neither his sedentary way of life nor regular employment allowed the courts to deduce racial persecution as the only logical explanation remaining. Most disgracefully, in 1961 a 'Gypsy' falsely imprisoned in 1938 for being 'asocial' — he owned two properties and had no criminal record — was denied compensation on the extraordinary grounds that his arrest might have been mistaken. The courts also exhibited in-built prejudices against Sinti and Roma as witnesses, with lawyers and judges making off-the-cuff comments which, had they been directed against Jews in the officially philosemitic climate of the Federal Republic, would have resulted in universal outrage. By contrast, considerable indulgence was shown to the very few men and women prosecuted for crimes against Sinti and Roma, as is evidenced by the fact that not a single individual has ever been convicted for acts of genocide against them, and that the perpetrators of yesterday frequently seem to have become today's 'experts on Gypsies'. It is literally a case of 'no perpetrator, no victims, no compensation'.

Because of a change in climate in the 1960s, in 1965 the Supreme Court decided to revise its arbitrary date for the onset of racial persecution of 'Gypsies', backdating this to 1938 and the mass arrests and confinement of the 'asocial'. Although this led to a reconsideration of compensation claims hitherto rejected, it still did not include those Sinti and Roma persecuted under laws in which they were not explicitly mentioned — such as the 1933 Law for the Prevention of Hereditarily Diseased Progeny or the 1935 Nuremberg Laws — or who had been detained in the *ad hoc* 'Gypsy' camps that were established throughout Germany in the mid-1930s. The Berlin historian Wolfgang Wippermann is a leading authority on the Nazi persecution of Sinti and Roma, and the author of an official report, which established the coercive and racist character of camps set up in Berlin in 1936 to 'sanitise' the image of the Olympic Games host city. In his chapter Wippermann highlights continuities between treatment of Sinti and Roma in the Nazi and post-war periods by telling the story of two individuals. The chapter also provides disquieting insights into the workings of a particularly inhuman type of bureaucracy and courts where the odds are firmly stacked against the victims.

The issue of individual compensation is not the only way in which the legacy of the Third Reich continues to haunt the European and German present, although it is often lost from view amidst the academic and publicistic handwringing about 'national identity'. Hundreds of thousands of Germans were compulsorily sterilised or killed because the Nazis deemed them to be of 'lesser racial value'. This fact gives a particular intensity to discussions about broad ethical issues, over and above the sort of passions aroused by abortion or euthanasia in other countries. In Germany, the experience of the Third Reich affects the words one uses, or indeed the questions one can pose, in ways that outsiders find perplexing, and in the following case, uncongenial.

During the 1980s, 'euthanasia' once again became a major issue especially in Germany, but also in Britain, the Netherlands and parts of the USA, where 'right to die' enthusiasts managed to put it back on the popular agenda and university centres of bioethics lent it academic credibility. Manuals on how to kill oneself apparently did rather well in London bookshops. A recent Dutch film chronicling the last days of a terminally-ill man showed the effects of recent legislation in moving detail. In Germany, much of the debate centred upon the controversial views of the philosopher Peter Singer, who teaches bioethics at Monash University in Australia, which also happens to include a Centre for Molecular Biology and Medicine heavily engaged in test-tube fertilisation. Singer was hitherto best known for his impassioned advocacy of 'animal liberation' and antipathy to factory farming; however in the summer of 1989, he was invited to speak at a European Symposium on 'Bioengineering, Ethics, and Mental Disability' held in Marburg. Singer wished to argue that 'the parents of severely disabled newborn infants should be able to decide, together with their physicians, whether their infant should live or die'. This would be so in the case of, for example, infants born with anencephaly (literally 'no brain'), major chromosomal disorders, or severe forms of Down's Syndrome and spina bifida.

In the event, Singer was abruptly 'disinvited' as the conference organisers baulked at the anticipated scale of public protest. In the end they cancelled the entire conference. Undeterred, Singer took up an invitation to speak at the University of Saarbrücken. Despite whistles and shouts, Singer endeavoured to convince his critics that he was not a spokesman of the far Right, and that since three of his Austrian-Jewish grandparents had died in Nazi concentration camps he could hardly be described as a 'fascist'. Singer obviously found his confrontations with people who wanted to debate whether there should be a debate about 'euthanasia' deeply unsettling, so much so that he converted his experiences into a full-blown defence of free speech in a New York literary journal given over to grand issues. Still reeling from the shock, Singer noted that Franz Christoph, leader of the self-styled 'Cripples Movement' had chained his wheelchair to the doors of *Die Zeit* when the weekly tried to hold a debate on the subject, while an audience in Zurich had chanted 'Singer raus' ('Singer out') in a manner that had unfortunate associations with an earlier era. Singer wrote 'there is . . . a peculiar tone of fanaticism about some sections of the German debate over euthanasia that goes beyond normal opposition to Nazism, and instead begins to seem like the very

mentality that made Nazism possible', in a pointed allusion to the phenomenon of 'Left-wing fascism'. He concluded, 'Germans and Austrians,
both in academic life and in the press, have shown themselves sadly lacking in the commitment exemplified by the celebrated utterance attributed
to Voltaire: "I disapprove of what you say, but I will defend to the death
your right to say it."'

One key theme in Singer's thinking is that our present attitudes
towards the sanctity of human life stem from the coming of Christianity
and would have been alien to the Greeks and Romans. He writes, 'Today
the doctrines are no longer generally accepted, but the ethical attitudes to
which they gave rise fit in with the deep-seated Western belief in the
uniqueness and special privileges of our species, and have survived.'
Secondly, he rejects what he calls anthropocentric or 'speciesist' distinctions between persons and non-human animals. Pointing to the conceptual capacities of chimpanzees and dolphins, which he feels give them
claims to 'personhood', Singer says, 'Some members of other species are
persons: some members of our own species are not . . . So it seems that
killing, say, a chimpanzee is worse than the killing of a gravely defective
human who is not a person.' Given the limited scope of amniocentesis,
Singer suggests controlled infanticide, which would also reduce the number of healthy foetuses aborted because of suspected defects. He concludes,

> We do not doubt that it is right to shoot a badly injured or sick animal . . .
> To 'allow nature to take its course', withholding treatment but refusing to
> kill, would obviously be wrong. It is only our misplaced respect for the
> doctrine of the sanctity of human life that prevents us from seeing that what
> it is obviously wrong to do to a horse it is equally wrong to do to a defec-
> tive infant.

How does Singer distinguish between these arguments and those used
by the Nazis to justify their campaign of mass murder? He attempts to
refute the slippery slope argument with the observation that 'The Nazis
committed horrendous crimes; but this does not mean that everything the
Nazis did was horrendous. We cannot condemn euthanasia just because
the Nazis did it, any more than we can condemn the building of new
roads for this reason', an argument which, as we shall see is enjoying
some currency among younger German historians. He is noticeably silent
on the Nazis' Weimar antecedents. Correctly pointing out that many
rational people would consider that a life of suffering could be construed

as not being worth living, Singer overlooks the fact that this description would not apply to most of the Nazis' victims. Rightly regarding racism and crude utilitarian calculations as the primary motivating forces behind the Nazi 'euthanasia' programme, Singer omits to mention that one of the essential elements of their propaganda was the denial of personality to the victims, who are referred to as 'beings', 'ballast existences', 'creatures' or 'useless eaters'. Suffering animals, like a blind old hunting dog or a lame laboratory mouse, were also frequently used in books and films of the Nazi period deliberately to sow precisely the sort of moral uncertainties which Singer so unselfconsciously then avails himself of. Displaying a remarkable naïveté regarding the perpetrators of the Nazi 'euthanasia' programme, who were of course leading academic psychiatrists and doctors, Singer counters the argument propounding the danger of an ever-widening circle of victims with the far from comforting observation, 'If acts of euthanasia could only be carried out by a member of the medical profession, with the concurrence of a second doctor, it is not likely that the propensity to kill would spread unchecked throughout the community', and states that the ancient Greeks and traditional Inuit were restrained and circumspect in their killing of, respectively, their sickly infants and elderly parents. Leaving the Inuit to one side, critics have pointed out that Singer's grasp of ancient history is as slight as his awareness of the Nazi period, and that the practices he regards as exemplary belong to the earliest period of Spartan history and were regarded as barbaric and unusual by the few Greek authors who bothered to describe them. Perhaps Singer's German critics were more incensed by his lack of historical awareness than by his utilitarian philosophy?

My own chapter describes the origins of the Nazi 'euthanasia' programme during the liberal Weimar Republic and its extension into the mass murder of the Holocaust. It includes discussion of the arguments used by Nazi propagandists to legitimise medicalised mass murder. Most of these arguments had been inherited from the Weimar period, when the moral brutalisation resulting from the First World War combined to deadly effect with economic crisis and questions of cost.

So far we have been considering the tensions between attempts to 'historicise' the Third Reich and its place in many people's memories. The argument is that direct experience of the period is still too raw for it to be amenable to treatment in the same way as any other historical 'subject', and that what historians regard as important about it may actually miss its universal message and significance. It is nice to know that life went on as normal in villages in the Hunsrück; that Nazi Germany shared certain characteristics with Stalin's Russia; that German psychiatrists and social planners believed they could 'modernise' health provision by killing their own patients; or that Hitler was an egalitarian, keen to implement his version of North American society, but what does this tell us about a society responsible for Auschwitz, the most abiding image of the entire Nazi period?

Academic debate on the Nazi period is itself often conducted with a passion and intensity, well beyond the usual rancour found amongst academics. Gradually the dust settles, as the debates are rehearsed in countless textbook surveys for regurgitation in student essays and exam papers. An almost 'textbook' case of this process is the debate between 'intentionalists' and 'structure-functionalists' over the origins of the 'Final Solution'. Eventually the simple restatement of what was once blindingly obvious, for example the centrality of racism to Nazism, takes on the character of a novel interpretation. The chapter by Paul Weindling, a medical historian, is a detailed attempt to reveal the complex and competing intellectual, scientific and social strands that informed the Nazis' racial vision, which, as his work shows, cannot be reduced to the simple implementation of the simple-minded *obiter dicta* of Adolf Hitler, but rather represented a specifically German solution to the medicalisation of the 'social question'.

Four chapters in this book represent some of the areas where historians are most in disagreement and where much interesting research is currently being done. They concern the putatively 'modernising' impact and intentions of the Nazi regime; the complicity of the *Wehrmacht* in ideologically-motivated atrocities on the Eastern Front; and, finally, the involvement and responses of the German people to the persecution of the Jews. The authors, Götz Aly, Omer Bartov, Avraham Barkai and Jeremy Noakes, have each made major contributions in these areas.

One does not have to go very far in Germany today to hear the opinion that the Third Reich had its good as well as bad sides. In the past it was possible to console oneself with the view that this was a product of an evasive and partial treatment of the subject in official discourse and the nation's schools, of the kind revealed in Michael Verhoeven's film *The Nasty Girl*, the story of a not so innocent schoolgirl who decided to write a prize essay about her own town's murky history, and paid the price in terms of social ostracism and acts of violence ever after. Sooner or later, the findings of recent research would filter through into popular consciousness through such 'multipliers' as teaching or television, or indeed through the widespread writing of *Alltagsgeschichte* (the history of 'everyday life') by laymen. None of this, of course, will have the slightest influence on those self-styled neo-Fascists for whom the facts of the period are so many fictions. As we saw at the beginning, recent trends in academic research have begun to undermine this last assumption. In the mid-1960s, Ralf Dahrendorf and David Schoenbaum drew attention to the real or imagined impact of the Nazi 'national community' upon traditional German society, the ways in which it destroyed older class, confessional or regional loyalties and thus paved the way for post-war liberal democracy, at least in that half of Germany not ruled by the Communists. Detailed studies of particular social classes have not on the whole confirmed Schoenbaum's vision of the 'triumph of egalitarianism'.

In a ground-breaking chapter on the highest echelons of German society, Jeremy Noakes charts the failure of Nazi attempts to fashion a new social élite and of their efforts to infiltrate the existing one. Although individual scions of the aristocracy may have fallen for the chic-cum-kitsch glamour of the SS black uniform, the Europeanised high aristocracy were 'more or less totally detached from the regime and regarded it with a mixture of contempt and disgust'. Parvenu Nazi officials were still consigned to meals alongside the servants. These subtle social realities continue to elude historians fashionably (and remotely) sensitive towards such colourfully marginal groupings as juvenile delinquents or prostitutes. By contrast, Schoenbaum's views upon the extent of working-class integration into the Nazi 'national community' seem to be being endorsed by recent research, despite the gallant attempts of some on the Left, such as the late Tim Mason, to sustain a picture of working-class solidarity in alienation. In his chapter, Ulrich Herbert, the author of the definitive account of 'foreign workers' in the Third Reich, takes a much more sceptical view of working-class reactions to the blandishments of the Nazi regime and deals honestly with the subject of working-class racism, something curiously absent from most histories of German labour. It is to be hoped that this lack will be remedied as the ranks of those writing about German history become more politically pluralistic than has been the case since the 1960s.

In the last decade modernisation theories have undergone a renaissance among younger historians of Nazi Germany writing from both ends of the political spectrum. If on the Left this is part of the ongoing project of discrediting the liberal capitalist Federal Republic by stressing its Nazi antecedents, motivation on the neo-Conservative Right seems obscurer. Adding their voices to Martin Broszat's plea for a 'demoralising' history of National Socialism, a group of scholars associated with Rainer Zitelmann, has recently put together a body of work which stresses the intentionally 'modernising' impact of National Socialism. Zitelmann argues that Hitler's principal aim was the creation of an egalitarian, performance-oriented society, and that his models were the Soviet Union and the United States of America, rather than retrograde visions of a medieval social order. This will come as something of a surprise to anyone who has even glanced through the Declaration of Independence or Lincoln's Gettysburg Address. Echoing Martin Broszat's plea for 'historicisation', Zitelmann writes:

> Historical writing, in which moral and political intentions will play at least a more limited role and in which popular pedagogical motives make way for detached points of view, will find it easier to recognise the modernising function of National Socialism.

This modernising function is illustrated with the by-now-familiar analogies between, say, the welfare plans for the post-war era of Robert Ley's German Labour Front and the Beveridge Report, although how the latter sits with Hitler's admiration for the USA is never made explicit. But leaving America aside, to regard Robert Ley as an equal of William Beveridge seems as ridiculous as it would be to equate the calculated philanthropic activities of the Mafia or the Colombian drug cartels among the poor of their respective milieux with the work of Roman Catholic missionaries.

During the 1980s, attempts to interpret the Third Reich with the aid of a variety of modernisation theories were augmented by groups of German 'alternative' historians, or researchers working outside a conventional academic framework to which they evince considerable, and sometimes quite understandable, hostility. It would not be doing violence to reality by associating these groups — sometimes misleadingly known as the 'Hamburg school' — with the far Left of the political spectrum. Some of the most interesting research on the 'euthanasia' programme, 'foreign labour', health and social policy in recent years has come from Götz Aly, Matthias Hamann, Susanne Heim and Karl-Heinz Roth. Much of their work concentrates upon the role of 'intellectuals', by which they mean the academics, psychiatrists and scientists churned out by German universities, rather than thinkers with independence of mind or creativity. Like similar extremely sectoral perspectives, for example that of the bureaucracy or indeed history 'from below', this approach has its merits and demerits. Recently, Götz Aly and Susanne Heim have developed their earlier work on one obscure population planner into a comprehensive account of the 'Final Solution'. They begin by rejecting both catastrophist and nihilistic explanations of the 'Holocaust', that is to say the idea that this was an event beyond human comprehension or an unparalleled instance of 'destruction for destruction's sake' which flew in the face of even economic rationality. They posit the existence of a group of academic experts — economists, agronomists, demographers, statisticians and so on, working under the aegis of the Four Year Plan apparatus and in the Generalgouvernement in Poland — who decided to modernise and rationalise the backward and overpopulated societies of Central and Eastern Europe by eliminating 'surplus' people, a task then carried out on their behalf by the SS Reich Main Security Head Office. This would have led to capital formation, the mechanisation of agriculture and the creation of a further industrial base subordinate to Germany. Killing the Jews of Eastern Europe would at once remove one of the most visible manifestations of urban poverty and create opportunities for social mobility for the 'surplus' non-Jewish rural proletariat, while facilitating the rationalisation of urban commerce through the removal of artisans and penny-capitalists.

Not that the Jews were the sole or primary objects of these policies. In the more grandiose versions, the 'Final Solution of the Jewish Question' became a detail amidst plans to 'evacuate', or in other words murder, thirty million people. Rational planning and racial fanaticism fused to terrible effect in this broadly conceived attempt to engineer a new social order. Not surprisingly, these ideas — elaborated here in Götz Aly's own contribution — have given rise to controversy, without, it should be said, managing to displace some of the more familiar academic debates about the origins of the 'Final Solution'. The importance of Aly and Heim's work lies in the light it sheds on the involvement of a previously unknown group in the 'Holocaust', and more importantly, in the element of deliberation it restores to a chain of events which some historians are inclined to view as almost the by-product of competing bureaucratic structures. Critics of their thesis have pointed to the lack of consensus evident among middle-ranking functionaries responsible for, for example, policy towards the inmates of ghettos in Poland, as well as to the obvious fact that the economic circumstances that the experts described did not fit Amsterdam, Paris or Rome, whose Jewish populations also perished. Aly and Heim also fail to connect the cogitations of their experts with what is known about the origins of the 'Final Solution' — Himmler, Heydrich and the Reich Main Security Office were not merely executants for Goering — and more seriously, run the risk of confusing the legitimisation and rationalisation of policy with the factors — notably race hatred or the transference of the ethics of colonial wars to Europe — that motivated it. Sanitation, military and security experts also provided 'cogent' grounds for mass murder, but no one has bothered so far to take them seriously.

In contrast to this rather localised, would-be historical controversy, the *Historikerstreit* or 'historians' debate' of the mid-1980s assumed almost global dimensions, spawning a vast and often highly acrimonious literature in the form of books and articles in journals and newspapers. The bull elephants of the historical profession (few women historians took part) roared at one another across continents. Several people who had never previously published a line on Nazi Germany now felt compelled to air their views on the Holocaust, Idi Amin, Pol Pot, Stalin and other mass murderers. The controversy began on 11 July 1986 when the philosopher and sociologist Jürgen Habermas published a coruscating attack upon what he deemed 'the apologetic tendencies in the writing of German contemporary history', evident, for example, in the recent work of Andreas Hillgruber and Ernst Nolte. Nolte, whose work utilises the outré products of the 'revisionist' far-Right, insinuated a causal relationship between Bolshevik and Nazi barbarities, with the latter taking on the character of 'preventive murder'. Hillgruber, an internationally respected authority on German diplomatic history, had just published a slim book entitled *Two Forms of Downfall: The Smashing of the German Reich and the End of European Jewry*, a title whose uneven emotional cargo deserves its own consideration. The book was widely criticised for its invitation to empathetic identification with German troops fighting on the Eastern Front, who, notwithstanding the resultant prolongation of the death camps, saved the eastern areas of the Reich from being overrun in an 'orgy of revenge' by the Red Army. This was a novel variant upon the pertinacious idea that the German Army had fought a normal war, and that relatively small units of the SS and SD had been responsible for all criminal enormities. This view obviously suited a society where virtually every family had a member who had been a soldier, and where the young soldiers were now workers and bureaucrats, professionals, teachers, novelists, industrialists and politicians.

The clichéd dichotomy between the decent German soldier and the ideological fanatics of the SS, served up incidentally in virtually every Anglo-American post-1945 war film, was first seriously challenged in the late 1970s with the publication of Christian Streit's *Keine Kamaraden*. This showed the ways in which the *Wehrmacht* moved from cognisance of, to complicity in, acts of brutality between the campaigns against Poland and Russia, culminating in the deliberate starvation and murder of three million Soviet prisoners of war and culpable involvement in the 'Final Solution'. Much of the research which ensued in the wake of Streit's work served to endorse his views concerning the high-level involvement of the military élite in National Socialist racial imperialism. Omer Bartov's book on *The Barbarisation of Warfare on the Eastern Front*, which appeared in 1986, was the first study to shift attention from élites to the everyday realities of combat as experienced by junior officers and their subordinates. A few years ago Bartov developed this work in an outstanding book entitled *Hitler's Army*. This reveals the degree of ideological saturation evident among ordinary soldiers, bereft of primary group loyalties because of the appalling casualty rates, and fighting under 'demodernised' conditions an enemy depicted as being racially 'subhuman'.

Bartov's account does not, of course, preclude the existence of decent dissenters and shirkers — the 'slipper soldiers' who opted out of the war — unearthed by Theo Schulte in his study of army rear areas in Russia. In line with much recent work on the social history of Nazi Germany, Schulte argues for the existence of pockets of normality in a highly abnormal situation. The American historian Christopher Browning has recently pushed this line a bit further with an outstanding study of the everyday life of an 'ordinary' police battalion engaged in mass murder. Bartov's chapter here outlines the unique character of the war in the East and relates this to debates about the social history of the Third Reich and on the comparability of *Wehrmacht* conduct with that of other armies. The final section of his contribution has bearings not only upon the revisionism of Ernst Nolte, but also upon facile and fashionable analogies between Auschwitz and the bombing of Dresden and Hiroshima.

In 1898, at the height of the Dreyfus affair in France, many European countries began to express reservations about whether to participate in the forthcoming 1900 Paris Universal Exposition. Influential circles in

Germany, apparently totally unaware of their own hypocrisy, were of the opinion that France 'was a country where all rights are violated, where only the anti-Semitic and chauvinist population makes the law, and where anyone who doesn't share their passions runs the risk of being hurled into the Seine'. If anyone at the turn of the century was to have predicted the probable location for eruptions of anti-Semitism, they would have alighted upon France, Poland, Rumania or Russia, rather than Germany.

The issue of German popular responses to, and involvement in, the Nazis' systematic persecution of the Jews has generated a considerable academic literature. Older studies which used a relatively narrow range of sources to substantiate quite sweeping generalisations about the Germans in general, have been superseded by careful and nuanced analyses of particular regions, confessional groups and social classes. Some of the most detailed and judicious work on this subject has been that of Ian Kershaw on Bavaria, which is conceived very much in the spirit of Broszat's plea for 'historicisation':

> Popular opinion on the 'Jewish Question' formed a wide spectrum running from the paranoid Jew-baiters at the one extreme, undoubtedly a tiny minority; through a wide section of the population whose existent prejudices and latent anti-Semitism, influenced in varying degrees by the virulence of Nazi propaganda, accepted legal restrictions on Jews amounting to economic exclusion and social ostracism whilst rejecting the blatant and overt inhumanity of the Jew-baiters; and finally including another minority imbued with a deeply Christian or liberal-humanitarian moral sense, whose value-system provided the most effective barrier to the Nazi doctrine of racial hatred.

In a memorable phrase, Kershaw remarked that 'the road to Auschwitz was built by hate, but paved with indifference'. Kershaw's views have not won universal acceptance, and would seem to be too cautious in the light of recent experiences in Rostock, where ordinary citizens enthusiastically egged on working-class neo-Nazi skinheads as they laid waste the block of flats occupied by asylum seekers. Michael Kater claims that Kershaw and others seriously underrate the durability and popular roots of German anti-Semitism and the extent to which manifestations of it were genuinely spontaneous rather than the product of state manipulation:

> Between 1933 and 1939, discrimination by Germans against Jews in the private sphere, without the involvement or sanction of state agencies and without heed to existing laws, was both spontaneous and calculated. It

spanned the entire spectrum from verbal humiliation to denunciation, depredation, and physical harm. It could be committed by individuals or by corporate bodies, who may have had formal connections with party or state, but were not under their directive at the time of the transgressions.

Israeli scholar, Otto Dov Kulka and American scholar, Aron Rodrigue, who have also extensively studied the sources on this issue, have questioned the typicality of Kershaw's rural Bavarian examples, and suggested the substitution of the term 'passive complicity' for his more neutral 'indifference'. They conclude:

> The concept of 'indifference', suggesting as it does only a lack of concern, is too limited in scope, and does not convey the full complexity of popular opinion. For example, it cannot account for the widely reported attitude that something, one way or another, had to be done to 'solve the Jewish Question'. This 'Question' might not have been high on the list of priorities for the population at large. Nevertheless, the attitude that measures had to be initiated to reach a solution of this problem was as much in evidence when the issue did come up, as the attitude of not caring one way or the other.

Discussing the period of deportations and extermination, Kershaw concludes that the former 'were apparently unaccompanied by much attention from the German population' and that the response to the killings in the East was 'that the Jews were out of sight and literally out of mind'.

Recent studies, notably by Willy Dressen, Ernst Klee and Völker Ullrich, present a much bleaker picture of avaricious neighbours squabbling over the household goods of Jews yet to be deported, and of housewives, reminiscent of the Polish peasant women interviewed in Claude Lanzmann's film *Shoah*, knowingly remarking, in their Berlin working-class argot, of a Jewish family being transported, 'They'll be gassed too.' Passengers on trains passing through the major rail-junction at Auschwitz were engulfed in a sweet-smelling fog and could see flames shooting up from the crematoria in the camp — a distance of fifteen to twenty kilometres. Many people were more or less directly involved in the 'Final Solution'; for example the local authorities, railway officials, diplomats, bank employees and the manufacturers of exterminatory technology, as well as ordinary soldiers, police and SS men. The photographer Joe Heydecker noted:

There were always soldiers, railwaymen, men from the Organisation Todt, civilians, sometimes in bathing trunks and frequently equipped with cameras who spectated at the dreadful scenes which were enacted at the mass graves where in place after place the Jewish inhabitants were bloodily butchered without regard to age or gender.

Letters home from the Front again and again registered considerable animosity towards the Jewish populations of Eastern Europe and the Soviet Union — 'The deeper we advance into Russia, the more Jews we encounter. The fellows are just as cheeky as they are in time of peace. One should shove many more of these monsters up against a wall than has been done so far' — and described the murder of thousands of people in terms of the utmost inhumanity. However, as Hans Mommsen has remarked in a careful study of these issues, it remains an open question as to how far knowledge of individual episodes of barbarity coalesced into an awareness of the terrible scale of the 'Final Solution'; knowledge of the depredations of the *Einsatzgruppen* killing squads did not mean awareness of Auschwitz.

Avraham Barkai is a leading authority on the German economy and on the economic exclusion and ruin of Germany's Jews in the Nazi period. In his chapter Barkai addresses himself to the relationship between the Nazis' 'national community' and the persecution of Germany's Jewish minority, exploring the long- and short-range aspects of both phenomena. He argues that a deep-seated tradition of Christian anti-Semitism — recycled in the secular terms of Nazi propaganda — as well as such perennial motives as sheer greed combined in powerful response to the open season on Jews licensed by the Nazi leadership. A constant barrage of propaganda and a steady extension of what was possible — stretching from the early boycott through informal and formal discrimination, 'aryanisation' of economic concerns, to the violence of *Kristallnacht* — gradually engendered a climate in which the murderous obsessions of the Nazis could become practicable. As Barkai remarks, 'the persecution of the Jews seems the necessary, although not sufficient precondition, for the murder of European Jews'. These things would not, and did not, occur in any other historical context.

The two final chapters in this book are concerned with questions of sexuality and gender. Hans-Georg Stümke's account of the Nazis' persecution of homosexuals is a timely reminder of the biologistic and collectivist thinking which determined the Nazis' treatment of all minorities. Homosexuals were not persecuted because they subverted the Nazis' notions of masculinity, still less because Nazi homophobia was driven by anxieties about the allegedly latent homosexuality in the ranks of an aggressively masculine Party, but because they considered homosexuality to be an 'illness' which was undermining the nation's racial–demographic vitality. The 'threat' posed by homosexuals was thus closely akin to that posed by Jews, who were held to be peculiarly responsible for the spread of syphilis and later typhus, or that represented by people with allegedly hereditary illnesses and psychiatric disorders who were compulsorily sterilised or murdered. Although, as Stümke shows, homosexuals suffered terribly under the Nazis, very few of them have ever received any form of compensation. Apart from the Federal government's refusal to regard Nazi legislation against homosexuals as 'abnormal', this also reflects the reluctance of older homosexuals to 'come out' in a hostile climate in order to qualify for compensation. People sterilised for allegedly hereditary illnesses or psychiatric problems often experience similar, and quite understandable, inhibitions.

Women's history has become a thriving area in modern German historiography. Jill Stephenson has made distinguished contributions both to the study of specific issues and by surveying the position of women in society as a whole. In her chapter, Jill Stephenson, takes a critical view of the degree to which women were successfully integrated. She notes, for example, that there were few alternatives to the associational life that the Nazi dictatorship had on offer, and rightly questions whether Nazi policy merely represented 'more of the same' by drawing attention to the regime's philogenerative fixations and its ruthless persecution of the 'racially unfit' through compulsory sterilisation and 'euthanasia', or indeed 'valuable' women who had liaisons with foreigners deemed to be 'racially inferior'. Other scholars are beginning to explore such issues as indirect female complicity in the crimes committed by their perpetrator husbands.

These essays are a coherent and representative cross section of work by some of the most active international researchers in the field. No one is here by dint of something they wrote twenty years ago, or the frequency or loudness with which they repeat the same old views about, say, the origins of the 'Final Solution'. Our authors do not represent the view of any self-conscious 'School' since it is unlikely that they would agree with one another. This approach, which leaves the reader to draw his or her own conclusions, seems more satisfactory than some dubious consensual 'evaluation' of arguments that sometimes remain obstinately irreconcilable.

Apart from introducing them to a body of work often published in German, the book is explicitly designed to stimulate sixth-formers and undergraduates to consider a range of issues that are sometimes encompassed by, but which more often go beyond, conventional historiographical debates about the period. Broadly speaking, these essays reflect the major currents of the 1980s and 1990s, that is an 'essentialist' emphasis upon biological politics and a rejection of neo-Marxism and sub-Weberism, the dominant intellectual fashions in many of our universities, if nowhere else. The issues discussed here include the pathologies of racial prejudice; the role of scientific 'experts'; the relationship between calculations of social utility and Nazi exterminism; why soldiers behaved barbarously on the Eastern Front; and how different social classes conducted themselves under a dictatorship, including that relatively understudied group — the German upper classes. Readers will at least have a good idea of how historians conceptualise these subjects, sharing the adventure of finding solutions to very difficult questions.

'THE REAL MYSTERY IN GERMANY'. THE GERMAN WORKING CLASS DURING THE NAZI DICTATORSHIP

Ulrich Herbert

How did the German working class conduct itself in the Third Reich? Almost no other question was so crucial during the early years of the National Socialist dictatorship. It was widely assumed that if any power in society was capable of endangering the Nazi regime and its partners among the traditional élites in industry, the military or civil service, then this would inevitably be the working class. The hopes of the exiled leadership of the working-class parties, as well as the fears of Germany's National Socialist rulers, hinged upon the working class. However, the picture of working-class behaviour under the Nazi dictatorship, relayed by the correspondents of the Social Democratic Party in exile (Sopade) through the 'Sopade' reports, was so diverse and contradictory that the analysts in the Party's makeshift headquarters in Prague were hardly in a position to offer accurate prognoses. In December 1935, a Sopade commentator described the response of the working class to the Nazi dictatorship as being 'the real mystery in Germany'. As well as references to labour stoppages and the almost universal rejection of the Nazi dictatorship by the workers, there was also talk of depression and humiliation; depoliticisation and opportunism; and even loud complaints about 'deserters', or assent and 'enthusiasm' for Hitler's regime. But a considered judgement was equally difficult in the case of those reports which provided a more coherent picture; for how and against what was one to measure the circumstances they described? Comparisons with conditions before 1933 were of limited value, because they neglected the peculiar circumstances of a dictatorship. Since there was no comparable experience in the entire history of the working-class movement, it was impossible to estimate the room for manoeuvre that the workers may or may not have had under the Nazi dictatorship. However, in general, the German workers' readiness to fight was over-estimated by the editors of the 'Sopade' reports from Germany, out-weighing the disappointment, or indeed bitterness, regarding 'the degree to which the Nazis' divide and rule tactics have already born fruit in the shape of class-betraying individualism'.

The obvious overestimation of the cohesion and strength of a working class schooled in the socialist labour movement was broadly endorsed by the National Socialists. The greatly expanded network of spies and informers established following the seizure of power in January 1933 thought that if domestic resistance to the Nazi regime should occur, then it would inevitably emanate from the working class. The panicky and pernickety investigation of even the most trivial occurrence attributable to working-class dissent can be attributed to this false assumption. The Nazi authorities breathed a sigh of relief a few years later as it became obvious that their initial apprehensions were exaggerated; however, the attitudes of the working class could never be taken entirely for granted.

The views expressed on this subject by later historians are equally con-fused by this difference between what people thought should happen and the actual course of events. The left-wing historian Tim Mason asked, 'Why were there only individual acts of protest or resistance? Why weren't there more mass protests from the working class?' This implied that, given the socio-political position before the Nazis came to power, another, more radical response might have been expected from the work-ing class to the Nazi dictatorship.

By way of an answer to these questions modern psephological research — reflecting the state of research in the early 1970s — came to the con-clusion that worker resistance was less strong than expected — in itself an interesting way of putting things — on the basis of the fact that in 1932 a mere quarter of workers voted for the National Socialist German Workers' Party (NSDAP), which went some way to explaining why 'there was a considerably greater level of working-class integration in the National Socialist national community than had commonly been assumed'. If this assumption, based as it was upon the expectations of contemporaries, had not existed, then the same findings could be inter-preted as indicating that in 1933 three-quarters of the working class was opposed to the Nazis, while only slightly more than a third of other social classes was similarly disposed. However, the period of exaggerated expectations among both contemporaries and contemporary historians was superseded by a phase — according to individual temperament — of relief or disappointment, in which the working class was now regarded as being the main social pillar of the Nazi regime. The particular attention paid to the conduct of the German working class during the Nazi dictatorship drew upon the image of the working-class and labour movement from the era before 1933. Behind this lay, on the one hand, an obvious concern to discover the genuine sources of opposition to the regime, and therewith a source of political legitimacy, and, on the other hand, concern with the question of how Nazi policies of control and integration functioned, with the extreme example of the working class assuming a particular saliency, while also promising a degree of moral unburdening for German society as a whole.

The widespread hope among many of the cadres of the labour movement that although the Nazis had smashed the workers' organisations and persecuted its leaders, nonetheless the semi-private network of social contacts in working-class housing districts or on the factory floor would endure, or that working-class solidarities might even be consolidated, as they had been at the time of Bismarck's 1878 anti-Socialist laws, proved illusory. The breaking-up of proletarian social milieux, including even leisure and sports clubs destroyed their sense of social identity. Certainly, the Nazis were unable completely to suppress worker solidarity within these milieux, but they did manage to largely depoliticise them. At the same time, the sense of being delivered up to an uncertain fate served to weaken worker self-confidence, while diminishing the attractions of the working-class movement and, above all, of the Communists, who a few weeks before the Nazis came to power in 1933 had been predicting the immanence of a proletarian revolution. Now, however, they were not even in a position to do anything about SA forays into working-class districts. The traditional division between a minority of political activists, who were determined to resist, and the mass of workers in the factories or working-class areas became deeper, resulting in a steady drift into two mutually incomprehensible realms of experience. But when in July 1933 Kurt Schumacher said that 'the process of conversion to fascism ... begins with the workers. One only has to listen to the conversations in working-class circles', this may be seen as somewhat exaggerated, at least in terms of the early years of the Nazi regime. Despite their sense of impotence and their exposure to Nazi terror, the workers also discovered that, notwithstanding the strident propaganda, nothing had changed as far as their economic circumstances were concerned. Thus, commentators agreed in describing the response of the workers during this phase as being characterised by surliness and a despondent form of acceptance. Only from 1935 onwards were their lives affected by new developments: the novel experience for many of having a stable job to go to, as well as the socio-political offensive of the National Socialist regime.

As far as the actual socio-economic position of the workers before the outbreak of war is concerned, two clear tendencies are evident, bearing in mind the differences in the various sectors of the economy.

First, real wages rose considerably in the wake of an armaments-led boom, achieving pre-war levels in certain sectors between 1936 and 1939. If one includes the number of hours worked per week and therefore the amount of overtime paid, one can see that before the war German workers probably achieved the highest rates of pay hitherto on offer in their entire history. The reasons for this were general economic recovery and a resulting labour shortage, with the regime's attempts to suppress wage rises — by, for example, the demand for expanding welfare provision in factories — being circumvented by lump sum payments. The regime's attempts to restrict labour mobility were also partially invalidated by aggressive recruitment or the widespread practice of informal or illicit changes of employment.

Second, these favourable developments for the workers were in part nullified by the acute food and housing shortages they experienced before 1936. In comparison with other social classes, who benefited more rapidly from the country's financial recovery, the workers continued to be at a disadvantage; their living standard remained at a low level. Since the middle of the First World War this had been a familiar experience for most workers. What was different now was that they had stable employment and at least the hope of a long-term improvement in their conditions. The politically crucial comparison with the situation before 1933 enabled the improvements achieved since then gradually to move to the foreground.

Any attempt to assess the impact of these developments upon the situation and political attitudes of the workers is complicated by the problem of identifying what was specifically National Socialist about them. Certainly, rationalisation, structural change and differential rates of pay would have accompanied recovery from a crisis in a non-National

Socialist Germany too. However, the terroristic marginalisation of representatives of organised labour meant that these developments could be introduced more radically, without having to pander to the demands of the working class.

However, it was also significant that links began to be forged between performance and eugenic criteria. The hierarchy no longer merely included those who worked well and thus reaped their rewards, but at the bottom end of the scale, those 'rejects' who failed or refused to perform were now not merely poorly rewarded, but rather actively punished and persecuted. One of the most important conceptual advances in recent research lies precisely in examining the relationship between, on the one hand, labour and social policy and, on the other, racism and extermination, two areas hitherto treated separately. The ideological foundation of National Socialist social policy was the conviction that a large part of social deviance, or phenomena that suggested social maladjustment had biological causes. This biologisation of the social — a core concern of racist thought — was based on the concept of the *Volk* as an autonomous, overarching supraindividual biological and cultural unity. Just as the various nations could be differentiated according to their biological substance, so the internal composition of a nation was determined by the biological worth of its individual members. According to this model, deviant behaviour could be attributed to the biological, inherited and heritable 'substance' of an individual, ranging from mental illness via physical abnormalities to criminality, alcoholism and 'asociality', all of which could be put down to his or her inherited constitution.

The aim of labour and social policies posited upon this model had to be to promote those 'valuable' members of the 'national community' (value was identified with social conformity and performance), by supporting their families and increasing their fertility in order to increase the proportion of 'valuable' substance in the body of the nation. At the same time, it was necessary to identify the 'less valuable' elements — who were regarded as being so many 'ballast existences' — who would then be deliberately disadvantaged, separated out or even 'eradicated'. The specifically National Socialist component of the labour and social policies developed during the Third Reich consists of this combination of promotion and separation, 'social policy' coupled with 'eradication'.

The working class was most affected by the National Socialists' racially informed social policies simply because they contributed the majority of those who were poor, inefficient and socially inadequate, as well as most

of the prostitutes and vagrants, even if one chooses to refrain from applying the problematic concept of *Lumpenproletariat* in the interests of
defining these groups out of the working class. This was particularly
apparent in connection with the campaign waged by the Gestapo and the
authorities running the Four Year Plan to boost the economy in 1937–8
against the 'workshy', a group that encompassed, among others, tramps,
beggars, 'Gypsies' and pimps. Such campaigns were used to exert pressure upon those working in factories, but also to 'cleanse' the 'body of the
nation' of those elements whose behaviour signalled their 'lesser value'.
The ruthless pursuit by the police and war economy bureaucracy of
'shirkers' and 'layabouts', which was stepped up following the outbreak
of war, reveals the close connection between social discipline and racially-
motivated 'eradication'.

Measures designed to separate and eradicate the 'less valuable' were
accompanied by various positive social policy measures which catered for
the 'valuable'; however, particularly in so far as they were directed at the
workers, these measures must be regarded as part of the regime's continuing attempts not merely to neutralise politically those who were distant
from or overtly opposed to the dictatorship, but actively to solicit their
acquiescence. These measures included the egalitarian rhetoric of the
regime, a form of propagandistic compensation for the repression of the
working class, which repeatedly referred to the 'honest worker' and
'German socialism', while mobilising resentments against 'reactionaries',
'bosses' and other putative privileged elements, including the Jews.
However, purely ideological compensation without social improvements
was insufficient reward for the loss of political rights. Many of the socio-
political offerings of the Nazis were little more than proof of a purpose-
less activism, which had no actual impact on the situation of the working
class.

Tangible social improvements were received much more positively,
and included family support and, above all, the leisure activities organised
by the regime — namely the introduction of a minimum annual holiday
period of, on average, six days — and the creation of an organisation,
called Strength through Joy, dedicated to mass tourism, which in 1938
organised some 10.3 million holidays. Naturally cruises to Madeira were
still virtually inaccessible to most workers, for whom organised short
trips to relatively close destinations were more usual. Nevertheless, the
cruises to Madeira signalled the arrival of fresh possibilities — symbolis-
ing not real, but at least prospective opportunities for social mobility, and

tangible proof of the hope of further improvements.

By contrast, the Nazi authorities' repeated insistence on the existence of a collective form of 'worker opposition', as evidenced in report after report, requires considerable qualification. For example, when in 1936–8 the Gestapo claimed it had detected 356 'strikes', this was no doubt, from the perspective of their self-styled totalitarianism, a scandalous alarm signal. It could also be taken to imply that the terror inaugurated after 1933 had simply failed to halt social conflict. On the other hand, in 1936–7 a 'strike' may have meant little more than fifteen unskilled building workers downing tools for three hours because of some disagreement about wages. Just as the economic recovery was, above all, an expression of a general economic upturn which was merely accelerated by Nazi rearmament, so the increase in inner-factory conflicts can mainly be attributed to a number of different factors whose extent and form were merely influenced or modified by the policies of the Nazi regime. What was crucial in terms of domestic stability and worker attitudes towards the political system was that inner-factory social conflicts were not directly related to the prevailing form of government, which meant that the Nazis' policy of intimidation and repression had been successful.

At the same time, the relationship of the overwhelming majority of the workers towards National Socialism was generally one of distance. However, it also appeared to be the case that the Nazis' economic and foreign policy successes resulted in a situation in which a fundamental antipathy to Nazism was accompanied by approval of some aspects of their policy. Explicit rejection of, or indifference to, the regime and its works, was superceded by a form of double-think, in which some policies were rejected while others won widespread approval; what Tim Mason called a 'disassociation of consciousness' ensued, a process which, by stifling exchanges of experience, prevented an overall analysis of individual experiences or occurrences. The main achievement of the working-class movement before 1933 lay precisely in this capacity to relate individual experiences to political outlook; this capacity did not arise from the relationships between workers themselves, but rather was a product of political analysis and the power of conviction. Bereft of this comparative political context, the individual was fully exposed to the suggestive power and dynamism of the socio-political developments which came into play before 1939. Thus it could be argued that it was less the heterogeneous nature of the experience that promoted working-class disassociation, than the individualisation of the process of analysis.

If the regime's leaders succeeded in at least politically neutralising the working class before 1939, by partially integrating at least part of it, they were also aware that this was largely due to economic recovery. Terror and threats were not enough to secure 'peace on the home front' in the event of war. It would be necessary to maintain the living standards of the pre-war period. However, the experience of the First World War suggested that a reduction in living standards was an inevitable result of sustained conflict. Upon the outbreak of war, the Nazi regime found itself precariously perched on the horns of this dilemma. When, in September 1939, the authorities began to try to implement wage reductions and increased working hours in order to finance the conflict, they did this in the hope that the impression made by the outbreak of war and its consequent appeals to patriotism would stifle ill-will among the workers. This calculation soon proved illusory: the number of people reporting sick increased, and reports of 'shirking' and other forms of discontent became more frequent.

The regime reacted tentatively and hesitantly to mounting worker discontent, because it still had vivid memories of the socio-political conflicts of the First World War. Rapid military successes made it possible to rescind the 'September decrees' by the Spring of 1940. The opposite of the wage reductions desired by the authorities ensued, with real weekly wages rising above average until 1942. Despite a considerable deficit in the supply of labour available, the overall number of women in employment fell by about 300,000 following the outbreak of war (only achieving pre-war levels again in 1943), with some six million German women capable of working being officially counted as not working in 1939. Generous separation allowances for the wives of soldiers meant that there was no pressure upon them to undertake paid employment. The fact that the Nazi leadership did little to reverse these trends was because of their fear that working-class discontent over the conscription of women would aggravate dissatisfaction with poor pay and inadequate rations to the point where the destabilising domestic experiences of the First World War would be repeated. On the other hand, following the defeat of Poland and the invasion of France, the arguments of the economic technocrats began to seem less convincing. Now, the Party in particular began to demand that as wartime economic constraints appeared to be at an end, priority should be given to labour and social policies of a *völkisch* type, which would benefit the German population. Nor did the industrial conscription of women accord with social policies posited upon racial criteria. Equally, of course, the fact that the number of working women in pre-war Germany was relatively high by European standards should be taken into account. Recently, Richard Overy has modified the picture of a 'peacetime-like war economy' between 1939 and 1941. In reality, the policies of the regime — tax increases, food rationing, cuts in consumer production, savings programmes designed to soak up purchasing power in the interests of financing the war — had considerable consequences for the standard of living of the population. An American observer found life in Berlin during the winter of 1939–40 'thoroughly spartanic', but since it had been like that for the working class before the war, they probably did not regard this as either novel or serious. In contrast with conditions in the First World War, food supplies remained at a high level. Large parts of the population, and in particular the workers, were obviously concerned to ensure that the living standard they had arduously achieved before the war was not going to be forfeited again.

Military successes also promoted working-class loyalty to the regime, and the victory over France was regarded as being the high-point of assent and enthusiasm among most sections of the population. If hitherto Hitler's foreign policy successes and approval of the Nazi regime had been two rather separate quantities, so now the boundaries became fluid and the discontent with this or that aspect of Nazi policy was superseded by basic acceptance of Hitler's regime among the workers. This was particularly so once there were no realistic political alternatives, especially after the pact between Hitler and Stalin of 1939 disoriented Communist support and isolated them from other opponents of Hitler.

Mounting working-class assent to the Nazi regime may also be ascribed to the success with which the authorities were able to shift the burdens of war on to the populations of countries occupied by the German military (*Wehrmacht*). The slogan went: 'First the Wehrmacht, then the German people, and only then the populations of occupied countries!' The extent to which this would be taken literally only became fully apparent with the economic preparations for the war against the Soviet Union. Domestically, a very tangible and immediate reminder of this principle of displacement were the mounting numbers of foreigners brought to Germany for 'labour deployment'. By the summer of 1941 some 3 million foreigners, mostly Poles and Frenchmen, were working in Germany; the use of foreign labour reached a peak in the autumn of 1944, with some 7.7 million foreign civilian workers and prisoners of war. The largest group were workers from the USSR, of whom there were 2.2

million (half of them women), including 630,000 prisoners of war. Until the autumn of 1941 most of these foreign workers were deployed in the agricultural sector; from the winter of 1941–2, when the fortunes of war altered, more of them were employed in industry. By 1944 foreigners comprised more than a quarter of all those employed in the German economy: in armaments factories, in construction work, mining and agriculture the quota of foreigners was over 50 per cent. In the last stages of the war, German workers were only active as foremen and mastercraftsmen, with 80–90 per cent of the workforce being foreigners. Among the workforce a strictly segmented racial and national hierarchy developed, with German workers at the apex, followed by workers of 'Germanic' origin such as the Danes or Dutch, and then down, via the Poles, to Soviet civilian workers and finally prisoners of war. This hierarchy determined the living and working conditions of workers. Germans were generally in supervisory positions where workers from Eastern Europe were deployed; and in large factories, Germans were usually there solely to train or to control the others. Certainly, German workers were also subject to increased pressure, but foreigners were much more adversely affected by the draconian punishments for 'shirking' or 'breach of contract' than their hosts. There was some potential for the development of common interests between Germans and foreigners in the factories, and the number of cases where people were ready to help 'foreign workers' was not inconsiderable. However, most German workers, like the population in general, were neither ready to help nor ready actively to maltreat foreigners, but rather regarded their presence with disinterest, an attitude that hardened as the war progressed and as the Germans became preoccupied with their own problems. Gradually, an attitude developed towards such foreigners which silently presupposed racial inequalities and did not regard effective participation in racial policy as being anything worthy of much comment.

This had long-term consequences for the German working class. Regardless of how individuals behaved towards foreigners, their presence set in motion a form of social restructuring that provided unprecedented prospects for social mobility. The conversion of the German economy from one of *Blitzkrieg* to a long war of attrition as a result of the military failure outside Moscow in the autumn of 1941, rapidly altered the living and working conditions of the German workers. The composition of the factory workforce altered. Although, apart from foremen and skilled craftsmen, those remaining in factories were mostly over fifty, conscription began to make inroads even into the workforce of armaments factories. An increasing proportion of German workers was called up, an event that dramatically and decisively altered their destinies, (although here we are entering the realm of supposition in the absence of hard evidence). What is certain is that, depending upon luck or otherwise, a couple of months or fifteen years in the army not only broadened a socially and geographically very narrow range of experience, but also profoundly influenced their political and moral values. In relation to this, squabbles about pay, socio-political improvements or the role of the German Labour Front — to take only a few subjects all too prevalent in recent historical literature — seem rather marginal.

The primary concern of those who stayed at home was to make sure they were categorised in reserved occupations or that their presence on the domestic front was essential. This became one of the most effective means of disciplining German workers. On the other hand, the working population was much preoccupied with erratic food supply and bombing raids. Given the decrease in available consumer goods, wage rates lost their significance and food became the primary subject of interest. The logical consequence of rationing and food shortages was a burgeoning second economy: panic buying, illicit slaughtering, hoarding and the black market quickly assumed great significance — an obvious, almost logical development, which certainly did not politically threaten the Nazi regime. However, it was an obvious challenge to that regime's totalitarian aspirations, because it threatened to puncture belief in the regime's administrative efficiency. Despite the brutal but obviously ineffectual intervention of the Gestapo, it was impossible to get rid of the black market; however, the Nazis were successful in limiting memories of its activities to the post-war era.

The decisive element in the disintegration of the pro-National Socialist consensus was undoubtedly the bombing campaign, which, because of the density of urban working-class residential districts, affected them worse than any other class. The concomitant burdens were considerable: the time and place of work frequently altered, and in many factories the workers had to work all day and then do air-raid service at night. The mood of the German population, especially in towns within bombing range, gradually switched to one of apathy and resignation; the reduction of social awareness to matters of day-to-day existence and the mounting disinterest in social or political questions, were all manifestations of this development. Nevertheless, there was no broadly based political opposition.

This political apathy was not merely a by-product of increased terror on the part of the security services, nor of a growing concern with individual survival. The air-raids themselves contributed not merely hopelessness and fear, but also, by promoting anger and bitterness towards a superior opponent, provided the National Socialist leadership with sentiments they could harness. Broad sections of the population, including the workers, were also afraid of a German defeat, particularly at the hands of the Soviet Union, which again provided Nazi propaganda with something to play upon in the last two years of the war.

It is, in fact, very difficult to separate the experiences of the working class from those of other groups during the third and final stage of the war. The reason for this lies not simply in the changes among the workforce brought about by conscription or the deployment of foreigners. Rather, as the effects of the war became more and more apparent, individual horizons narrowed and other criteria assumed vast importance: whether one was called up or not; whether one ended up on the Eastern or Western Front; whether one was wounded or not; whether one's family lived in a small country town or a major industrial region; in the suburbs or the town centre; whether they had been bombed out or not; whether the children had been evacuated; whether they had taken in refugees or had had to seek shelter themselves; whether one lived in eastern Germany and had had to flee, or in the west where the bombing raids were severer — these were the questions that primarily determined individual destinies and comprised people's experiences. Ties to the collective development of a class to which one once belonged lost their significance. Instead, people formed communities of destiny, whose fate was determined by geographical, military and political factors, and, last but not least, by luck. This was important for the German workers because, more than any other class, their lives had been focused upon a class-bound collectivity even though the cohesive power of the proletarian milieu had diminished in recent years.

The initial problem of how to interpret the development of the working class under Nazi rule has led to the stressing of consensus, integration and agreement rather than such factors as nonconformity, opposition and resistance. When looking at the pre-war years as a whole what seems striking in terms of the Nazis' assumption of power is the relative continuity of development in the context of favourable economic circumstances as well as the form assumed by social conflict. What was new was the changed political framework which favoured employers, following the destruction of organised labour and the terrorising of the working population, rather than any automatic material consequences for the workers themselves. The National Socialists' specific contribution in this phase consisted in introducing racial-hygienic principles into social policy: by excluding the 'unfit' or 'biologically burdened'. If one compares these developments with the corporatist social policies of the Italian Fascists, then the difference would seem to lie, above all, in the Nazis' more modern conception of not excluding the workers explicitly from a share in economic development, but rather attempting to include the 'valuable' elements among them in the 'national community', something achieved by promoting a vision of society in which the dividing lines were horizontal rather than vertical. In view of the miserable socio-economic condition of the German workers since the middle of the First World War this strategy was successful, because it gave the workers stability, albeit on a very modest level, while simultaneously opening up prospects of longer-term social mobility. The Nazis were therefore reacting to the workers' primary social concerns, against which political repression seemed quite secondary, especially since terror was limited to resistance activists, while the persecution of the 'racially' or 'biologically' inferior did not directly concern them. In any case, one could hardly say that many younger workers, including supporters of bourgeois and Right-wing groups and indeed the Communists, had a very profound acquaintance with the notion of democratic freedom before 1933. Thus, political criticism of the Nazi regime abated with improvements in personal circumstances, while the continuation of social conflict in the factories was not directly connected with the political rule of the National Socialists. Put differently, it was not a case of political consensus, but rather socio-economic improvements that neutralised and partly integrated the workers, with the regime going to considerable lengths until the last year of war to appease the German worker.

This occurred principally through the imposition of burdens upon the populations of occupied countries, which radicalised existing domestic racism while simultaneously turning it outwards. But while those elements excluded from the German population — Jews, the disabled, Gypsies, the asocial and others — were lost from view, the arrival of millions of foreign workers whose presence explicitly worked to the advantage of a German population deemed to be racially superior was a tangible everyday reality. At the same time, a considerable proportion of the working class became part of the Nazi war machine for such long periods that the effects and influence of this upon their own self-esteem and political outlook were probably extraordinary and considerable.

Nonetheless, neither experience — as privileged German workers or German soldiers — was sufficient to achieve political cohesion; working-class adherence to National Socialism was bound up with the regime's success. If there was no success, Nazism lost its attractions. The bombing war destroyed the preconditions for acceptance of the regime without, it should be said, resulting in active political opposition. The political ties to the regime that existed among the workers quickly lost their power and were replaced by a disillusioned pragmatism, with experience contradicting the regime's ideologically determined models of a perfect society. But at the same time, people's first experience during the late 1930s of the interplay of security of employment, relatively high wages, welfare provision, leisure activities and a focus upon family life left lasting and positive memories. In the light of these experiences, all future policy would be judged by German workers in accordance with these standards.

'The Real Mystery in Germany'
M. Burleigh and W. Wippermann, *The Racial State: Germany, 1933–1945* (Cambridge, 1991; 2nd edn. 1992); David F. Crew, *Nazism and German Society, 1933–1945* (London, 1994); N. Frei, *National Socialist Rule in Germany: The Führer State. 1933–1945* (Oxford, 1993); U. Herbert, *Fremdarbeiter, Politik und Praxis des 'Auslander-Einsatzes' in der Kriegswirtschaft des Dritten Reiches* (Berlin, 1985); ibid, *Arbeit, Volkstum, Wettanschauung* (Frankfurt au Main, 1995); L. Niethammer, 'Heimat und Front', in L. Niethammer (ed.), *Die Jahre Weiss Man Nicht, Wo Man die Heute Hinsetzen Soll* (Berlin, 1983); D. Peukert, *Inside Nazi Germany* (London, 1989); M.-L. Recker, *Nationalsozialistische Sozial-politik im Zweiten Weltkrieg* (Munich, 1985); J. Stephenson, 'Triangle: Foreign Workers, German Civilians, and the Nazi Regime', *German Studies Review*, 15 (1992).

CHAPTER II

RACIAL DISCRIMINATION AT WORK: FORCED LABOUR IN THE VOLKSWAGEN FACTORY, 1939–45

Klaus-Jörg Siegfried

O N 26 MAY 1938 ADOLF HITLER laid the foundation-stone for the Volkswagen factory at Fallersleben which was being constructed under the auspices of Robert Ley's German Labour Front (DAF). The Volkswagen plant was built for the mass production of a cheap 'people's car' — costing a relatively modest RM990 — designed by the Stuttgart-based engineer Ferdinand Porsche, the only private sector car manufacturer to regard such a vehicle as either feasible or desirable. Other manufacturers such as Opel had explored the idea, principally to offset the prospect of a Nazi takeover of the automobile industry. When they retired from the quest for a cheap popular vehicle, Porsche and a colleague from Daimler-Benz stayed on to run the whole project, which was essentially a state concern run by private sector managers. The factory was to be equipped with its own power plant, foundry, rolling-mills and facilities for the manufacture of glass and tyres, with assembly lines copied from the Ford factory at Rouge River. A 'model town' was to be built near Fallersleben, to be called 'the town of the Strength through Joy car', 'Strength through Joy' being the DAF subsidiary organisation dedicated to shaping the leisure time of the working-classes. At a time when car ownership was still a luxury enjoyed by the middle classes, the Nazis wanted to demonstrate that their policies would benefit the working classes. Ley and the DAF took an interest in the scheme chiefly because involvement in one of the Führer's pet projects would counter the DAF's reputation for corruption, mismanagement and scandal. Paradoxically, the idea of approaching the DAF seems to have come from the chairman of Bayerische Motorwerke (BMW), who by linking ownership of a 'people's car' with DAF membership, was clearly hoping to preserve intact his own firm's share of the middle-class market.

In the event, following the outbreak of war the Fallersleben factory was gradually subsumed by the arms industry, becoming a regionally significant producer of arms for the duration. The plant produced military vehicles, such as the Kübelwagen or 'bucket car' (in 1943: 28 per cent of output); aircraft parts for Junkers 88 bombers (in 1942: *circa* 40 per cent of output; in 1944: *circa* 8 per cent of output); becoming from 1944 the largest manufacturer of V-1 flying bombs, of which between 13,000 and 14,000 were produced before the end of the war. The factory also turned out a range of smaller weapons, such as mines, bazookas, ammunition, tank tracks and stoves for the troops on the Eastern Front.

Although the initial transformation from civil to military production was accompanied by a number of setbacks, the factory became a flourishing part of the armaments sector as industrial capacity was mobilised for total war. However, this was only achieved through increasing resort to foreign forced labour, prisoners of war and inmates of concentration camps. Like most other armaments manufacturers, the Volkswagen plant made up the deficit of skilled workers lost to the armed forces by participating in the conscription and deportation of millions of people from countries under German occupation. Even as the plant was being established, management had had difficulties recruiting labour due to competition from other armaments manufacturers in the Brunswick area, notably the Hermann Göring-Werk at Salzgitter. Workers had to be recruited from Austria, the Saarland, Upper Silesia and the Sudentenland. A factory training school was established at Brunswick to provide future skilled workers. However, with the outbreak of war the management was faced with the loss to the armed forces of the nucleus of skilled workers they had carefully assembled. Many of the eager trainees at Brunswick enthusiastically volunteered for the *Waffen*-SS. Arms contracts, which were accompanied by allocations of forced labour, were one way of solving the firm's labour crisis. Initially, Volkswagen acquired foreign workers either on a voluntary basis, or through agreements with Allied or neutral countries. For example in 1938 the management could replace 3,000 construction workers drafted to the 'Westwall' fortification project with a corresponding contingent of Italians, under an agreement between the DAF and the Fascist Confederation of Industrial Labour. This element of voluntarism increasingly disappeared in the case of Germany's defeated opponents. In mid-1943, about 1,500 French workers arrived at the factory to perform labour service. Their number included members of the collaborationist Vichy youth organisation. They were followed shortly by 150 Belgian civilians, about 300 Dutch students and smaller contingents from other occupied countries.

The extent and method of labour recruitment were determined by political factors and by the Nazi regime's all-pervasive racial ideology. The main criterion was the racial proximity of any given nationality to the so-called 'Aryan master-race'. The Dutch, Flemings, Danes and Norwegians received better treatment because of their alleged racial affinity with the Germans. By contrast, workers from Poland and the Soviet Union were regarded as being of 'lesser racial value' or 'sub-human', and hence lived in conditions that were designed merely to keep them alive. Accordingly, in eastern Europe and the Soviet Union the Nazi regime rapidly resorted to conscription and deportation, with entire villages being ringed by the police, SS or army, and the inhabitants shipped to Germany in railway cars designed for freight or livestock. In this fashion, the Volkswagen plant acquired about 1,500 Poles, many of them under fifteen years of age, and four to five thousand so-called 'eastern workers' from the Soviet Union, the majority of whom were women aged between sixteen and twenty.

A further 1.9 million prisoners of war were also deployed in the armaments industry, although this was expressly prohibited by international law. Some 850 French and 850 Soviet prisoners of war worked in the Volkswagen factory, with their ranks eventually being augmented by 1,500 Italian 'military internees', that is soldiers loyal to Marshal Badoglio rather than Mussolini. These prisoners were subject to the discipline and orders of the German armed forces, lived behind barbed wire and were denied the freedom to move about outside their camps. Their allocation to armaments factories was carried out by the labour authorities.

In the case of concentration camp prisoners, compulsory labour was inseparable from the organised terror perpetrated by the SS. Industrialists applied directly to the SS department responsible for concentration camps in order to satisfy their labour requirements. As a result of this initiative by the management of the Volkswagen plant, about 600 prisoners were contracted to build a light metals foundry; in 1944 a satellite camp of Neuengamme concentration camp was established with about 860 prisoners who then constructed a camp for forced foreign labour there. In the same year, 650 Jewish women were transferred from Auschwitz to the Volkswagen plant to work on the manufacture of bazookas and mines. Finally, about 7,000 concentration camp inmates were distributed among a number of outlying or underground work-shops established as a consequence of worsening Allied air-raids. Concentration camp labour, both in the Volkswagen plant and in the armaments sector as a whole, contributed little to the regime's ever-growing production targets.

How did the management of the Volkswagen factory control this army of forced foreign workers, prisoners of war and concentration camp inmates? In the Nazi state armaments factories were areas where normal rights were suspended and the management could call on the SS to dis-cipline the workforce. In practice, this meant that the Volkswagen factory was organised according to the Führer principle; the workforce lost any form of independent representation (the 'works council' was a sham) and was subjected to the totalitarian control and propaganda of the German Labour Front. Surveillance of the workers, designed to obstruct any form of political activity, was carried out by informers who reported to the Gestapo and the representative of military intelligence. The factory guard or *Werkschutz*, consisting of SS men, patrolled the factory corridors and floor with guns and dogs, arresting workers for the slightest infraction of rules; they were then beaten, confined in the factory cellars and taken to a special works (punishment) camp, or in more serious cases for three weeks' detention in Labour Camp 21 at Hallendorf near Salzgitter. Those who were not killed there returned to their workplaces in a desolate con-dition or were sent to hospitals to recover from their injuries.

Foreign workers were particularly subject to these terror practices; they were entirely under the control of German master-craftsmen and foremen whose instructions had to be obeyed without demur. Much therefore hinged upon the character or political persuasion of individual German workers; whether they abused the foreign workers, making them work at a frenzied tempo or whether they treated them sympathetically when hunger and exhaustion meant that they could not fulfil their pro-duction quotas. Foreign workers were further subject to control and sur-veillance in the camps where they lived. The camps were under the direction of commandants from the German Labour Front who were also employees of the Volkswagen factory. They relied upon a subordinate hierarchy of camp spokesmen and auxiliary police to maintain control. Concentration camp prisoners, who were housed in total isolation from the rest of the workforce, were guarded exclusively by the SS.

It was characteristic of National Socialist rule that terror and violence were augmented by integrationary strategies so that consensus accompanied coercion. These included not only ideological and propagandistic conditioning or concessions of a socio-political type, but also cultural events and the organisation of leisure time. The Volkswagen factory had a vast leisure centre known as the Cianetti Hall. The eponymous Tullio Cianetti was the President of the Fascist Confederation of Industrial Labour who concluded the arrangement with Robert Ley to deploy thousands of Italian construction workers in order to build the 'town of the Strength through Joy car'. The Cianetti Hall was designed as a monument to Italo-German friendship, a fact suggestive of the political function of the various cultural activities — concerts, ballet, plays, films, exhibitions and sporting events — that took place there. These were primarily designed to influence German and Italian workers, although the Belgians, Dutch and French were allowed to participate too. The Poles and 'Eastern workers' and naturally prisoners of war and concentration camp inmates were excluded from the events held in the Cianetti Hall. Italian military internees were admitted or debarred from these events in accordance with the degree of submission and willingness to work they evinced. In other words, the official cultural offerings of the leisure organisation 'Strength through Joy' themselves reflected racial criteria in accordance with the patterns of discrimination which governed the working and living conditions of all 'foreign workers'. How did this work in practice?

Discriminatory racial criteria also determined living and working conditions. Foreign workers deemed to be racially akin to the Germans were to all intents and purposes treated like Germans. Political considerations also played a part. Workers from allied states, for example until 1943 the Italians, or workers from collaborationist Vichy France were regarded by the Germans as 'workmates' and enjoyed a relatively privileged position. This was particularly so in the case of members of a Vichy organisation who volunteered to work in the Volkswagen factory. These 'Western workers' were properly fed and received adequate medical attention. They could leave their barracks after work and could go about the town if they wished to. They were also allowed to organise their own cultural activities. The French seem to have been particularly active on the cultural front, organising concerts, exhibitions and Christmas festivities in the Cianetti Hall, and taking part in an orchestra and choir which were occasionally allowed to undertake outside engagements.

Matters were otherwise for Polish and Soviet 'eastern workers'. They had to wear discriminatory identificatory markings on their clothing, analogous to the Star of David worn by Jews: a 'P' for Poles and 'OST' for people from the Soviet Union. They were highly vulnerable to abuse by fanatical master-craftsmen, foremen, camp commanders and the factory guards, and were usually forbidden to leave the camps in which they were housed. There they were certainly permitted their own cultural activities, but it was highly unlikely that any of them were keen on taking part in amateur dramatics when they were starving and having to work ten or twelve hours a day. Any enthusiasm for cultural activities soon evaporated and they sank into the dull monotony of the camp's daily routine. While many of them sickened and died as a result of exhaustion and hunger at an unusually premature age, none of the Dutchmen or Frenchmen at Volkswagen died.

The weakest were worst affected. Inevitably, intimate relations developed which resulted in many Polish and Russian women becoming pregnant. The regime stipulated that female forced labourers had to part with their children two weeks after delivery in order to return the mothers to the productive process as rapidly as possible. The children were to be raised in a 'children's home of the simplest sort'. From the autumn of 1944 all newly born children taken to the Volkswagen children's home at Rühen died on account of this officially inspired neglect of basic hygiene. Because of this, after the war the British occupying forces tried and executed Dr Körbel, the doctor responsible for the home.

Living conditions of prisoners of war were also determined in accordance with racial criteria. They were subjected to greater control and more stringent discipline than civilians from the same countries. Conditions were especially atrocious for Soviet prisoners of war. Demonised as the 'Jewish Bolshevik enemy', many of them never survived the long treks into captivity or confinement in vast camps with nothing to shelter them from the harsh Russian winter. Millions of them simply lost the will to live and died. Those Soviet prisoners of war who arrived at the Volkswagen plant were often in a deplorable condition, with many of them suffering from typhus from which they soon died. Economic, rather than humanitarian, considerations led the management

to give these men food and medical attention so that they might be incorporated into the productive process. Notwithstanding this initial concern, most of them soon vegetated in lice-ridden rags at the margins of
human existence. The same fate awaited the Italian 'military internees' —
known colloquially as 'Badoglio swine' — or those Italian soldiers captured by German troops after the fall of Mussolini in 1943. They became
the special targets of the fury and frustration of German workers and
foremen, who regarded them as traitors and who blamed Germany's erst-
while ally for setbacks on the battlefields. Many of these Italians committed suicide or died of hunger and exhaustion. Soviet and Italian
prisoners of war were almost on the same level as concentration camp
prisoners. In the latter case, discrimination against foreign workers escal-
ated into the deadly maxim 'extermination through labour'. The SS were
not concerned to conserve the labour capacity of the prisoners —
although this sometimes happened in the interests of productivity — but
rather to 'exhaust' it (i.e. not to restore them from hunger and exhaustion). By the end of 1944, the Volkswagen plant and its outlying work-
shops had incorporated the deaths of these prisoners into their business
calculations.

How did the foreign forced workers and concentration camp prisoners
react to their fate? One of the objectives of the racially discriminatory
measures considered here, was to stimulate antagonism and resentment
between the various categories of foreign workers, thus making it impossible for them to unite in the interests of resistance to Nazi terror. By and
large this strategy failed. No durable enmities developed between
'Western' and 'Eastern' workers, or between civilian workers, prisoners
of war and concentration camp inmates. Even the policy of physically
isolating the various groups failed. Although they lived in separate camps,
the foreign workers mingled in the factory, with the sole exception of
concentration camp inmates who worked separately. This resulted in
numerous contacts and expressions of solidarity: French, Dutch, Belgian
and Italian men developed close personal relations with Polish or Russian
women; Dutchmen learned Russian, while Ukrainian girls acquired a
smattering of Dutch; French civilian workers shared their food with
starving Soviet prisoners of war; an Italian doctor secretly smuggled
medicines to women Jewish concentration camp prisoners; two unknown
Polish Jewish nurses cared for sick Dutch foreign workers in hospital.

Cultural activities were a means of counteracting the deleterious
psychological effects of forced labour. Even though the cultural activities

offered by the regime had a transparent ideological and political message, they nonetheless contributed to the inner stability of the individual in the comfortless milieu of the camps in which the workers lived. Autonomous cultural activities strengthened national group solidarities and hence powers of resistance. For example French forced labourers produced their own newspaper, which was tolerated by the camp commandant and factory management because of its supposedly non-political content. They and the Gestapo simply failed to note the hidden ironies of much of the content, which hence became a platform for the expression of French opposition.

All of the forced foreign workers were united in their rejection of the Nazi regime, regardless of differences in their conditions and treatment; for even the Dutch, Belgians and Frenchmen, including collaborationist Vichy workers, were victims of SS and Gestapo repression if they expressed undesirable political views, let alone participated in spontaneous demonstrations. This universal opposition to the regime did not result in every group of forced foreign workers participating in active resistance. Gestapo and factory militia control were far too tight and the punishments too draconian for this to happen. Accordingly, there was only passive resistance, consisting of innumerable minor acts of individual sabotage, which were difficult to detect: machinery was wrongly set, small parts were incorrectly assembled and so on. Moreover, individuals endeavoured to overcome hunger and exploitation by deliberately working at a slow pace, pretending to be sick or stupid, by smuggling food from the kitchens or by surreptitiously cooking stolen potatoes at the work-bench with the aid of buckets and electric cable. Many Dutchmen and Frenchmen took the opportunity of home leave to disappear entirely, before home leave was cancelled for all 'west workers'. Among those who stayed behind, a few had the courage to tune in to foreign radio stations to learn of Allied military advances.

Exploitation of foreign forced labour at the Volkswagen plant ceased when Fallersleben was occupied by American troops on 11 April 1945. The Nazi functionaries and SS men fled, and the machinery finally lay still. Soviet forced labourers and prisoners of war, who had suffered the most in the preceding years, armed themselves and went on a looting spree in the town, killing anyone who tried to stop them. Former 'west workers' supported the efforts of Allied forces and what remained of the German administration to restore law and order. Subsequently, all foreign workers were repatriated. The concentration camp inmates had been taken away by the SS before the town was liberated by the Allies. Many of them were so debilitated that they died before they too could be liberated.

What was the significance of armaments production and forced labour for the Volkswagen concern? While other firms were swiftly integrated into the armaments sector, the outbreak of war initially threatened the very existence of Volkswagen. Planned as a car factory and only partially completed, the factory could not immediately be converted to military production. It faced the real danger of being left incomplete and idle, or of being taken over by an existing arms manufacturer. This gave a certain urgency to the concern's quest for arms contracts and the forced labour that went with them. Since the Volkswagen factory had had considerable difficulties recruiting labour in the year of its foundation, and then had to relinquish many of those it managed to recruit to the armed forces, the firm felt obliged to bridge the labour shortage by resorting to foreign forced labour and concentration camp inmates. The problem was compounded by the management's attempts to expand its share of armaments manufacturing, a policy that was only possible by increasing the number of those foreign workers most subject to the Nazi regime's repression. Since these groups comprised the greater part of the army of forced labour in the Volkswagen factory (with about 8,000 Polish and Soviet civilian workers and prisoners of war as well as Italian 'military internees') it can be seen that the Volkswagen factory became a leading participant in the regime of terror that the Nazis created in the armaments sector. The result was massive dependence upon forced labour, consisting of 70 per cent of the total workforce in 1943, a figure that far outstripped the numbers employed in other factories.

Which of the directors and managers of the Volkswagen plant were responsible for these decisions? The Nazi war economy was dirigiste. Allocations to factories of raw materials and labour were in accordance with state production programmes established by the Ministry of Armaments in response to military priorities. The private sector itself was involved in allocating as well as implementing government contracts. This permitted businessmen from the more powerful concerns to exert influence upon state planning. The Volkswagen plant enjoyed this sort of influence, since the firm's foundation was intimately bound up with one of the regime's favoured social projects. Moreover in 1943 Volkswagen derived additional prestige from being designated a 'model wartime concern', a title augmented a year later into 'model National Socialist concern'. More important was the fact that the chief executive was Ferdinand Porsche, the designer of the 'people's car'. The other executive directors were the DAF functionary Dr Bodo Lafferentz and Jakob Werlin, a member of the board of Daimler Benz. Porsche was a confidant of Hitler, who used Porsche's reputation as a designer of genius to identify the regime with technological progress. In 1941 Hitler put Porsche in charge of a commission concerned with tank manufacture, the most important weapon on the eve of, and during, the invasion of the Soviet Union. Porsche's role was to act as a conduit for Hitler's own ideas on tank warfare. He used his contacts with the Führer to achieve the integration of Volkswagen into the armaments sector, but he also had a personal interest in doing so, since he was in charge of a firm in Stuttgart-Zuffenhausen which fulfilled contract work on behalf of the Volkswagen factory. What benefited Volkswagen benefited Porsche too. Ferdinand Porsche was thus responsible for Volkswagen's conversion to an armaments factory. He eagerly sought out fresh defence contracts, including one for the V-1 flying bombs which were used to destructive effect against London from 1944. A representative of Porsche roamed the occupied Soviet Union in search of 'eastern workers'. Engineers from the factory also had their pick of Soviet prisoners of war caged at Fallingbostel, as well as of hundreds of Jews from the extermination camp at Auschwitz. Porsche's keenness eventually ensured his ensnarement in the conflicts of competence and interest within the Nazi polyocracy. He crossed swords with the Minister of Munitions, Albert Speer, who eased Porsche from the chairmanship of the commission on tank production. In order to realise his ambitions in the armaments sector, Porsche sought for a powerful ally, finding one in the shape of Reichsführer-SS, Heinrich Himmler, who was interested in securing a share of the arms sector for his ramified concentration camp empire. In 1937 Porsche had already put out 'feelers' to Himmler by requesting SS men to test drive the Volkswagen Beetle (so-called because of its shape). Later, he availed himself of the SS to provide guards for the workers forced to toil in the Volkswagen factory. The Waffen-SS in turn backed his plans to convert the Beetle for military purposes. In 1942, Porsche used his connection with Himmler to secure from Hitler the authorisation to build a concentration camp at Volkswagen whose inmates would construct a foundry. In return, Porsche agreed to supply the SS with 4,000 'bucket' vehicles (jeep-type military vehicles). Porsche's aim was eventually to use the foundry for the production of civilian vehicles; whether he still harboured these ideas by the end of the war is doubtful, since he was still trying to secure military contracts in 1944, by which time they were much reduced in number. For example, he requested from Himmler 3,500 concentration camp inmates for the production of V-1 rockets and aircraft in a subterranean factory. Himmler rewarded his commitment and enthusiasm by granting him the honorary rank of SS-Oberführer and a death's-head ring for his finger.

The historian Hans Mommsen, who for some years has been producing a history of the Volkswagen plant during the Nazi period on behalf of Volkswagen AG, which has so far not appeared in print, has characterised the behaviour and personality of Porsche as follows. Porsche was 'tantalised by the technological opportunities which the regime made available to him' and did not shrink 'from exploiting the personal relationship which existed between him and Hitler in the interests of both his design bureau and then the plant'. Mommsen continues, 'Especially in the later stages of a war which was effectively already lost, Porsche revealed himself to be a champion of armaments production at any price', and 'as a supporter of a policy of soldiering on to the bitter end . . . He himself never questioned the system of forced labour. He also proceeded relatively unscrupulously when it came to the implementation of his projects.'

However, it would be wrong to judge Porsche in isolation from the historical circumstances of his actions or to explain them solely through reference to the nature of his character. The biases of the car manufacturer were typical of German industrialists in the Nazi period, and many of his decisions could certainly also have been made by other entrepreneurs. It has already been noted that the German armaments industry was closely involved with the apparatus of the Nazi state. The regime wanted to direct arms production in accordance with its policies and military strategies and thereby availed itself of the private sector, upon which it was necessarily dependent. However, this dependence gave the most powerful concerns the chance to maintain themselves *vis-à-vis* the state, or indeed to use its institutions and organisations in their own interests. Without being necessarily convinced of the racial ideology of the Nazi regime, many industrialists colluded with the racially-motivated imperialist goals of the Nazis' war effort since arms production meant vast, state-guaranteed profits, while the regime's military expansionism promised a considerably enhanced sphere of economic activity and influence. Mommsen writes that 'In this respect the management of the Volkswagen factory was no different from any other large concern.' The political horizons and economic activities of industrialists such as Porsche progressively lost their moral dimension the more hopeless the war appeared and the more brutally the regime practised its policies of extermination during the phase of 'total war'. The cumulative desensitisation that accompanied this process saw a progressive loss of scruple regarding the employment of forced labour and concentration camp prisoners, and the ruthless exploitation of their labour, until only purely economic and technocratic aims counted. This may explain why, for example, Porsche intervened to improve the rations of half-starved Soviet prisoners of war, while doing nothing to prevent the mass demise of the children born to forced workers in the Volkswagen factory.

'Moral deadening, a professionalised loss of a sense of reality and National Socialist indoctrination, went hand in hand in the attitudes of functionaries at various levels' is how Mommsen characterises the behaviour of Porsche and other members of the management in the last phase of the war. But even though contemporary circumstances and the climate of the times may determine the behaviour of individuals, they do not exonerate them from responsibility. It remains the historian's task to distinguish and evaluate the degree to which the behaviour of an individual was influenced by social circumstances, or the result of individual decisions that also carry the burden of personal responsibility.

THE MASS DEATH OF THE CHILDREN OF POLISH AND SOVIET FORCED LABOURERS IN THE VOLKSWAGEN PLANT.

1942: The Nazi regime decides to halt the repatriation of pregnant foreign workers since it needs their labour capacity for armament production. The children are to be removed from their mothers and raised in children's homes 'of the simplest type'.

February 1943 to the end of 1943: The management of the Volkswagen factory establishes a maternity ward and a children's home within the camps for pregnant foreign workers. Ten children die of malnutrition.

October 1943 to May 1944: The children fall ill with scabies, boils and ulcers. Thirty-five of them die.

14 June 1944: The home is moved to Rühen (about 15 kilometres from the Volkswagen plant). The children contract gastroenteritis. The death rate rises to 100 per cent.

BIOGRAPHY OF A PERPETRATOR: DR HANS KÖRBEL

1909 born in Höchst. Attended a grammar school and then studied medicine.

1927 Membership of the Nazi Party.

1929 Joined the SA.

1934 Graduated with a doctorate from Heidelberg. Practical training in Darmstadt, Mainz and Heidelberg. Served as a factory doctor with Opel, I.G. Farben and other concerns. Promoted to SA *Obersturmführer* and awarded a golden Nazi Party decoration.

1935 Assistant physician in the university medical clinic at Heidelberg. Resigned from the SA and joined the SS. An *Untersturmführer* in the SS Security Service (SD), promoted to SS-*Obersturmführer* in September 1936.

1939 Promoted to SS-*Hauptsturmführer*. Became leading factory doctor in the Volkswagen plant, simultaneously assuming the following functions:

1940 Medical adviser to the factory health insurance scheme.

1941 Chief of the factory insurance scheme.

1943 Chief of the 'town of the Strength through Joy car' municipal hospital.

1946 Sentenced to death by a British military court for killing Polish and Russian children through deliberate neglect.

7 March 1947 Executed.

Forced Labour in the Volkswagen Factory

Bernard P. Bellon, *Mercedes in Peace and War: German Automobile Workers, 1903–1945* (New York, 1990); Ulrich Herbert, *A History of Foreign Labour in Germany* (London, 1990); ibid., *Fremdarbeiter. Politik und Praxis des Ausländereinsatzes in der Kriegswirtschaft des Dritten Reiches* (Berlin and Bonnn, 1985); Heinz Hohne, *The Order of the Death's Head* (London, 1972); Edward L. Homze, *Foreign Labor in Nazi Germany* (Princeton, 1967); Hans Mommsen, *Die Geschichte des Volkswagenwerks im Dritten Reich* (Bochum, 1991); Klaus-Jörg Siegfried, *Rüstungsproduktion und Zwangsarbeit im Volkswagenwerk,*

1939–1945 (Frankfurt am Main and New York, 1987); ibid., *Das Leben der Zwangsarbeiter im Volkswagenwerk, 1939–1945* (Frankfurt am Main and New York, 1988); Alfred Streim, *Die Behandlung Sowjetischer Kriegsgefangener im 'Fall Barbarossa'* (Karlsruhe, 1981); Christian Streit, *Keine Kamaraden* (Stuttgart, 1978).

CHAPTER III

NAZISM AND HIGH SOCIETY

Jeremy Noakes

'HIGH SOCIETY' IS NOT A TERM that has a respectable academic pedigree. Nevertheless, it expresses a social reality, namely the existence — at any rate from the 1920s to the 1940s — in the major capitals of Europe of an élite group whose basis was their social intercourse, their participation in an endless round of social engagements — dinners, balls, banquets, receptions, teas, soirées, concerts, theatre performances, race meetings and other social events of a similar nature. According to Martha Dodd, the daughter of the American ambassador to Berlin (1934–7), 'During the winter months most people got in two to four teas a day and a lunch or a dinner.' Membership of this group was determined by birth, official position or status, money, or — a trend that was beginning to develop during the 1920s — popular prestige as reflected in the mass media, or a combination of these attributes. High society was not identical with the political élite. Nevertheless, since it was widely regarded both by its own members and, through the influence of the media, by the population at large as the social élite, it invariably included a substantial proportion of the political élite.

At the centre of high society in Weimar Germany was the diplomatic corps. This marked a shift from the pre-war period when the central role had been performed by the Court and the diplomatic corps had formed simply a part of Court Society. During the first years of the Republic, much of the nobility associated with the Court had avoided social engagements with the despised new regime presided over by the ex-saddler, Friedrich Ebert, as President of the Reich. But, with the election of Field-Marshal von Hindenburg as President in 1925, they began to return to the capital and to play a role in high society. Until the outbreak of war, the Crown Prince continued to act as a focus for some members of the old aristocracy — retired generals and former ladies-in-waiting, who were known collectively and somewhat disparagingly as 'the

Potsdam Set' — entertaining at his 'stockbroker Tudor' mansion, the Cäcilienhof in Potsdam, or in his palace on Unter den Linden. In addition to the diplomatic corps and members of the former nobility, there were a number of wealthy businessmen who entertained on a grand scale. Some, such as the head of the Siemens electrical engineering combine, Werner von Siemens, were 'old money'; others had done well out of the war or the inflation and tried to make up for their lack of breeding by the lavishness of their entertainment. Then there were leading politicians, top civil servants, generals, artists and musicians, the occasional academic, film stars and the odd sports personality (tennis star, racing driver or flying ace).

Although most of the conversation that went on at these events was of a purely formal or conventional kind ('dull beyond belief' according to Martha Dodd), they did provide the opportunity for contacts and conversations of a more political nature — hence the intense involvement of the diplomatic corps. Moreover, acceptance within this circle implied social approval and so would confer a degree of legitimacy on any politician or political movement whose members could gain admittance. For the Nazi movement in the years before it came to power in 1933 the need to gain social acceptance among the élite was of considerable, indeed growing, importance. The abortive Munich Putsch of November 1923 had demonstrated that the Party could only come to power legally within the rules laid down by the Constitution. At the same time, it had tainted the movement with the reputation of being a group of violent revolutionaries. During the period 1925–9 the Party had to struggle against its image of being wild men on the political fringe. After the effective ending of parliamentary democracy with the appointment of Heinrich Brüning as Reich Chancellor in March 1930, political power became increasingly concentrated in the hands of the small group of men who had access to and influence over the Reich President. These men — Franz von Papen, Kurt von Schleicher, the young Hindenburg, Otto Meissner — were leading members of German high society. In these circumstances, the Nazis' need to transform their image, to convince the German élites that they were *salonfähig* (socially acceptable), formed an important part of the wider requirement to convince such groups that they were acceptable as a future government or at least as part of a future government.

Hitler was well aware of the political importance of social acceptability; he had owed his initial success in Munich to a significant extent to his ability to win friends and influence people within Munich high society. The post-war Munich high society suffered, like that of Berlin, from the loss of the Court. There was a small diplomatic corps in the shape of the foreign consuls — Munich was a relatively important posting after 1918 because of the importance and sensitivity of relations between Bavaria and the Reich, but its role in high society was not nearly so significant as that of Berlin. Munich high society was dominated by leading members of the upper middle class, particularly from the educated bourgeoisie — publishers, academics, artists, officials and professional men. Some of them were already associated with such extreme Right-wing *völkisch* organisations as the Thule Society and the Deutschvölkische Schutz und Trutzbund: men such as the publishers Julius Lehmann and Ernst Boepple, and the writer and translator, Dietrich Eckart. Others were impressed by Hitler's gifts as a demagogue, for example Munich University's Professor of Forestry, Karl Escherich, and the Professor of History, Karl Alexander von Müller.

Hitler had a particular appeal for upper-middle-class society ladies. With his shabby blue suit, long trench-coat, his dog whip and his revolver, Hitler was an exotic figure in the salons of Munich high society, either providing a frisson of radical chic or awakening the motherly instincts of his hostesses. Frau Erna Hanfstängl, the wife of 'Putzi' Hanfstängl, an early Nazi admirer whose family owned a prestigious international art publishing firm, sheltered Hitler after the abortive Munich Putsch. The Bechsteins, the famous piano manufacturers, invited Hitler to their suite in the Bayerischer Hof hotel and to their country house at Berchtesgaden. Frau Bechstein even loaned jewellery to the Party for use as collateral and gave Hitler advice on etiquette. But she had to compete for Hitler's attentions with Frau Bruckmann, the wife of the publisher of the works of Houston Stewart Chamberlain, the son-in-law of Richard Wagner. Hitler met Chamberlain when the Bechsteins introduced him to the Wagner household at Haus Wahnfried in Bayreuth in October 1923. Although this was not the most politically useful or financially lucrative of the numerous introductions provided by these society figures, it was undoubtedly the one that gave Hitler most personal satisfaction. Chamberlain's letter to Hitler, written following the meeting and shortly before his death, and praising him as the future saviour of Germany, not only boosted Hitler's self-esteem but impressed Winifred Wagner and laid the foundations for Hitler's long association with Haus Wahnfried.

More significant politically and, above all, financially were the contacts that were established through the Bavarian industrialist, Dr Emil Gansser, and the 'Baltic baron' Max Erwin Scheubner-Richter. Through Gansser's contacts, for example, Hitler spoke twice in the influential 1919 National Club in Berlin in May 1922 and received financial contributions from the two leading Berlin industrialists, Ernst von Borsig and Siemens, among others.

Although clearly Hitler's success during these early years depended primarily on his demagogic talents, nevertheless, it is difficult to see how he or his party could have survived, let alone prospered during 1922–3, years of hyperinflation and authoritarian government in Munich, without the protection of elements within Munich high society and among the Bavarian political and military establishment.

Following Hitler's abortive putsch in November 1923, the Nazi movement was obliged to spend several years in the political wilderness, a period in which, inevitably, it lost much of its appeal to high society in Munich or beyond. At the time of his trial in the spring of 1924, Hitler was still able to attract the favourable attention of some members of Munich society and, during the years 1925–8, he still had influential supporters, such as the coal magnate, Emil Kirdorf, who in 1926, for example, arranged for him to speak to Ruhr industrialists in Essen and to the élite 1919 Club in Hamburg.

However, the year 1929 was the turning-point in terms of the renewal of the attractiveness of the Nazi movement for high society. Moreover, this appeal was no longer largely confined to Munich but existed at national level. This development reflected both the changing electoral fortunes of the Nazi Party as apparent in the state and local government elections in the autumn of 1929 and, above all, the inclusion of the Party in the campaign against the Young Plan regulating German reparations payments organised by Alfred Hugenberg, the leader of the Right-wing German National People's Party. The fact that the Nazis were now officially allied to such socially respectable bodies as the Reichslandbund, the pressure group representing agriculture in general and the Prussian Junker landowners in particular, and the veterans' organisation, the Stahlhelm, of which Reich President von Hindenburg was the honorary president, removed from them the stigma of being a fringe group of wild men; the movement was now officially part of the right-wing anti-Republican establishment. This position was strengthened by the Party's massive gains in the Reichstag election of September 1930.

In fact, some members of the nobility had begun to gravitate towards the Nazi movement even before its electoral breakthrough in September 1930. Initially, the SA, the Stormtroopers' organisation, was the Nazi unit which proved most attractive, since its paramilitary style clearly appealed to the ex-officers and Free Corps leaders who were the first noble recruits. By August 1929, many of the leading positions within the SA were held by noble ex-officers. Its leader was Captain von Pfeffer; the deputy leader for West Germany was Lieutenant-Colonel Kurt von Ulrich and his adjutant was Werner von Fichte; the deputy leader for central Germany was Naval Commander, Manfred von Killinger, while the adjutant of the deputy leader for South Germany was Hanns Günter von Obernitz. Moreover, in that year a number of leading members of the German aristocracy joined the SA: Prince August-Wilhelm of Prussia, the fourth son of the Kaiser, Prince Friedrich-Christian of Schaumburg-Lippe and Prince Philipp of Hesse, who was the son-in-law of King Victor Emmanuel of Italy. The motorised division of the SA (the NSKK) was joined by Duke Eduard of Saxe-Coburg. Over the next four years, the higher ranks of the SA were full of members of noble families: Karl Friedrich Freiherr von Eberstein, Wolf Heinrich Count von Helldorf, Dietrich von Jagow, Hans von Tschammer und Osten, among others. However, although the SA had secured a head start in attracting members of the German nobility, in the event it was not the SA that was destined to become the élite Nazi formation but its rival, the SS.

Even before the appointment of Heinrich Himmler as its leader on 6 January 1929, the SS had the reputation of being an élite unit. In 1926 it was ordered that the SS 'must consist of specially selected, able, and cir-cumspect human material' and, at the first Party rally in Weimar in the same year, Hitler entrusted it with the 'blood banner', the swastika flag that had survived from the Munich Putsch of 1923, a signal honour. However, it was Himmler who was primarily responsible for turning the SS into the élite corps of the Third Reich, a goal that he sought from the moment of his appointment.

Like Hitler, Himmler had no great respect for the German nobility, regarding it as substantially degenerate. However, he shrewdly recog-nised that one way of rapidly achieving élite status for his organisation was to attach to it the prestige of the existing high society, and so he deliberately set out to win them over. His success was impressive. Between 1930 and 1933, nobles began to join the Nazi movement in ever-increasing numbers and these new recruits tended to prefer the smart tailored black uniform of the SS to the more plebeian brown shirt of the

SA. Among the German aristocrats who joined the SS before 1933 were the Hereditary Grand Duke of Mecklenburg, the Hereditary Prince of Waldeck and Pyrmont and the Princes Christof and Wilhelm of Hesse, as well as a string of lesser nobles.

With its electoral gains of 1930, the Nazi Party had for the first time become a serious player on the national political stage. During the next two and a half years, the Nazis set about integrating themselves into Berlin high society. Many of the nobles who had been recruited hitherto — for example, most of the ex-Free Corps SA leaders — were not members of high society as such. The Party still needed to gain an entrée into the drawing-rooms of Berlin. Bella Fromm, the society correspondent for the *Vossische Zeitung*, who had remarkable social connections, particularly with the diplomatic corps, noted in her diary on 29 January 1932: 'Society slowly gets accustomed to the originally plebeian National Socialist movement. People from the upper crust are turning to Hitler.'

As in Munich during the early 1920s, an important role in this process was played by individual society hostesses, notably Helen ('Mammi') von Carnap, the ambitious wife of the Kaiser's last Chamberlain, Viktoria von Dirksen, wife of a wealthy monarchist, whose palace was a meeting place for the highest aristocracy and members of the royal family, and Manna von Winterfeld, wife of a general in the Imperial army. On 19 October 1932 Bella Fromm noted:

> They get in everywhere these National Socialists. They are patient, they bore from within and from without ... Frau von Dirksen, relic of the *Geheimrat* Willibald von Dirksen, always a monarchist, has for years been an eager hostess of the National Socialists in her magnificent palace ... She has acted as a mediator between the National Socialists and the old courtiers. Her brother, Karl August von Leffert, the German 'Jules Verne', attends his sister's receptions in the full splendour of his SS uniform. 'Auwi', Prince August Wilhelm, is generally to be found there in his brown uniform, and both the hostess and her youngest daughter wear the swastika pinned conspicuously on their bosoms.

In addition to these salon Nazis, there were one or two figures closer to Hitler who performed a key role in mediating between the Nazi movement and the German establishment, of whom the most important were Hermann Goering and Joachim von Ribbentrop. Both of them in their different ways were well-equipped to play the part. Goering's father had been a low-ranking diplomat, consul-general in Haiti, and Goering had been brought up in a castle in Bavaria owned by his mother's lover. During the First World War he had won Germany's highest military award, the Pour le Mérite, while leading the élite Richthofen squadron. Thus, although not a member of the social élite, Goering's background made him sufficiently *salonfähig* to move easily in high society and establish and maintain the right contacts. He was also an appropriate figure to take on the post of President of the Reichstag, the most prominent public position held by a Nazi before the takeover of power.

Ribbentrop lacked Goering's war record but made up for it with the wealth he had acquired from his marriage to Annette von Henckell, whose family owned the largest German champagne business. Ribbentrop, whose 'von' was acquired rather than inherited, had travelled widely abroad and, his excellent manners made an urbane impression. He entertained lavishly at his villa in the exclusive Berlin suburb of Dahlem, providing one of the best tables in the capital. His villa was the venue for the key negotiations that preceded Hitler's appointment as Reich Chancellor.

The recruitment of large numbers of nobles and other figures from German high society in the years 1929–33 ensured that the immediate impact of the Nazi takeover of power in this sphere was limited and was felt more as a stage in a transitional process. In the months before January 1933 brown and black Nazi uniforms were already part of the social scene; Magda Goebbels and Annette von Ribbentrop were already members of high society; by the autumn of 1932, much of the social élite was already coming to terms with the possibility if not the prospect of a Nazi victory, and some were already seeking a place in the new order.

After the Nazi takeover in January 1933, the stream of noble recruits to the Nazi movement became a flood as German nobles scrambled to position themselves advantageously for the opportunities offered by the new regime and to protect the positions they already had. Both the ex-Kaiser and the Crown Prince sounded out the prospects of a restoration of the monarchy and, for a few months, Hitler let them and their supporters keep their illusions — until his regime was well established. In this behaviour the nobility were of course no different from their bourgeois compatriots. However, whereas the mass of the 'March violets' or 'March casualties' (as those who had joined the NSDAP after March 1933 were called) joined the Party, the noble recruits preferred the SS. The result was that, as one author put it: 'the membership lists of the SS soon began to resemble pages from the Gotha [the official record of the German nobility]'.

Despite his contempt for what he regarded as the degeneracy of much of the nobility, Himmler approved of its two traditional foundations, namely careful breeding from approved stock and the ownership of land, and he urged his SS officers to try and win over the good blood in the nobility by seeking out their society. As he told a meeting of SS leaders in 1936:

> I refer, for example, to the horse-riding sports in which the Prussian landed nobility are heavily involved. If you take a look at the individuals involved, you have to admit there is some damned good blood among them; and you have to admit further that the Party has not won over this good blood. That is a sober statement of fact . . . We must try to fill the sons and daughters of those who are now opposed to us with our ideology, which after all is not so very far removed from the ideological principles of the nobility . . . Sometimes, when I was in the society of such people I commented maliciously: I expect you're surprised that we use a knife and fork, that we can do it too. At first, they found it in bad taste that one said something like that, but then one could talk to each other frankly about many things which one otherwise wouldn't have been able to discuss . . . But if we succeed in winning over one or two society people then they will gradually come to understand: that's right, they too have a shortage of leaders . . . And so I want you to have a word with your Gauleiter and other leaders of the movement and tell them: you must attend these social occasions. And if they refuse, saying that there's no point, that as old revolutionaries they're not going to meet this reactionary, then you must reply: we didn't carry out a revolution for the sake of carrying out a revolution. And that among those who move at this level there are a number who are worth winning over, just as there were a number among the workers who were worth winning over.

As part of this strategy, in 1933 the SS had succeeded in taking over the most important of the élite riding clubs in the most important horse-breeding areas of East Prussia, Holstein, Oldenburg, Hanover and Westphalia.

By 1938, the nobility made up 18.7 per cent of the SS *Obergruppenführer*, 9.8 per cent of the *Gruppenführer*, 14.3 per cent of the *Brigadeführer*, 8.8 per cent of the *Oberführer* and 8.4 per cent of the *Standartenführer*. However, it would be wrong to assume from this relatively high proportion of nobility in the upper ranks of the SS that the nobles as such had any significant impact on the goals and ethos of the SS.

The figures tell us more about the German nobility than about the SS. In the first place, some of these ranks were effectively honorary ones carrying no real influence. Secondly, the key positions in the SS were held by those, whether noble or not, who had joined relatively early and who were committed to its ideology.

Himmler's intention was to create a new synthetic élite based on 'good blood'. Some attempt was made to measure 'good blood' through pseudo-scientific techniques involving the assessment of alleged racial characteristics through physical examinations, most notoriously in the SS Marriage Order of 1931, which required the physical examination of both an SS man and his fiancée before marriage. However, in practice 'good blood' was generally assumed to be present in those who demonstrated loyalty, commitment and efficiency in the pursuit of SS goals. As the SS journal *Das Schwarze Korps*, put it on 13 May 1935:

> We have new standards, a new way of appraising. The little word 'von' no longer means to us the same thing as it once did. We believe that a nobility has the right to exist, not a nobility of class, not a nobility of birth or property, but a nobility of achievement . . . the best from all classes . . . that is the nobility of the Third Reich.

The fact that so many members of the German élites, including many among those elements who formed Berlin high society, had either joined the Nazi movement or were, at least, contemplating doing so before 30 January 1933 ensured then that there was a transition from the old to the new order rather than a sharp break. Nevertheless, the changes became increasingly noticeable. Bella Fromm, who as a Jewess felt the changes particularly acutely, noted in her diary on 16 March 1933: 'We had our fourth charity tea. I can't put my heart into the work any longer. A Nazi "lady" at every table. Mrs Meissner [wife of the State Secretary of the Reich President's office] basked in the presence of so many Brown stars. She just loves to raise her arm in the Hitler salute. She is not aware of how unbecoming the gesture is to her.' A year later, on 2 February 1934, she commented on the Foreign Minister, von Neurath's, ball on the eve of his sixty-first birthday:

> A very formal affair . . . Uniforms of all shades and designs were prominent. The Nazi officials felt uneasy in the crowd of nobility. They function best when braced by quantities of alcohol. It is not very becoming. They lost control over their heads and feet and were soon unable to conduct any kind of lucid conversation. Impressively towering Frau von Neurath was

escorted by one of the younger members of her husband's staff who introduced 'that crowd', as she called them, to her.

Strange that, in spite of their behaviour, they gain social ground steadily.
I think the reason is the curiosity, the thrill, which the foreigners find in
associating with the Brown hordes. Also, perhaps their naive pleasure in
gathering uniforms at their parties, if only brown uniforms . . .

The fact and form of social entertaining in German life has changed considerably during the last twelve months, Rolf [an anonymous noble friend]
and I concluded, as we sat in the corner of the Ballroom. The contrast
between what was before us and what we had known all our lives was so
strong that we could not help commenting on it.

'The old elegance has gone,' said Rolf sadly.

The reference to the diplomatic corps is significant. It continued to be
at the heart of Berlin high society and, since one of the main functions of
diplomats is to gain information, it was inevitable that they would be
obliged to engage in social intercourse with the new political leadership.
At the same time, however, the indigenous section of Berlin high society,
now with a substantial injection of 'new men' to replace those members
of the old order who for various reasons were no longer acceptable or —
fewer in number — who found the new order unacceptable to them, continued to flourish with the usual round of receptions, dinners, balls and
gala performances. Thus, whereas previously there had been gala performances in aid of the Winter Aid Programme for disadvantaged 'National
Comrades' sponsored by President von Hindenburg, now Gigli sang for
the new Nazi Winter Aid Programme. And society ladies now attended
charity teas for the Nazi welfare organisation, the NSV (or National
Socialist Peoples Welfare).

The leading members of the regime varied in the extent to which they
— and most importantly — their wives played a role in high society.
Hitler himself was well aware of the importance of representational
obligations and he fulfilled them when necessary. He purported to
despise the nobility. In *Mein Kampf* he referred to its 'degeneracy'. In
practice, however, he was prepared to make individual exceptions of
those who had demonstrated their fitness by joining his movement.
Indeed, initially at any rate, he displayed an Austrian petty-bourgeois
awe of the nobility. Thus, at his first formal social appearance at a large
party after his appointment as Reich Chancellor — a reception given by
Vice-Chancellor von Papen, Bella Fromm reported that

Hitler's eagerness to obtain the good graces of the princes present was subject to much comment. He bowed and clicked and all but knelt in his zeal
to please oversized ugly Princess Luise von Sachsen-Meiningen, her
brother, hereditary Prince George, and their sister, the Grand Duchess of
Sachsen-Weimar. Beaming in his servile attitude, he dashed personally to
bring the princesses refreshments from the buffet. He almost slid off the
edge of his chair after they had offered him a seat in their most gracious
company ... Upon the arrival of the immensely rich Prince Ratibor-
Corvey and his two daughters, Hitler was again overwhelmed.

In fact, however, although convinced of the need for an élite, Hitler,
like Himmler, believed it should no longer be based on birth or inherited
wealth but rather should become a meritocracy based on achievement in
the service of the national community. But he recognised that this could
only develop gradually and, in the meantime, was prepared to pay lip-
service to the traditional German high society.

Of the other leading Nazis, Goering, Goebbels, Ribbentrop, and —
until his murder in July 1934 — the SA leader, Ernst Röhm, were the
main participants in Berlin high society. The other leaders — Hess,
Himmler, Frick and Rosenberg made only occasional appearances. This
was partly because they and/or their wives lacked social flair and partly
because their political roles within the regime made it unnecessary for
them to play a significant part in high society. Robert Ley, although
uncouth himself, had an elegant and sophisticated wife and they participated to some extent.

The outbreak of war soon put an end to the form in which high society
had operated hitherto. Apart from the restrictions created by wartime
exigencies, much of the diplomatic corps, which had provided the core of
high society, had left within the first nine months. There were still opportunities for high living. For example, Horchers, the exclusive restaurant
in Berlin's Lutherstrasse, which was effectively not subject to rationing
regulation, continued to do good business throughout most of the war.
But high living was not the same as high society.

The war years demonstrated above all that the regime had failed in its
goal of integrating the old upper class of birth and property with the new
Nazi élite. For, although, on the one hand, the Nazis had succeeded in
recruiting members of the nobility while, on the other hand, individual
Nazi leaders successfully asserted their claim to membership of high
society on the basis of their official positions, and although the two
groups mingled at the various social engagements that they attended,

there was never a true integration. In particular, the traditional nobility had never been wholly won over to the new regime, despite the large numbers who had joined various Nazi organisations at the beginning. Some of its members had regarded the new order with greater or lesser hostility from the start and, by the end of the 1930s, the numbers of those who were distancing themselves from it was growing. In some cases the motive was disappointed hopes for personal advancement; others became increasingly aware of the contempt of the Nazis for their values and disgusted by the regime's mendaciousness and widespread corruption. As their concern at its totalitarian and revolutionary policies — for example, vis-à-vis the Churches — grew, so their disillusionment increased. In some cases, as for example with Count Gottfried von Bismarck-Schönhausen, a grandson of Otto von Bismarck, who was an early enthusiast, becoming an SS *Standartenführer* and District Civil Governor of Potsdam, this disillusionment led to active participation in the Resistance and eventual death, others merely distanced themselves from the regime as best they could.

As this process of disillusionment increased so the networks of family and friendship which bound the nobility together began to create a sphere that the totalitarian thrust of the regime found difficult to penetrate. This sphere acquired a semi-institutional basis in certain ministries, or certain departments within ministries, and within sections of the officer corps — for example, in the Foreign Office or, more particularly in its Indian Special Department under Adam von Trott zu Solz, and in the Military Intelligence (Abwehr) section of the Army High Command. These provided niches within which resistance to the regime could be discussed and planned. Similarly, the fact that so many senior officers should have been sounded out about the possibility of a coup against the regime during 1938–44 without them betraying the instigators to the Gestapo, even when they themselves were not prepared to participate, suggests that the professional and social *esprit de corps* of the military continued to act as a barrier to Nazi control — at least at the highest levels. Here, the process of social dilution or levelling and of ideological penetration had not yet had time to take effect.

The best source for the social relations of the traditional noble élite during the war years is *The Berlin Diaries of Marie 'Missie' Vassiltchikov*. Marie Vassilitchikov was a young Russian aristocrat living and working in Berlin during the war. The picture that emerges from her diaries is of a group of nobles, many of whom were from the highest ranks of the

European aristocracy — the Hohenzollerns, the Wittelsbachs, the Metternichs, the Bismarcks, the Lichtensteins, the Schwarzenbergs, the Fürstenbergs and many others — who, although doing their patriotic duty as fighter-pilots, tank commanders, civil servants, office workers, or nurses, were more or less totally detached from the regime and regarded it with a mixture of contempt and disgust. Their international connections, both family and social, acted as a barrier to its extreme nationalism and their upbringing led them to despise the crude and parvenu behaviour of its officials. In short, their common background, shared set of values and their family and social links provided a kind of insulation from the regime, and the basis for a critical perspective, even for those — like Bismarck-Schönhausen or Fritz-Dietlof von der Schulenburg — who still held senior positions within it.

The insulation was not total. There were still a number of members of the nobility who supported the regime and, for example, 'Missie' Vassilitchikov's mother was denounced to the Gestapo by Count Carl-Friedrich von Pückler-Burghaus, the husband of a childhood friend with whom she was staying, for her criticisms of German policies in Russia. Pückler-Burghaus became a *Brigadeführer* in the SS and the German police chief in Prague. Nevertheless, social and family loyalties normally prevented such denunciations even when there might be a conflict of views.

Through its social activities this group of nobles formed a kind of alternative high society to the official one, which increasingly atrophied under the impact of the war. There were informal lunches and dinners at Horchers or the leading Berlin hotels — the Eden, the Adlon and the Kaiserhof. There were dinners and receptions at those embassies that were still functioning, such as those of Latin America and Spain. There were parties at their homes in the villas of Potsdam and Dahlem. When the stresses of life in wartime Berlin became too great, Marie Vassiltchikov could seek rest and recuperation at the castles and palaces of various friends where of course there were plentiful supplies of home-grown food. There were skiing holidays up until as late as February 1943. Moreover, the fact that some members of this social set still had influential positions within the regime enabled strings to be pulled on occasions.

The biggest society event during the war was the marriage of Princess Maria-Adelgunde of Hohenzollern to Prince Konstantin of Bavaria, which took place at Sigmaringen Castle on 31 August 1942. According to the description by Marie Vassiltchikov, it was an extraordinarily feudal occasion in which the local officials of the regime were allowed to pay court but were kept in their proper place:

> At 10 a.m. on the dot we started off, again in pairs. I myself arm-in-arm with Didi Tolstoy. Slowly and solemnly the procession, the guests first, the bridal party and the immediate family last, wound its way out of the castle, across the many courtyards, down the wide ramp, through the town and into the church. The whole neighbourhood seemed to line the streets to watch, as had a score of photographers and newsreel cameramen . . . When we arrived back at the castle we found the main reception rooms crowded with people gathered to congratulate the newly-weds, each room being allotted to a given group according to their position, i.e. the local officials in one, the staff in another, the outside guests in a third, and we, the house guests, in a fourth. Luncheon, a veritable banquet, was served in the so-called Portuguese Room (named after its magnificent wall tapestries). The food was delicious, starting with crab cocktail and vol-au-vents filled with caviar, and the wines out of this world.

These upper-class activities provoked some popular resentment which was exploited by the Nazi Security Service (SD) in its reports. For example, on 12 March 1942, the SD reported that

> there are increasing complaints about the life-style of well-off families, above all of young women, which is particularly crassly apparent in the winter-sports districts. The young women in their ski outfits and with sun-burnt faces have a really provocative effect on the national comrades who are working. There are also frequent complaints from soldiers, who are travelling south and can hardly get a seat on the overcrowded trains, about the fact that the 'upper classes' are going skiing. Exhausted officers and soldiers have to put up with spending hours standing in the corridors watching the ladies sitting in the compartments playing a cosy game of bridge. People do not understand why the state cannot prevent this and ensure that these national comrades adopt a life-style which is more in line with that of the rest of the community (Berlin, Munich, Vienna, Stuttgart).

Goebbels, who increasingly took the lead in matters of morale was particularly sensitive to these popular criticisms. In March 1943, for example, he tried to close down Horchers, organising a night-time demonstration in which windows were broken. But he was confronted with the implacable opposition of Goering, who, unlike Goebbels, was a gourmand and a regular patron of Horchers. This indeed was the point.

Much of the Nazi leadership indulged in various forms of high living, despite regular reminders from Hitler and Bormann of the need for them to set a good example. But, by now, although the two groups — the Nazi leaders and the traditional German élites — visited the same restaurants and hotels, they indulged themselves separately. High society, in the sense in which it had operated even into the late 1930s, that is as a group whose basis was their social intercourse, had ceased to exist.

Nazism and High Society

Bella Fromm, *Blood and Banquets* (New York, 1942); Michael Kater, 'Hitler in a Social Context', *Central European History*, vol. 14 (1981); Jeremy Noakes, 'Nazism and Revolution', in N. O'Sullivan (ed.), *Revolutionary Theory and Political Reality*; ibid., 'German Conservatives and the Third Reich: An Ambivalent Relationship', in M. Blinkhorn (ed.), *Fascists and Conservatives* (London, 1990); *The Berlin Diaries of Marie 'Missie' Vassilitchikov, 1940–1945* (London, 1985); Herbert Ziegler, *Nazi Germany's New Aristocracy: The SS Leadership, 1925–1939* (Princeton, 1989); Hellmuth Auerbach, 'Hitlers politische Lehrjahre und die Münchener Gesellschaft 1919–1923' in *Vierteljahrshefte für Zeitgeschichte* 25 (1977); Martha Dodd, *My Years in Germany* (London 1939); Gerhard Grainer, *Magnus von Levetzow. Seeoffizier, Monarchist und Wegbereiter Hitlers. Lebensweg und Ausgewählte Dokumente* (Boppard 1982); G.H. Kleine, 'Adelsgenossenschaft und Nationalsozialismus' in *Vierteljahrshefte für Zeitgeschichte* 26 1978, pp. 100–141; *The Berlin Diaries of Marie 'Missie' Vassiltschikov, 1940–1945* (London 1985); Albrecht Tyrell, 'Der Wegbereiter. Hermann Göring als politischer Beauftragter Hitlers in Berlin 1930–1933' in M. Funke et. al. *Demokratie und Diktatur, Geist und Gestalt politischer Herrschaft in Deutschland. Festschrift für Karl Dietrich Bracher* (Düsseldorf 1987), pp. 178–197.

CHAPTER IV

UNDERSTANDING NAZI RACISM: PRECURSORS AND PERPETRATORS

Paul Weindling

A FTER THE SECOND WORLD WAR an American intelligence officer investigating the Kaiser Wilhelm Institute for Anthropology, Human Heredity and Eugenics in Berlin commented that one German scientist was a thousand times more guilty than 'an idiotic SS man'. Although Nazi Germany has been paradigmatic for the abuse of medicine and biology in human experiments and in justifying killing of the mentally ill and of Jews, 'Gypsies' and Slavs, until the 1980s there had been little study of the role of doctors, biologists and anthropologists in the formulation and implementation of Nazi racial policies. Given that during the Cold War there was concern to protect genetics and human genetics from Lysenkoism, eugenics was seen as a legitimate branch of medicine and public health, and sharply differentiated from non-scientific racial ideology. The concentration on a handful of criminal doctors and human vivisectors meant that normal science and medical systems were not scrutinised. The burden of guilt could be shifted on to racial ideologists. It was overlooked that eugenicists had commandeered public health and welfare services in order to make Germany an all-embracing medical utopia, in which health and the reproduction of future generations sound in body and mind were priorities.

Nazi racism has been interpreted primarily as a populist variant of a Germanic ideology of racial purity and cultural regeneration, harking back to archaic rural and aristocratic values of a pre-industrial society. Less historical attention has been given to other variants of race propagated by social groups associated with scientific, medical and welfare experts, and institutions with an interest in social modernisation. The distinctive composition and influence of professional and scientific élites under Nazism have until recently been overlooked. Most of the burden of guilt could be shifted on to party-political racial ideologists. The concentration on a handful of criminal doctors and human vivisectors meant that conventional science and medical systems under Nazism did not come under scrutiny until the publication of a recent wave of historical studies generated by concern over the power wielded by professional experts.

The notion of a one-nation community, or *Volksgemeinschaft*, was central to Nazi propaganda and racial policy: it was reinforced by the ideology of Germanic racial purity. The Nazi attempts to inculcate sentiments of social cohesion were underpinned by a sense of common ancestral roots and notions of communal health, blood and genetic inheritance. The population policy for large 'child-rich' German families had implications for the disciplining of women and in setting models for the family in domestic welfare measures; the required living space (*Lebensraum*) was a justification for territorial expansion. Given the dispersal of Germanic ethnic groups throughout central and Eastern Europe, racial ideologies legitimated the military expansion of Nazi Germany and the inexorable brutality and killings that followed.

The extermination of those deemed to be threats to the biological and cultural unity of the race was an expansive programme. Racial pathology was liberally applied not only against so-called 'aliens', notably Jews and other ethnic groups such as Gypsies and Slavs, but also against the so-called 'asocial' — the mentally and physically ill and disabled, homosexuals, vagrants and criminals. Population policy meant women were either dragooned into motherhood or subjected to eugenic abortion and sterilisation. Heavy drinking, tobacco consumption or simply being 'workshy' or 'feeble-minded' could all be construed as deviant racial traits. Indeed, there were cases of Nazi Party members being brought before sterilisation tribunals, and some eugenicists darkly hinted that Hitler was himself a degenerate psychopath. Thus it can be seen that race, while intended to be a unifying ideology, was ultimately divisive, as the circle of degenerates was so enlarged it could foment disunity among élite social groups.

While Nazi racial ideology was part of the vapid rhetoric of a one-class society, or *Volksgemeinschaft*, historians should not be seduced by such propaganda into believing that race was a monolithic, standardised, simple and self-evident concept. Whereas there is consensus that the political structure of Nazi Germany consisted of diverse and overlapping authorities, Nazi racial ideology is often conceived of in simplistic terms of Germanic racial purity. It is ironic that the intensive historical research on the competing political structures, regional diversities and conditions in various economic sectors has not resulted — at least until very recently — in any attempt to work with anything more than a formulation of Nazi racial ideology so simplified that it is more a caricature than a true likeness. The mismatch between polycratic political structures and a supposedly monolithic racial ideology is a glaring inconsistency; if the Nazi state was a 'racial state' then the developing ideological forces, which integrated and created possibilities for further development, require analysis. Moreover, seen from an international perspective, given that there was wide variation in the racial and eugenic components of diverse fascist movements and states (notably Italy, where racial concepts were low on anti-Semitism but high in pronatalism and maternal and child welfare) the possibilities of divergent racial ideologies under Nazism become evident.

That racial ideology and movements contained conflicting elements and interests prompts the question whether the Nazis appropriated a science of eugenics that would have led to the biological categorising of the population, to incarceration and sterilisation as in Britain and the United States of America, but could have stopped short of anti-Semitism and genocide? Or whether the removal of democratic controls on the scientific community allowed a coercive and lethal potential in eugenics and more broadly in biology and medical research to become manifest? These issues become more complex when it is realised that the Nazis maintained massive investment in biological research programmes, resulting in innovations in ethology, virology and human genetics, which need to be assessed as powerful extensions of the racial state. Given that Hitler and Himmler were prepared to mix opportunistically quite divergent strands of scientific eugenics and mystic notions of Germanic racial purity, the way in which conflicting types of racism interacted provides insight into the ability of Nazi leaders to manipulate and control antithetical social interests. Racists had different targets: some were primarily anti-Semites and others were ideologists of rural peasant utopias, like H.F.K. 'Rassen' Günther for whom industry was a pathologically degenerative factor, whereas supporters of industrial social welfare schemes could regard rural populations as slow-witted and prone to in-breeding.

The question is did Nazi racial policies accord with the aims of scientific experts who wished to establish a professionally administered dictatorship replacing civil laws by the laws of biology, or did the Nazis give the eugenics movement lethal new marching orders? To understand the position of eugenicists under the Nazis, it is helpful to take a long-term view of German eugenics since the 1880s. Eugenicists, keen to assert their autonomy and authority in 1933, reminded the Nazis of their long pedigree as a scientific movement. A longer-term perspective shows not only the variations among racial groupings that continued to metamorphose under Nazism, but also the processes of social transformation that gave rise to eugenics and kindred forms of racism. The origins of eugenics indicate how it provided an alternative to notions of class conflict, being of interest to revisionist socialists seeking alternatives to Marxism, feminists and campaigners for social welfare measures.

The 1880s and 1890s in Germany were decades of rapid industrialisation; with the largest cities showing the highest rates of population increase, fears arose of physical and psychological degeneration. Chronic degenerative diseases such as tuberculosis, alcoholism and sexually transmitted diseases (all rife among youth and students of the period) were regarded as 'racial poisons', threatening the health of future generations. In protest against urban degeneration there was a spate of utopian colonies. The natural values of air, sun and light were the basis of utopian communes which cultivated a reformed lifestyle, nudist open-air bathing and organic foodstuffs. Dissident young artists, students and doctors condemned industrial society and the repressive politics of Bismarck's anti-socialist laws. One group of students formed a society called 'Pacific' and collected money to send a delegate, a medical student called Alfred Ploetz, to study utopian settlements in the United States. After working at a colony in Iowa, Ploetz returned home to condemn egalitarianism; instead, he drew up a scheme for a racial colony based on sound health as a means of recovering primitive racial vigour that had been sapped by urban life. Biology was to be a source of social salvation and to ensure that future generations would be sound in body and mind. The utopian values of a reformed way of life were to be scientised. Here lay the roots of Pletz's new philosophy of 'racial hygiene' — a term he introduced in 1895.

There was a demand for scientific solutions to the social problems of urban squalor and disease, as well as a disenchantment with liberal individualism as destructive of human lives and of the sense of common national and social interests. As a scientifically based creed of social corporatism with selective welfare benefits to promote health and fitness of future generations, eugenics represented a biologically based variant of revisionist socialism. Even such orthodox socialists as August Bebel and

Karl Kautsky had a critical interest in eugenics, and a number of early eugenicists had been socialist activists, for example Ludwig Woltmann, who launched a journal for political anthropology in 1903. Ploetz considered that the more one could understand the biological causes of the reproduction of weak progeny, the less the exterminating process inherent in the struggle for survival would be necessary. He hoped that it would be possible to have a science of reproductive hygiene by controlling the selection of favourable reproductive cells. Ploetz argued for scientific solutions to social problems — rejecting education, sexual selection and Francis Galton's suggestion that marriage be restricted to the hereditarily healthy.

Advances in therapeutic medicine and the boost that sickness insurance gave to individual doctor-patient relations were considered to be keeping the weak and degenerate alive. Thus, another young doctor, Wilhelm Schallmayer, suggested that there should be screening of the entire population by means of a system of health passports, annual medical inspection and the official notification of all diseases; instead of working for the individual sick patient, the doctor was to be a state official. The obligation to the state would mean that medicine would act in the interest of future generations.

A transition occurred from utopian counter-cultures to attempts to reform society as a whole by bringing social legislation into line with biology and medical science. In 1905 Ploetz founded both a periodical for racial and social biology and the German Racial Hygiene Society, in which doctors and biologists predominated. While rejecting notions of race based on cultural myths and psychological stereotypes, Ploetz attempted to base race on biology — to shift from a static classificatory concept of race to a dynamic concept of a *Vitalrasse* based on Mendelian genetics and reproductive biology. The 'rediscovery' of the Mendelian laws in 1900 prompted analysis of both paternal and maternal lines of inheritance for a range of medical conditions like spastic debility, short-sightedness, cancers and tuberculosis, for physical traits or reproductive tendencies like the birth of twins (by Wilhelm Weinberg) and for psychiatric illness, as with Ernst Rüdin's statistics on the incidence of schizophrenia which were linked to his calls for compulsory sterilisation. Medical researchers pointed out that attention to individual cases of illness obscured information about the incidence and transmission of diseases. They argued for research on entire populations and for measures that would give priority to the health of future generations. Such thinking undermined liberal notions of the individual's right to health and of choice in reproduction. Eugenic science supported authoritarian and collectivist forms of society, maintaining its appeal over a wide political spectrum. Certain eugenicists (for example Schallmayer) drew up models offering eugenic controls on reproduction as a means of eliminating poverty and disease in future generations.

The presence of eugenicists who also happened to be Jewish or part-Jewish (like Weinberg) indicates an interest in non-racial socio-biology in which population groups and medical problems were analysed according to biological categories. While Ploetz sought to keep eugenics separate from organised anti-Semitism, privately he and a number of other members were anti-Semitic — there was a secret Nordic inner group in the Munich Racial Hygiene Society. There was thus a complex interaction with other variants of racial ideology. Ploetz was critical of the Gobineau Society and of such racial philosophers as the Gestalt-theorist Christian von Ehrenfels, who advocated polygamy, seeking to marginalise them while remaining on good terms with their leaders. Other areas of ambivalence were those that involved the feminists, particularly the Nietzschean radical Helene Stöcker, who dominated the League for the Protection of Motherhood and Social Reform.

At the beginning of the new century there were competing schemes of racial and social biology, hygiene and sexual reform. These focused on reproduction and demographic issues as the key to the solution of the social problems of crime, poverty and disease. Abortion, the effects of sexually transmitted diseases in causing congenital syphilis and sterility, and birth control were much debated. Biological ideas were applied to explain homosexuality — including Magnus Hirschfeld's idea of an intermediate third sex. Eugenicists promoted maternal health with improved infant welfare: the League for the Protection of Mothers and Social Reform shifted from folkish rural colonies to schemes for maternity allowances. The anthropologist Eugen Fischer returned from studying the Rehoboth mixed race tribe in German south-west Africa to call for a national institute for the study of human heredity to correlate data on genealogy and disease. By 1912 state medical officials were asking to what extent degeneration was a cause of the declining birth-rate. Hereditary biology was permeating not only medical science but was also under consideration by the central state administration.

During the First World War the state sought to promote improved health and welfare provision on the domestic front, and the war can be seen as midwife to a eugenically based welfare state. One wing of the Racial Hygiene Society became committed to welfare and support for a population policy to raise the birth-rate. The other wing demanded foreign conquests for *Lebensraum* (literally, 'living space') and was politically on the ultra-Right with links to the *Vaterlandspartei*. Racial hygienists were horrified at the mass slaughter of the fittest in society, but were enthusiasts for the conquest of new territories for rural settlement. Although ideas of the unified nation waging a biological struggle for survival and the expansion of *Lebensraum* became a folk memory on the ultra-Right in the 1920s and were later to be appropriated by Nazism, this should not blur the conflicts among the eugenicists.

The fact that welfare became a state responsibility under the Weimar constitution opened the way to state-sponsored eugenic research and medical practices. For a time the German Racial Hygiene Society was taken over by leading medical officials, who regarded eugenics as part of the post-war reconstruction policy to overcome famine and wartime losses. Among the health administrations most active in pursuing a welfare oriented eugenics were Prussia, with a welfare minister from the Catholic Centre Party, and socialist controlled Saxony. New health centres included marriage advice clinics providing a eugenic premarital health examination, and there were hereditary databanks correlating the records of health centres, schools, police, the churches and hospitals. The aim was hereditary prognosis; by studying the patterns of inheritance, it was hoped that effective medical and crime prevention schemes could be implemented. State authorities supported schemes for 'total registers of biological populations'. For example the Saxon eugenicist Eugen Fetscher recorded mental and physiological disorders, alcoholism, character and indebtedness, as well as a range of sexual information. Eugenics entered academic curricula. Among the students of the geneticist Walther Haecker at Halle were Heinrich Himmler (studying agricultural science; later to be in control of the SS) and Joachim Mrugowsky (who was to head the Hygiene Institute of the *Waffen*-SS). Eugenic notions flourished throughout the political spectrum and there was acrimonious debate about eugenics, sexual and reproductive issues among feminists, socialists and welfare experts, as well as among the ultra-Right. Birth-control, sterilisation and abortion were political battlegrounds. Notions of *Lebensraum* were supported by those seeking to disperse the high-density (and often socialist) urban populations into rural settlements, and by diplomats, who supplied eugenic literature and material assistance to ethnic German communities in Eastern Europe.

Schemes for biological politics culminated in the opening of the Kaiser Wilhelm Institute for Anthropology, Human Hereditry and Eugenics in Berlin in 1927 as a national eugenics institute. This organised a scheme for a nation-wide programme of anthropological surveys correlating physical with psychological traits. By the time of the economic crisis there was a favourable atmosphere for the scientific experts of the Kaiser Wilhelm Institute to launch schemes for a scientific dictatorship. Eugenic experts were to tackle the root-causes of poverty and associated diseases: eugenics was thus integral to biologically-conceived systems of state welfare. Positive eugenic incentives with premiums for child-rich families of sound eugenic quality were matched by calls for sterilisation as well as other eugenic controls on reproduction for those of constitutionally less value. Biological concepts of a human economy thus displaced the categories of liberal political economy just as the concept of eugenic and medical controls supplanted notions of individual rights. In the telling formulation of Karl-Heinz Roth, eugenics represented the 'Final Solution' of the social problem of poverty, disease and crime. While racism flourished on the ultra-Right, Weimar eugenics was primarily concerned with offering scientific solutions to social problems, so countering radical socialist demands for a redistribution of wealth and property.

Yet the view of eugenics as a programme of bourgeois social rationalisation and modernisation does not satisfactorily account for the cultural force of racial ideologies and anti-Semitism. In contrast to the sophisticated genetics of the Kaiser Wilhelm Institute, Hitler's racial biology was scientifically antiquated, and much more closely linked to currents of mystic Germanic and Nordic racial purity. He might have been given the textbook of human heredity and eugenics by Baur, Fischer and Lenz while imprisoned after the Munich Putsch, but certainly its eugenics left little impact on his notions of racial purity, except perhaps regarding the possibilities of sterilisation and the problem of syphilis. Burleigh and Wippermann judiciously remark that Hitler's racism had 'inner contradictions': we do not know exactly which men provided the sources of Hitler's racism and many crucial aspects of policy-formulation of racial measures still require clarification. Hitler's *Mein Kampf* of 1924 relied on blending heredity in order to show the evils of racial intermarriage as leading to the sterility of hybrids, but had no understanding of particulate genetic characters. This had repercussions for the Nuremberg Laws of 1935, which banned racially mixed marriages. Hitler and Himmler were scornful of the snail's-pace of medical research, and called for a new dynamic action-oriented style of science. Racial policies relied on public health administrations to seek out the medically, socially and racially undesirable, and to implement such measures as sterilisation and, ultimately, the killing of mental patients and other racial undesirables.

The rifts over eugenics were reflected in criticisms of the concept of a Germanic branch of an Aryan race. Anthropologists pointed to the mixed racial composition of Germany and some privately commented (to their cost) that Hitler was a dark Alpine racial type with psychopathic and hysterical traits. Apart from a major role in drafting the Law for the Prevention of Hereditarily-diseased Progeny of July 1933, eugenicists were unsuccessful in the pursuit of their strategy of an expert dictatorship. Examples of tensions between the Nazi concept of race and such socio-biological measures as the sterilisation laws included the protest by the Reich Doctors Führer, Gerhard Wagner, that Nazi Party members were being forcibly sterilised under the law drafted by the veteran Mendelian psychiatric researcher, Ernst Rüdin. In-fighting between groups of eugenic experts was in the interests of the Nazi state, as eugenic pluralism — equivalent to what political historians term the polycratic structure of Nazi Germany — resulted in the radicalisation of racial policies. Wagner exploited these divisions to place the killing of mental patients and crippled children on to the political agenda. For eugenicists to survive, links had to be forged with the racial priorities of groupings in the Nazi Party, state and the SS, and racial categories increasingly dominated the social programme of the eugenicists.

A few years ago Müller Hill, a geneticist, showed that such SS doctors as Josef Mengele acted in league with the leading human geneticists. We know that the Nazis supported innovative research in areas such as population genetics: for example the Soviet geneticist Timoféef-Ressovsky remained as a researcher in Berlin throughout the war and Konrad Lorenz certainly endorsed views that domestication of animals led to degeneration being applied to human society, arguing that patients with hereditary diseases should not be treated. One trouble with Müller Hill's work is that he does not differentiate various levels of engagement in the Nazi racial machinery. His work exemplifies the interpretative approach, which can be characterised by borrowing the Nazi prescription for a more economical and nutritious way of cooking meals in a single pot — as the *Eintopf* school — for every eugenicist is seen to be part of a homogeneous racial ideology. A eugenicist supporting compulsory sterilisation for schizophrenics would not necessarily have supported their killing in the 'T-4 euthanasia' programme (see p. 101ff). Müller Hill and Robert Proctor (the author of an overview on Nazi racial hygiene) throw all eugenicists and racists into the same historical melting-pot, regardless of their different views and political affiliations.

The case of Wilhelm Weitz, a clinician expert in human genetics during the Nazi period, is instructive. The funding and scale of his research increased because the Nazi public health authorities needed geneticists in sterilisation tribunals. In 1936 Weitz established a Department for Twin and Hereditary Research in the Hamburg University Hospital, collecting data on 8,000 pairs of twins. Weitz supported the ideology that the duty of the German doctor was to defend the hereditary health of the population. While believing that hardly a disease was free from the taint of heredity, he was also interested in the interaction of hereditary and environmental factors. He established a central registry of medical records — with over a million records by 1939 — in order to locate monozygote twins. Such a databank was open to use by social workers and the police. Weitz was keen to extend compulsory sterilisation to neurological conditions, and joined the Nazi Party in 1937 and the SS in 1938. But this exact geneticist was also accused by a Nazi official of a complete lack of understanding of Nazi ideology. Weitz resigned in 1943 from the SS, apparently because an assistant informed him about the Holocaust. This resignation illustrates how participation in the Nazi medical killing programmes was essentially voluntary. Weitz's shock at the Holocaust did not deter him from continuing to build up his hereditary databank.

The case of Weitz suggests that concentration on eugenics provides only limited insight into Nazi racial policies. Other types of racism and the ultimate aims of the Nazi racial utopia need to be considered. The Holocaust was not self-contained, nor was it the result of a single coherent programme under a unitary authority (although the SS came close to achieving this) was an end in itself, but a stage in a vast programme of population engineering to be achieved by moving populations throughout Eastern Europe and Germanic rural settlement programmes (see pp. 140ff). Anthropologists were deployed to screen populations and to distinguish racially 'valuable' from 'worthless' populations. There was also a need for infectious diseases to be controlled to make such settlement possible. Ideologies of Germanic racial superiority reinforced the technical skills of eugenicists.

In acknowledging that professional élites and experts extended the capacity of the Nazi state to pursue its racial ends, the problem of the sheer lack of uniformity arises. The vacillations of policymakers, and the competition of different interests to attain control over the machinery of anti-Semitism are echoed in other areas of social policy. A state that was irresolute in deciding the fate of half and quarter Jews, showed a similar broad spectrum of opinion with conflicting interests and definitions of race. For if 'National Socialism was applied biology' (as Hess once said), biologists and other medical experts were divided over a wide range of issues associated with heredity and race, to which must be added competing allegiances (for example SS membership) and sectional interests. The implications of a polycratic interpretation of racial ideology are far reaching. Historians have to understand that the place of diverse groups of racial experts in the Nazi machinery was subject to continuing change and conflict. Thus the psychiatrist Ernst Rüdin, who advised on the Sterilisation Laws of 1933 was marginalised by the time of the killing of psychiatric patients, and was under severe pressure from the SS to allow them to control the German Institute for Psychiatry. By this time the SS were concerned with the implementation of genocidal policies in the East. Although the agenda was set by Hitler's *Mein Kampf* and by *völkisch* ideologists of *Ein Volk ohne Raum* (a nation without space), its realisation depended on technical expertise.

Eugenics has been studied with reference to domestic social policies in Germany — but not *vis-à-vis* foreign policy and strategic aims. The integration of eugenics with Holocaust history remains problematic. Many aspects of the Holocaust cannot be explained by reference to leading eugenicists, for example the geneticists portrayed by Müller-Hill had, at most, a marginal role in the planning and (apart from Mengele) implementation of the Holocaust. Similarly, the disillusion of Richard Walther Darré and Hans F.K. Günther as agrarian ideologists with the power of industrial lobbies in the Nazi state suggests the insufficiency of *völkisch* racism to explain Nazi genocidal policies. The 'utopian programme' has been limited to Hitler's visionary statements concerning 'the destruction of the Jewish race in Europe'. Self-interest is seen as taking priority over ideological rationales. The control of the Final Solution by the SS was strengthened by personal lust for status and power, and by departments seeking to justify their existence and economic motives.

The importance of a broader, biologically-driven aim of exterminating the causes of disease can be seen in Nazi medical killing programmes. The positive side to public health was the promotion of physical fitness through sport and exercise. There was also much emphasis on vaccination as a crucial element of preventive medicine. Ironically their very success in eradicating diseases made Germans vulnerable, something well illustrated in the case of typhus. When they invaded Russia, the Germans had to face the problem that they were encountering infectious diseases (including typhus) that could not only be hazardous to the troops, but might be brought back to Germany where the population could be non-immune and therefore highly susceptible. These epidemics also posed risks for any settlement programme. Given that ethnic Germans were to be brought back from the East and that peasant stocks from the heartland of Germany were to be transplanted to the East, there was a double risk of epidemics. Finally, the destruction, deportations, ghettoisation and concentration camps also posed severe epidemiological threats. The SS commanding concentration and extermination camps were fearful for their own health. The epidemiological threats that dogged the racial engineering and the Holocaust prompted a racialisation of epidemiology.

The Nazis were incapable of recognising that their actions were the causes of epidemics. Instead, they attributed these to congenital filth and the racial degeneracy of Slavs and Jews. Anti-typhus measures have been seen as simply providing a convenient rationalisation and cover-up for the brutality of racially motivated killings. Medical terminology of 'disinfection' and 'special treatment' were used to disguise the Holocaust, and sanitary engineering provided techniques of mass murder, including the disguise of gas chambers as showers. The Nazi perversion of preventive medicine provides insight into the rationales, implementation and extent of the Holocaust as extending from apparently harmless research by biochemists examining the effects of gases on the cellular metabolism or entomologists involved in louse-control studies, to those who manufactured, serviced and operated the gas chambers.

The routines of delousing developed by German military medical officers in the First World War shaped the routines of the concentration and extermination camps. Refugees had come to expect delousing at railway junctions and on entry to transit camps. The body of the concentration-camp prisoner was under the dictatorial regime of hygienic delousing requirements of short hair, a change of clothing and a

scientifically calculated starvation diet. While the SS wished to acceler-
ate the deaths of concentration-camp prisoners from starvation, harsh
work-regimes and overcrowding, the SS feared epidemic infections arising
from such conditions to which they themselves were vulnerable. It is in
this context that the Hygiene Institute of the *Waffen*-SS under Joachim
Mrugowsky merits consideration. An examination of Mrugowsky's
career reveals that this key (and hitherto overlooked) figure whose career
linked public health and the Holocaust, was a character of considerable
complexity.

The image of the medical experimenters like Mrugowsky (who was
condemned to death in the Nuremberg Doctors' Trial) has been that of
abusers of science. Mrugowsky fits into the pattern of a Nazi activist of
the younger generation: while Mengele had doctorates in anthropology
and medicine, Mrugowsky had doctorates in botany and medicine.
Mrugowsky's studies of the ecology and sociology of plant communities
were applied to the teaching of racial hygiene from 1934 and in research
on the health of the mining community of Mansfeld (published in 1938).
His biological approach to the social problems of a mining community
with a reputation for revolutionary socialism shows the importance of
internal social problems of Germany in generating concepts and methods
later to be applied in the Holocaust. In 1930 Mrugowsky joined the Nazi
Party and SA and from 1931 he was in the SS. In 1937 he joined the sanitary department of the SS, and he had special responsibility for the health
of the armed SS as director of the Hygiene Institute of the *Waffen*-SS.
Mrugowsky's qualifying lecture in Berlin was on ethnic groups and disease in the 'German South East' (the Sudetenland, Ostmark and Slovakia)
and marked a transition from domestic sanitary measures to issues associated with the expansion of German *Lebensraum*.

The organisation and expanding responsibilities of Mrugowsky's
Hygiene Institute of the *Waffen*-SS merit comment. It had three
departments: one each for epidemic control (by means of bacteriology
and serology), chemistry and hereditary (or constitutional) medicine.
Thus, measures were appropriated from a eugenically oriented public
health system, in order to maintain the SS at the peak of racial health.
These methods had a highly destructive potential when applied in the
military context of Nazi expansion in the East. Mrugowsky also
supervised typhus research in Buchenwald, where human experiments
were conducted while testing vaccines. He personally undertook
'experiments' concerning the efficacy of different types of bullet, which

involved the shooting of Soviet prisoners. The Hygiene Institute of the *Waffen*-SS supplied Zyklon (a fumigant gas) to concentration and extermination camps and received gold from the teeth of murdered victims.

The genocidal role of preventive medicine is revealed in the sanitary codes for SS units; the men were warned that all civilians were potential typhus carriers and thus their extermination could be justified. Despite such crude prescriptions, epidemiological rationales used sophisticated statistical and geographical methods to explain the vulnerability of the more civilised German to the lethal parasites carried by Jews and Slavs. As Browning has shown, high rates of typhus provided the pretext for sealing off the Warsaw Ghetto. Mrugowsky viewed this in the context of a vast system of geographical epidemiology (or geomedicine). The Ostgrenze (eastern frontier) as a cultural divide between Germans and menacing racial Slavs could be correlated with high rates of infectious diseases, for example typhus, typhoid and dysentery in Russia and Lithuania. Mrugowsky considered that control of cities such as Warsaw, Lublin and Lvov, crossing-points for communications to Ukraine and Belorussia, was the key to the control of epidemic threats from the East. Eugenics thus took a key role in combating 'Asiatic threats' of epidemic infections which were linked to the inferior races of Jews, Slavs and Gypsies.

The conventional view that the 'technical' implementation of the Final Solution was carried out by a few officials, implies that the processes of the implementation are reduced to be a mere working-out of the logic of genocidal policies. While Hans Mommsen has recognised that 'technocratic and subordinate attitudes could be as important as blind racialism or the mere parroting of National Socialist anti-Jewish clichés', there remains an unexplained gulf between the technocrats and the racists, and the distinctive forms of racism that might have motivated the technocrats are never considered. By leaving the distinctive constituents of Nazi racial utopias unexamined important elements of motives and the forms that the Holocaust took are obscured.

An example of the Nazis' complex blend of ideology and technology is the cremation movement, which combined medical notions of a pure earth, Nordic beliefs in fire as eternal life and Germanic cultural traditions. The Nazified cremation movement was under the direction of public health officials and there were complex links with other branches of Nazified medicine. Mrugowsky's interest in the holistic roots of German medicine reveals the ideology of clearance and of a purging fire with the flames of destruction necessary for a momentous scientific discovery. Doctors can be seen as supplying the methods and ideological rationales for the Holocaust and thus for the realisation of the Nazi racial utopia.

Race and its medical extensions were neither administratively nor ideologically monolithic. Thus, the eugenicist Fritz Lenz criticised Mrugowsky for advocating the holism of Adolf Meyer, who at this time was under attack from SS human geneticists and anthropologists, so revealing the in-fighting among the SS ideologists linked to non-SS eugenicists (like Lenz). In June 1942 Lenz resisted Mrugowsky's promotion in Berlin university to professor, arguing that his services in combating typhus on the Eastern Front were insufficient for an academic honour. While the SS was moving into a controlling position in universities and in the German Research Council, there was still pluralism within its ranks. There were racial mystics associated with the SS *Ahnenerbe* (Ancestral Heritage) and genetic reductionists, advocates of herbal medicines or of industrially produced drugs and vaccines. It might be argued that the co-existence of diverse strands within the SS strengthened its influence as a directive and controlling organisation.

The interpretation of public health and eugenics as modernisers by such historians as Aly and Roth has resulted in an impressive array of new evidence that brings academics into the mainstream of the Nazi power structures. Their important analysis of statisticians and demographers in the service of the state and SS shows how the state relied on experts to define categories and to implement policies. Yet they also rigidly defend a linear interpretation of eugenics as unchanging between the population policies formulated during the First World War and those of the Federal Republic, policies basically generated and sustained by economic demands for a healthy and fertile workforce. Denying any cultural relativism, ideas are reduced to the underlying interests of capitalism. Indeed, race hardly figures in Aly and Heim's account of economic planning as the key to Holocaust. I would suggest that once the diversity of competing groups of racial experts continually forming and dissolving alliances with diverse groups in the Nazi power structure has been mapped, then the social interests underlying key decisions in racial and social policies can be determined. Greater use can be made of the social history of ideas, of academic institutions, of the professions and of health and welfare in order to bridge the gap between studies of the ruling élite and of public opinion.

Returning to the problem of what weight to give to the Nazi ideologies of blood and soil, *Lebensraum* and racial health and purity, some deficiencies of the historical approach that marginalises the importance of race for the underlying economic conditions and political organisation of Nazi Germany should now be evident. Racial ideology was far more complex than just a chilling distillation of utterances emanating from Hitler, implemented by Himmler and the SS and disseminated by the Nazi Party's Racial Political Office (Rassepolitisches Amt). While it has been acknowledged that there was an impressive propaganda machine, these ideas have been reduced to manipulative techniques of social control. Historians dealt with the functions and organisation of the state and party, the effects on policies and the people, and indeed the complex problem of popular perceptions and responses. For all the sophistication of the categories used, this rested on assumptions of a rather simplistic binary social structure: of a ruling élite and the people. There was a lack of attention to middle-class professional groups such as doctors, lawyers and teachers, who were simply reduced to the status of purveyors of a uniform Nazi ideology, rather than recognised as interacting with the Nazi ideology and power structures. Instead, critical analysis concentrated on the interaction of party political groupings, functionaries and leading Nazis within the state, military, Party and SS.

The stress on the crucial importance of the interactive process of decision-making in the Nazi state, led to the conclusions that racial ideology could reveal little about the planning and decision-making that led to the Holocaust. With the Holocaust reduced to 'a complex political process', mass extermination was one more act of wartime social policy with complex origins — just as (to choose a humane counter-example) the British National Health Service might be seen as arising from wartime expediencies, and complex and controversial decisions among politicians and decision-makers. Instead, I would suggest that the types of ideologies and methods of extermination deployed can be used to indicate the power of involved groups in the Nazi ruling élites. Moreover, racial values provided connections to other related areas of Nazi social policy. That there was indeed a Nazi plan for the unification of health services as part of the medical campaign to boost Germany's racial élite indicates how racial concepts shaped health and welfare, as well as the Holocaust. It is all too easy to see Nazi Germany as positively innovative in the modernisation of social institutions, in the provision of medical care and in the generation of science and technology, if the values of race are artificially limited to the bloody rhetoric of Nazi anti-Semitism.

KARL ASTEL

Karl Astel exemplifies the transition made by those involved in the Munich Racial Hygiene Society before 1933 to their implementation of racialised medicine in the service of the SS. As director of public health in the Nazi state of Thuringia and as administrator of the university, he racialised public health and biology. He was responsible for surveys of the fertility of the élite party members and the peasantry, and screened the population for such 'asocial' groups as homosexuals. Despite the homogeneity of Thuringia's racialised public health services, Astel was, for personal and ideological reasons, at loggerheads with numerous Nazi officials. He was a believer in direct action, thus he discouraged smoking by punching cigarettes out of the mouths of students. He committed suicide in 1945.

Understanding German Racism

Götz Aly and Susanne Heim, *Vordenker der Vernichtung* (Hamburg, 1991); Götz Aly and Karl Heinz Roth, *Die restlose Erfassung* (Berlin, 1984); Gisela Bock, *Zwangssterilisation im Nationalsozialismus. Studien zur Rassenpolitik und Frauenpolitik* (Opladen, 1986); Christopher R. Browning, 'Genozid und Gesundheitswesen. Deutsche Ärzte und polnische Juden, 1939–1941', in Christian Pross and Götz Aly (eds), *Der Wert des Menschen. Medizin in Deutschland, 1918–1945* (Berlin, 1989), pp. 316–28; Michael Burleigh and Wolfgang Wippermann, *The Racial State: Germany, 1933–1945* (Cambridge, 1991); Michael Burleigh, *Death and Deliverance: Euthanasia in Germany 1990–1945* (Cambridge, 1994); Michael Kater, *Doctors under Hitler* (Chapel Hill and London, 1989); Alfons Labisch and Florian Tennstedt, *Der Weg zum 'Gesetz über die Vereinheitlichung des Gesundheitswesens'* (Düsseldorf, 1985); Hans Mommsen, 'The Realization of the Unthinkable: "The Final Solution of the Jewish Question" in the Third Reich', in Hans Mommsen, *From Weimar to Auschwitz. Essays in German History* (Oxford, 1991), pp. 224–53; Benno Müller Hill, *Murderous Science: Elimination by Scientific Selection of Jews, Gypsies and Others: Germany, 1933–1945* (Oxford, 1988); Jeremy Noakes, 'Wohin gehören die "Judenmischlinge"? Die Entstehung der ersten Durchführungsverordnungen zu den Nürnberger Gesetzen', in U. Büttner (ed.), *Das Unrechtsregime* (Hamburg, 1986);

R. Proctor, *Racial Hygiene: Medicine under the Nazis* (Cambridge, Mass., and London, 1988); Paul Weindling, '"Mustergau Thüringen". Rassenhygiene zwischen Ideologie und Machtpolitik', in Norbert Frei (ed.), *Medizin und Gesundheitspolitik in der NS-Zeit* (Munich, 1991), pp. 81–98; ibid., *Health Race and German Politics Between National Unification and Nazism* (Cambridge, 1989).

CHAPTER V

THE GERMAN VOLKSGEMEINSCHAFT FROM THE PERSECUTION OF THE JEWS TO THE 'FINAL SOLUTION'

Avraham Barkai

RACIAL ANTI-SEMITISM, AS IS generally well known, was a central theme of National Socialist ideology and propaganda. Nevertheless, many historians continue to question whether the electoral successes of the Nazis before 1933 can be attributed to the purchase exerted by crude and virulent anti-Jewish propaganda. As early as the 1870s, there were political parties in Germany whose programmes and solutions to the nation's problems were pronouncedly anti-Semitic. Moreover, from the mid-nineteenth century, German academics and scientists attempted to give racial ideology, particularly that concerning the Jews, an air of scientific respectability, although they were assisted in this enterprise by French and British popular writers. Despite this, it is impossible to maintain that the German people were more hostile towards the Jews than, say, the peoples of Eastern Europe; violent pogroms occurred during the 1880s in Russia and Romania, but nowhere in Germany. The most public, turbulent and politically divisive manifestation of anti-Semitic resentment was the Dreyfus Affair in France between 1894 and 1906. By this time, the fortunes of German anti-Semitic parties had waned and German Jews comforted themselves with the thought of increasing security and progressive integration into German society as a whole.

The ascendancy of the National Socialist German Workers' Party, or NSDAP, after 1930 was primarily a consequence of mass unemployment and the political crisis of the late Weimar Republic. However, the Nazis' anti-Jewish demagogy also contributed much to the unstable climate, and culminated in the vicious street fighting and pugnacious meetings characteristic of the final phase of the Republic. These disturbances did not deter potential voters because traditional hostility towards Jews was deeply rooted in almost every section of the population. This also explains the willing acceptance of racial anti-Semitism by the population at large once this had been elevated by the Third Reich to a state ideology and substitute religion. Anti-Semitism was integrated into a comprehensive, internally consistent, *völkisch* ideology, characterised by a number of specific features that may be described as being peculiar to Germany.

The concept *völkisch* is even less amenable to precise translation than the word *Volk* from which it is derived. The term 'nation' is conventionally used to describe the contractual coming together of a community of people sharing a common origin, language or other common characteristics and interests in a unified community. A 'people' represents the multiplicity of individuals living in a society; by contrast, in the German tradition the word *Volk* has profounder, mystical significance. In German the word signifies an autonomous, living organism from which the individual members of the *Volk* derive the true meaning and essence of their existence. A metaphor frequently used to make these distinctions comprehensible is of a heap of stones, juxtaposed against a seamless, indissoluble rock. The origins of these ideas lay in German Romantic literature and philosophy of the early nineteenth century. They were frequently, but not necessarily, associated with fanatical nationalism and also with anti-Semitism. *Völkisch* and anti-Semitic ideology were not always synonymous. Although their complex evolution need not detain us here, both *völkisch* and anti-Semitic ideas and organisations were intimately linked in the period under consideration.

In 1919 Adolf Hitler joined the German Workers' Party, one of the many *völkisch* splinter-groups operating in the Munich area, as an undercover *Reichswehr* (or military) agent. Most of these sects were led by cranky middle-class ideologues and demagogues; the support of reactionary conservative elements of the upper bourgeoisie, who preferred to stay out of the limelight in the revolutionary climate of the years following the First World War, enabled these groups to produce and disseminate vast quantities of propaganda. Hitler managed to merge these *völkisch* societies and sects into the National Socialist German Workers' Party under his own leadership. He had grasped the fact that *völkisch* ideas would only achieve considerable purchase in a modern industrial society if they became part of the programme of a broad mass-based party. Therefore he saw his specific task in terms of 'winning the workers once more for the German national community'.

The notion of a 'national community' (*Volksgemeinschaft*) was the National Socialist counterpart of the classless society to which Marxist and revolutionary parties aspired. Every racially pure German employer and worker, peasant and intellectual was to occupy his or her rightful place in the national community. The success and welfare of the national community in the worldwide struggle for power would determine the destiny of every individual 'national comrade'. The 'national community' therefore occupied the highest rung in the National Socialist scale of values. All individual rights and received moral norms were subordinated to the interests of the national community, which encompassed every sphere of life and justified any action. During the Third Reich these interests were determined solely by the Führer, who alone could establish the national community's goals and the stages for their implementation.

This total concentration of power in the hands of a dictatorial regime was by no means predetermined at the outset. It was achieved in stages, albeit with remarkable speed. Although the political terror exercised by the Gestapo may always have hovered in the background, this was not the decisive factor. More significant was the degree of consensus the regime enjoyed among broad sections of the population as a result of its economic and foreign policy triumphs, which led to increasing identification with the Nazis' ideological and political goals.

In January 1933, most Germans felt resigned and disappointed about democratic parliamentary politics. They were therefore ready to give the self-confident-seeming Nazis a chance to deliver them from economic and political crisis. The surrender of basic freedoms and the brutal use of terror against political opponents and the Jews were regarded as unpleasant side-effects, which had to be accepted even if one did not necessarily care for them. This mood of cautious expectancy was soon superseded by the ecstatic enthusiasm of jubilant masses of people celebrating their Führer.

The reasons for this phenomenon lay in the many tangible achievements of the regime. Dirigiste control of the economy enabled the Nazis to overcome unemployment more rapidly than the government of any other country affected by the Depression. The Nazis also effectively exploited the helpless inactivity of the Western Powers in the face of rearmament and an aggressive foreign policy. All of these things were celebrated as the achievements of a national community united behind the Führer, which had finally left behind the old class antagonisms and divisions of the Weimar Republic. Propaganda encouraged the feeling of belonging to a united people encompassing every 'national comrade'. A new social élite gradually emerged in the shape of such party organis-ations as the paramilitary SA and SS, which offered the reckless and talented members of the lower classes unheard of opportunities for social advancement. All of these factors, as well as the sense of belonging inher-ent in any mass movement, created the illusion of an egalitarian society, which gave every German rather more than he or she had had before.

These sentiments were accompanied by tangible, as opposed to illusory, benefits. The German Labour Front, the largest mass organis-ation in the Third Reich, endeavoured to achieve improvements in work-ing conditions and gave the working class a sense of enhanced status. Its leisure organisation, Strength through Joy, enabled many people to go on outings, ski trips or visits to sanatoria, which would have previously been beyond their reach. Ideological considerations led to preferential treat-ment for the farmers who had been badly hit by the Depression. They received higher prices for their produce, state subsidies and agronomic advice, all of which served to improve their standard of living. The regime's propaganda celebrated them as 'bearers of Germandom', and, dressed in colourful traditional costume, they were honoured by the Führer at mass harvest festivals. Even impoverished national comrades were catered for by a special Nazi organisation, the National Socialist People's Welfare (NSV). Annual collections for 'winter aid' were cele-brated in the regime's propaganda as a demonstration of national solidar-ity. One Sunday a month rich and poor families tucked in to a simple 'one pot meal', donating the money saved to national comrades in distress. On these occasions prominent Party figures ostentatiously rattled collection tins on street corners as living proof of a national community that had transcended the barriers of social class.

In the years before the outbreak of war, the cost in terms of loss of personal freedom or existential security was only paid by a minority of political opponents, socially marginal elements such as homosexuals, 'Gypsies', the chronically ill and, in particular, Jews, who are the subjects of this chapter. Since in the Nazi view of things Jews were not national comrades and, following the promulgation of the 1935 Nuremberg Laws, were no longer citizens of the Reich, they were excluded from the benefits outlined above. Only a few Jewish firms briefly benefited from the general upturn in the economy. Jewish workers and salaried employees were excluded from obligatory membership of the German Labour Front. They were therefore dismissed *en masse* from large firms, including those still owned or operated by other Jews. Despite the achievement of 'full employment' by late 1936, Jewish workers remained unemployed. Most of those still in work with Jewish firms lost their jobs in the course of the progressive liquidation of 'non-Aryan' businesses. Jewish academics, civil servants, doctors, lawyers, teachers and other professionals had already mostly lost their livelihoods following special discriminatory legislation in April 1933. In 1935 Jews were excluded from the general provision of 'winter aid'. Those in need — almost a quarter of those Jews living in Germany required welfare — were assisted by the Jewish community in a separate Jewish Winter Aid.

The people who were on the receiving end of this Nazi campaign of hatred were a small, demographically and economically declining minority group. In 1933 about half a million Jews lived in the German Reich or, in other words, about 0.7 per cent of the total population. Like most other small minorities, historical circumstances — even in an age of general and rapid industrialisation — had given them a specific demographic and economic profile. A higher proportion of Jews dwelled in the major cities than was true of the population at large. Their birth-rate had declined considerably since the turn of the century and from 1925 the number of deaths exceeded that of births. This means that the Jewish population was ageing and declining before the onset of persecution under the Nazi regime. Almost half of all Jews employed were independent small businessmen. The commercial sector accounted for almost half the Jews in employment. The largest concentration was in trade, particularly in the clothing industry. Jews were also strongly represented among self-employed doctors and lawyers. Because of the crisis occasioned by the Depression in these competitive professions, the large number of Jews concentrated in these sectors suffered grave consequences during the Nazi period.

During the nineteenth century, the general process of secularisation had led to the displacement of religious by economic arguments as the chief rationalisation for anti-Semitic hatred; Jews were accused of having enriched themselves unfairly through trade and banking, in ways prejudicial to the German economy, which was increasingly described as having been 'Jewified'. Nazi propaganda employed the hate-figure of an 'international Jewish financial oligarchy', as a sort of counterpart to the socialists' dilation upon major and monopoly capitalists. A totally spurious distinction between 'parasitic Jewish capital' and 'creative Aryan industrial capital' enabled the Nazis to appear to be anti-capitalist at a time when many German capitalists were nonetheless giving them their support. In Nazi and conservative ideology, the enemy stereotype of 'the Jew' embodied all the negative characteristics of a modern industrial society, whose principal casualties were the old *Mittelstand* of small farmers, craftsmen and merchants. Nostalgia for a bucolic society and the idealised harmony of a traditional way of life, easily degenerated into aggression against Jews, who were blamed for the absence of these values in the present. Jews were simultaneously held responsible for the Bolshevik Revolution in Russia and similar manifestations in Germany. They were identified as the so-called 'November criminals' of 1918, who by 'stabbing the armed forces in the back' had (according to the Right) denied the latter victory, in order to assume the leadership of the German people in the subsequent 'Jewish Republic of Weimar'. In this manner, the Jewish *Volksfeind* (enemy of the nation) was deployed as a simple and effective opposite to the ideology and propaganda of the *Volksgemeinschaft* or 'national community'.

This does not mean that anti-Semitism played a purely instrumental role in National Socialist propaganda before and after the 'seizure of power'. Nowadays, no serious historian holds the view that anti-Semitism performed a merely functional role, designed to offset the real or imagined prospect of a revolutionary upheaval through deployment of the Jewish scapegoat. Naturally, broadly based anti-Semitic resentments among the population were effectively exploited by Nazi propaganda; beyond this, however, the struggle against the Jews constituted the constant, unalterable core component in Hitler's world view. In National Socialist ideology, to which Hitler's personal contribution was greater than anyone else's, anti-Semitism enjoyed pride of place alongside the utopian vision of *Lebensraum* conquered and settled by racially pure German 'Aryans'. The murderous 'Final Solution of the Jewish Question' and the war of conquest against the Soviet Union were constant, fixed and interrelated objectives of National Socialist policy. Certainly, the successive stages of policy implementation were far from unilinear and were affected by changing political circumstances and possibilities. However, Auschwitz was latent in the anti-Semitic obsessions of Hitler and his Party from the beginning, in the way in which the embryo is in the egg or fruit within a bud.

This alone explains why persecution of the Jews not only failed to slacken following what the Nazis referred to as their 'seizure of power', but rather became ever more vicious, escalating into increasingly radical measures against Jews residing in Germany. In this phase, anti-Semitism was no longer necessary as an instrument of political mobilisation. On the contrary: henceforth the basest instincts of suppressed aggression, personal envy and sheer greed could be directed against Jews. Because of this, the National Socialists' initial measures were directed against Jewish economic activities.

Acts of violence against Jews, and attempts to take over their businesses, began immediately after the 1933 'seizure of power'. As trusted 'old fighters' of the movement, SA and SS men believed that the time had come to implement the Party's slogans, and to enrich themselves at the expense of the Jewish enemy of the people. The government, which included such coalition partners from the German National People's Party as the Minister of Agriculture Alfred Hugenberg, could not tolerate these so-called 'individual actions'. Individual attacks on the economic activities of the Jews were channelled into the more orderly lines of systematically implemented policy. In this phase, the objective was to undermine the economic base of the victims' existence, to isolate them from society as a whole and to force them to leave their homeland through mass emigration.

These policies commenced on 1 April 1933 with the officially inspired enforced boycott of Jewish businesses. Within a few days, 'action committees' were formed in even the most remote villages, which, accompanied by noisy propaganda, undertook measures against Jewish shopkeepers, doctors and lawyers. Uniformed and sometimes armed Nazis were stationed outside Jewish shops and legal and medical practices in order to deter customers and clients. People who refused to be intimidated were insulted and photographed so that they might subsequently be denigrated as 'traitors to the *Volk*' in the Press or public display cases. Shop windows were daubed with viciously offensive slogans or covered with specially prepared posters and flysheets. Although the official boycott only lasted for one day, it gave the signal for the beginning of officially sanctioned and remorselessly pursued exclusion of the Jews from the economy. From now on, the same scenes were sporadically repeated on the streets, particularly in the provinces but also in primarily Jewish residential quarters of the bigger cities.

Jewish lawyers and professors were forcibly expelled from the courts

ERSCHEINT WÖCHENTLICH EINMAL • PREIS 20 PFG., Kc 1,60
30 GR., 30 SCHWEIZER RP. • V. b. b. • NEUER DEUTSCHER
VERLAG, BERLIN W8 • JAHRGANG XI • NR. 42 • 16. 10. 1932

DER SINN DES
HITLERGRUSSES:

Motto:
**MILLIONEN
STEHEN
HINTER MIR!**

Kleiner Mann bittet um große Gaben

1 John Heartfield's 1932 illustration of the standard Marxist 'line' on Fascism explains 'the meaning of the Hitler salute' with the ambiguous slogan 'Millions stand behind me!' The millions of votes cast for the Nazis suggest that the party was more than the creation or 'tool' of a small class of industrialists and bankers.

2 Hitler attending the opening of a section of the Autobahn network. Nazi popularity in the early 1930s was in part a result of their success in putting the unemployed back to work through a range of economic policies including improvements to the infrastructure.

3 The German Labour Front was designed to integrate the working classes into the 'national community'. Its strategies included improvements to the workplace itself, and attempts to make a middle and upper class 'High' culture accessible to the workers. The photograph shows a symphony orchestra playing in a tram depot.

4 During the war, German agriculture and industry became increasingly reliant upon foreign forced labour, primarily to avoid conscripting German women for labour service. Treatment of foreign forced labour reflected racial criteria, with 'eastern workers' from Russia or the Ukraine experiencing the worst conditions. This photograph shows a group of Soviet prisoners of war huddled around a stove in a camp attached to the Volkswagen factory.

5 A children's home run by the Volkswagen factory at Rühen. It was stipulated that all female forced labourers had to give up their children two weeks after birth. They were raised in the most basic conditions, and from the autumn of 1944, all newly born children taken to the home at Rühen, died.

6 The patrician Jewish painter Max Liebermann passing a man canvassing for Hitler during the 1932 presidential elections in which the other candidates were Hindenburg and the Communist, Thälmann.

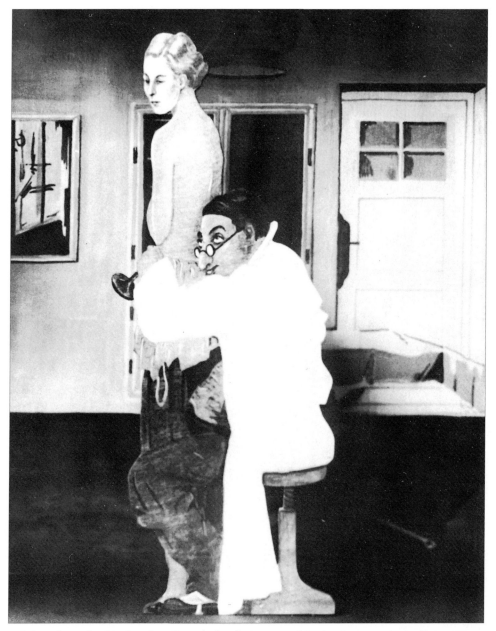

7 *A cheap slur used to drive Jews from the medical profession was to claim that they were misusing their positions of trust to sexually abuse female 'Aryan' patients, a claim given visual form in this 1935 illustration of the new Reich Doctors' Decree.*

Mann und Frau sind körperlich und seelisch verschieden

8 *After the Dresden Hygiene Exhibition of 1911, gigantic anatomical figures were used for mass public health education. During the 1920s, the 'visible man' and 'visible woman' were devised using an innovative new technique of anatomical preparation. Under the Nazis, the tone of educational displays became more authoritarian and directive, including propaganda on race, euthanasia and eugenics. The photograph (above) shows a man and woman from the 'Gesundes Leben – frohes Schaffen' exhibition on the Kaiserdam, Berlin in 1938.*

9 *(left) The Nazi racial scientist, Karl Astel.*

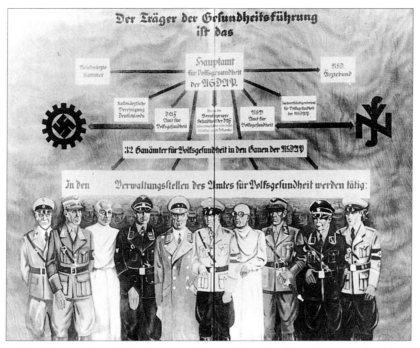

10 Doctors played a key role in the implementation of Nazi racial policies. No longer concerned with the health of the individual, they constituted a new class of 'experts' patrolling the hereditary health of the entire nation.

11 The enforcement of Nazi racial policies depended upon the willingness of the public to denouce people to the authorities. This photograph, taken by a member of the Nazi Party, proves that a fellow member was socialising with Jewish people. The cross identifies the house where these 'crimes' took place; the arrow indicates the Jews.

12 Jewish people assembled with their meagre belongings in Wiesbaden prior to their deportation to extermination centres in the East, 1941.

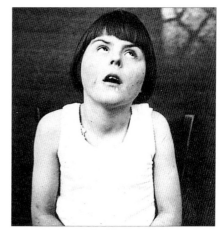

13 Handicapped child killed during the so-called 'children's euthanasia' programme. In 1939 Hitler authorised the medical murder of mentally and physically handicapped infants.

14 A registration form used to identify victims of the adult 'euthanasia' programme (left). This form concerns an elderly patient suffering from arteriosclerotic dementia. Among the non-medical 'symptoms' described here is that the man is 'inactive, and looks very bad'.

15 Buses from the 'Community Patients' Transport Service' were used to transport selected groups of patients to one of six asylums used as extermination centres.

16 Gypsies were persecuted because they were deemed to be both racially 'alien' and 'antisocial'. This picture shows a traditional Gypsy wedding.

17 The National Socialist persecution of Gypsies built upon earlier traditions of hostility towards this minority. They were persecuted for being 'racial aliens' and because of their allegedly biological predisposition towards criminal patterns of behaviour.

18 This painting (1942-43) by Emil Scheibe allegedly shows Hitler visiting the Front. In fact, despite his habitual identification with the ordinary soldier during the First World War, an experience with which he regularly used to browbeat his generals, Hitler rarely, if ever, visited any Front, and was utterly indifferent to the sufferings of ordinary soldiers.

19 A German armoured column advances through a Russian village in June 1941. The Germans sought a swift victory, but the Allies' economic power, fierce Russian resistance and the hostile climate proved to be insurmountable.

20 The Nazi soldier was required to sacrifice all for the Fatherland, but was also likely to succumb to the strain.

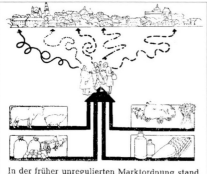

21 *The main guard house (above) leading onto Auschwitz II-Birkenau and a railway siding used from 1944 to transport Jews to their deaths. In addition to Chelmno, Belzec, Sobibor and Treblinka, Auschwitz was the main camp used to murder the Jewish population of Europe.*

In der früher unregulierten Marktordnung stand der Jude als Vermittler der landwirtschaftlichen Erzeugnisse.

22 Before and after graphics (left and right) illustrating
the supposed economic benefits resulting from the
rationalisation- meaning removal- of Jewish middlemen
from the rural economies of eastern Europe. Such
arguments may have been a means of rationalising
racially-motivated hatreds.

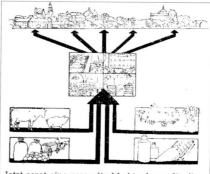

Jetzt sorgt eine geregelte Marktordnung für die
Erfassung und Verteilung der Produktionsgüter

23 Homosexuals were persecuted by the Nazis because they did not contribute children to the 'national community' and because they undermined conventional notions of masculinity. Ironically, Nazism itself was partly based on the idea of intense male camaraderie, with women relegated to subordinate functions.

24 Peasant women in folk costume at the annual Bückeberg harvest festival in 1935 welcoming their Führer. Photographs like this were used to demonstrate the allegedly hysterical enthusiasm of women for Hitler, as if he was an early version of a modern popstar. There is, however, no substantive evidence of this phenomenon.

25 During the 1930s, housewives were encouraged to 'buy German', in this case in order to feed their families with German salt herrings, rather than imported foodstuffs. The role they were expected to play in developing a self-sufficient national economy may have contributed to a reevaluation of the housewife and mother in line with Nazi ideological imperatives.

and lecture theatres even before a law promulgated on 7 April 1933 ordered the dismissal of Jewish civil servants, academics and teachers from the public service, schools and universities. Doctors were excluded from hospitals and health insurance schemes. Initially, Jewish war veterans and relatives of war dead were allowed to pursue their trades and professions, following the intervention of President Hindenburg. But even they were affected by the progressive boycott and soon their clients consisted almost entirely of other Jews. Craftsmen and other business-men were also increasingly dependent upon the isolated Jewish sector of the economy. Local authorities ceased to grant them official contracts. Trade associations and co-operative credit associations took it upon themselves to issue 'Aryan paragraphs', whose effect was to render Jewish businesses uncompetitive, before the introduction of correspon-ding legislation.

The direct effect of these measures was the gradually escalating liquida-tion of Jewish economic activity. Some 100,000 individual businesses were owned by Jews in late 1932; this number included a few large mer-chant banks and a smaller number of major department stores or industrial concerns. Most, however, were middling, small or one-man enterprises. By mid-1935 almost a quarter, and by mid-1938 over two-thirds, of these enterprises had already ceased to exist. Their owners had either gone into liquidation or been obliged to sell at knock-down prices to 'Aryan' buyers. In most cases the Jewish sellers were ruthlessly pressurised by 'Aryan' purchasers. Since each 'Aryanisation' sale had to be confirmed by Nazi Party agencies, with preference being given to 'old fighters' wishing to make a killing, the years before 1938 represented an 'open season' for minor Nazis on the make. However, even major industrialists were not slow to join in when the chance arose to 'Aryanise' Jewish businesses. Threats from the Gestapo, followed if necessary by arrest and consign-ment to a concentration camp, were used without restraint to render Jewish businessmen more amenable to selling.

The indirect influences of the boycott and Aryanisation programme were far more portentous. The propaganda that accompanied them gave the vulgar jibes of the boycott and the greed manifested by Germans in the course of Aryanisation the nimbus of ideological legitimacy. The special status of the Jews was gradually anchored in popular conscious-ness. In their case, the received norms of civilised behaviour and com-mercial probity were no longer valid. The Nazi Press published bemused and laudatory reports about 'holiday-making schoolchildren' who mobbed and traduced elderly Jewish shopkeepers and also their non-Jewish customers on the streets. The pressure exerted upon commercial values by the most extreme Aryanisers was also effectively sanctioned by Nazi ideology. Since all property was regarded as part of the 'nation's wealth', Jews were not entitled to any part of it. Moreover, since in the eyes of anti-Semites, the Jews had come into possession of their wealth through the fraudulent exploitation of German 'national comrades', removing their property was a service to the nation rather than a criminal offence.

Economic marginalisation was only one aspect of a comprehensive policy designed to isolate the Jews within German society and as human beings. Even the education of young children was included in this process. The publishing house which produced the paper *Der Stürmer* on behalf of the rabidly anti-Semitic Gauleiter of Franconia, Julius Streicher, produced illustrated childrens' books which warned the very young against the Jewish enemy of the people. Racist sentiments were also encouraged in the schools and among the Hitler Youth who played an active part in the hooliganism which accompanied the boycotts. *Der Stürmer*, which was exclusively dedicated to the most primitive and quasi-pornographic type of anti-Semitic propaganda, was displayed everywhere in special showcases. Jews were depicted in caricatured form, with beards and sidelocks and clothed in a medieval style of dress which was still only used by the Jews of Eastern Europe. Represented with unattractive features and gestures, they were accused of seducing German women and girls, as bloodthirsty ritual murderers or as crafty participants in a world conspiracy. Real Jews living in Germany, who of course looked quite otherwise, were identified as being merely a more cunningly disguised version of the same species.

Identification of one's Jewish neighbours, with whom one frequently enjoyed amicable relations, with the travesty represented by the Nazis' 'traitor to the *Volk*' was only possible because of a tradition of Christian anti-Semitism. The Nazis did not need to invent any of the odious anti-Semitic stereotypes that they employed. They were able to find most of them in ecclesiastical teaching, in the folklore of antiquity or the Middle Ages, or in the secular anti-Semitic literature which circulated in nineteenth-century France, Germany or Russia. At Christmas 1933 the Munich cardinal Michael von Faulhaber delivered a number of sermons which are often interpreted as evidence of resistance to the Nazis irreligious policies. It is striking what he had to say about the Jews:

Following the death of Christ, Israel was debarred from the task of revelation. They had denied the Lord's Anointed, depraved, they expelled him from the City and nailed him to the Cross. The veil of the Temple of Zion was rent asunder and therewith the union between the Lord and his people. The Daughter of Zion [the Jewish people] was cast aside and henceforth the eternal Ahasver wandered ceaselessly across the earth.

It is significant that one of the most murderously anti-Semitic films produced and shown during the Third Reich was entitled *The Eternal Jew*. Even though traditional anti-Semitism was no more widely diffused in Germany than in other countries, it had sufficiently deep roots to provide a receptive breeding ground for systematic indoctrination in which the *Volksgemeinschaft-Volksfeind* polarity was a central element.

However, this objective was not achieved overnight. The Nazis needed a number of years to clear aside the received moral inhibitions of the average German citizen. In the early years, the violent scenes that frequently accompanied the boycotts often encountered popular disapproval. A man called Richard Schneider, who described himself as a veteran Party member, wrote in disgusted terms to the Ministry of the Interior in December 1934 regarding the boycott in Frankfurt am Main:

> Half-grown boys of 16 to 17 years of age barred the entrances . . . Elderly, but rather distinguished-looking gentlemen, including men who had made the greatest sacrifices fighting for four years for their Fatherland, had to ask leave to enter from these rascals and scallywags, having to answer the question: 'Are you a German?' And this was done with police protection, by a vulgar pack of people whose inclusion in the national community should be absolutely rejected.

Nothing in the records tells us about the Minister's reply or the fate of the man who signed off with the words: 'Ugh to the Party! Ugh to the new Germany!'

In summer 1995 an increase in the boycott was accompanied by violence. The Minister of Economics Hjalmar Schacht protested to his colleagues in the government about the illegal behaviour of the Party, which was endangering economic recovery, relations with foreign countries and thereby Germany's rearmament programme. This time there was much less evidence of negative popular response. When Hitler promulgated the notorious Nuremberg Laws on 15 September 1935, the population accepted these measures without demur. Evidently, it was no longer regarded as objectionable that a group of people should lose elementary civil rights and be socially marginalised up to and including the forfeiture of the most intimate human relations. Following the so-called Law for the Protection of the German Blood marriages between Jews and Gentiles were prohibited and extra-marital sexual relations thenceforth constituted the punishable offence of 'miscegenation'. In order to 'protect' German girls, Jews were no longer allowed to employ Aryan domestic servants. In one small town local Nazi leaders took this stipulation so seriously that, accompanied by the drunken cries of those who took part, they dragged housemaids out of Jewish households on the very same night the law was promulgated.

The next and most notorious station in the continuing exclusion and depersonalisation of the Jews was the pogrom of 9 and 10 November 1938. The pretext was the assassination of a German diplomat in Paris by the seventeen-year-old Hershel Grynszpan, in revenge for the forced expulsion of his entire family. During the night of 28 October about 18,000 Jews of Polish nationality had been taken from their beds by the police and hounded across the Polish border. There is no record of disapproving reactions on the part of the German population *vis-à-vis* this first deportation of 'Eastern Jews', who in any case enjoyed little sympathy among the wider population. Nazi propaganda used the murder in Paris to whip up support for a campaign of hatred orchestrated by the Minister of Propaganda Josef Goebbels. During the night of 9 November, every synagogue in Germany went up in flames on Goebbels's instructions. The 7,500 businesses still in Jewish ownership, as well as many Jewish homes, were ransacked and their occupants violently mishandled. The following day about 25,000 Jews were sent to the concentration camps. About 100 Jews died in the pogrom and hundreds more were badly injured; how many died subsequently in concentration camps is not known.

This time, broad sections of the population were shocked by the brutality of the pogrom and a small minority bravely gave vent to their opposition. A considerably larger minority took an active part in these attacks, plundering Jewish businesses and rejoicing with open expressions of *Schadenfreude*. Most Germans silently shook their heads and averted their gaze. Criticism was mostly directed against the destruction of material goods, which might have benefited the 'German national economy', or concerned incidents that disturbed public law and order. The majority of Germans had so internalised the exclusion of the Jewish 'enemy of the people' by this time, that the physical abuse of Jewish neighbours and sacriligious incendiarism against their places of worship were regarded as unavoidable.

The November pogrom marked the opening of the final, tragic stage in the existence of German Jewry. The Jewish businesses that had been wrecked could not be re-opened. All firms still in Jewish hands were liquidated or compulsorily 'Aryanised' through transfer to state-appointed trustees. Half of the property still owned by Jews went to the Nazi state. Hermann Goering imposed a collective 'payment of atone-ment' of a billion Reichsmarks for the murder in Paris. Jews, who were now fleeing en masse, had to pay a large part of their capital in the form of a 'tax on flight from the Reich'. The state, as well as individual Party members and national comrades, prised out further considerable sums through a whole series of 'gifts' and supplementary deductions. Those Jews who remained in Germany were able to subsist for a few years more on the remains of the property of Jewish communities, organisations and private persons. From the end of 1941 even the costs of their own deport-ation to the extermination camps were withdrawn from these funds by the Gestapo.

About two-thirds of the Jewish population in Germany in 1933 had emigrated or died before mass deportations to extermination camps began in October 1941. By this date about 165,000 Jews still lived within the pre-1938 borders of the Reich, i.e. before the annexation of Austria and parts of Czechoslovakia. The majority were elderly, with more women than men, and lived a desolate existence totally isolated from the non-Jewish population in special 'Jewish houses' or forced labour camps. A few thousand of them survived the war, thanks to the courageous assis-tance of a few Germans who sustained their underground existence. Many more were delivered into the hands of the Gestapo by neighbours and acquaintances. The rounding up and deportation took place in full public view, without protest from either the population or the Churches.

Between 1933 and 1941 the National Socialists succeeded, through education and propaganda, in totally isolating the Jews in Germany. A striking exhibition of Jewish everyday life in this period is entitled 'From neighbours into Jews'. Real Jewish people were converted into a collec-tive and depersonalised mythical enemy stereotype. It was only a small step from that figure to the total dehumanisation that made possible the murder of six million European Jews. How that was achieved can be seen from the film *The Eternal Jew*, which was shown everywhere in Germany and occupied Europe from 1940 onwards. It compared the

Jews with vermin who, emanating from 'breeding grounds' in the ghettos of Poland, streamed across the entire world in different garb in order to spread sickness and pestilence, and finally to achieve power. Deliverance from this threat was identified in the film with the words Hitler delivered in a speech to the Reichstag on 30 January 1939 when he prophesied:

> If the international Jewish financiers in and outside Europe should succeed in plunging the nations once more into a world war, then the result will not be the Bolshevising of the earth, and thus a victory of Jewry, but the annihilation of the Jewish race in Europe.

In thousands of books and articles historians seek to explain how a civilised people in the heart of Europe could cause or, at least, passively watch the state murder millions of people — men, women and children — in a bureaucratically superbly organised operation, solely on account of their membership of a 'race'. So far none of them has found a satisfactory explanation. Many conclude that the Holocaust was a unique, totally inexplicable phenomenon, beyond the understanding of historical research. This overlooks the fact that the perpetrators were not extraterrestrial monsters, but rather tens of thousands of perfectly ordinary people. After carrying out their abominable activities, they spent evenings with their children, played cards at their regular tables in bars and canteens or delighted themselves through the music of Mozart or Beethoven. Because of this it is simply not possible to give up the attempt to understand and explain what happened. The account given here does not claim to supply a complete or final answer to these frightening questions. It simply seeks to show how seven or eight years of fanatical ideological indoctrination and concrete visual instruction in racial matters could befog the consciences of millions of Germans and corrode their moral inhibitions. Without these prior developments the Holocaust would not have been possible. From this perspective, the persecution of the German Jews seems the necessary, although not sufficient precondition, for the murder of European Jews.

Point 4 of the National Socialist German Workers' Party Programme dated 24 February 1920
Only national comrades can be citizens of the State. Only persons of German blood can be national comrades, regardless of religious affiliation. No Jew can therefore be a national comrade.

Reich Citizenship Law of 15 September 1935
A citizen of the Reich is that subject only who is of German or kindred blood and who, through his conduct, shows that he is both desirous and fit to serve the German people and Reich faithfully.

Express letter from the Reich Minister of Finance dated 4 November 1941
Jews who are not employed in concerns of major national economic importance are to be pushed out to a town in the eastern territories in the coming months. The assets of those Jews who are to be deported are to be confiscated in the interests of the German Reich . . . The deportation of the Jews will be carried out by the Gestapo. The Gestapo will take care of the securing of Jewish assets.

SS Economic and Administrative Main Office instruction to the commanders of the concentration camps dated 6 August 1942
The Head of the SS Economic and Administrative Main Office has decreed that all human hair collected in the concentration camps is to be utilised. Human hair is to be recycled into industrial felt and spun into thread. Therefore it is hereby decreed that the hair of female prisoners collected after disinfection is to be preserved.

The German *Volksgemeinschaft*

Avraham Barkai, *From Boycott to Annihilation: The Economic Struggle of German Jews 1933–1943* (Hanover and London, 1989); Michael Burleigh and Wolfgang Wippermann, *The Racial State: Germany, 1933–1945* (Cambridge, 1991); Hermann Graml, *Antisemitism in the Third Reich* (Oxford, 1992); Raul Hilberg, *The Destruction of European Jews* (New York and London, 1985); Ian Kershaw, *The 'Hitler Myth': Image and Reality in the Third Reich* (Oxford, 1987); Robert Gellately, *The Gestapo and German Society: Enforcing Racial Policy* (Oxford, 1990).

CHAPTER VI

SAVING MONEY, SPENDING LIVES: PSYCHIATRY, SOCIETY AND THE 'EUTHANASIA' PROGRAMME

Michael Burleigh

IN GERMANY PSYCHIATRY EMERGED FROM the First World War with its already poor image as a futile and scientifically dubious branch of medicine tarnished even further. Some 70,000 patients had died during wartime from a combination of hunger, disease and neglect. Exhausted or 'neurotic' soldiers had been systematically abused by crude shock therapies. Revolutionaries arrested after the abortive Munich Soviet were regularly diagnosed as 'psychopaths' by forensic psychiatrists. Post-war austerity engendered a decline in the physical fabric of the asylums, while economy cuts affected everything from books, drugs and heating to light-bulbs and soap.

In Wilhelmine Germany criticism of psychiatry had often come from the Right, for example from the anti-Semitic court chaplain Adolf Stöcker, and was primarily directed against psychiatry's medicalised denial of individual liberty. In Weimar Germany a temporarily powerful psychiatric reform movement, including groups demanding patients' rights, went on the attack, demanding enhanced patients' rights, checks on committal procedures and an effective inspectorate. On the Right many questioned the efficacy and value of the entire psychiatric project, for there was frequently no tangible 'cure' for mental illness. And in 1920 the lawyer Karl Binding and the psychiatrist Alfred Hoche, dared to raise the delicate question of whether a nation faced with a dire emergency could actually afford to sustain what they dubbed 'life unworthy of life'. In a controversial tract, which was essentially a search for a post-Christian utilitarian ethics, Binding and Hoche deliberately conflated the issues of suicide and voluntary 'euthanasia' with the non-consensual killing of the mentally ill; stressed the historical relativity of such notions as the 'sanctity of human life'; highlighted the objective futility of such emotions as 'pity' — 'where there is no suffering there can also be no pity' — and emphasised the emotional and economic burden allegedly represented by 'entirely unproductive persons'. The altruistic heroism of British Polar explorers, such as Captain Robert Scott, was invoked to justify jettisoning 'dead ballast' from the 'Ship of Fools'. The tract was symptomatic of how received liberal or humanitarian values were breaking down, with concern for narrow or wider collectivities, such as the good of a class, the economy, race or nation usurping respect for the rights and value of the individual.

Faced with such variegated assaults upon their activities, German psychiatrists began to think more kindly of a handful of farsighted reformers in their own midst who had hitherto been cold-shouldered. Two rather remarkable men, Gustav Kolb and Hermann Simon, had long advocated breaching the walls between asylums and the wider society, and between sickness and the world of work. Their liberal recommendations found a ready response from Weimar governments obsessed with cutting costs. Patients were discharged into the arms of a new range of urban outpatient clinics or perambulatory community psychiatrists in rural areas or, indeed, into paid family fostering, where a family was paid a fee to house a former patient. The economic advantages of this were clear: whereas the annual overheads of an outpatient clinic in Munich were RM2,000 a year, it cost RM1,277 to keep one patient for a year in Munich's Eglfing-Haar asylum. However, patients in asylums were not free from the attentions of the reformers either. Depressed by the effects of long-term institutionalisation in environments with next to no therapy, the psychiatrist Hermann Simon decided to use occupational therapy to engender self-satisfaction and hence repress the depressed or excitable moods that resulted from enforced idleness. Soon, asylums were humming with patient activity, with the complexity of the work performed, and hence the degree of freedom and responsibility enjoyed, being the objective indicator of recovery. In many asylums, up to 80 per cent of patients did some form of work, which made the asylums largely self-sufficient or capable of generating modest surpluses. Judging by the flood of articles devoted to community care and occupational therapy published in the professional journals in the 1920s, psychiatry began to be a more optimistic profession.

Inevitably, there was a disadvantage to these developments. First, as psychiatrists began to follow their discharged patients out into the wider world, they inevitably encountered hitherto unknown ranges of 'abnormality'; what had passed before them in the asylums was literally the tip of an iceberg. Being of an increasingly hereditarian cast of mind, they began to construct genealogies of the patients' families. Instead of addressing themselves to questions concerning the socio-economic environment, which in any case they were powerless to effect, they opted for the control function of registering widespread deviance in primitive databanks. The sheer scale of illness they discovered engendered a certain pessimism, and hence their susceptibility to radical eugenicist solutions. Experience had taught them that people they deemed degenerate or feck-less could not be counselled into voluntary birth control, so many psychiatrists began to think in terms of compulsory sterilisation. This would enable the person to return to the productive process without risk of reproductive damage ensuing to the collective biological substance of the race or nation. Furthermore, the widespread introduction of occu-pational therapy in asylums increasingly meant that patients were measured in terms of their economic productivity. Unfortunately, not all patients were capable of rolling cigars, weaving baskets, running errands or answering the telephone. Each asylum therefore had a quantity of 'incur-ables', languishing 'unproductively' in back wards, where conditions were often parlous. The adoption of occupational therapy implicitly meant separating the able-bodied and willing from the therapy-resistant chaff. Long before the National Socialist government appeared on the scene, some psychiatrists advocated (or considered) killing this per-manent reminder of the limits of their own therapeutic capacities and permanent burden upon the nation's scant resources. Paradoxical as it may sound, psychiatric reform had actually established most of the con-ceptual framework for the sterilisation and later elimination of psychi-atric patients. The year 1933 did not mark a decisive break; most of the policies of the Nazi period were more or less latently evident in the Janus-faced health and welfare apparatus of the Weimar Republic.

Nonetheless, the advent of a National Socialist government had dire consequences for the asylum population. Asylums became freak-shows, with thousands of members of Nazi formations being given tours to illus-trate the inherent uselessness of the patients. Between 1933 and 1939 21,000 people trooped through Eglfing-Haar, including 6,000 members of the SS, some of whom came out recommending setting up machine guns at the entrance to mow down the inmates. Party newspapers and journals such as the *Völkischer Beobachter* or *Schwarze Korps* dilated upon the Goyaesque scenes in the asylums and advocated killing the mentally ill, often coupling this with heroic instances of 'mercy killing' carried out by individuals.

With the regional health authorities increasingly in the hands of men who explicitly advocated killing mental patients, it is hardly surprising that conditions in the asylums soon deteriorated sharply. Specialist facilities were closed and patients were removed from the private or religious sectors and crammed into cheaper state institutions to save money and increase control. An asylum such as Eichberg in the Rheingau had 793 patients in 1934 and 1,236 by 1940. The ratio of doctors to patients deteriorated from 1:162 to 1:300 between 1935 and 1938. In some institutions it was as high as 1:500, which made basic care — hygiene, watering and feeding — let alone any treatment, totally impossible. The meagre sums expended upon patients' food were cut, for example, at Haina in Hessen from RM 0.69 per day in 1932 to RM 0.54 in 1935; this was against a background of general economic recovery. Enthusiastic lower-class National Socialist administrators replaced disinterested boards of upper-class philanthropists in the running of institutions such as the Idstein reformatory (also in Hessen), gradually marginalising medical control in these institutions. With doctors no longer necessarily in charge, economic efficiency became the primary goal. Many of the psychiatrists — who tended to be recruited from the dross of the medical profession anyway — were SS members inherently antagonistic towards their patients. Below them, a host of thoroughly unsuitable people, armed with Party cards and SA membership, flooded into nursing in order to escape the dole queues in many cases. Nursing had always been an occupation for those who had failed in other fields or for women who had yet to find a husband. Independent inspectors, some of whom deplored the fact that patients were sleeping on straw on the floor or going about virtually naked, and who objected to the brutal language used by senior health administrators, were simply barred from further visits.

Apart from the continuing deterioration of general conditions, psychiatric patients were directly affected by the 1933 Law for the Prevention of Hereditarily Diseased Progeny, which sanctioned compulsory sterilisation for a range of putatively hereditary illnesses. This Law was promoted through various forms of propaganda, including film, whose intention was to degrade and stigmatise mental patients. Psychiatrists were responsible for initiating the procedures leading to a patient's sterilisation and, indeed, often sat on the 220 local Hereditary Health Courts that made the final decisions. At this time, the hereditary character of the illnesses concerned was more a declaration of faith than a matter of scientific certitude. Leaving aside the fact that one genuinely hereditary illness — haemophilia — was actually omitted, the prefix 'hereditary' was dropped from schizophrenia in order to sterilise those where the cause was exogenous, while reformed drunks or people with low alcohol tolerance who did not actually drink much, were sterilised as 'chronic alcoholics', on the grounds that alcoholism reflected some underlying 'asocial or psychopathic disorder', neither of which separate conditions was specified in this legislation. Nor did the courts confine themselves to the people who actually came before them. In Bavaria, for example, after he had ordered the sterilisation of a young woman, the Kaufbeuren psychiatrist Hermann Pfannmüller, who was also a judge in the court at Kempten, spent a week isolating twenty-one additional 'degenerates' in her family, recommending the sterilisation of ten of them as being 'highly urgent since the danger of reproduction appeared immanent'. In a thoroughly pernicious development, schoolteachers were encouraged to set their pupils the task of constructing their own family trees, with a view to helping identify any defective members, while mayors reported single mothers primarily to curtail the costs involved in looking after their illegitimate children.

Apart from the permanent psychological damage sterilisation caused those affected, it was not uncommon for people to die on the operating table or to commit suicide shortly afterwards. The regime's remorseless propaganda campaign to sell these policies inevitably entailed generating mass resentment against the 'burden' represented by the asylum population. Propaganda films also regularly disputed the human 'personality' of the mentally ill and severely handicapped, deliberately and indiscriminately conflated criminals and the insane, and advocated a reversion to Social Darwinian elimination of the weak and the abandonment of a counter-selective welfare apparatus.

From the mid-1930s, what had once more become a very desolate psychiatric landscape was temporarily brightened by the arrival of a new range of somatic therapies. The Viennese psychiatrist Manfred Sakel pioneered insulin coma therapy for schizophrenia, which essentially involved starving the central nervous system of the glucose circulating in the blood, for it cannot metabolise substitutes for even short periods. Glucose solutions were used to arrest the drop in blood-sugar levels before they became critical. This was in turn augmented by Ladislaus von Meduna's cardiazol convulsive therapy, based upon the alleged biological antagonism of epilepsy and schizophrenia, and which employed the cerebral stimulant cardiazol to induce epileptic fits. Finally, in the late 1930s the Italians Bini and Cerletti developed electro-convulsive techniques, which had the advantage over other therapies of not involving injections and which rendered the subject instantaneously unconscious. However, none of these therapies was free from serious risks to the health of the patients treated in this fashion.

The major psychiatric journals quickly filled with enthusiastic accounts of these therapies. They often included detailed 'before and after' case-histories and the testimonies of people who felt miraculously relieved of isolating and oppressive illnesses. For example, a young woman treated for persecution mania with insulin and cardiazol wrote to relatives:

> Now I can write to you as once more as the Hilde of old! Imagine Mummy, Saturday evening in bed, it just dawned following a conversation with the others. Naturally I am eating again, for not eating was just part of the persecution mania. You cannot imagine the feeling of being freed from every fear. One is born again, so to speak. Now I look forward to Sunday and to seeing you dear Mummy. It should have clicked together before, then you would have noticed something, but nonetheless, we should thank our lucky stars. How are you then? I am so very happy.

A new optimism was abroad, for with these therapies, psychiatrists could argue that they actually cured people.

Paradoxically, these limited psychiatric successes with acute patients only heightened psychiatric embarrassment about that proportion of patients for whom they could do nothing. Acute cases could be treated with occupational therapy or one of these new somatic therapies. Any danger they might represent to the collective hereditary health of race and nation could be neutralised through compulsory sterilisation before, or as a condition of their release into the community. But this still left the problem of, the incurable or refractory, upon whom these therapies made no impact whatsoever, and whose care still cost money. In November 1939 director Hermann Pfannmüller of Eglfing-Haar responding to a report from local auditors, commented on this last group of patients, 'The problem of whether to maintain this patient material under the most primitive conditions or to eradicate it has now become a subject for serious discussion once more.' Selective therapeutic intensity had once again pushed a certain patient constituency to the margins, but this time, in a political climate where the masters of the state had no moral inhibitions about murder, and wished to clear the economic decks for the war they were bent on waging.

Before turning to the 'euthanasia' programme, one final element needs to be introduced into this discussion, namely the extent to which these policies were consensual. Matters are a little more complicated than the conventional polarised triad of victims, bystanders and perpetrators, because mental illness and severe disability are issues where attitudes are not clear cut and prejudice and social stigmas operate. Most discussions of the National Socialists' justification of their policies quite reasonably alight upon the intellectual influence of Binding and Hoche's utilitarian tract for the times, without noticing that very often they actually refer to an author who was, in fact, the tract's main critic. In 1925 Ewald Meltzer, the director of the Katharinenhof asylum for backward juveniles at Grosshennersdorf in Saxony, published an extremely powerful critique of Binding and Hoche, which stressed both the joy handicapped people took in life and the positive sentiments caring for them engendered in others, and which condemned the inflationary and materialist character of the arguments used by the two professors.

Unfortunately, Meltzer decided to carry out a poll of the views on 'euthanasia' held by the parents of his young charges. His assurance that the results of the poll would be non-consequential did not stop one or two people removing their relatives from his asylum. Much to Meltzer's surprise, some 73 per cent of the 162 respondents said that they would approve 'the painless curtailment of the life of [their] child if experts had established that it is suffering from incurable idiocy'. Many of the 'yes' respondents said that they wished to be relieved of the burden represented by an 'idiotic' child; some of them expressed the wish that this be done secretly and that they should be told that the child had died of some illness, in a manner which resembled later National Socialist practice. Only twenty of the forty-three 'no' respondents in fact rejected all four propositions put to them by Meltzer — for example some countenanced killing in the event of their own deaths leaving the child orphaned — it thus being a minority who, either from ethical and religious convictions or powerful bonds to their child, would not sanction their deaths under any circumstances. Surveying National Socialist propaganda on these subjects, it is not entirely surprising that Meltzer was as much cited as Binding and Hoche. Silent collusive assent was as much involved as outrage and protest.

Indeed, the origins of the 'euthanasia' programme were very much bound up with requests for 'mercy killing'. The reason Hitler decided to assign the task to the Chancellery of the Führer was not simply because this small prerogative agency could act secretly outside the regular channels of government, but because the Chancellery handled incoming petitions, which included requests for 'euthanasia'. These came from, for example, a woman dying of cancer, a man blinded and severely injured after falling into a cement mixer, and the parents of a handicapped infant called Knauer, languishing in a Leipzig clinic, blind and without a leg and part of an arm. Hitler despatched Karl Brandt, the accident surgeon attached to his retinue, to Leipzig to authorise the death of this child. He then empowered both Brandt and the head of the Chancellery of the Führer, Philipp Bouhler, to make further authorisations in similar cases in future. A Reich Committee for the Scientific Registration of Serious Hereditary and Congenital Illnesses was formed, consisting of three leading paediatricians, whose task was to make decisions on euthanasia killings on the basis of information they received following the introduction of compulsory registration of such conditions. A number of special paediatric clinics was established, which promised the parents the latest forms of treatment, with the revealing rider that there were real risks involved. Parents who had exhausted every medical avenue and who were worn down by having to cope with several children had few reservations about handing their child over to these clinics, in some cases in the knowledge that he or she would be killed there. An army of welfare snoopers equipped with coercive powers could easily bring pressure to bear on the recalcitrant by, for example, conscripting single mothers for labour service.

The children concerned were killed by a combination of starvation and powerful sedatives. The nurses involved may have found the work disturbing, but they also thought it right to 'release unfortunate creatures from their suffering', and appreciated the regular bonus payments. The doctors were volunteers. That it was possible to refuse such work is demonstrated by, for example, the case of Dr Friedrich Hölzel, who used the opportunity of a vacation ruined by rain, to write to Pfannmüller declining the post of running Eglfing-Haar's paediatric killing centre.

Although he approved of these policies, it was another matter to carry them out in person, a distinction that 'reminded [him] of the difference which exists between a judge and executioner'. He thought he was too weak and too concerned with helping his patients to be able to 'carry this out as a systematic policy after cold-blooded deliberation'. Pfannmüller never pressed him any further on the matter. In total, as many as 6,000 children were killed in this programme, with the age range being surreptitiously extended to include adolescents.

Hitler's wartime authorisation of an adult 'euthanasia' programme was conceived as an economy measure, a means of creating emergency bed space for military casualties, and, although this has not been much explored, hostels for ethnic German repatriates from Russia and eastern Europe. In the eastern areas of the Reich, SS units under Kurt Eimann and Herbert Lange were subcontracted to shoot psychiatric patients to create army and SS barrack space in a parallel operation. The Chancellery of the Führer created an elaborate covert bureaucracy based at Tiergartenstrasse 4 (hence the code name Aktion T-4), whose task was to organise the registration, selection, transfer and murder of an anticipated, and previously calculated target of 70,000 victims. This apparatus was run by a group of economists, agronomists, former businessmen and commercial lawyers — many of whom were old friends — with an expanded panel of academics and psychiatrists whose job was to handle the medical side of mass murder. Many of the professors were of modest social origin, men for whom education was hence a form of social mobility, with their fragile egos being bolstered by titles and semi-official positions in Hereditary Health Courts or by working for the SS on a freelance basis. For instance T-4's first medical chief, Werner Heyde of Würzburg, had worked part-time in concentration camps since the mid-1930s, and was a provincial, latently homosexual, university professor of modest social circumstances, literally tantalised by the indirect power radiating from the Chancellery of the Führer.

Together this odd assortment of highly educated, morally vacant humanity set about registering and selecting victims; finding asylums quietly to kill them in; establishing an effective means of so doing; and, last but not least, a staff of people willing and able to commit mass murder. Both Herbert Linden, the desk officer responsible for asylums in the Ministry of Interior, and regional health bureaucrats such as Walter 'Bubi' Schultze in Munich or Ludwig Sprauer in Stuttgart proved very co-operative, because they had already been advocating these policies for several years. They either identified suitable asylums, organising transfers of ownership, or recommended doctors, orderlies and nursing staff whose track-record and level of ideological commitment singled them out as suitable; Heyde provided the names of his past students. The SS, which was at one remove from these policies, provided a pool of insensate hard men from the concentration camps who could deal with the horrible physicality of murder. Teams consisting of these people were sent to six asylums in order to convert them into extermination centres: the former hard labour prison at Brandenburg; Bernburg, near Halle; Grafeneck, high in the Swabian Alb; Hadamar, near Limburg; Schloss Hartheim, near Linz, and Sonnenstein, outside Dresden. The doctors who monopolised killing were gradually inducted into their grim work, beginning by watching and moving on to turning a gas-valve themselves, a simple enough task, but one apparently requiring a medical degree. Most of these doctors were quite young, socially insecure and hugely impressed by big names and grand places, i.e. the usual accompaniments of petty-bourgeois academic ambition. Their narrow professional training added no element of moral inhibition. The nurses and orderlies were the products of a professional and societal culture of obedience, and often had proven records of ideological commitment, believing in the rightness of these policies. It was a culture of compliance.

Registration forms were completed for every patient and then despatched via T-4 to various assessors. Many asylum directors made the fatal mistake of deliberately underestimating a patient's capacity to work in order not to lose valuable workers, a depressing reminder in itself of how the asylums had been turned into units of production. Low productivity, and the length of institutionalisation, usually signed a patient's death warrant. The T-4 assessors received batches of 200–300 forms at a time, and were paid on a piecework basis, which probably accounts for the diagnostic virtuosity of such Stakanovites of the psychiatric profession as Josef Schreck, who alone completed 15,000 forms in a month. On the basis of these forms, batches of patients were then removed by the Community Patients' Transport Service either directly to the gas chambers or to holding asylums, designed both to mislead relatives and to stagger the burden on the crematoria.

These killings inevitably meant contacts between T-4 and a host of private, state and religious asylums. Ecclesiastical resistance to these policies was slow in coming, not least because many directors of religious asylum networks, such as the director of the Protestant Inner Mission Hans

Harmsen, had supported negative eugenic strategies in the 1920s and 1930s, and because the Church hierarchies preferred high-level private talks to open confrontation with an anti-clerical government. Indeed, the chief Roman Catholic negotiator with T-4 headquarters (in itself a striking development), Bishop Heinrich Wienken, seems to have made a series of unfortunate compromises, impressed, no doubt, by the elaborate theological arguments T-4 had elicited beforehand to justify 'euthanasia'. Half of the 70,000 victims of T-4 came from asylums and homes which were part of ecclesiastical charitable networks. Protests from individual churchmen came too late to be effective and were simply sidestepped. Difficulties with individuals within the judiciary or state prosecution service were ironed out by inducting their superiors into an operation that had no formal legal sanction whatsoever.

Some asylums tried to subvert the operation by delaying completion of the registration process once they realised that this had a malign hidden agenda. This practice was countered by roving teams of T-4 assessors, some of whom would go off sight-seeing leaving their students to process entire cohorts of patients. A few asylums tried pre-emptive discharge, or indeed hid a few vulnerable patients. But discharge depended upon the willingness of families to have the patient at home; in many cases the response was that there was no room in the inn. Refusing to have his brother home from the Mariaberg asylum, a man wrote that Otto 'would never be forgotten' and promised a 'little something' in the post for Christmas. Otto did not last until Christmas — he was gassed at Grafeneck on 13 December. Most asylum staff co-operated, rationalising what they did by the weak excuse that they had haggled over the life of this or that patient, for T-4 naturally included room for a little plea-bargaining to anticipate the element of bad conscience. It was always possible to point to this or that saved individual, quietly overlooking the disappearance of bus-loads of others. Capacity to work, the dominant therapeutic criterion, now became the basis of selection. In many cases, psychiatrists had no difficulty effecting the transition.

In total, T-4 killed over 70,000 people. A final report translated the monthly kill-rate into graphs, while precisely calculating how much money or foodstuffs would be saved by 70,273 'disinfections', extrapolated down to 1951. These graphs, discovered by the Americans in a safe at Hartheim, showed actual savings on, for example, marmalade — assuming each person consumed 700 grams a year — of 5,902,920 kilograms with its money equivalent of RM7,083,504.

Following the cessation of the mass gassing of patients in August 1941, because the initial target had been slightly exceeded and protests were mounting, the T-4 medical assessors were turned loose on the inmates of concentration camps, where they perfunctorily rediagnosed people the SS had already deemed 'sick' and hence dispensable. Many of the 20,000 or so victims of 'Aktion 14f13' — the code designating the death of a sick camp inmate — were killed simply because of their criminal records, or because they were Jewish. In the winter of 1941, a T-4 team under Viktor Brack was despatched to Minsk where it is very probable they quietly disposed of seriously injured German soldiers *en route* from field hospitals to rear areas. That autumn, a busy Brack had also met Himmler, for whom he had once been a driver and for whom his doctor father had once helped Frau Himmler with a difficult pregnancy, who allegedly said that 'Hitler had some time ago given him the order for the extermination of the Jews. He said that preparations had already been made, and I think that he used the expression that for reasons of camouflage one would have to work as quickly as possible.' The T-4 men were to be one of the separate groups involved in the various competitive, experimental pushes set in motion finally to 'solve' the European 'Jewish Question'. As experts in mass gassing, they were given the largest part of the operation, apart from Rudolf Hoess's death factory at Auschwitz.

Some ninety-four temporarily redundant T-4 personnel were 'loaned' by Philipp Bouhler to the Higher SS and Police Leader in Lublin, the ex-bricklayer Odilo Globocnik. With the SS 'euthanasia' expert Herbert Lange already disposing of the Jewish population of the Warthegau at Kulmhof, this T-4 team formed the hard core whose task was the massive operation of murdering the entire Jewish population of the Generalgouvernement, the part of Poland not simply absorbed into greater Germany. Thus, a motley array of former cooks, lorry-drivers, labourers and ex-policemen, such as Kurt Franz, Lorenz Hackenholt, Josef Oberhauser, Franz Stangl, Christian Wirth, together with T-4 doctors such as Irmfried Eberl, moved up several social notches to pre-side over the murder of nearly two million people in what came to be called 'Aktion Reinhard', i.e. the extermination camps of Belzec, Sobibor and Treblinka, which wiped out the poor Jewish masses of Poland and the Jewish bourgeoisie of Western Europe. These men were hardened killers, inured to death and destruction, although few of them were con-victed psychopaths like Hoess at Auschwitz. They did not become extremely violent; most of them started off like that, indefinitely deferring and evading recognition of their own awfulness through black humour and talk of production targets. Indeed, the final statistical reckoning, drawn up by Globocnik in December 1943 precisely enumerated the vast sums garnered in the process, as well as nearly two thousand waggonloads of bedding, towels and clothing, and such things as sunglasses, opera-glasses, powder-puffs and silver cigarette cases.

Following the silent eradication of these three killing centres, many of the T-4 men involved were despatched southwards to the Dalmatian Coast to operate an extermination and torture centre in the Risiera — or rice warehouse — at Trieste. There they killed bottlenecked transports of Jews *en route* to Auschwitz, as well as Italians and Yugoslavs vaguely suspected of partisan activities.

Meanwhile, in the asylums of Germany, 'euthanasia' killings went on, using slow starvation on specially conceived diets, designed to minimise the cost of lethal drugs necessary to complete the process. At meetings in the regional health ministries, psychiatrists exchanged 'menus' consisting of nothing more than root vegetables in fluid, whose express object was to kill patients. There were no actual food shortages, since most asylums produced large surpluses on the backs of patient labour, which the administrators then sold at profit to Nazi organisations. There is also the matter of doctors such as Friedrich Mennecke and his wife Eva gorging themselves to excess while his patients expired through hunger. Death was visited upon anyone deemed unproductive or whose behaviour or manner irritated the staff, with patients sometimes being co-opted into killing their fellow inmates. Many of the victims were foreign forced labourers, for killing them on the spot was deemed cheaper than repatriation. In cases where nurses were drawn from religious orders, hardened T-4 killers such as Pauline Kneissler were brought in, with the recorded mortality rate spiralling high, only to fall when, in her case, she went on holiday for a week or two. In other institutions, the nursing staff participated in killings because their training had told them to do what they were told, because institutional culture desensitised what little sensitivity they possessed and because they were often bitter, frustrated, disillusioned, tired, underpaid and undervalued.

Obviously, policies like the ones described above, which were impossible to keep secret, did nothing for the image of either asylums or psychiatry. More importantly, they were like sawing off the branch upon which one was sitting, for depopulated asylums were usually alienated for non-medical purposes. In order to counteract these unwanted tendencies, psychiatrists working for T-4, such as Paul Nitsche or Carl Schneider, put forward various proposals for the 'modernisation' of psychiatry by using the funds saved through these killings to provide up-to-date therapies for acute cases. The more or less explicit subsidiary agenda was to build up university-based research activities by integrating them with the neurological 'material' made available to the professors through the 'euthanasia' programme. These plans were thus about reasserting professional psychiatric control over policies that were economically driven, whose effect was to put young recruits off entirely and whose logic threatened the existence of this entire branch of medicine. They were thus a form of *ex post facto* rationalisation, a means of evading the fact that these men had in fact created conditions in the asylums which a few enlightened doctors there described as a 'reversion to the psychiatry of the Middle Ages', with untended and skeletal patients lying naked in their own excrement and urine on straw sacks, and people locked alone in dark vermin-infested bunkers. Doctors strode the wards not as 'modernising' idealists but as self-styled 'soldiers' for whom the patients, particularly if they were people who spoke not a word of German, had literally become 'the enemy'.

Saving Money, Spending Lives
Michael Burleigh, *Death and Deliverance: 'Euthanasia' in Germany c. 1900–1945* (Cambridge, 1994); Jeremy Noakes and Geoffrey Pridham (eds), *Nazism, 1919–1945: A Documentary Reader* (Exeter, 1989), vol. 3; Paul Weindling, *Health, Race and German Politics Between National Unification and Nazism, 1870–1945* (Cambridge 1989).

CHAPTER VII

CHRISTINE LEHMANN AND MAZURKA ROSE: TWO 'GYPSIES' IN THE GRIP OF GERMAN BUREAUCRACY, 1933–60

Wolfgang Wippermann

O N 17 JANUARY 1942 TWENTY-TWO YEAR OLD Christine Lehmann was summonsed by the criminal police in the Ruhr town of Duisburg. She was ordered immediately to abandon the 'marriage-like relationship' she was having with the van driver Karl H. Refusal would result in 'assignment to a concentration camp', for Christine Lehmann was 'a member of the Gypsy clan Lehmann', and 'membership of a clan' constituted 'an impediment to marriage'. There was also no question of Christine Lehmann and Karl H. continuing to live together out of wedlock, for this would prejudice 'the maintenance of the purity of Aryan blood'.

In order to understand what lay behind the inhumanly pedestrian language used in this and further communications with Christine Lehmann, it is necessary to say a little about the legal position of so-called 'Gypsies', or Sinti and Roma as they prefer to call themselves in the Third Reich. The Roma, or Romany, differed from Sinti — many of whose forefathers had been in Germany since the fifteenth century — with respect to their customs and pronunciation of the Romanes (or Romany) language. However, few outsiders beyond a handful of so-called experts on 'Gypsies' were aware of these differences. The authorities certainly did not differentiate between Sinti and Roma. As far as they were concerned, both ethnic groups were simply 'Gypsies', who were subject to special laws, and who could be summarily deported if they could not prove German citizenship.

Strictly speaking, Sinti and Roma were already second-class citizens before Hitler's accession to power. By virtue of the Bavarian Law for the Combating of Gypsies, Travellers and the Workshy of 16 July 1926, Sinti and Roma could be sent to a workhouse for up to two years if they were unable to provide proof of regular employment. Following the National Socialists' abrogation of all residual civil rights between 1933 and 1934, Sinti and Roma were in even less of a position to protect themselves against discrimination than before. Low-ranking officials and some local authorities used this new situation further to inhibit their right to earn a living or their freedom of movement. From 1934 onwards various towns endeavoured to confine Sinti and Roma in so-called 'Gypsy camps', which were hardly fit for human habitation. Initially there was no legal sanction for this, since Sinti and Roma were not specifically mentioned in National Socialist racial legislation. This was true of, for example, the Law for the Restoration of the Professional Civil Service of 7 April 1933, which licensed the dismissal of Jewish civil servants; the law of 14 July 1933 sanctioning the compulsory sterilisation of the allegedly hereditarily ill; and finally, of the Nuremberg Laws of 15 September 1935 which effectively took away the citizenship of German Jews and forbade them to marry or have sexual relations with 'citizens of German or related blood'. Sinti and Roma were not even mentioned in the so-called Marriage Health Law of 18 October 1935 to which the Duisburg criminal police were referring in their summons to Christine Lehmann. These deficiencies were remedied in the successive decrees that accompanied the implementation of these laws. For example the 'first decree concerning the implementation of the Law for the Protection of German blood and honour' stipulated that marriages could not be contracted if, in general, 'the progeny would constitute a threat to the purity of German blood'. A decree issued by the Minister of the Interior on 26 November 1935 concluded that this would be so in the case of 'marriages between persons of German blood with Gypsies, Negroes and their bastards'.

In the absence of formal legislation concerning Gypsies, the Duisburg criminal police availed themselves of this decree in the case of Christine Lehmann. How, one might ask, had she and Karl H. managed to stay together until 1942? As early as 8 December 1938 Heinrich Himmler had ordered the 'final solution of the Gypsy Question in accordance with the nature of their race' and in May 1940 some 2,500 German Sinti and Roma had been deported from westerly regions of the Reich to the Generalgouvernement in occupied Poland. Among the latter were the parents and six siblings of Christine Lehmann, who may herself have been spared because at that time 'Gypsies married to persons of German blood were to be excluded from deportation'. Such caution was no longer in evidence by 1942. The Duisburg criminal police now regarded the 'marriage-like relationship' of Christine Lehmann and Karl H. as being 'asocial'. They put the town health authorities, with their army of professional snoopers, on the case. A few months later, a zealous female welfare official reported that she had 'encountered' Christine Lehmann 'with her husband'. Christine Lehmann had cooked for him and 'the home looked as though two persons with children slept (!) there'. Christine also delivered express letters for Karl H.

In other words, Christine Lehmann was exactly what the authorities normally wanted Gypsies to be, in the sense that she was manifestly socially conformist. She looked after her family as a wife, mother and provider of income. Paradoxically, it was precisely these prosaic activities that led to her being categorised as 'asocial' on racial-ideological grounds. She was summonsed once more on 30 January 1943 by the Duisburg criminal police, who by this time had compiled a comprehensive 'hereditary and life history questionnaire' about both her and her entire family. In the box asking: 'Which members of the clan have led a markedly irregular, unsteady, drifting way of life, or have frequently changed their habitation and place of work? Which are workshy or vagrants? Which seem to be criminals?' the Duisburg criminal police wrote: 'The Lehmann clan belongs to the Gypsy people and, until they settled, continually moved around, deriving their living from the sale of haberdashery. With the exception of the person under consideration here, the entire clan was resettled in the East on 16 May 1940.' This was a *de facto* death sentence for Christine Lehmann. However, at first she appeared to be fortunate. Unlike the majority of German Sinti and Roma she was not deported to the 'Gypsy camp' at Auschwitz in early 1943. The records are imprecise as to why this oversight occurred. Perhaps the reason was that at this time she had not yet been subjected to 'racial investigation', which was one of the necessary preconditions for the 'regularised' deportation of a Sintiza (a Sinti woman) to Auschwitz.

This deficiency was remedied in June 1943, according to a communication dated 10 June from the Essen criminal police to their colleagues in neighbouring Duisburg. They used Christine Lehmann's 'Gypsy' name and added the letters 'ZM' after it to signify (*Zigeunermischling*) or 'Gypsy halfcaste'. This took care of all the preliminaries needed to send someone to Auschwitz. However, this still appeared impossible. The criminal police in Essen went on to remark that 'assignment of Gypsy persons to the concentration camp at Auschwitz is not possible at present on sanitary grounds'. Of course, the criminal police did not simply release Christine Lehmann. She was detained in 'police preventive custody by virtue of the general provisions for the 'preventive fight against crime'. Her 'asocial' and 'community-endangering behaviour', as the pleonastic jargon had it, or in other words her illicit sexual relationship with a German, was sufficient pretext for her continued detention. The gentlemen from the police also drew attention to 'her constant efforts to flee so as to avoid the projected confinement'.

Without evidently realising it, the criminal police in Duisburg had made an error. People taken into 'police preventive custody' were normally detained in nearby concentration camps rather than sent to the extermination camps in the East. A higher department of the Essen criminal police spotted the error, drawing attention in a letter dated 10 June 1943, regarding the 'detention order' issued against Christine Lehmann — for this was paper dealing with more paper — to the fact that 'in her case one is dealing with a Gypsy person whose transfer to the Gypsy camp of the concentration camp at Auschwitz is in accordance with the decree of the Reich Main Security Office of 29 January 1943'. This recommended improvement was relayed to the Reich Criminal Police Office in Berlin. They, in turn, decreed that Christine Lehmann should not be sent to a concentration camp in Germany, where her chances of survival would have been marginally better, but rather to the extermination camp at Auschwitz-Birkenau, where her chances would be practically nil. Almost as an afterthought, the Reich Criminal Police added that since Christine Lehmann's children were 'Gypsy half-castes', they should accompany their mother too. They meant four-year-old Egon and twenty-month-old Robert.

Executing these orders proved difficult for the criminal police in Duisburg. The parents of Karl H. — who by this time was serving at the Front — refused to surrender the two children. The criminal police in Duisburg decided, *faute de mieux*, to deport Christine Lehmann unaccompanied by her small children. Somewhat frustrated they reported on 3 February 1944 that Christine Lehmann was on her own in the concentration camp at Auschwitz. In the meantime, baby Robert had been taken in by a sister of Karl H. who lived in Luxemburg. This presented the police with a taxing problem; their colleagues in the Duisburg welfare department refused to oblige by making available a nurse to pick up the child, because Allied bombing had made travel more than usually arduous.

Eventually, the criminal police in Duisburg nerved themselves to send an officer to bring the child back. The 'costs . . . up to the handing over of the prisoner to the concentration camp' were 'defrayed by the responsible criminal police office under heading 14, item 33'. On 12 March 1944 the police could finally regard the job as having been properly done. They reported that five-year-old Egon and Robert, who was almost two, had 'been transferred to Auschwitz by individual transport'. It is doubtful whether the family enjoyed even the briefest of reunions. Christine Lehmann died on 28 March 1944, 'as a result of enteritis and physical weakness in the sick-bay of the camp at Auschwitz'. The criminal police officer responsible for the case made a final laconic entry in his records: 'There are no known relatives here. In so far as there was a relationship between Lehmann and the van driver H. — who is in the army at present — the latter's mother has been informed of the demise. The legal heirs are Lehmann's two children Egon and Robert who are in the camp at Auschwitz.' Egon, Robert and Christine Lehmann were among the 500,000 people whom the National Socialists murdered because they were Sinti and Roma.

Mazurka Rose was spared this fate. However, although he survived persecution by the National Socialists, he was not recognised as a victim by the Federal German authorities after 1945, and indeed experienced continued discrimination in the post-war period. He shared this fate with many other Sinti and Roma who had survived Nazi persecution.

Mazurka Rose was born on 20 July 1911 in Bärwalde near the East Prussian city of Königsberg. He came from a Roma family which had migrated to Germany from Hungary in the nineteenth century. In common with other Sinti, Roma or, for that matter, Polish or Jewish nineteenth-century immigrants, the Rose family had acquired German citizenship.

In 1937 Mazurka Rose, his wife, mother and some of his brothers and sisters were confined in the 'Gypsy camp' set up at Marzahn in Berlin, where they occupied 'waggon 75'. This camp was established in the summer of 1936 on the joint initiative of the municipal welfare authorities, the police and the Racial Political Office of the National Socialist Party. The ostensible motive was the desire of the National Socialist government to remove 'blots' on the image of the city currently hosting the summer Olympic Games. The blots included sites occupied by Sinti and Roma scattered across the city. On 16 July 1936 the police herded together about six hundred Sinti and Roma in a so-called 'Gypsy camp' on an insalubrious site in the north-eastern suburb of Marzahn, which was thenceforth put under permanent guard and ringed with fencing. The inmates of the camp received inadequate accommodation, elementary sanitary facilities, poor food and minimal medical attention. In early 1939 the authorities noted 'numerous cases of scarlet fever, diphtheria and tuberculosis', and were concerned about 'the danger that the population of Marzahn might contract these diseases'. They therefore recommended the 'physical reconstruction' of the camp, and the introduction of a strict regime along the lines of a concentration camp. Such an arrangement would also have the merit of regular legal status. In 1941 the camp's one-class school was closed. At the same time it was decreed that 'in so far as they are still capable of work, aged and infirm Gypsies should carry out . . . clearing work,' while able-bodied Gypsies should be employed in construction work or in factories. Mazurka Rose was sent to work at Soff, the cap manufacturers. However, shortly afterwards he was denounced to the Gestapo and sent to the work training camp at Berlin-Wuhlheide.

This forced labour camp was established in early 1940, following an agreement between the Gestapo and the national railway construction department in Berlin. There were similar forced labour camps in other towns or attached to large concerns. They were retrospectively legitimised by a decree issued by Himmler on 28 May 1941, who simultaneously ordered every Gestapo regional office to set up camps of this sort. Conditions in the camp at Wuhlheide seem to have been particularly squalid. The barracks were overcrowded and food and medical provision were totally inadequate. A large number of inmates fell ill. Prisoners were beaten up by their guards, thrown into drainage ditches and cesspits, or subjected to sadistic tortures such as being crushed between two portable cement-mixing trays. Many of the inmates did not survive. The local registry office at Berlin-Karlhorst gave false information on death certificates, using such stereotypical formulae as 'died from pneumonia', 'heart failure' or 'circulatory disorder' to account for deaths due to maltreatment.

After a few weeks, Mazurka Rose was released and allowed to return to the camp at Marzahn. He was rearrested on 5 October 1942 by the criminal police in Berlin. The latter handed Rose over to the Gestapo, who consigned him to Sachsenhausen concentration camp on 16 December

1942. This was done on the authority of Himmler's circular of 14 December 1937 categorising Sinti and Roma as 'asocial' and sanctioning their detention in police 'preventive custody'. In Sachsenhausen, Mazurka Rose was categorised as 'Aso [asocial] Gypsy'. On 17 July 1944 he was transferred to Dachau, where he was categorised under the rubric 'AZR' (Reich Forced Labour) in reference to the large-scale raids against the 'asocial' conducted under the operational heading 'Action Workshy Reich' in June 1938.

In 1945 Mazurka Rose was liberated by the Americans from Blaichach, a satellite camp of Dachau. Although he had survived, his wife, children and mother had been murdered in the extermination camp at Auschwitz following their deportation from Berlin on 5 May 1943. After the war, Mazurka Rose resumed his job as a carpet and rug dealer and remarried. On 21 December 1950 he applied to the Bavarian regional compensation office for compensation for the physical and material damage he had incurred in various concentration camps between 1942 and 8 May 1945. In other words, he failed to claim compensation for his detention in the 'Gypsy camp' at Marzahn or the 'work training camp' at Wuhlheide, which he would certainly be entitled to do today with considerable chance of success. This reticence turned out to be mistaken, for on 10 August 1953 the Bavarian regional compensation office rejected his application on the grounds that 'he had not been imprisoned because of his race, but because he was not engaged in regular employment'. Mazurka Rose decided to contest this decision in the courts. However, on 18 August 1954 the third compensation chamber of the Munich regional court rejected his appeal. The court argued that in contrast to his relatives, Mazurka Rose had been sent to a concentration camp 'too soon', that is before Himmler's decree of 16 December 1942 despatching all German Sinti and Roma to Auschwitz. Mazurka Rose had actually been sent to Sachsenhausen on the day this decree was issued. Unfortunately, on 7 January 1956 the Federal Supreme Court decided to endorse the view that Sinti and Roma had only been subject to racial persecution following the decree sending them to Auschwitz. All previous measures, notably the deportations of April 1940, whose legal status was the question at issue in this hearing, were evidently not inspired by racial-ideological motives. This had particular relevance for those Sinti and Roma who had been categorised as 'asocial' by the decree issued by Himmler on 14 December 1937 and had thence been sent to concentration camps. In other words, the Federal Supreme Court had decided that it was completely legitimate to confine Sinti and Roma and the 'asocial' in general in concentration camps.

The decision of the Munich regional court reflected this thinking, managing to emulate the language and outlook of the Nazis in the reasons given for their judgement. The court declared that Mazurka Rose had been sent to Sachsenhausen and Dachau as an 'Aso Gypsy' because 'he was workshy, refusing to work', and had 'carried out sabotage at the workplace'. In the concentration camps he had worn the 'black triangle which designated the workshy'. The court came to the following conclusion: 'All of these circumstances suggest that the plaintiff was not categorised as being workshy on account of his membership of the Gypsy people; rather, how [the authorities] regarded one individual proved crucial, and this cannot be taken to justify the claim of persecution upon racial grounds.' Setting aside the unfortunate choice of words in the second part of this sentence, with its implication that it might be possible to justify racial persecution, it is necessary to emphasise that the National Socialists did indeed deduce 'asociality' simply from 'membership of the Gypsy people'. Even a passing acquaintance with the publications of a Nazi expert on Gypsies, such as Dr Robert Ritter, would have been enough to set the court to rights on this question.

The court's judgement had certain untoward consequences for Mazurka Rose. The only 'expert' witness called was a criminal police inspector called Geyer. This was the same Georg Geyer who, along with other colleagues, had been responsible for the deportation of Bavaria's Gypsies before 1945, but who nonetheless was still operating in the Travellers Department of the Bavarian Regional Criminal Police. On 19 August 1954, one day after the completion of the oral hearing of Mazurka Rose's case, Geyer put in a special request to the residents' registration office in Essen and both the trade inspectors and criminal police in Hamburg. Because the Munich criminal police had Mazurka Rose in their records as a 'traveller', and because he had been unable to produce a birth certificate at the time of his second marriage, and finally, because he had described himself to the court as 'a member of the so-called Romany people', Geyer had decided that Rose's 'nationality remains unclear'. Henceforth, the Munich criminal police office had decided to regard Rose as being 'stateless . . . until such time as unimpeachable proof exists concerning his nationality'. Geyer asked the authorities he contacted 'carefully to re-examine the information which led to Rose being issued with identity papers, including both his passport and itinerant trading licence'.

This threatened Rose's entire professional existence. Without German identity papers he would find it very difficult to obtain an itinerant trading licence which he needed in order to continue to purchase and sell rugs and carpets.

On 30 August 1954 Geyer asked the criminal police in Hamburg to check whether Rose's brothers Karl Rose, Alfred Weiss and Josef Rose had legitimately acquired German citizenship. Geyer justified this request by remarking that the Rose family were 'Roma Gypsies, whose forefathers had illegally entered Germany from Hungary in about 1870'. In a further communication, dated 14 October 1954, the Bavarian criminal police openly admitted where they had got the intelligence that the forefathers of Rose and his family had illegally come to Germany in about 1870. They had discovered 'watertight evidence' in the Bavarian regional criminal police headquarters gleaned from 'investigations of individuals'. What they omitted to mention was that these records were those of the Reich Central Office for the Combating of the Gypsy Nuisance, the Nazis' central agency involved in persecuting Sinti and Roma, and also the findings of the 'racial hygienic research institute in the Reich Office of Health', the agency run by the notorious Robert Ritter. The department for nationality questions within the office for legal affairs of the city of Hamburg also referred on 18 August 1955 to the research materials of Ritter's agency which, during the Nazi period, 'had refereed every Gypsy'. This material led the department for nationality questions to conclude on 27 April 1956 that there were no grounds for claiming that Mazurka Rose had 'ever possessed or acquired German citizenship' and that therefore he was to be regarded as being 'stateless'. It is almost incomprehensible that the scientifically dubious findings of Ritter's agency, which before 1945 had played a critical role in the persecution of Sinti and Roma, should have been used by the Federal authorities after the war not only to deny claims to compensation, but even to challenge the victims' right to German citizenship.

The 'research' on the Roma in question was carried out first by Ritter's colleague Dr Karl Moravek, and then by Ritter's girlfriend and quondam postgraduate pupil Eva Justin. She wrote an article about her research in the journal *Neues Volk* published by the National Socialists' Racial Political Office in 1944. She began by remarking that 'in the sixties and seventies of the last century several clans of a semi-nomadic Gypsy tribe from the Hungarian-Slovakian border region traversed the open frontier with Germany'. Once there, they had 'paid large sums of money to native

Sinti Gypsies, German travellers and even indigeneous Germans in order to acquire documents and identity papers' and thus 'had illicitly come into possession of German citizenship'. This same claim was repeated almost word for word by the post-war officials of the Bavarian regional criminal police. Naturally, Eva Justin had no hard evidence for her assertion that all Roma had illegally assumed German citizenship. Today it is possible neither to prove nor disprove this assertion, any more than it is to establish the exact origins of all those Germans — and a glance at a telephone book would reveal the scale of the problem — who have Polish, Russian, Czech, Slovak, Huguenot or Hungarian names, whose deportation on the grounds of illegal entry is presumably on no one's agenda.

In any case it is indisputable that many Roma, including the Rose family, were in possession of German citizenship, and that not even the notoriously racist Nazis had endeavoured to contest this. Mazurka Rose's mother Lisa and some of his sisters were only formally declared 'enemies of the state and nation' or 'enemies of the Reich' after their deportation. The object of this strategy, which was also used in the case of German Jews deported to the East, was to facilitate confiscation of the goods they left behind under the provisions of the Law for the Confiscation of the Property of Enemies of the State and Nation of 14 July 1933. In the case of Mazurka Rose's mother, some RM30 was confiscated 'for the benefit of the Reich'. As seen above, Mazurka Rose himself was sent to a concentration camp following Himmler's decree of 14 December 1937, something that could only be done in the case of German citizens. Put briefly, in the eyes of the Nazis the Roses were indisputably German citizens.

In this respect therefore, the Bavarian regional criminal police were far more radical and hostile to Gypsies than the Nazis had been, and were content merely to rely upon the research 'findings' of Ritter's racial hygienic research bureau to legitimise their actions. It is time to return once again to Eva Justin's article about the Roma Gypsies. In order to prove her claim that the Roma had illegally acquired German citizenship, Eva Justin referred to a number of anthropological and sociological characteristics of the Roma that allegedly distinguished them in a negative light from indigenous Sinti. She was not referring to alleged or real differences in language or their system of taboos, but rather to differences in appearance and behaviour. While the 'undemanding' Sinti 'eked out a miserable living through music-making and seasonal work, but mainly through begging, fortune telling and minor acts of deception, and almost without exception had more or less lengthy criminal records consisting of short spells in prison', the Roma were by contrast 'casually but elegantly dressed textile dealers', the 'most intelligent of whom' were wealthy people who 'even in the first years of the war had driven past our institute in heavy foreign lorries'.

However, in ways reminiscent of Christine Lehmann's unimpeachable lifestyle, it was precisely this evidence of socio-economic success that both Eva Justin and her disciples in the Bavarian criminal police used negatively against the Roma. According to criminal police officer Eller, 'all Roma Gypsies . . . were extremely cunning and for the most part well-off dealers . . . who once used to be horse dealers, but who for the last twenty years or so have mostly worked as textile traders'. The same claim can be found in Eva Justin's article, which moreover claimed that 'up to 1942 most of the 2,000 odd Roma Gypsies in Germany managed to make a living from large-scale black-market trading in textiles and other consumer goods in short supply'. Predictably, there was no evidence for this claim. Justin merely referred to the painstaking and tenacious endeavours of Berlin-based experts in Gypsy matters under one Leo Karsten, who had succeeded 'in bringing about 200 of the 400 adult Roma in Berlin before the courts as parasites on the nation'. Among those 'parasites' brought before the courts by the Berlin 'Gypsy' police was Mazurka Rose.

Justin considered it 'of racial-biological interest' that 'the worst Roma blackmarketeering families . . . evinced fewer physical characteristics typical of Gypsies'. Indeed, a few of them were beyond racial 'diagnostic classification' altogether. It was difficult to ascertain whether they were Gypsies or South-East Europeans. This was an involuntary admission of just how difficult it was to achieve precision in this branch of 'scientific' research, none of which stopped Justin from further flights of academic fancy. She went on to claim that in the case of a few Roma, 'their overwhelmingly Near Eastern or oriental physical characteristics, their gestures and smoothly cunning trading practice left a pronouncedly Jewish impression'.

It is more than shocking that racial differences between Sinti and Roma 'discovered' by Nazi 'experts' should have been perpetuated by Federal German authorities after 1945, and that the latter frequently had recourse to the findings of the former. This is evident in a letter written by a senior police official in Hamburg on 3 November 1960 which referred to materials left on file by the 'former expert on Gypsies L. Karsten'. This was the same Karsten who had decided that Mazurka Rose and a further 200 Roma Gypsies were 'parasites on the nation', and who had sent Rose's mother and sisters and another 252 Berlin Gypsies to Auschwitz. Relying upon his expertise in this matter was tantamount to asking Adolf Eichmann for expert testimony in compensation cases brought by Jews. But this was precisely what the Hamburg criminal police were doing as they wrote in this letter of the 'valuable materials' from the Racial Hygienic Research Bureau which 'according to the testimony of former staff members of the archive on Gypsy clans had survived the collapse of 1945' and now lay 'in the form of microfilm with the Bavarian regional criminal police'.

Mazurka Rose never regained his German citizenship. He died prematurely on 14 July 1962 at the age of fifty-one, quite possibly because of damage to his health sustained during his spells in various camps. An official physician whom Rose had asked for a report on his state of health, had categorised his condition as 'hereditary'. Mazurka Rose's son Georg Rose, who was born in 1949, was still 'stateless' in 1992; his attempts to gain German citizenship had been totally unsuccessful. The judgements against his father were confirmed, notwithstanding the fact that they were unjust and unconstitutional. Article sixteen of the German Constitution says: 'German citizenship may not be withdrawn. Loss of citizenship can only ensue following the promulgation of a law and against the will of the person affected in so far as the person affected is not thereby rendered stateless.' Article sixteen is a basic law. Like other basic laws, such as freedom of the Press, of assembly and the inviolability of one's own home, 'its essentials ... can never be challenged' (Article 19.2 Basic Law).

Two 'Gypsies' in the Grip of German Bureaucracy
Ute Brucker-Boroujerdi and Wolfgang Wippermann, 'Die Rassenhygienische und Erbbiologische Forschungsstelle im Reichsgesundheitsamt', *Bundesgesundheitsblatt*, vol. 32 (Bonn, 1989); Michael Burleigh and Wolfgang Wippermann, *The Racial State: Germany, 1933–1945* (Cambridge, 1991); David Crowe and John Kolsti, *The Gypsies of Eastern Europe* (New York, 1991); Donald Kenrick and Grattan Puxon, *The Destiny of Europe's Gypsies* (London, 1982); Wolfgang Wippermann, 'Nationalsozialistische Zwangslager in Berlin, 1936–1945', in Wolfgang Ribbe (ed.), *Berlin-Forschungen*, vol. 2 (Berlin,

1987); Michael Zimmermann, *Verfolgt, Vertrieben, Vernichtet. Die Nationalsozialistische Vernichtungspolitik gegen Sinti und Roma* (Essen, 1989).

CHAPTER VIII

SAVAGE WAR

Omer Bartov

B ETWEEN 1941 AND 1945 THE THIRD REICH conducted the most savage military campaign in modern history. The invasion of the Soviet Union, code-named Operation Barbarossa, cost the lives of between 20 and 30 million Soviet citizens, well over half of whom were civilians, and devastated vast areas of western Russia from Leningrad in the north to Stalingrad in the south. Over three million Red Army prisoners of war, or 60 per cent of the number of Soviet soldiers captured, died in German captivity. Although the Soviet Union emerged from the war as a military superpower, it took decades to recover from the human tragedy and economic disaster of the German occupation.

The German war in Russia raises a number of important questions, relevant both to the history of the Third Reich as a whole and to the history of modern warfare. First, why Barbarossa was conducted in such a savage manner and what ends this policy was expected to serve; second, to what degree the soldiers fighting at the Front participated in the murderous actions of the regime and what effect the character of the fighting had on their morale, motivation and perception of reality; third, whether the war in the east was indeed a unique and unprecedented phenomenon in modern history by comparison to other instances of brutal warfare.

War played a central role in Nazi ideology. It was no coincidence that Hitler called his book *Mein Kampf*, that is, 'my battle'. According to the Nazi world-view, life consisted of a constant struggle for survival in which the best would win, or rather, in which the very fact of victory and survival would show the inherent physical and spiritual superiority of the winner, on the one hand, and the inferiority and moral depravity of the vanquished, on the other. Traditional norms of behaviour, ethical conventions and legal restrictions had nothing to do with this eternal battle; all that mattered was survival through victory and total annihilation of the enemy. Conversely, battle did have a profoundly ennobling effect, for in it the best qualities of the individual were called forth and the nation was purged of all slackness and degeneration. Thus war was not merely an inevitable condition, but also a necessary and welcome one. War forged a community of battle, a *Kampfgemeinschaft*, which in turn would produce the community of the people, the *Volksgemeinschaft*, that Nazi ideal of a racially pure, militarised, fanatically determined society, where affinities of blood and endless conquest would compensate for class inequality and lack of political freedom.

The ideal war, according to Hitler, was one of conquest, extermination and subjugation; the ideal area in which to conduct such a war was in the east, where the German people would win for itself the living space, or *Lebensraum*, necessary for its moral and racial purity, as well as for its ultimate emergence as the master race (*Herrenvolk*) of Europe and Asia, if not indeed the whole world. However, due to political and military constraints, this ideal could not be immediately realised. Before turning to the east, the Third Reich first had to make certain that its western flank was secure. Germany had experienced a two-front war between 1914 and 1918, and Hitler was determined to prevent a recurrence of such a hopeless strategic situation. Also, while the Western Powers were quite willing to let Germany fight it out with Bolshevik Russia, Stalin was unwilling to take the main brunt of Nazi military might and concluded a pact with Hitler which enabled the Third Reich first to smash Poland and divide its territory with the USSR, and then to turn against France.

The fighting in the west was inherently different from what was soon to be seen in the east. This had to do both with ideological determinants and with political calculation. Nazi racial theory placed the Jews at the very bottom of the racial ladder; they were to be simply done away with, whether by exclusion and expulsion (as was done in the early years of the regime) or by extermination, which began to be practised on a mass scale simultaneously with the attack on the Soviet Union. Only slightly higher were the Slavs, who were considered subhumans (*Untermenschen*), to be either murdered, worked and starved to death, or used as slave labour for the German colonisers of their lands. As for the French, and even more so the English, Nazi racial 'experts' remained rather vague, whether because of what they perceived as racial affinities with the German 'Aryans', or because of the 'higher' culture of Western Europe. Thus, while France was seen as a 'degenerate' civilisation, it was not marked for subjugation, but rather for a secondary role in the Nazi scheme of a German-dominated Europe. Politically, Hitler was always keen on reaching some settlement with the British, both because of his ambiguous view of the 'Anglo-Saxon race', and because of his fear of a two-front war.

Consequently, the German army fighting in the west was given strict orders to conduct itself according to the rules of war. This was easier also because the average German soldier had far fewer prejudices about the French and the English than about the Russians, and because Western Europe seemed to him more similar to his homeland than the Russia he was soon to invade.

Once France was defeated, and following Hitler's realisation that he would be able neither to persuade the British to reach an agreement with Germany nor to destroy British military strength whether from the air or by a landing from the sea, the German army was given orders to prepare for an invasion of the Soviet Union. Now at last Hitler could have the war of destruction (*Vernichtungskrieg*) and ideologies (*Weltanschauungskrieg*) he had always wanted to fight. In this he was far from alone, for his generals were in full agreement with the need to conduct a wholly different kind of war against what they called 'Judeo-Bolshevism' and the 'Asiatic hordes' of the east.

The Barbarossa Decree was composed of the operational orders for the attack on the Soviet Union, as well as of what have come to be called the 'criminal orders', a set of instructions regarding the manner in which the army was to conduct itself during the campaign. These included the infamous 'commissar order', calling for the immediate execution of all Red Army political officers captured by front-line units; the curtailment of military jurisdiction, which stipulated that soldiers could not be tried for offences committed against enemy soldiers and civilians as long as they did not thereby impinge on combat discipline; regulations regarding the behaviour of soldiers in the occupied territories, which called for ruthless punitive action against guerrillas and anyone assisting them, as well as against members of the Communist Party and Jews; and orders for the army closely to collaborate with and furnish military and logistical assistance to the death squads (*Einsatzgruppen*) of the SS, whose task was the mass murder of Jews and all other Soviet citizens belonging to 'biological' and political categories deemed unworthy of life by the authorities of the Third Reich.

To these orders the army added a series of logistical instructions, based on the assumption that in order to conduct a rapid campaign deep into Russia the units should not be hampered by a cumbersome supply apparatus, whose maintenance was expected to confront numerous difficulties because of the Soviet Union's primitive transportation infrastructure and a serious shortage of vehicles in the *Wehrmacht*. The conclusion was that, as far as possible, the army should sustain itself from the resources of the (often wretchedly poor) occupied population, with scant regard for the obvious repercussions this policy would have on the civilians' chances of survival. Moreover, the cold utilitarian calculation of operational efficiency was allied with the determination of the Nazi leadership not to allow any undue hardship among the German population in the rear as a result of the war, thereby preventing the outbreak of protests and demoralisation of the kind that had swept Germany during the latter phases of the First World War. Consequently, the army and the civil administrative authorities that followed it into the Soviet Union were ordered to exploit the agricultural, industrial and demographic resources of the occupied territories to the benefit of Germany. It was estimated that this would cause the death by deprivation of tens of millions of Russians, but this was greeted with satisfaction in view of the perceived need to 'depopulate' the eastern *Lebensraum* so as to make it ripe for German colonisation.

Closely tied to the military aspects of the operation was the decision to use this opportunity to 'eliminate' European Jewry once and for all, a policy officially sanctioned (though actually already in an advanced stage of execution) at the Wannsee Conference of January 1942, during which the work of the various agencies involved in the Final Solution was brought under the overall control of the SS six months after the attack on Russia was launched. The so-called 'Final Solution of the Jewish Question' by mass, industrial murder of the Jewish population of Europe, could hardly have taken the form which characterised it between 1941 and 1945 had the *Wehrmacht* not created the necessary military, logistical, demographic and psychological precondition for its implementation by its invasion of the Soviet Union and the vicious war it conducted there.

Thus it is clear that Barbarossa was conceived as an ideological war of extermination and enslavement; its goal was to wipe out the Soviet state, to enslave the Russian people after debilitating it by famine and all other forms of deprivation, systematically to murder all 'biological' and political enemies of Nazism, such as the Jews, the Gypsies, members of the Communist Party, intellectuals and so forth, and finally to turn western Russia into a German paradise of Aryan colonisers served by hordes of Slav helots.

For many years after the Second World War it was commonly assumed that although the Nazi regime was obviously criminal and had made use of murderous organisations such as the SS to carry out its policies of extermination, the army was not involved in such actions and in many ways resisted them, or at least kept itself in a position of critical isolation from the more unsavoury aspects of Nazi rule. It is therefore necessary to emphasise that this is a wholly erroneous view, based mainly on apologetic post-war literature by German veterans and its indiscriminate acceptance by Western military historians who remained quite ignorant of the realities of the Eastern Front and tried to apply their experience in the west to the totally different conditions that reigned in Russia between 1941 and 1945.

The fact of the matter is that, once Barbarossa was launched on 22 June 1941, the German combat troops on the ground showed little reluctance, indeed often demonstrated much enthusiasm, in carrying out the 'criminal orders' issued by the regime and the high command of the army. Nor did the field commanders do much to restrain the troops; quite the contrary, in many cases formation commanders exhorted their soldiers to act with even greater ferocity and determination against the 'racial' and political enemies of the Reich.

The commander of the Sixth Army, Walthar von Reichenau, appealed to his troops on 10 October 1941:

Regarding the conduct of the troops towards the Bolshevik system many unclear ideas still remain.

The essential goal of the campaign against the Jewish-Bolshevik system is the complete destruction of its power instruments and the eradication of the Asiatic influence on the European cultural sphere. Thereby the troops too have *tasks*, which go beyond the conventional unilateral soldierly tradition [*Soldatentum*]. In the East the soldier is not only a fighter according to the rules of warfare, but also a carrier of an inexorable racial conception [*völkischen Idee*] and the avenger of all the bestialities which have been committed against the Germans and related races.

Therefore the soldier must have *complete* understanding for the necessity of the harsh, but just atonement of Jewish subhumanity. This has the further goal of nipping in the bud rebellions in the rear of the *Wehrmacht* which, as experience shows, are always plotted by the Jews.

On 20 November 1941 General Erich von Manstein, commander of the Eleventh Army, issued the following order:

> Since 22 June the German *Volk* is in the midst of a battle for life and death against the Bolshevik system. This battle is conducted against the Soviet army not only in a conventional manner according of the rules of European warfare ...
>
> Judaism constitutes the mediator between the enemy in the rear and the still fighting remnants of the Red Army and the Red leadership. It has a stronger hold than in Europe on all key positions of the political leadership and administration, it occupies commerce and trade and further forms cells for all the disturbances and possible rebellions.
>
> The Jewish-Bolshevik system must be eradicated once and for all. Never again may it interfere in our European living space.
>
> The German soldier is therefore not only charged with the task of destroying the power instrument of this system. He marches forth also as a carrier of a racial conception and as an avenger of all the atrocities which have been committed against him and the German people.
>
> The soldier must show understanding for the harsh atonement of Judaism, the spiritual carrier of the Bolshevik terror ...

On 25 November 1941, the commander of the Seventeenth Army, Colonel-General Hermann Hoth, issued this order:

> It has become increasingly clear to us this summer, that here in the East spiritually unbridgeable conceptions are fighting each other: German sense of honour and race, and a soldierly tradition of many centuries, against an Asiatic mode of thinking and primitive instincts, whipped up by a small number of mostly Jewish intellectuals: fear of the knout, disregard of moral values, levelling down, throwing away of one's worthless life.
>
> More than ever we are filled with the thought of a new era, in which the strength of the German people's racial superiority and achievements entrust it with the leadership of Europe. We clearly recognise our mission to save European culture from the advancing Asiatic barbarism. We now know that we have to fight against an incensed and tough opponent. This battle can only end with the destruction of one or the other; a compromise is out of the question.

The enormous death-toll among the Russian prisoners of war and civilian population was thus a direct result not merely of the heavy fighting but to a large extent of the implementation of Nazi policies in the occupied regions of the Soviet Union. Hitler had stated unambiguously before the campaign that German troops should not recognise their Soviet enemies as 'comrades in arms'; there were to be, in his words, *keine Kameraden*. Consequently, in the first few months of fighting, the *Wehrmacht* shot out of hand some 600,000 political commissars, and by the end of the first winter in Russia some two million prisoners were already dead. Unlike the Western campaign, the *Wehrmacht* had made no provisions for the very high number of prisoners it expected to capture thanks to its tactics of encirclement. Instead, captured Red Army troops were marched hundreds of miles to the rear or carried in open freight trains in midwinter, and those who survived were then herded into empty fields surrounded by barbed wire and armed guards and allowed to starve to death. The troops became so used to this treatment of Soviet soldiers as *Untermenschen* that even when the orders were changed due to the decision to conscript prisoners for forced labour in the Reich, they refused to relent and kept shooting them out of hand against the express orders of their direct superiors.

As the logistical situation of the *Wehrmacht* deteriorated during autumn and winter 1941, the troops were ordered to resort to extensive requisitions which stripped the population of its last reserves of food and caused widespread famine and death. Intensified guerrilla activity against the *Wehrmacht*, caused not least by desperation occasioned by the horrifying conditions in occupied Russia, brought brutal retaliatory measures which included not merely the hanging of anyone suspected of partisan activity, but also the destruction of thousands of villages and the murder of their inhabitants as part of a policy of collective punishment. Following the Red Army's counter-offensive of December 1941, and thereafter whenever the *Wehrmacht* was forced to retreat, German combat units resorted to a policy of 'scorched earth' which devastated vast regions of abandoned territory and led to the death by deprivation of whoever was not killed right away by the withdrawing troops or sent back to the Reich as slave labour.

Wehrmacht commanders were initially anxious lest such policies should cause demoralisation among their troops. In fact, the result was quite the opposite, for the fighting morale and motivation of the troops seem to have been fortified by the increasingly savage nature of the fighting.

This can be explained by reference to the perception of reality among the troops fighting in the east, which in turn owed much to their ideological training before and during their service in the army. The combat troops of the *Wehrmacht* were young men who had spent their formative years under the Third Reich and were exposed to large doses of indoctrination in Nazified schools and especially in the Hitler Youth and the Reich Labour Service. Thus, by the time these young men were conscripted many of them had already accepted the Nazi view of the war as a racial and ideological struggle for survival against a horde of demonic enemies. This was strongly reflected in their letters home, just as much as in their actual conduct at the front.

In mid-July 1941 Private Fred Fallnbigl wrote from the front:

> Now I know what war really means. But I also know that we had been forced into the war against the Soviet Union. For God have mercy on us, had we waited, or had these beasts come to us. For them even the most horrible death is still too good. I am glad that I can be here to put an end to this genocidal system.

A soldier's letter from Russia in late August 1941:

> Precisely now one recognises perfectly what would have happened to our wives and children had these Russian hordes . . . succeeded in penetrating into our Fatherland. I have had the opportunity here to . . . observe these uncultivated, multi-raced men. Thank God they have been thwarted from plundering and pillaging our homeland.

On 1 September 1941 Lance-Corporal O. Rentzsch wrote:

> It is good to know that this confrontation has already come. If otherwise those hordes had invaded our land, that would have . . . made for great bloodshed. No, now we want to shoulder ourselves all endeavours, in order to eradicate this universal plague.

A non-commissioned officer's letter in July 1942:

> The great task given us in the struggle against Bolshevism, lies in the destruction of eternal Jewry. Once one sees what the Jew has done in Russia, one can well understand why the Führer began the struggle against Jewry. What sorrows would have come to our homeland, had this beast of a man had the upper hand?

Moreover, it was precisely because they were allowed to vent their anger and frustration at the enemy in the course of a costly and increasingly hopeless war, that the soldiers accepted without opposition the extremely harsh, indeed brutal combat discipline enforced by their commanders, which resulted in no less than 20,000 executions of soldiers charged with offences such as desertion, cowardice and self-inflicted wounds. Both the absence of any serious mutinies in the *Wehrmacht* throughout the war and the outstanding determination with which the German army kept fighting until almost the very end, testify to the fact that the troops were both terrified of their own commanders' wrath and, even more so, of the enemy, whom they viewed as a faceless, Satanic entity out to destroy everything they believed in and cherished.

Social historians of the Third Reich have pointed out that the Nazi ideal of creating a *Volksgemeinschaft* where class tensions and inequality would be replaced by national and racial unity under a benign Führer was, in fact, never achieved. Instead, German workers retained a strong class-consciousness and kept up the struggle to improve their material condition and, by implication, to gain political recognition. Evidence has been found of resistance to the regime among the working class, manifested in strikes and intentional lower productivity, as well as in political organisation, quite apart from active resistance to the dictatorship (which was ruthlessly curbed in the first years of the regime). However, what such historians have neglected to address, is the extent to which the tensions between the working class and the regime were expressed once the younger workers were conscripted to the *Wehrmacht*. Although this issue has not been thoroughly researched, it does seem that, contrary to expectations, from the moment such workers became soldiers they no longer presented the regime or their military superiors with any problems of discipline and motivation. We have no evidence of mutinies of soldiers stemming from class-consciousness and lingering opposition to a regime that had obviously not fulfilled its perceived promises of at least partial equality. On the other hand, some recent work on attitudes among workers in the Ruhr industrial region, based on interviews conducted in the 1980s, seems to indicate that many workers were in fact quite pleased with the economic achievements of the Nazis, which meant that unemployment was drastically reduced (thanks to a vast programme of rearmament) and consequently led to a significant improvement in the standard of living. Moreover, it now seems that Nazi ideology was also much more successful in penetrating the strongholds of the working class than had been previously thought, particularly among the young. Men interviewed forty years later stated that they had joined the Hitler Youth with a great deal of enthusiasm, and did not view it as contradicting their identity as workers.

Gustav Köppke, son of Communist workers in the Ruhr industrial region, was interviewed in 1981. On watching the *Kristallnacht* pogrom in 1938 at the age of nine, he said:

> It was terribly impressive, when the SA marched . . . I was on the side of the strong guys; the Jews, they were the others.

On being a member of the Hitler Youth:

> Our workers' suburb and the Hitler Youth were in no way contradictory . . . this idea of the Hitler Youth versus the people, you shouldn't see it as if we young lads had to decide for something or against something; there was nothing else . . . and whoever wanted to become something belonged to it . . . The Hitler Youth uniform was something positive in our childhood.

On experiencing the defeat of Germany as a volunteer to the SS Hitler Youth Division:

> I was raised then, in the National Socialist time and had seen the world just as they had shown it to us . . . And suddenly nothing made sense any more.

Gisberg Pohl, another son of a working-class family interviewed in 1981, had this to say on participating in the suppression of the Warsaw rising as a member of an SS Division:

> Being a young man one easily made too much of it. We had after all gone to Russia, we wanted there [to destroy] subhumanity — That is, I was, strongly convinced of my task, that I was right. And once it goes that far, then you don't think about it much, then only one thing remains, then you know very well, either him or me.

These findings, taken together with the general high motivation of German troops, seem to indicate that even if the *Volksgemeinschaft* remained largely a myth (though a highly potent one nevertheless), its military counterpart, the *Kampfgemeinschaft*, or the community of battle, served not only as a powerful ideal but was very much seen by many soldiers as a true reflection of reality. Hence, by observing the conduct of soldiers at the front we can now gain a new perspective on the social history of the Third Reich as a whole. Furthermore, considering that once the war was over the survivors returned to their previous occupations, one must ask to what extent their experience as Hitler's main instrument of conquest and subjugation moulded their self-perception in the post-war era. This is a particularly pertinent question, because the *Wehrmacht* was in every sense of the word the army of the people, namely a vast conscript army composed of members of all social strata. It was these young men who, following the capitulation, built German post-war society, and it was they who gave it the character it has retained ever since, for better or for worse. The collective memory of the war is thus a crucial element in the new/old German national identity, and still plays a major role today as the newly reunited Germany regains its political stature and increases its already considerable economic might.

This brings us to the question of comparability and uniqueness, key factors in what has come to be known as the process of 'coming to terms with the past' (or as the Germans call it, *Vergangenheitsbewältigung*, roughly translated as 'overcoming the past'). This somewhat ambiguous term stands for the complex confrontation between personal and collective national memory (and its repression), on the one hand, and the memory (or amnesia) of individuals and groups belonging to other national entities, along with historical documentary evidence, on the other; it also refers to the use and abuse of the past by individuals and groups with the view of legitimising either past actions or current opinions and aspirations. While the past is constantly interacting with the present (both forming it and being informed by it in return), some past events and periods are of greater impact and significance than others. There is little doubt that the Nazi regime still plays a major role in the political consciousness and individual psychology of many Germans today. This was witnessed in the 1980s in a number of public debates in the Federal Republic and, particularly, in the German historians' controversy, or the *Historikerstreit*, which began in 1986, and in spite of (or perhaps very much due to) the upheaval of reunification, has remained in the background of much recent scholarship and public debate, thereby reflecting the growing political relevance of the Nazi past to a Germany searching for a new definition of national identity.

The *Historikerstreit*, as the subtitle of one German publication on the issue had it, concerned 'the controversy over the uniqueness of the National Socialist extermination of the Jews'. However, in an even wider sense, the debate was over the uniqueness of everything and anything that took place under the Third Reich, indeed over the meaning of uniqueness in history. From the purely scholarly point of view, the argument against uniqueness raised a valid point; namely, that if uniqueness implies incomparability, then it introduces an ahistorical terminology, that is, it decontextualises the event by wrenching it out of the course of history and thereby rendering it inexplicable, even mythical. In other words, the historian cannot accept that any event in the past is wholly unique, since that would mean that this event would defy any rational historical analysis and understanding. More specifically, however, the argument regarding the uniqueness of the Holocaust does not necessarily mean that it is incomparable. Comparison does not aim to show that two things or events are the same, but rather to shed light on two or more objects or phenomena by demonstrating both their similarities and their differences. Yet the 'revisionists', that is, the German scholars who called for a revision of the history of the Third Reich by means of 'contextualising' it through comparison and 'demystifying' it through 'detached' analysis, had a different aim in mind when they objected to the presentation of Nazism as unique. As their opponents claimed, the 'revisionists', or at least their more extreme representatives, were interested in 'relativising' the history of Nazism, that is, in demonstrating that although the Nazi regime was indeed evil and criminal, there were many others like it, and therefore the Germans had no reason to feel more guilty about their past than any other people, and could calmly go about re-establishing a proud national identity based on a history of great political and cultural achievements.

While these arguments met with fierce opposition in Germany and abroad in so far as they concerned the murder of the Jews, they were received with far more sympathy when applied to the German army's conduct of the war. When the 'revisionist' Ernst Nolte claimed that the only difference between the Holocaust and the Soviet gulags was the use of gas for killing, and that in any case the gulags were the begetters of Auschwitz because Hitler behaved as he did out of fear of the Bolsheviks, both the ethical import of and the documentary evidence for his assertion were forcefully challenged by many of his colleagues. But when Andreas Hillgruber, another highly respected 'revisionist', argued for the need of the historian to identify with the German soldiers' 'heroic' defence of the

Reich from the 'orgy of revenge' with which the Red Army threatened the German civilian population, he touched on a sensitive point for the Germans. The murder of the Jews could be ascribed to a relatively small circle of criminals, that is, could be isolated from the main bulk of the German population (and, as some would have it, from the main current of German history). Not so in the case of the *Wehrmacht*, based as it was on mass conscription and therefore highly representative of German society as a whole. Moreover, the powerful sense of abhorrence of war in post-war Germany, following the destruction visited upon it during the closing phases of the Second World War, has made many Germans view war, any war, as hell. Paradoxically, this view has in turn legitimised the actions of German soldiers in the war as being in no way essentially different from those of all other soldiers. Thus, one finds a combination of anti-war sentiment, apologetics and a sentimental admiration for the men who 'saved' Germany, indeed the whole of Europe, from the 'Bolshevik-Asiatic hordes', along with a powerful rejection of the notion that the *Wehrmacht* had served as Hitler's main instrument in implementing his policies of conquest and genocide.

The view of the *Wehrmacht* as an army like any other is shared by many non-German scholars, especially in the West, and reflects a wider trend in public opinion. This was given expression in former President Reagan's assertion that the soldiers of the *Wehrmacht* buried in the military cemetery of Bitburg were also victims of the Nazi regime. It is therefore of some importance to point out in what respects the German army's conduct in the war was essentially different from that of any other army in modern history.

War is a highly brutal affair, and there is little doubt that individual soldiers can and do become brutalised in the course of fighting. On the individual level there is no difference between, for instance, the killing of civilians by a *Wehrmacht* soldier in Russia, an American soldier in Vietnam or a Soviet soldier in Prussia. Once we shift a little from the individual level, however, we begin to see the differences. German soldiers fighting in Russia were allowed, indeed were ordered, to commit mass killings of people who were clearly not of any direct military threat to them. This was not the case of American GIs in Vietnam, nor of Red Army troops in occupied Germany, even if many such instances did occur. And because this was not the policy, but rather an unauthorised action, the scale of the killing was smaller. The Red Army in Germany had no policy of decimating the German population and turning

Germany into a wasteland fit for Russian colonisation. Had this been the case, we would not have seen the recent reunification of Germany, for there would have been nothing to reunite with. The German army in Russia, on the other hand, followed a clear policy of subjugation and extermination. Had Germany won the war, Russia would have disappeared as a political entity and millions more Russians would have been murdered, with the rest being enslaved by their German colonisers. Nor did the US Army have a policy of genocide in Vietnam, even if it did cause the deaths of hundreds of thousands of innocent civilians. If the Soviet Union installed brutal dictatorships in the East European countries it conquered, these were nevertheless not genocidal regimes, just as an American victory in Vietnam would not have meant the destruction of the Vietnamese people (whose existence under the victorious Communists has not been particularly cheerful either). The strategic bombing of Germany, another example often used by Germans, had no intention of wiping out the German people, even if it was of dubious military value and morally questionable. Moreover, one cannot forget that both the English and the Americans, as well as the Russians, were fighting against Nazi aggression: it was the Third Reich which had striven to conquer Europe, not the British, Americans or even the Soviets.

The *Wehrmacht* did not behave in the same manner everywhere. As has been seen, it was on the Eastern Front that the German army conducted a uniquely savage war. This was possible because of the agreement between the regime and its soldiers on the need to wipe out the Soviet Union, its political system and much of its population. Shared racist sentiments acted as a powerful motivation in the conduct of war in the east. Doubtless, many other armies have known the effect of racism; the US army, both in the Pacific War and in Vietnam, as well as the Japanese army have acted brutally, not least because of a racially-oriented perception of the enemy. Yet racism was not the official policy of the US government, nor was the education of American youths as deeply grounded in racism as that of the German youths of the 1930s. When Japan was occupied by the US army it was not enslaved, even if many American GIs had clearly evolved strongly racist views of the Japanese. The Japanese, on the other hand, did carry out highly brutal policies of occupation motivated by a mixture of imperialist policies and a sense of racial superiority propagated by the regime; it is true that the Japanese army's conduct in China, for instance, comes close to that of the *Wehrmacht* in Russia, just as their treatment of prisoners of war was abominable. Yet even here one must make the qualification that the Japanese did not adopt a policy of genocide. Hence, for instance, the rate of survival of prisoners of war in Japanese hands was twice as high as that of Soviet soldiers in German hands.

It is, indeed, on the issue of genocide that the German army must surely come out worse than any other modern army. This is both because the army itself actively pursued a policy of mass killing of Russians and because it was an essential instrument in the realisation of the Final Solution. The attempt to differentiate between the *Wehrmacht* and the SS, between the fighting at the front and the death camps in the rear presents a wholly false picture of the historical reality. As a number of highly detailed and thorough works have shown, the army was involved in the implementation of the Final Solution at every conceivable level, beginning with the conquest of the areas that contained the highest concentrations of Jewish population, through rendering logistical and manpower support to the *Einsatzgruppen* and the death-camp administrations, to the bitter determination in which it resisted the final and inevitable defeat of the Third Reich at a time when the rate of the industrial killing of millions of human beings reached its peak. The *Wehrmacht* was thus a crucial factor in the most horrendous crime perpetrated by any nation in modern history.

Savage War

O. Bartov, *Hitler's Army: Soldiers, Nazis and War in the Third Reich* (Oxford, 1991); A. Dallin, *German Rule in Russia, 1941–45*, 2nd ed. (London, 1981); W. Deist (ed.), *The German Military in the Age of Total War* (Oxford, 1985); R.J. Evans, *In Hitler's Shadow* (New York, 1989); G. Hirschfeld (ed.), *The Policies of Genocide: Jews and Soviet Prisoners of War in Nazi Germany* (London, 1986); E. Klee et al. (eds), *Those Were the Days: The Holocaust as Seen by its Perpetrators and Bystanders* (London, 1991); C.S. Maier, *The Unmasterable Past* (Cambridge, Mass., 1988); K.-J. Müller, *The Army, Politics and Society in Germany, 1933–45* (New York, 1987); R.J. O'Neill, *The German Army and the Nazi Party, 1933–39* (London, 1966); T. Schulte, *The German Army and Nazi Policies in Occupied Russia* (Oxford, 1989).

CHAPTER IX

THE PLANNING INTELLIGENTSIA AND THE 'FINAL SOLUTION'

Götz Aly

THERE IS A BROAD CONSENSUS among scholars that no rationally conceived motives informed the Nazis's murder of European Jews. The political philosopher Hannah Arendt, for example, emphasised that what made this crime unique was not the number of victims, but rather the absence of any concern for the economic utility of the victims on the part of the perpetrators. When it comes to motives, historians prefer to stress 'irrational racial hatred', 'destruction for destruction's sake', a 'black hole of historical understanding', or the self-propelling radicalising capacities inherent in modern bureaucratic structures.

For many years historians have sought in vain for an order from Hitler to destroy the Jews of Europe. However, from a careful examination of the documents that are assumed to have ordered the murder of German psychiatric patients or the deliberate starvation of 'many millions' of Soviet citizens, it is clear that they 'commission' or 'authorise', which means that recommendations or concrete plans were submitted to Hitler, Himmler or Goering for a decision: to be approved or rejected, redrafted or put on hold. Goering also expressed wishes about how these measures should best be disguised. Regarding the murders perpetrated by SS task-forces in the former Soviet Union, Hitler simply remarked: 'as far as the world at large is concerned our motives must be in accordance with tactical considerations . . . we will carry out all necessary measures — shootings, resettlements etc. — regardless of this.' This raises questions about the authorship of these 'necessary measures', and above all questions regarding aims and motives.

My starting point is that the Nazi regime relied to an exceptional degree upon academically-trained advisers and that it made use of their skills. Their ideas were transmitted upwards to the highest echelons by civil servants, especially by the secretaries of state attached to the various ministries, many of whom belonged to the General Council of the Four Year Plan agency, in which capacity they ranked higher than their own ministers. The Four Year Plan was designed to boost production in strategically vital areas of the economy and it reached the apogee of its power between 1938 and 1942, during which time programmes for the socio-political and economic reorganisation of Europe were developed and converted into both policy and military strategy.

The concept of an 'economy of the Final Solution' was developed by German experts — above all economists, agronomists, demographers, experts in labour deployment, geographers, historians, planners and statisticians. They made up the planning committees of such agencies as the Reich Office for Area Planning, the Reich Commissariat for the Strengthening of Ethnic Germandom and the Four Year Plan authority. They conceived and discussed solutions to the various 'demographic questions', and calculated the possible 'release of pressure' that would be the result of excluding Jews from the economy. They recommended converting the Ukraine into Europe's breadbasket — taking into their calculations the deliberate starvation of 'many millions' of Soviet citizens. They calculated the losses occasioned by the economies of the ghettos and thus delivered arguments for the mass murder of their inhabitants.

The approach adopted in this study is not that of the conspiracy theory, but to name those who were responsible, and to expose the role of a careerist, academically-trained, intelligentsia in the extermination of millions of people. There were probably a few thousand members of this 'scientific community', who, notwithstanding the usual animosities and petty institutional and personal jealousies, contributed to the formation of the prevailing opinion. It has sometimes been said that these people were not 'real' scholars, but rather half or totally crazy third-rate figures, but arguments such as this fail to explain the involvement of people more usually described as being major intellects, for example the historians Werner Conze and Theodor Schieder, who went on to dominate their profession in the post-war period. The expertise of this 'community' was not a form of *ex post facto* rationalisation of policies upon whose formulation they had exerted no real influence, but rather the basis upon which decisions were made by ministers and state secretaries. The reports produced by the Reich Committee for Economic Affairs concerning the 'conversion' of trade in Vienna or later in the Generalgouvernement in Poland provided the basis for decisions subsequently taken which sought to combine the 'dejudaisation' with the 'rationalisation' of their economies. The Reich Commissar for the Strengthening of Ethnic Germandom had detailed information regarding the optimum distribution of commercial and manufacturing firms in the areas from which Jews and 'Aryan' Poles were dispossessed in the interests of incoming ethnic German repatriates. In other words, both expulsions and compulsory 'germanisation' were carried out according to calculated economic, as opposed to racial-biological criteria. On the basis of these initial practical steps, in whose conception they had played a material part, the economists, demographers and planners could develop yet more elaborate plans. Thus, the Aryanisation of Vienna served as a model for all similar policies, and the expulsion of undesirable ethnic groups to the Generalgouvernement resurfaced later in discussions regarding the economic reconstruction of this territory, in the form of solutions to a self-imposed dilemma. Population pressure urgently demanded 'disburdenment'.

The reason why the links between long-term economic planning and the extermination of people have scarcely been investigated may largely be attributed to the initial connections forged between the uniqueness of the Holocaust and the alleged or assumed absence of any rational, utilitarian calculation. It is also the result of a gross underestimation of the power wielded by professional experts in a regime whose ideological statements were imprecise, vague and open-ended. This can be illustrated by looking at the various 'contributions' to the Nazi 'euthanasia' programme. On 3 April 1940 Viktor Brack, a senior official in the Chancellery of the Führer, speaking at a meeting of senior mayors, outlined recent developments in German psychiatric hospitals. (In what follows, the agencies, individuals or interests responsible for various elements within the 'euthanasia' programme have been included in brackets):

> In many of the asylums in the Reich there are innumerable incurable patients of all descriptions [the doctors and psychiatrists], who are of no use to humanity [Hitler, the doctors]. They only serve to take away resources from other healthy people [military logistics experts, Hitler], and often require intensive nursing [doctors]. The rest of humanity has to be protected from these people [Hitler]. If today one has to make decisions regarding the maintenance of healthy people, then it is all the more essential first to remove these creatures, if only to ensure better care of curable cases in the asylums and hospitals [doctors]. One needs the vacant bedspace

for all sorts of important military purposes [army medical corps experts]: sickbays, hospitals, auxiliary hospitals [army medical corps experts]. For the remainder, the action will greatly disburden the local authorities, since each individual case will no longer occasion any future costs for care or maintenance [war finance experts, local authorities].

To this list should be added the bureaucratic ambitions of the officials in the Chancellery of the Führer itself. A close examination of this relatively well-documented decision-making process should disabuse anyone of the idea that 'the bureaucratic machinery functioned automatically', as Hans Mommsen repeatedly states with reference to the murder of European Jews, where there is much less surviving evidence of the decision-making process. Three successive stages can be distinguished in deciding whether there was an 'economy of the Final Solution'.

1. Pogroms and Rationalisation

On 12 November 1938, two days after the pogroms of Reich Crystal Night, an important part of the Nazi leadership gathered for a discussion on the Jewish Question. The chair was taken by Hermann Goering, the Plenipotentiary for the Four Year Plan. Among those invited were Goebbels, Reinhard Heydrich and an array of economic experts: the Ministers of Finance and the Economy, a representative of the insurance sector and about one hundred experts, policy advisers and senior civil servants. Goering, the leading light in the economic affairs of the Greater German Reich, introduced himself with the modest disclaimer that he was 'not well versed enough in economic affairs', but then informed the participants that 'since the problem is mainly an economic one, it will have to be tackled from an economic perspective'. The measures necessary to Aryanise the economy would have to be taken 'one after another', with the Jews being excluded from the economy and 'put into the poorhouse'.

It was not a matter of enriching the petty-bourgeois grassroots supporters of the National Socialist German Workers Party (NSDAP), or, indeed, of Aryan competitors expropriating Jewish banks or department stores, but rather that there were too many one-man stores, artisan workshops and small factories in Germany in general. Within a few weeks of the conference state agencies closed two-thirds of all Jewish-owned one-man concerns and small businesses, selling off their stock to Aryan traders and adding the profits to national funds. This was part of what Goering called 'an action to convert non-essential units of production into essential ones', which was also scheduled to take place in the near future. So-called Aryanisation was therefore primarily a matter of economic rationalisation and concentration, what is now known as 'restructuring'.

The decisions taken at this conference were informed by the experiences derived from the annexation of Austria, experiences that were relayed to the participants by the Minister for the Economy and Labour in Austria, Hans Fischbock, who made the trip to the conference from his office in Vienna. According to calculations by the Reich Committee for Economic Affairs, 90 per cent of Jewish concerns in Vienna had been shut down entirely, with only 10 per cent being put up for sale. Fischbock boasted that the closures were based upon studies of each sector of the economy and had been determined in accordance with local needs. This *modus operandi* was adopted a few days later in Berlin and then by the German occupying authorities in Czechoslovakia, Poland and The Netherlands.

Any concerns about adverse socio-political consequences stemming from the Viennese model were allayed by Heydrich who, referring to co-operation between the Ministry of Economics, foreign humanitarian agencies and Adolf Eichmann's SS office for Jewish Affairs, pointed to the 50,000 Jews who had been removed from the economy since the Anschluss by being forced to emigrate. Only some 19,000 Jews had been removed from the Old (pre-expansion) Reich in the same timespan. The Special Plenipotentiary for Jewish Emigration was the President of the Reichsbank Hjalmar Schacht. Only one person present evinced any scepticism, the conservative nationalist Minister of Finance Schwerin von Krosigk who remarked: 'the crucial point is that we don't end up with the whole proletariat. Dealing with them will always be an appalling burden.' The conference ended with the slogan 'out with what can be got out', by which they meant the Jews. At the same time it was immediately obvious that because of shortages of foreign exchange this would only be partially successful, and that those Jews who remained — the old, sick and unemployed — would 'be a burden on the state'. If before Reich Crystal Night in November 1938 there had been rivalries and clashes of competence between the various agencies occupied with the Jewish Question, this changed dramatically after 12 November 1938. Goering declared: 'Once and for all I prohibit any separate action. The Reich has taken the matter in hand.' Thenceforth, anti-Semitic measures were co-ordinated by the Four Year Plan apparatus; special responsibility devolved upon Erich

Neumann, the State Secretary for Exchange Questions and 'special tasks of a general economic nature'. The business of deportations and later extermination was transferred to the Reich Main Security Office of the SS.

2. Developmental Policy and Demographic Questions
The second phase in the economically motivated radicalisation of policy towards the Jews began after September 1939 with the conquest and deliberate territorial fragmentation of Poland. In the eyes of German economic planners, Poland was underdeveloped and its economy both badly organised and starved of capital. Above all, however, too many people derived their livelihood from the land. The economy was characterised by subsistence agriculture: the rural population satisfied most of its own demands for foodstuffs and consumer goods, and in the villages barter rather than money was the normal means of exchange, in other words it was 'a system insufficient for rationalisation', basically impervious to the logic of capitalist penetration and exploitation. In the minds of German, and indeed other international economists, Poland's main problem lay in rural overpopulation. A third of the population would be deemed surplus to requirements should modern means of cultivation be adopted. The 'surplus population' was a 'burden on the national economy', or what Theodor Oberländer called, 'a symptom of socio-economic sickness'. Overpopulation had nothing to do with the density of population, but was rather a question of perceived deviation from an allegedly normal or 'optima' population.

The theory of optimum population had been developed at the turn of the century by a number of economists with the aid of Paul Mombert's theory of diminishing returns, or what is known as the Mombert Formula. Mombert (1876—1938) was Professor of Political Economy at Giessen until his compulsory retirement as a 'non-Aryan' in 1933. His formula consists of a simple equation which relates population numbers to economic resources. According to this formula, $F = P \times L$, food-supply (F) equals population numbers (P) times living standard (L). This reductionist abstraction enables the 'explanation' of every misrelationship between resources and living standards to be made in terms of population figures, regardless of such factors as unemployment, lack of capital or raw materials, absence of markets or low productivity and so forth. Every type of economic crisis, including those occasioned by war, could be redefined in terms of the 'population question'.

According to this theory, population becomes an economic variable like any other, which can therefore also be manipulated like any other. Mombert himself seems to have expressly ruled out this possibility, but this was overlooked by his disciples. To German economists, with their sights set upon a vast, dependent, integrated European economy under German hegemony, the size and composition of a population became the factor which, given wartime conditions and the relative scarcity of raw materials, they could adjust most easily. Population policy in the form of 'resettlement' became a way of overcoming capital and foreign currency shortages, of regulating wartime finances and of releasing foodstuffs and raw materials, while at the same time achieving the longer-term goal of a more rational economic structure and enhanced exploitation of labour.

By 1932 Mombert had already calculated the burden upon the national economy of the surplus population created by the Depression. The cost to the state of maintaining the unproductive was of the order of four billion Reichmarks, money which could otherwise have been employed productively by expanding the economic base in the form of domestic investment or export capital. At the time Mombert was thinking in terms of financing colonial projects in Africa, however his model also suggested ways in which capital could be more rapidly accumulated via a 'cessation of population growth'. According to the academics who serviced the occupying authorities in Poland — and who again and again referred to the 'irrefutable Mombert formula' — this was precisely the answer they needed to the underlying problems they discerned in the Polish economy. A reduction of the population would simultaneously break the vicious circle of overpopulation and lead to capital accumulation necessary for the modernisation of the economy. If this did not succeed, then occupied Poland would become a 'burden' upon the entire German-dominated *Grossraum*. The extermination of millions of people would halt population growth in eastern Europe for a few critical years, 'thus' releasing capital resources, which could be used to promote industrialisation and the mechanisation of agriculture, or in other words developments that were in Germany's economic interest. The German academic planners generated quantities of plans and developmental models, which at a stroke rendered entire peoples surplus to requirements and therefore subject to resettlement or deportation as forced labour. 'Negative demographic policy' was the lever of a new type of German developmental economics.

According to German calculations, every second rural Pole was 'nothing more than a dead weight', and overpopulation 'effectively a barrier to capital formation'. Theodor Oberländer, subsequently a minister in Konrad Adenauer's post-war cabinet, reckoned that in many areas of Poland the population was as much as 75 per cent superfluous. Expressed in absolute terms, this meant that some 4.5 to 5.83 million Poles were surplus to requirements. Thinking bigger, the economists calculated that in south-eastern Europe, whose overpopulation would also have to be regulated, there were between twelve and fifteen million workers on the land who would have to be 'set in motion'. If one included their families, then there were about fifty million people who would have to be pushed out of their domestic subsistence lifestyle if the German industrial economy was to benefit. Having occupied large parts of the Soviet Union, the German economic and agrarian experts revised their figures upwards by another thirty million, in other words by precisely the increase of population in Russia that had occurred between 1905 and 1939.

This theory of overpopulation described relatively backward economies. Underactivity and unemployment were the norm, or as economists would say, labour capacity was being only partially used. Disharmony between people and capital resulted in considerable rural and urban poverty; outside intervention designed to rationalise this state of affairs, would necessarily result in the population being divided into those who would have to work more intensively and those who would not be working at all. The state would decide who was deemed to be productive or non-productive. This was precisely the point at which Nazi racial criteria fused with the scientific criteria of population economy.

3. The War against the Soviet Union

The third phase in this demographically conceived programme of mass murder began with the planning for the war against the Soviet Union. The initial aim was to achieve a '180 degree turn' in the direction of the economy of the Ukraine, which should no longer feed Soviet workers, but rather secure the foodstuffs and hence immunity to blockade of Central Europe. The plan of attack incorporated the deliberate starvation of 'many millions' of people in order to secure food for the inhabitants of Western and Central Europe. According to printed guidelines:

> Many tens of millions of people will become superfluous to requirements in these areas [i.e. the forests and industrial towns of the north] and will die or have to move to Siberia. Attempts to prevent the population there from

starving by moving food surpluses from the black earth zone, can only be done at the cost of supplying Europe. This would undermine Germany's capacity to prevail during the war, and would undermine Germany and Europe's capacity to resist blockade.

Underlying these bleak calculations was the knowledge that Germany was only able to provide some 87 per cent of her food requirements, that the only occupied country able to deliver food supplies without starving its own citizens was Denmark and that the rest actually needed to import foodstuffs from Germany. Because of the way in which agriculture tended to become more and more extensive during wartime, involving the cultivation of unsuitable land, the food situation was bound to deteriorate from harvest to harvest. This problem, the only one that might have adversely affected the mood of the German population, was to be resolved by organising the deaths of about thirty million Russians. The plans, which were unparalleled in their clarity, never mentioned the word 'race', but constantly referred to the logic of economic circumstances. 'Negative demographic policy' was the imperative of the hour, with hunger acting as a form of geo-strategic tourniquet. These plans, which were developed some months before the 'Final Solution of the Jewish Question' once again emanated from Goering's Four Year Plan agency. The two million Soviet prisoners of war who died of starvation in German camps before the end of 1941, did not die because of any problems in food supply, but were victims of deliberate murder. In November 1941 Goering remarked that 'this year twenty to thirty million people will starve in Russia. Perhaps that's a good thing, since certain people will have to be decimated'.

These plans connected with the supply of food were accompanied by others — notably the Generalplan Ost — which were concerned with strategies of power and settlement policy. During the preparations for the war against the Soviet Union, the horizons suddenly appeared limitless to German planners. The Institut für Deutsche Ostarbeit in occupied Cracow considered inter alia 'the resettlement of the Poles', while a Berlin professor of anthropology who carried out studies of Soviet prisoners of war recommended 'the liquidation of Russiandom'.

The invasion of Russia opened up new ways of solving every social problem, not just in the occupied areas, but also in the Reich itself. As the chief of the Generalplan Ost project noted: 'the victory of our arms and the expansion of our frontiers has destroyed all of the old limitations.' The massive tasks which had 'arisen' for the German nation were not just a matter of 'germanisation' and the reconstruction of conquered territories. Rather, a 'profound reordering of nation and available space' in the old Reich would ensue as a result of the new order created on the new frontiers. It would begin with the reorganisation of the economy and with the cleansing of overfull occupations. Production, markets and prices would be streamlined in accordance with purchasing power. Finally, the whole structure of settlement would have to be reorganised. The Generalplan Ost, which covered the whole area between Leningrad and the Crimea, presupposed the 'evacuation' of thirty-one million people. In the eyes of the authors of these documents, the Solution of the Jewish Question (for some five million Jews lived in the areas covered by the plan), was merely part of their 'great task'.

In the German Reich, in occupied Poland and, finally, in the entire area subject to German hegemony it was overwhelmingly people designated as being unproductive — the chronically sick, the so-called asocial, and then the Jews — in other words, groups who were already discriminated against and who were hence easy to isolate, who were to be removed from the economic process and denied any form of social security. This meant that in addition to Jews and Gypsies, vast parts of the Slav population were to be victims of extermination. The extermination of the Jews carried out under cover of war was the part of this agenda most fully realised. These plans were founded upon demographic and economic criteria as well as theories of racial hierarchy. Their initial premise was that the population of Europe had to be reduced for medium- and short-term economic and strategic reasons. The dynamics of extermination and the actual course of decision-making can only be understood if the demographic and economic goals which underpinned them are borne in mind.

In destroying the Jews one of the most tangible manifestations of poverty in Eastern Europe would be destroyed, in other words the poorest parts of the cities and towns. Genocide was a means of solving the social question. Because most of the Jews lived in towns, their deportation would set the surplus rural population moving in the direction of the towns, giving them the possibility of social advancement into trade and handicrafts. At the same time, these overcrowded sectors in the towns themselves could be modernised and rationalised, without creating a discontented, declassé, national petty-bourgeoisie which would have been a threat to the German occupiers.

Both in Eastern Europe and, above all, in Germany itself, the expropriation of Jewish property provided an unbureaucratic form of self-help, which provided household goods, housing, new jobs and so forth. In the case of large-scale capital, expropriation enabled German banks and industry to consolidate their holdings. All that remained were unemployed and propertyless people or, in other words, an artificially achieved population surplus. Liquidified assets set free as a result of the deportation of Jews and non-Jewish Poles were taken over by the Main Trustees for the East set up for the purpose and then distributed in the form of development credits in order to strengthen undercapitalised sectors and regions.

Similar calculations informed the cogitations of virtually every German economist, agronomist, demographer and statistician. One example from many is the Berlin economic adviser Alfred Maelicke. Writing in the journal *The German Economy* in 1942, Maelicke remarked:

> Only the total dejudaisation of economic life will facilitate the solution of what is still the main problem in many countries, such as south-eastern Europe and elsewhere, namely overpopulation and other social questions. The elimination of the Jewish trader mentality and profit-mindedness and the exclusion of the Jews will create space and security (full employment) for many hitherto rootless and impoverished workers and peasants, artisans and others ... By observing the fundamentals and practices of dejuda-isation as applied in Germany one could effect profound changes in demo-graphic relations, and even wider structural changes, without violently upsetting the nature of any given economy. There will be no need to dis-miss workers and no difficulties of supply. One does not even need to worry about a contraction of turnover.

Maelicke had described a racially informed 'cleansing of the population problem' — the structural preconditions for the long-term re-ordering and exploitation of the *Grosswirtschaftsraum* (greater economic space) that once was Europe.

This explains the apparent contradiction between an economic or mil-itary interest in exploitation and the mass-extermination of potential sources of labour. In the eyes of German economists, overpopulation confirmed the alleged economic backwardness of economic structures and retarded the implementation of 'optimum labour productivity' within the *Grosswirtschaftsraum*. In other words, the economic experts presupposed that part of the overpopulation would have to be 'erad-icated' if the labour potential of the *Grossraum* was to be effectively exploited by being rendered 'mobile'. The Germans were not prepared to think in terms of capital investment designed to broaden overall resources. The low level of mechanisation to which the Jews were reduced in the ghettos and labour camps following their exclusion from the wider economy was further evidence of 'an effective brake upon capital', because resources were being tied up which, with the better organisation of labour and a more favourable combination of capital and labour, could otherwise have been used to produce greater profits. Himmler and Speer were in full agreement on this issue. The low wages paid to Jews working for German and Polish firms prevented rational-isation because in the short term, a Jewish labour force was a cheaper alternative than new machinery; the advantages that cheap labour obviously had for individual concerns were not mirrored by advantages for the economy as a whole. According to these criteria, it was economic-ally more rational to kill the Jews than to put them to work.

The fact that even Jewish munitions workers were only temporarily reprieved from the gas chambers suggests that these concepts were racially determined. Even the last Jewish craftsman was replaced by an 'Aryan' one. However it is incorrect to talk (as some historians do) of the 'primacy of racially-motivated exterminatory plans above any economic factors'. Rather, especially in the second half of the war, the imperatives of munitions production collided with other economic imperatives, namely the no less acute crisis of food supply, which demanded a reduc-tion of the population numbers and long-term economic restructuring by means of mass murder. Selection in accordance with racial criteria did not contradict economic calculation, rather it was an integral part of it.

Just as contemporary anthropologists, doctors and biologists regarded the marginalisation and extermination of allegedly 'less valuable' ele-ments as a scientific way of improving mankind or 'healing the body of the nation', so economists, agronomists and planners thought their work would result in the 'healing of the structure of society' in underdeveloped regions of Europe. The mere 'co-eaters' would be separated from 'economically really active people'. In so far as the Jews, active in such sectors as trade and handicrafts, which the Germans regarded as over-crowded and superfluous, were not already doomed, socio-political and economic restructuring pushed them yet further into a position where they lost their property and all means of earning a livelihood. In this way racial and economic selection criteria were harmonised, with a consensus replacing alleged conflicts of interest between rational planners and racial fanatics. This consensus and the social sanitising concepts which under-lay it gave the systematic and centrally planned murder of millions of people its own gruesome dynamic. Evidence of a technocratically ration-al agenda does not make these crimes 'comprehensible' let alone 'under-standable', in the sense of having empathetic understanding for something. But looked at in this way, the crimes Germans committed in these years assume a rather different character, and require us to under-take the search for causes and continuities afresh and perhaps with yet greater seriousness.

Finally, there is the question of uniqueness. We began by considering Hannah Arendt's statement that no rational motives informed the Final Solution, a view with which most historians concur. In her important work on the origins of totalitarianism, Arendt made the following pertin-ent observation:

> The imperative 'Thou shalt not kill' fails in the face of a demographic policy which proceeds to exterminate systematically or industrially those races and individuals deemed unfit and less valuable, not once in a unique action, but on a basis obviously intended to be permanent. The death penalty becomes absurd when one is not dealing with murderers who know what murder is, but rather with demographers who organise the murder of millions in such a way that all those who participate subjectively consider themselves free of guilt.

What did the demographic policies of both of the major dictatorships of this century have in common? The Stalinist population policy of the 1930s — the eradication of the kulaks (peasant farmers) — corresponded in many respects to the policies pursued by the Nazis between 1939 and 1944. Discrimination against minorities, the mobilisation of the rural population, forcible colonisation, slave labour, cultural and linguistic homogenisation, and progressive forms of extermination. Both dictator-ships pursued strategies of more or less violent modernisation, based upon the degradation of people into 'human contingents', to be adminis-tered, dispossessed, resettled, privileged or marginalised at will. At the heart of such policies was the belief that in this way socio-economic structures could be revolutionised more rapidly, indeed almost overnight. Of course this belief was not unique to either Nazi or Soviet thinking. There are echoes of it in the progressive thought of the century as a whole, in the form of the 'agrarian or industrial question', or the 'refugee or overpopulation question'. The most striking example of this can be

seen in the 1946 report of the United Nations on the economic reconstruction of Europe: 'In eastern Europe the large-scale elimination of the
Jewish population has left the distribution system in a state of virtual disorder. On the other hand the pre-war phenomenon of agricultural overpopulation still prevails.' Only once, in Germany, did such ideas result in
Auschwitz. The deed and the crime is unique. However, Auschwitz is
part of European as well as German history. Only when one has fully
understood this context is it possible to talk meaningfully of the 'limits of
understanding'. The Holocaust was not a 'reversion to barbarism', nor a
'break with civilisation', still less an 'Asiatic deed'. But it was also far
from being a 'historical black hole', somehow beyond language, poetry
and historical understanding, but rather a possibility inherent in
European civilisation itself.

The Planning Intelligentsia and the 'Final Solution'
Götz Aly and Susanne Heim, *Vordenker der Vernichtung* (Hamburg,
1991); ibid., 'The Economics of the Final Solution', *Simon Wiesenthal
Center Annual*, vol. 5 (1988), pp. 3–48; Zygmunt Baumann, *Modernity
and the Holocaust* (Ithaca, 1989); Michael Burleigh, *Germany Turns
Eastwards: A Study of 'Ostforschung' in the Third Reich* (Cambridge,
1990).

CHAPTER X

FROM THE 'PEOPLE'S CONSCIOUSNESS OF RIGHT AND WRONG' TO 'THE HEALTHY INSTINCTS OF THE NATION': THE PERSECUTION OF HOMOSEXUALS IN NAZI GERMANY

Hans-Georg Stümke

FOLLOWING THE FOUNDATION of the German Reich in 1871, male homosexuality was declared illegal and punishable as an 'unnatural sexual act'. By contrast, female homosexuality remained non-criminal. Paragraph 175 of the Criminal Code regulated the precise details of the offence, and massive pressure from the state of Prussia ensured that this legislation was incorporated into the new unified national criminal code. This effectively marked the end of the comparatively liberal epoch that had prevailed for about fifty years in some of the other constituent states. A relatively enlightened understanding of the law meant that these states regarded sexuality as a private affair, which did not require punitive intervention by the authorities. The leading power in Germany proved unable to emulate their example.

In order to defend itself against enlightened critics of its policy on this issue, the Prussian state made uncharacteristic play with references to 'the people'. An official commentator noted that 'The people's consciousness of right and wrong condemns these activities not merely as vice but also as a crime.' Therefore the state had a duty to defend this conception of the law by punishing homosexuality. Admittedly, only 'activities resembling sexual intercourse', that is to say where penetration similar to that practised by heterosexuals had occurred, seem to have offended 'the people's consciousness of right and wrong'. Since most homosexual relations seem to have been consensual, it was forensically difficult to establish the offence. Accordingly, the number of convictions was relatively modest. Between 1871 and 1924 some three to seven hundred people were convicted each year; between 1925 and 1933 between eight and eleven hundred.

However, from the turn of the century there was a clear tendency to punish homosexuality more severely. In 1909 a draft law recommended not only sentences of five years' hard labour in certain cases, but also the criminalisation of female homosexuality. Continuities in the state's interest in persecution were implicit in the comment 'The stipulations of Paragraph 175 do not merely correspond with the healthy outlook of the people . . . rather they also serve above all the interests of the community, and the direct interests of the state.' However, the Empire collapsed before this draft could be submitted for parliamentary approval.

There was a further attempt to bolster the law in 1925 on the part of the conservative cabinet of the Roman Catholic Chancellor Wilhelm Marx. Minister of Justice Hergt from the German National People's Party was responsible for the new draft legislation. Although this no longer sought to criminalise female homosexuality, it did specify the nature of homosexual offences and sought to punish these with sentences of up to five years' hard labour. The author of the draft commented that, according to 'the German view of things', homosexuality was 'an aberration' which would lead to 'the degeneration of the nation and the collapse of its power'. Despite practical impediments to the law's implementation, Paragraph 175 nonetheless constituted a barrier 'which one could not remove without harm being done to the health and purity of our people's way of life'. There were already echoes in this of the terms and tone employed a few years later by the National Socialists. After 1933 these racial preoccupations would take over entirely.

Protests against these attempts to stiffen the penalties for homosexual activities largely came from the burgeoning homosexual civil rights movement, which since the late nineteenth century had campaigned for the abrogation of Paragraph 175 under the slogan that homosexuality was 'neither an illness nor a crime'. The best-known homosexual organisation was the Scientific-Humanitarian Committee (WhK), founded in 1897 by the doctor and sexual reformer Magnus Hirschfeld (1868–1935). In 1897 the Committee had submitted a petition to parliament calling for the abolition of Paragraph 175, and the signatories included August Bebel, the chairman of the Social Democratic Party. Moreover, from 1926 onwards, members of the Committee combined with other organisations promoting sexual reform to produce an alternative draft law, calling not only for the abrogation of Paragraph 175, but also for reforms in the entire field of sexual offences and the decriminalisation of abortion.

The rapid changes of government during the Weimar period also meant sudden shifts in attitudes towards Paragraph 175. In 1929, when the government was in the hands of the Social Democrat Hermann Müller, a parliamentary committee responsible for criminal law voted by a slim majority to decriminalise homosexual acts between two consenting adults. Those in favour included the Social Democrats, Communists and sections of the Liberals; those against included the Catholic Centre Party and the German National People's Party, which in 1933 entered a coalition government with the National Socialists (NSDAP). The NSDAP was not represented on the committee, however, their Party Press reacted to the decision to alter the law with predictable expressions of fury and outrage. On 2 August 1930, the *Völkischer Beobachter* warned the (Jewish) sexologist Magnus Hirschfeld 'Don't you believe that we Germans will allow such a law to exist for one day when we achieve power.' The Nazi paper described homosexuality as 'an evil lust of the Jewish soul', and vowed that it would be punished as a crime in the most severe fashion, 'with the noose and deportation'. The recommendations of the parliamentary committee were never put to the vote in the Reichstag. Paragraph 175 of the 1871 law continued in force until its modification by the Nazis in 1935.

If one views this period as a whole then two trends are apparent. Firstly, following the suppression of enlightened legal traditions in the various states in the interests of Prussia's hegemonic aspirations, the threat of punishment and exemplary application of Paragraph 175 was designed to contain homosexuality through a form of general prevention. Increasing nationalism resulted in attempts to extend the scope of the law. Phrases such as 'healthy instincts of the people', 'the strength of the nation', or 'the health and purity of the people's way of life' signalled the state's claims. The National Socialists would abandon the preventive aims of earlier legislation and policy in favour of a radical 'Final Solution'. Second, enlightened legal traditions which sought to decriminalise homosexuality were supported not only by homosexual civil rights activists, but also by Social Democrats, the Communists and some Liberals. The accession to power of the Nazis effectively terminated these traditions.

Following Hitler's appointment as Chancellor, the Nazis' immediate concern was to secure and consolidate their power. In this initial phase the Nazis' persecution of homosexuals had a spontaneous character. Marauding SA men and SS thugs, with a violent hatred of everything foreign, Leftist or 'un-German' were symptomatic of the Brown mob's intoxication with victory. The historical record reveals attacks on homosexual meeting-places, arrests, detention in 'wild', or *ad hoc*, concentration camps, violent attacks on individuals and the destruction of Magnus Hirschfeld's world-famous Institute for Sexual Studies. The homosexual rights movement quietly disappeared in a manner so far not investigated by modern historians. The centrally organised and systematic persecution of homosexuals only began in the wake of the 1934 Röhm affair.

As early as 1930 many people were aware of the homosexuality of the SA chief Ernst Röhm (1887–1934). At the time the Social Democratic Party (SPD) Press published private letters written by Röhm, which left no doubts as to his sexual orientation. The SPD traduced the 'intolerable hypocrisy' of the NSDAP's desire for a 'cleaner Germany' in view of its apparent tolerance of a homosexual in a very prominent position within a major Party formation. The purpose behind the SPD's resort to gutter-Press tactics of personal exposure was to weaken the NSDAP politically, or even to divide the Party. Whereas in 1930 leading Nazis, including Heinrich Himmler, had been fulsome in expressing support for their comrade, by 1934 the situation had altered drastically.

Once in power, the Nazis decided to make the discovery of Röhm's homosexuality their own exclusive property. The widely publicised revelations regarding Röhm and the simultaneous liquidation of the SA leadership contributed decisively towards the consolidation of the Nazi dictatorship. Tensions between Left and Right within the Party and, more significantly, between the para-military SA and the army, were resolved by spreading the rumour that Röhm was plotting a putsch in order to transfer power to a group of 'degenerates' and 'perverts'. As the historian Eugen Kogon noted, the Röhm affair also provided the 'window of opportunity' for the inauguration of the SS state. As far as homosexuality was concerned, what Hitler called the 'well-known unfortunate inclinations of Röhm' served to mobilise the 'healthy instincts of the nation' for the political aims of the NSDAP. In a radio broadcast, the propaganda chief Joseph Goebbels announced 'We want the co-operation of the entire nation, rich and poor, high or lowly ... bubonic plagues, dens of corruption, sickly symptoms of moral decay will be burned out, and moreover right down to the flesh'. The state-controlled media now embarked upon a systematic propaganda campaign against homosexuals.

In 1935, the year of the Nuremberg Racial Laws, the existing version of Paragraph 175 was amended. A legal commentary noted 'The new state, which is striving for a quantitatively and qualitatively strong, morally healthy people, must combat all unnatural instincts with vigour', thereby explicitly articulating the *völkisch* impetus behind the new legal thinking. An article in the journal *Deutsche Justiz* said that 'the principal deficiency in Paragraph 175 as it stands', was 'that it only encompasses activities resembling sexual intercourse, so that neither the prosecutors nor the police can intervene in cases of public intimacy between men'. By extending the scope of the law to include every instance of inter-masculine sexual contact, the Nazis simplified the business of proving it in courts of law. In 1938, the Reich Supreme Court decided that even evidence of physical contact was no longer essential: 'The purely optically arousing function of the male body is sufficient proof.'

In 1935 the lawyer Rudolf Klare took the opportunity presented by his dissertation to present a justification for the 'eradication' of homosexuals. In what became a standard work of National Socialist jurisprudence, Klare advocated a reversion to ancient Germanic legal customs, involving the killing of homosexuals as an expression of 'racial instinct'. He described homosexuality as 'a racially exterminatory manifestation of degeneracy', and called for the ceaseless 'cleansing' of homosexuals from the Reich, recommending that 'the courts make increased use of expert witnesses in order to achieve an increase in the number of cases resulting in custodial sentences'.

While anti-homosexual propaganda continued to run in the media, the Nazis quietly established a central organisation to gather data on homosexuals as a prelude to systematically persecuting them. On 1 November 1934 a special department responsible for homosexuality was established in the Berlin Gestapo headquarters; its first task was to centralise personal data on homosexuals throughout the Reich. The Gestapo was particularly interested in learning whether the police 'had knowledge of homosexual weaknesses on the part of political personalities', a turn of phrase which suggests that the object of the exercise was to blackmail political opponents into oblivion. Tactics such as these were later employed against Roman Catholic religious orders, the leadership of middle-class youth movements and against the relatively independent-minded General Werner von Fritsch, who was successfully 'framed' in a homosexual scandal by his opponents. On 10 October 1936 this special unit was taken over by the equally secret Reich Central Office for the Combating of Homosexuality and Abortion. The conflation of the two offences was not accidental. Both homosexuality and abortion signified the privatisation of sexuality and its products, thus flatly contradicting the *völkisch* view, whereby sexuality was construed in terms of collectivist biology. The decree that established the Reich Central Office made the connection explicit:

> The considerable dangers which the relatively high number of abortions still being performed present for population policy and the health of the nation, and which constitute a grave infringement of the ideological fundamentals of National Socialism, as well as the homosexual activities of a not inconsiderable proportion of the population, which constitute a serious threat to young people, demands more effective measures against these national diseases than has hitherto been the case.

In other words, persecution of homosexuals was a product of 'population policy and national health', rather than as is sometimes claimed, a defensive psychological reaction on the part of a Nazi 'male state' whose homophobia was driven by anxieties about its members' own 'latent' homosexuality.

According to the decree that established the Reich Central Office, its tasks were the central registration of homosexuals and instances of homosexuality, and the combating of the latter in accordance with systematised directives. This meant that the Reich Central Office became the clearing office for information from a host of agencies and for the results of medical research in this area. In the spring of 1937 Heinrich Himmler informed senior police officers of the necessity for the campaign against homosexuals, saying 'Homosexual men are enemies of the state and are to be treated accordingly. It is a question of purifying the body of the German nation and the maintenance and strengthening of the power of the German nation.' It was the task of the police to 'reduce all cases of homosexuality and abortion so that the demographic losses resulting from these offences will be kept to a minimum'. At the same time, police chiefs were given detailed instructions on how to avail themselves of the developing network of spies and informers operating in this area. The racial-biological imperatives that informed the *Reichführer*-SS's thinking were apparent in a secret speech he gave before SS leaders in 1937. Here he spoke of 'deficits in the sexual balance-sheet' of the nation, and estimated the number of homosexuals in Germany as being 'one or two million'. He continued:

> If you further take into account the facts ... that with a static number of women, we have two million men too few on account of those who fell in the war, then you can well imagine how this imbalance of two million homosexuals and two million war dead, or in other words a lack of about four million men capable of having sex, has upset the sexual balance-sheet of Germany, and will result in a catastrophe.

Later, in January 1942, when the German armed forces were suffering heavy casualties on the Eastern Front, Hitler observed, regarding the connection between the production of human beings and warfare, 'The child will be our salvation! Even if this war should cost us a quarter of a million dead and 100,000 crippled, the surplus of births which the German people has achieved since the seizure of power will give them back to us again.' In fact, there was no surplus of births and the casualty figures he mentioned were decidedly optimistic.

The creation of the Reich Central Office inaugurated the period of centralised and systematic persecution. If in 1934 there were 948 convictions, the number quickly rose to 5,320 in 1936, 8,271 in 1937 and 8,562 in 1938, falling off again following the outbreak of war. According to official statistics, between 1933 and 1945 some 50,000 persons were convicted. Most homosexuals ended up in the hands of the police either through denunciations by their fellow-citizens or through large-scale raids. A typical newspaper announcement on 28 August 1936 read:

> A special commando unit of the Berlin Gestapo was deployed in a cleansing operation in Berlin and many other towns. This resulted in raids within a short space of time on a large number of so-called sex joints. Some hundreds of people were detained ... a special bureau was created in Hamburg which brought charges before a special court of jurors. The accused were sentenced to between one year and twenty months imprisonment.

What this meant for those on the receiving-end can be gauged from an eyewitness account of persecution in Reinbek, at the time still a village on the outskirts of Hamburg:

> With one blow a wave of arrests of homosexuals began in our town. One of the first to be arrested was my friend, with whom I had had a relationship since I was twenty-three. One day people from the Gestapo came to his house and took him away. It was pointless to enquire where he might be. If anyone did that, they ran the risk of being similarly detained, because he knew them, and therefore they were also suspect. Following his arrest, his home was searched by Gestapo agents. Books were taken away, notebooks and address books were confiscated, questions were asked among the neighbours . . . The address books were the worst. All those who figured in them, or had anything to do with him, were arrested and summoned by the Gestapo. Me too. For a whole year I was summoned by the Gestapo and interrogated at least once every fourteen days or three weeks . . . After four weeks my friend was released from investigative custody. The fascists could not prove anything against him either. However, the effects of his arrest were terrifying. Hair shorn off, totally confused, he was no longer what he was before . . . We had to be very careful with all contacts. I had to break off relations with my friend. We passed each other by on the street, because we did not want to put ourselves in danger.

Another eyewitness reported that in Hamburg there were systematic attempts to remove homosexuals from large concerns:

> At first they detained a few and then put them under pressure to reveal the names of other queers. When the Gestapo had enough names, they appeared in the personnel office one morning, got themselves taken through the individual departments and arrested the relevant persons. One raid alone on the Alsterhaus department store resulted in the arrest of about fifty queers. The same thing happened in the Hamburg power station.

In a 'strictly confidential! Official use only' situation report issued in 1941 by the Youth Leader of the German Reich the scale of these police activities was made explicit. Between 1936 and the first half of 1939 the police investigated 37,707 persons for infractions of Paragraph 175. Between 1937 and the first half of 1939 the Gestapo recorded the names of 77,990 persons in its records. In the following table these figures have been augmented with the number of persons convicted of homosexual offences.

YEAR	REGISTERED BY GESTAPO	INVESTIGATED BY POLICE	CONVICTED
1937	32,360	12,760	8,271
1938	28,882	10,638	8,562
1939	33,496	10,456	7,614
TOTAL	94,738	33,854	24,447

In a quantitative sense, the years between 1936 and the outbreak of war were the high-point of persecution of homosexuals. In this period alone, almost one hundred thousand people were registered by the Gestapo. About a third of them were then investigated by the police, with every fourth person being successfully convicted in accordance with the amended version of Paragraph 175.

Already in 1939, the Reich Central Office made a point of relaying the names of homosexuals of military age to the armed forces. Following the outbreak of war, when a large proportion of men 'capable of bearing arms' had been called up, persecution expanded within the military while the number of civilian arrests contracted. At the same time, persecution assumed a qualitatively different character. As early as 1935 the SS began demanding the death penalty for homosexuals. On 12 July 1940 Himmler ordered that 'in future all homosexuals who have seduced more than one partner are to be taken into police preventive custody following their release from prison'. Detention in a concentration camp was tantamount to a death sentence since the camps operated a programme of 'extermination through labour'. Homosexuals were also taken into preventive or protective custody throughout the Nazi period in order to protect the 'national community' from 'habitual and professional criminals', the 'asocial', 'community aliens' or 'parasites upon the people'. Already in 1933 the concentration camp at Hamburg-Fuhlsbüttel included a category designated homosexuals. On 15 November 1941 Hitler personally decreed the death penalty for homosexual members of the SS.

Although the SS managed to destroy a considerable proportion of records relating to concentration camps before the war ended, it is possible to find evidence for the presence of homosexuals in most of the camps. On the basis of an assessment of all of the available evidence, Rudiger Lautmann has estimated that about 10,000 men were forced to wear the degrading pink triangle in the camps, although 'it could have been 5,000 or 15,000'. Eugen Kogon, a political prisoner in Buchenwald until 1945, described their situation as 'deplorable'. Most of them simply died. They occupied the lowest rung in the prisoner hierarchy. In Buchenwald, according to Kogon, they made up the highest proportion of inmates transported to the extermination camps. According to R. Schnabel's eyewitness recollections of Dachau, the prisoners with the pink triangle 'never lived very long, and were rapidly and systematically eliminated by the SS'. A remarkable number of former political prisoners are in agreement that the SS treated homosexuals in a particularly brutal fashion. The writer Günther Weisenborn, who was sent to a concentration camp in 1942 on account of his activities in the Resistance, recalled that during his captivity he encountered 'many homosexuals who had been tortured', and that 'their sufferings were unspeakable; they were not sustained by any form of idea. They were absolutely defenceless and died rapidly because of this.'

The Nazis themselves were conscious that the terror they directed against homosexuals was ambivalent in character. Himmler himself remarked in 1936 that 'the great question of aberrant sexuality will never be regulated through policing'. In several scientific publications, the Nazi biologist and racial hygienicist Theo Lang cautioned against propelling homosexuals into marriage and 'normal' forms of sexuality. He wrote that one had to consider that 'the failure of homosexuals to reproduce had to be viewed not simply from the perspective of a quantitative, but also a qualitative population policy'. According to his theories, homosexuality was caused by chromosomatic disorders, from which he deduced 'that severe punishment and moral condemnation will drive homosexuals to at least attempt to marry and have children, or in other words [we will achieve] precisely the opposite of what harsh penalties are designed to prevent, namely the probable increase in the number of homosexuals in successive generations'.

These hypotheses reveal the fundamental dilemma the Nazis faced in combating homosexuality. As long as they were unable to satisfactorily answer the question 'What causes homosexuality?' the regime was effectively unable to embark upon a Final Solution in this area. Even if they succeeded in eliminating sections of the homosexual population, they would still be confronted with fresh generations of bisexuals and homosexuals. This made the situation of homosexuals rather different from that of other minorities persecuted during the Third Reich, for example Jews or Sinti and Roma, who were murdered regardless of whether they were eight or eighty years old, and thus for whom genocide meant the end of any possibility of reproduction. What connected the mostly Aryan homosexuals with these other groups, was that they were also categorised as being of 'lesser racial value' within the Nazis' programme of racial selective breeding. They shared this classification with those Aryan men and women who were compulsorily sterilised in order to inhibit their capacity to reproduce.

As far as homosexuals were concerned, from the mid-nineteenth century, science had been attempting to discover the causes of their 'illness'. Although the Nazis' research drew upon many of the resultant theories, an annual report by the Reich Criminal Main Office for the year 1939–40 suggested continued uncertainty on the facts of the matter: 'In order to discover further possibilities for the containment of this plague, and so as to leave no method unexplored, we will be examining the suggestions of various persons whose aim is to deepen scientific understanding of the problem of homosexuality.'

Science and research began to be employed more intensively, although precisely how remains largely unexplored. The most notorious example is of the hormonal experiments conducted in 1944 by the Danish SS doctor Carl Vaernet upon homosexual inmates in Buchenwald concentration camp. Himmler personally took a keen interest in Vaernet's work, supplying him with a secret letter of recommendation in November 1943: 'I request that you treat Dr V. with the utmost generosity. I myself also require a monthly report of between three to four sides in length since I am very interested in these questions.' According to Vaernet's correspondence with the SS, his experiments were designed 'to establish on a broad basis whether it is possible to implant an artificial sexual gland which will normalise abnormal sexual desires'. Should he be successful, Vaernet wanted to know 'whether one can normalise all homosexuals with these methods'. In the event that the experiments led to marketable offshoots, Vaernet agreed in advance to concede the SS exclusive rights both at home and abroad. Himmler's letter of recommendation indicated that the *Reichsführer*-SS and police had great expectations of these experiments. Himmler anticipated the mass application of Vaernet's future discoveries and planned to establish an institute where people would be treated with artificial gland implants. A few months before the collapse of the Third Reich he received information from Vaernet that a high dosage of the male hormone testosterone could obliterate any trace of homosexuality. On 10 February 1945, Vaernet dedicated his final report to Heinrich Himmler with gratitude 'for your lasting and generous support'. Apart from the suffering which these human experiments caused the 'subjects', two of whom died because of Vaernet's surgical incompetence, they are also an example of the process whereby a prejudice against a minority could be lent 'scientific' rationalisation.

It remains to note that the Nazis' modified version of Paragraph 175 remained on the statute books of the German Federal Republic until 1969. Between 1950 and 1965 about 50,000 people were convicted of homosexual offences. The highest Federal Court actually decided that the modifications to Paragraph 175 introduced in 1935 had been 'in order' and that they reflected 'no typically National Socialist way of thinking'. With a few exceptions, homosexuals received no compensation. Between 1 January 1958 and 31 December 1959 surviving homosexual concentration camp inmates were entitled to apply for compensation of DM150 for each month they had endured in a camp. On 20 December 1982 the statistical office of the Federal parliament responded to the question 'How many surviving homosexuals have received any compensation?' with the answer that it was impossible to say since 'no separate statistical data was kept concerning applications for compensation by homosexuals persecuted by the Nazis'. However, on 31 October 1986 the Federal government was able rapidly to provide the information that there had been twenty-three applications for compensation so far, with a further nine on the way as a result of a television programme shown in 1980 which drew attention to the compensation for hardship on offer. Even though funds have recently been made available for the so-called 'forgotten victims of National Socialism', the question of compensation for homosexuals persecuted by the National Socialists has largely been 'solved' simply by letting biology taking its course.

The Persecution of Homosexuals in Nazi Germany

Michael Burleigh and Wolfgang Wippermann, *The Racial State: Germany, 1933–1945* (Cambridge, 1991); Heinz Heger, *The Men with the Pink Triangle* (London, 1980); B. Jellonnek, *Homosexuelle unter dem Hakenkreuz. Die Verfolgung der Homosexuellen im Dritten Reich* (Paderborn, 1990); Rüdiger Lautmann, 'Gay Prisoners in Concentration Camps', in Michael Berenbaum (ed.), *A Mosaic of Victims: Non-Jews Persecuted and Murdered by the Nazis* (London, 1990), pp. 200–21; C. Limpricht, J. Müller and N. Oxenius (eds), *'Verführte' Manner. Das Leben der Kölner Homosexuellen im Dritten Reich* (Cologne, 1991); Richard Plant, *The Pink Triangle: The Nazi War against Homosexuals* (New York, 1986); Hans-Georg Stümke, *Homosexuelle in Deutschland.*

Eine politische Geschichte (Munich, 1989); Hans-Georg Stümke and Rudi Finkler, *Rosa Winkel, Rosa Listen. Homosexuelle und 'Gesundes Volksempfinden' von Auschwitz bis heute* (Reinbek, 1981); Günter Grau, *Hidden Holocaust? Gay and Lesbian Persecution in Germany 1933–45.* (London 1955).

CHAPTER XI

WOMEN, MOTHERHOOD AND THE FAMILY IN THE THIRD REICH

Jill Stephenson

HITLER'S INSISTENCE ON RACIAL ORIGIN as the fundamental criterion for determining citizenship in the Third Reich affected all the inhabitants of Germany and also those of countries occupied by German forces during the Second World War. 'Racially desirable Aryans' had special duties as well as rights and were subjected to incessant propaganda and 'political education' campaigns, while the 'racially inferior' were outcasts from the 'people's community', suffering discrimination and often outright persecution and physical violence. Some whose racial credentials ostensibly entitled them to membership of the Aryan community were less valuable in Nazi eyes because of some actual or perceived physical or mental ailment — profound deafness, perhaps, or chronic illness, or the loosely-defined disorder of 'feeble-mindedness'. Also less valuable were Aryans who were, by Nazi criteria, delinquent or deviant, for example homosexuals or rebellious youth. Both men and women, and therefore also families, could be 'racially and hereditarily valuable', or 'worthless', regardless of social class or occupation. Almost all of the characteristics that indicated value in this sense were either inherent or involuntarily acquired: that is, most of those who manifested them had no power to control or alter them, and were therefore condemned at best to live on the margins of society in the Third Reich, with physical abuse and death either a palpable threat or grim reality.

The overwhelming emphasis on allegedly racial or inherited characteristics as criteria for belonging to the German nation meant that all aspects of reproduction and the nurturing of the young were regarded as being of paramount importance. By contrast with revolutionary Russia, where, at first at least, the aim was to diminish the influence of the 'bourgeois family', in the Nazi view the family was the 'germ cell' of the nation — its fundamentally important basic unit and a microcosm of the 'national community'. The family, claimed the Nazis, had been damaged and corrupted by a number of recent developments: effective birth-control methods, an increase in female aspirations and employment outside the home, and a materialistic ethos had together helped to promote the 'one- and two-child family' of the Weimar 'system'. The Nazi leadership aimed for a return to the large families of the later nineteenth century, but fecundity was to be encouraged and supported only among those who conformed to the Nazi criteria of 'racial and hereditary value'. These 'desirable' families were to submit to Nazi demands and to reorientate their attitudes, from being inward-looking self-interested collective entities to being the agents of Nazi policies, giving priority to the interests of the 'Aryan race' — as these were defined by the Nazi leadership.

The family was, then, to cease to be a private institution, becoming instead an instrument of Nazi policy, one partner in a triangular relationship, along with school and the Hitler Youth organisation of the National Socialists (NSDAP). These three agencies were to co-operate in the continual and unceasing indoctrination of the young. Further, the legitimacy of parental authority in the Third Reich depended on the subordination of private aspirations and gratification to the demands of the Nazi state. Disqualification from parental rights and responsibilities could follow if a child were encouraged to adopt a negative or hostile attitude towards the regime, its agencies and its policies. The fundamental duty of the family was to maintain and propagate itself as a 'racially and hereditarily desirable' unit, protecting the purity of its blood through the choice of equally 'desirable' marriage partners for all its members and promoting the strength of the 'Aryan race' through generous reproduction [see p. 169]. The emphasis on reproduction ensured that the roles fulfilled within the family by the two parents would be different and complementary. While father necessarily spent much time away from the family, earning the money to sustain it, mother was 'the first educator of children'. Men involved themselves in the world outside the family, which included their role in the armed forces in time of war, while 'the smaller world of the home' was women's preserve: but man remained the head of the household and guardian of his family, while woman was the homemaker within his domain.

> *'Marry! — but whom?' — Ten Commandments for choosing a spouse*
> 1. Remember that you are a German.
> 2. If you are hereditarily healthy, you should not remain single.
> 3. Keep your body pure!
> 4. You should keep your heart and mind pure.
> 5. As a German, choose only a spouse of the same or of Nordic blood.
> 6. When choosing your spouse, ask about his/her forebears.
> 7. Healthiness is also the precondition of physical beauty.
> 8. Marry only for love.
> 9. Seek out a partner for marriage, not a playmate.
> 10. You should hope to have as many children as possible.
> (*Der Deutsche*, 11 August 1934)

All of this affected policies and propaganda towards both Aryan and non-Aryan young and adult males, but to a much greater extent it conditioned Nazi attitudes towards women's nature and role in all aspects of life and society. To the Nazi leadership, the female of the species was, above all, an actual or potential mother. Thus, the 'racially desirable' woman, together with her equally 'desirable' partner, was to produce Aryan, 'hereditarily healthy' offspring — as many of them as possible, to counteract the 'pollution' that was alleged to have occurred in the past with non-Aryans and the 'diseased' and 'delinquent' breeding with each other, or even with Aryans, to produce 'less valuable' children. To reverse this perceived development, the Nazis embarked on a horrific and bizarre exercise in reproductive engineering, heavily influenced by two parallel developments. On the one hand, the evidence of a steadily declining birth-rate from around 1900 was a source of anxiety to many Germans, especially as it plummeted during the Depression years around 1930. Equally, scientific interest in human genetics and in the nature of inherited diseases, dating again from about the turn of the century, had created a climate (not only in Germany) in which manipulation of the quality of a population seemed not only possible but also desirable. The Nazis, then, in generating hysteria about the nation dying out, wanted Germans to produce not merely *more* children but specifically more 'racially and hereditarily valuable' children, born to families who had not demonstrated 'asocial' behaviour patterns. The grotesque corollary of this was that 'undesirable' persons were to be prevented from procreating.

Compulsory sterilisation of those judged to be less than valuable was inflicted on women as well as on men, with doctors, lawyers and administrators, among others, instrumental in the procedures to seek out and compel unwilling victims to undergo sterilisation and, if a pregnancy were under way, abortion as a preliminary to it.

These racial and 'eugenic' obsessions and practices formed the essential basis of Nazi policies involving women in the Third Reich. Valuable women were to be treated in ways that protected and promoted their reproductive capacity, with enhanced labour protection laws, for example, and to be constantly reminded of their personal responsibility for raising the birth-rate. But while the role of housewife and mother was the ideal state for all valuable women, it was recognised that some would work outside the home, certainly before marriage; this would preferably be in an area where they could express their 'womanly' or 'motherly' attributes — such as nursing or kindergarten teaching, or in agriculture or domestic service.

To instil in them an awareness of their responsibilities and an acceptance of their biological destiny, women were to be 'politicised'. In a state without conventional politics, this meant little more than indoctrination. But the regime's aim was not simply to suppress opposition and dissent: for valuable women, politicisation was to mean being informed of the regime's policies and requirements in all areas of life, enthusing about them, and implementing them in their daily life, under the guidance of the Nazi women's organisations. Above all, this meant safeguarding the future of the Aryan race, which would involve ostracising the less valuable, and ensuring that their children did the same. If they were employed in teaching, nursing or social work, for example, they might be expected to contribute to the exclusion, humiliation and even the physical abuse of individual adults or children who were labelled 'inferior', in Germany itself or, during the Second World War, in occupied countries.

It was in the realm of motherhood and family life that the women's organisations associated with the NSDAP found their niche. In reality, the élite Party formation, the NS-Frauenschaft (NSF — Nazi Women's Group), and its subordinate mass organisation, the Deutsches Frauenwerk (DFW — German Women's Enterprise), under the leadership of Gertrud Scholtz-Klink, herself a prolific mother, were politically impotent and generally insignificant in the male-dominated Nazi system. They were, however, entrusted with the sensitive task of indoctrinating the valuable female population and with supervision of individuals' child-care and household duties by approved visiting welfare workers, who were used to monitor pregnant women and therefore discourage resort to abortion. The NSF and DFW were also to instil a sense of 'social responsibility' in women, so that they would bring up their children to accept Nazi norms and requirements and to participate enthusiastically in the activities of the Nazi youth organisations. Nazi women's magazines ran articles reassuring mothers that the activities of the Hitler Youth were wholesome and healthy, and that the emphasis on physical endeavour was not taken to dangerous lengths. The NSF and DFW also had the task of trying to wean women away from the Christian Churches, both Evangelical (Protestant) and Roman Catholic, whose influence remained strong, especially in rural areas. But attempts to break the habit of church-going among women and, even more importantly, their children, proved to be virtually impossible, especially when the crises and tragedies of war brought an increase in Christian observance.

The other major activity of the NSF and DFW lay in the provision of courses on housekeeping, child-care and cookery, to try to ensure that valuable families were being nurtured in conditions of cleanliness with healthy (and thrifty) meals, and that the health and growth of infants and small children were being promoted. None of this was merely for the benefit of individual German Aryan families: all these efforts were geared singlemindedly to promoting the regime's racial and power-political objectives. For example, as housewives, women were to buy German goods and shun imports; to this end, they were to use second-hand goods, substitute foods and produce in season. Above all, they were to manifest restraint as consumers and to mend and recycle existing clothes and utensils instead of 'wastefully' demanding goods that were new. This drive for frugality, while thoroughly unpopular, was an integral part of the regime's quest for autarky, or self-sufficiency, in foodstuffs and other essential commodities, in preparation for the coming struggle to achieve the goal of Aryan domination of all of Europe. While the complementary policies of autarky and the damping down of consumer demand were intensified during the war, they were already being pursued before it, particularly after the introduction of the Four Year Plan for the economy in September 1936.

The full-time housewife and mother, caring for her children and providing domestic support for her husband, remained the Nazi ideal. Particularly once her children were of school age, much of her day was to be spent on careful shopping and thrifty housekeeping — mending and altering clothing, making jam and bottling fruit, washing clothes by hand and eschewing 'unnecessary' labour-saving devices. It was hoped that she would also throw herself into the DFW's recreational activities, attending sewing circles or learning about German folk customs and popular culture under the watchful guidance of a reliable NSF member, or learning new skills such as air-raid protection or first aid, allegedly in the spirit of community service. It soon emerged that DFW courses in practical skills, especially child-care and cookery, were quite popular, but there was consistently poor, even derisory, attendance at courses and events in which there was a high overt component of 'political education' and virtually no practical or entertainment value. Participation in the DFW's activities was, of course, restricted to valuable Aryans. But participation did not necessarily indicate enthusiasm for the regime, the Party or its women's organisations. The early *Gleichschaltung* (co-ordination) process, which had eliminated most independent social groups as well as political organisations, created a situation where, if women wanted some kind of associational life, there was little alternative to accepting Nazi structures and leadership. The major exceptions to this were the Christian Churches, because even where local Party zealots succeeded in closing down church social clubs, like women's guilds or youth clubs, regular church services still continued.

The activities of the Nazi women's organisations were geared to promoting Nazi values and aims, with special emphasis on reminding women constantly of their 'duty' not only to cherish existing children but to accept the need to have more. But although there was a rise in the birth-rate from 1934, after the extremely low levels of the Depression years, it soon became apparent that Germans were not prepared to reproduce themselves in sufficient numbers to provide a return to the large families of the later nineteenth century. This was hardly surprising, because German population development had followed the general modern demographic pattern of growth at a time of rapid industrialisation, followed by stabilisation and decline in mature urban society in the twentieth century. But beyond this, part of the problem for the Nazis was a self-inflicted handicap: because the aim was to achieve fewer births in the less valuable sections of the population, the valuable families would have to compensate for that shortfall and then, in addition, contribute extra children to raise the German birth-rate from its low level. This helps to explain the manic nature of large-scale Nazi campaigns to try to persuade the racially valuable to procreate and to add an element of coercion by banning abortion

— on pain of imprisonment — and endeavouring to make contraceptives unavailable. Nevertheless, illicit abortions continued at the rate of between half a million and a million a year during the 1930s, no doubt partly because of the greater difficulty in obtaining contraceptives.

There were also material incentives to propagate, to encourage the valuable to produce large families. These families were designated *kinderreich* (rich in children), whereas 'worthless' large families were simply *Grossfamilien* (big families) which were disqualified from receiving any of the benefits conferred on the *kinderreich*. Benefits took the form of recurrent children's allowances and one-off grants paid to the parents (in practice, to the father) of a large family, and were financed by taxing the childless. Beyond that, mothers of large families were to receive preferential treatment in public places: for example, in some towns they were given free seats at the theatre, while staff in government offices were ordered to give priority to a mother with several children before other people in a queue. To indicate the esteem in which the regime held valuable and prolific mothers, in 1938 the Honour Cross of the German Mother, for women with four or more children, was introduced, with a gold Mother's Cross awarded to those with at least eight children. But perhaps the most practical innovative incentive, was the Marriage Loan Scheme, introduced in June 1933, which provided a small grant for valuable couples intending to marry, on condition that the wife-to-be gave up her job. In reality, the grant was paid in vouchers which were to be redeemed for household goods from approved shops — that is, shops run by Aryans, not Jews. The carrot was that, on the birth of a valuable child, one quarter of the loan would be cancelled, with a year's moratorium on repayments to encourage a new pregnancy in order to have a further quarter of the repayments cancelled.

While encouragement to the valuable to procreate was primarily directed at married couples, with corresponding pressure on the single to marry, any valuable child was welcomed, even if its mother was unmarried. This led to an easing of official prejudice against unwed mothers and their illegitimate children which has given rise to popular rumours about positive encouragement being given by the Nazi leadership to young women to 'give the Führer a child' by a valuable consort, whether or not within the context of a stable relationship. Himmler's *Schutzstaffel* (SS) is particularly associated with this, given his obsession with all issues of population policy, which was extreme even by Nazi standards. Certainly, especially during the Second World War, the SS leadership was in the vanguard of those calling for equal treatment of married and unmarried valuable mothers, and its *Lebensborn* (Fount of Life) homes for expectant and nursing mothers welcomed both. Himmler had already declared, in 1938, that he, through the agency of *Lebensborn*, would assume guardianship of all valuable illegitimate children whose mothers were alone and vulnerable [see box below]. But, contrary to rumour, the *Lebensborn* homes were not established as 'stud farms' for the pro-creation of SS stock. If such things did exist, they were local initiatives by SS zealots. The reality was more sober: the illegitimacy rate in the 1930s was lower than it had been in the 1920s. But, during the war, Himmler was anxious that his men, having had to provide evidence of especially 'pure' ancestry as a condition of admission to the SS, should leave heirs for the future, and that a young woman left to carry an SS man's child after his death in battle should be cherished.

In future, each SS doctor, as a member of the *Schutzstaffel*, must stand up for the honour of the expectant mother, irrespective of whether she is preparing to give birth to a premarital or illegitimate child, to protect her from the possibility of social ostracism and to advise her in the fullest measure ... The present position of the unmarried expectant mother above all necessitates special *legal pro-tection*, the particular safeguarding of her legal interests. The ex-perience of our few months' work has taught us that the unmarried mother is more often than not in a completely helpless position, and since her financial means, too, are generally limited, she cannot call on the necessary legal assistance. Therefore to create a remedy once and for all, the *Reichsführer SS* [Himmler] has decided himself to assume the guardianship of all illegitimate children, through the association *Lebensborn* insofar as it seems necessary. He will there-fore undertake the representation of mothers before both the courts dealing with matters of guardianship and the Youth Offices, and will supervise the payment of maintenance by the child's father.
(*Institut für Zeitgeschichte Archiv, MA 387, 5190/92* (?1936))

While illegitimate children were, therefore, not to be disparaged or dis-advantaged, the Nazi leadership felt that a better alternative to irregular relationships was the facilitating of marriage. Accordingly, a new Marriage Law was enacted in 1938 which unambiguously clarified the official Nazi view of the nature and purpose of marriage. This included an indication of what constituted an invalid marriage between otherwise 'desirable' couples: the new law made premature infertility in a childless union and also refusal by either partner to have children grounds for divorce. It also introduced the (then) radical principle of 'irretrievable breakdown' as grounds for divorce, without a 'guilty party' and after three years' separation. This, it was hoped, would enable those legally locked into a failed marriage either to enter a new relationship, which would be more likely to produce children, or to regularise an existing extra-marital relationship where there already were children. The new divorce law proved popular, with a sharp rise in both the divorce and marriage rates in 1939.

In addition to encouraging more pregnancies among the valuable, while (often forcibly) terminating those among the less valuable, the regime was anxious to get the best value from each conception, through a reduction in rates of miscarriage (spontaneous or contrived), dead births, infant and maternal mortality and childhood disease. Certainly, there was success in achieving a modest reduction in the infant and peri-natal mortality rates, continuing established trends. But, in spite of Nazi measures for incentives, coercion and surveillance, the rise in the marriage and birth-rates during the 1930s was modest, leaving the birth-rate still far short of pre-1914 levels. Whereas in 1910 there had been 128 live births per 1,000 women of child-bearing age, and 90 in 1922, the best that the Nazi regime could achieve was marked recovery from the Depression's nadir in 1933 of 59, with figures of 85 in 1939 and 84 in 1940. Thereafter, the Second World War saw a renewed decline in the marriage and birth-rates, with desperate attempts to combat this through such tactics as engineering postal romances between soldiers at the front and young women at home, using official 'letter centres' as supervisory match-making agencies [see box on page 176], and sanctioning weddings by proxy. Until the later stages of the war, efforts were made to allow husbands in the armed forces regular home-leave in the hope that this would stimulate conceptions.

The Nazi leadership thus seemed to have clear and ambitious objec-tives both for the control and manipulation of valuable women and their reproductive capacity, and for the marginalising of the less valuable. It was all too successful in the latter, pursuing a singleminded policy of dis-crimination against and persecution of the 'racially or hereditarily dis-eased', women and men alike. But its success in trying to persuade the valuable to procreate on a large scale was at best limited. Further, it soon

Letter Centre for the Marriageable in Gau Bayreuth
With the permission of the Party Chancellery, the Reich Association of German Families, in collaboration with the Racial Policy Office of the regional Leadership, a Letter Centre is opening in Bayreuth . . . The agency meets a need arising from the exigencies of war. For four, five and more years, young men of marriageable age have been in the forces. Many German girls are employed in war service, often far from home . . . The longing of the healthy German man and the healthy German woman for a happy marriage and the blessing of children is, however, unchanging. If even in peacetime not everyone finds a mate, the consequences of total war pose considerable new difficulties.

This is where the Letter Centre can and must play a role. The Letter Centre arranges introductions, gives young Germans who want to get married the chance to get to know each other by post and, if it is desired after this acquaintance through correspondence, to meet in person. The final choice of a partner, from several possibilities, is for the applicant to make . . . The nature of the Letter Centre's work carries the guarantee that applicants who are accepted for the scheme are hereditarily healthy, racially and personally unblemished fellow-citizens, who fulfil all the preconditions for a healthy and happy marriage . . .

The strictest confidence is guaranteed and also expected from all applicants. Thus anyone can take part in this project without regard to educational level, occupation, age, confession or property.

If someone is unwilling to take the first step in this, a relative or friend can get in touch with the Letter Centre as his/her sponsor. In accordance with the National Socialist conception of a German marriage, however, each applicant is expected to manifest a readiness to start a racially desirable, clean, child-loving and therefore also a happy family . . .
(*Völkischer Beobachter* (Süddeutsche Ausgabe), No. 238, 25 August 1944 in the Archives of the Wiener Library, London)

became clear that the regime's short-term power-political ambitions were vitiating its attempts to pursue a coherent policy towards valuable women. While the image of the full-time housewife and mother remained an ideal, it ceased to be unambiguously propagated as a goal from the mid-1930s because of a radical change in the employment market. Whereas in January 1933 there had been well over six million Germans unemployed, by 1938 there was a shortage of labour in key sectors of the economy; during the Second World War, German industry and agriculture suffered from acute labour shortages, even with the forced recruitment of prisoners-of-war and coerced civilians from occupied countries, to a total of over seven million in 1944. These foreigners, including in the end at least a million and a half women, had the advantage, as the Nazis saw it, of not requiring to be treated humanely: most came from Eastern Europe and were classed as 'racially inferior'. They could be deployed in areas where conditions were dangerous or insanitary, for long hours, in a way that might be (reproductively) hazardous for valuable Aryan women.

German women had, of course, figured in a wide variety of occupations long before 1933, including factory work, domestic service, clerical and other white-collar jobs and, especially, agriculture, where large numbers of wives and daughters of farmers worked as 'assisting family members' without a formal wage. A tiny number of well-educated women had breached male chauvinist professional bastions such as medicine and law, with larger numbers in school-teaching and the 'caring professions'. But in the shrunken jobs market of the Depression, prejudice against women in the workplace, especially if they were married, was strong before 1933 and the new Nazi government reflected a significant section of public opinion in calling for the return of women to home and family life. Restrictive legislation in 1933 against employing married women in the public service built on a pre-Nazi law of May 1932, while a quota system for female students was welcomed by many male professionals. Such measures gave the clear impression that the Nazis' aims in population development and employment policy would be compatible and mutually reinforcing. The Marriage Loan Scheme, after all, was introduced in a section of the Law to Reduce Unemployment of 1 June 1933, with the stipulation that the intending wife must relinquish her job on marriage as the crucial condition aimed at easing the straitened labour market.

While the Depression persisted, until the mid-1930s mass unemployment in all sectors of the economy and overcrowding of the universities seemed to provide double justification — over and above population policy considerations — for the Nazi policy of trying both to remove women, particularly married women, from jobs outside the home and to reduce the number of young women in higher education. These tactics were aimed at giving men (actual and potential 'fathers of families') priority in employment and educational opportunities, while recalling women to their 'natural sphere' of home, family and 'womanly work'. But the rapid revival of the economy meant that from the mid-1930s there were increasing shortages of labour in some sectors and later throughout the economy. With the exclusion of non-Aryans and political opponents of both genders from influential or promoted positions in thoroughgoing purges in 1933, German male labour and professional expertise were not alone sufficient for the regime's ambitions — which included the use of labour and expertise in programmes for compulsory sterilisation, 'euthanasia' and the extermination of the less valuable. Women were therefore encouraged to enter the employment market, even in areas that had previously been designated 'men's jobs'.

This contributed to an increase in women's presence in both higher education and the professions even before the war, once the graduate unemployment of the early 1930s had been absorbed, although women continued to figure overwhelmingly in the lower levels of the professions. While there were some new restrictions on women's employment and promotion prospects — from 1936, for example, women lawyers were excluded from participation in court-room work — the later 1930s provided increasing scope for individual women graduates. Some of this was due to the peculiar and pernicious nature of the Third Reich. For example, women doctors were in particular demand in the Nazi women's organisations, including the Bund deutscher Mädel (League of German Girls) and the Women's Labour Service, where not only the general health of young females, but also the detail of their reproductive development, was monitored. In addition, the involvement of doctors, lawyers and civil servants in the sterilisation and 'euthanasia' programmes created new jobs for those prepared to prostitute their professional training. There were also completely new occupations deemed to require graduate expertise, including work in the genealogical records offices, which were kept busy by the requirements of the 'racial and hereditary health' qualifications for both citizenship and the right to marry in the Third Reich.

By 1939 it was clear that the available *and willing* reserves of female labour had been exhausted, and that increasing recruitment in one sector meant a loss to another. In particular, young women in rural areas saw in the demand for labour in urban occupations an opportunity to escape from the long hours, low pay and physical exhaustion involved in farm work. It is an indictment of the harshness of life on the land that many viewed manual labour in a factory as preferable. By 1939, there were 50 per cent more women employed in industry than there had been in the depressed year of 1933, with increases in other sectors too, especially white-collar clerical work. Women industrial workers formed about half of the labour force in consumer goods industries throughout the 1930s, but only around 10 per cent in producer goods industries. They were much more likely to be found in textiles production than in armaments factories. Even so, by 1939 almost half of all German women classed as 'fit for work' were not employed, of whom the overwhelming majority were married: 36 per cent of married women, compared with almost 90 per cent of single women, were in work of some kind, whether as employees, proprietors or 'assisting family members' in small businesses, including farms. By the later 1930s, strenuous efforts were being made to attract more married women into work, with half-day shifts and the promise of more crèches — a promise never adequately fulfilled.

From the start of the war, the key labour problem that exercised the regime's leaders was how to mobilise more German women for the war effort without using outright coercion against these valuable citizens. The idea of labour conscription was repeatedly discussed but not enacted until January 1943; even then, it was imperfectly enforced. It has been argued that this was because Hitler was reluctant to risk women's reproductive health by forcing them into factory work, but it is clear that other factors were more important. Firstly, Hitler believed that unwilling and inexperienced female workers would be of little value, especially in compensating for skills shortages. And secondly, Hitler and some of his henchmen were reluctant to risk antagonising women and their families: middle-class women and their husbands, particularly, resisted appeals for more female labour in industry and found loopholes in the 1943 legislation. The regime had itself provided good reason for women's reluctance to go out to work in introducing an allowance to be paid to the wife of a serving soldier. The solution to the problem was the large-scale use of foreign forced labour, with skilled French workers and unskilled Soviet (and sometimes female) *Ostarbeiter* (literally, 'eastern workers'), under German supervision, providing some compensation for the loss of German male labour.

The foreign workers mostly lived and worked under oppressively segregated and policed control, especially in urban areas. Towards the end of the war, especially, many were close to starvation. But some foreigners — especially in the freer conditions of agrarian society — struck up relationships with Germans. While there were cases of foreign women workers becoming involved with German men or boys, more often the relationships were between German women and foreign men, especially, in rural areas, Poles. Sometimes this was the result of genuine affection, sometimes it was born of pure sexual need. A farmer's wife whose husband was at the front might voluntarily embark on a sexual liaison with a foreign male worker allocated to her as a replacement, or else she might accept it as the price to be paid for having a compliant worker without whose labour the farm could not function [see box below]. In the towns, too, a woman left on her own might strike up a friendship with a foreign worker, especially as he became more confident once the war turned against Germany. To the Nazi authorities these relationships were anathema, amounting to 'racial pollution'. The penalties for offenders, which were well-publicised, clearly demonstrated a gender-based double standard: a foreign woman and her German male lover often suffered little more than official disapproval, while a 'racially inferior' foreign man was hanged and his Aryan female lover sent to prison after being ritually physically abused by Nazi vigilantes, usually by having her head shaved in a public ceremony.

> After the call-up of almost all able-bodied male workers, agricultural concerns were allocated, almost exclusively, Poles, Serbs and prisoners of war to work alongside the female workers already available. There are complaints about the rampant unruliness of these foreign elements which, one hears, leads not infrequently to the Germans actually being afraid of foreigners who at one and the same time make great demands and, in the face of stricter discipline and supervision, threaten to withdraw their labour. So the proprietors cut down on their own provisioning in order to please the foreigners, grant them various comforts, and, in spite of official prohibitions, let them eat at the same table, simply to prevent damage to their business ... Farmers' wives are afraid of them, especially because of frequent reports in the press of acts of violence and the murder of proprietors. The ever-increasing symptoms of prohibited contact with prisoners of war, especially pregnancies in German girls and women, are not least attributable to these circumstances. Frequently, women who are accused plead under questioning that they gave in to the prisoner of war so as not to lose his labour.
> (*Bundesarchiv*, R22/3387, the Stuttgart Public Prosecutor to the Reich Minister of Justice, 31 May 1943)

The public humiliation and imprisonment of an Aryan German woman who had a sexual relationship with a foreigner indicates the ferocity with which even the valuable were punished when they violated Nazi racial prescriptions. There could be few sins greater than 'polluting

German blood', as a valuable woman was deemed to have done when she permitted the invasion of her body by a 'racial enemy', and the sanctions were accordingly draconian. Similarly, the death penalty was introduced in 1943 for anyone performing an abortion to terminate a valuable pregnancy, because this was 'racial sabotage', contributing to the 'dying out' of the German nation during the crisis of war. Beyond these specific sanctions, and those against overt political opponents, there was little direct brutality against valuable women, whose reproductive capacity had to be safeguarded at all costs. At the same time, the second half of the war saw an intensification of persecution of the Nazis' 'racial enemies' and the implementation of a systematic extermination programme in which they and the 'asocial' or 'deviant' were targeted with almost no discrimination between men and women. The chief exception was that male homosexuals were treated with appalling brutality, as 'racial saboteurs', while lesbians were seen as simply deviant, not as a racial threat. There were women villains as well as victims, including, most infamously, concentration camp guards. And a small band of committed NSF workers — regarded with contempt by large sections of the German population — not only tried to win valuable women's compliance with Nazi demands, but also assisted in the segregation of the valuable from the 'worthless', and in the dispossession of the latter, in occupied countries (see box below).

From the work of the NS-Frauenschaft in the Wartheland
The Border/Foreign Section [of the NSF/DFW] participates in the tasks associated with the German People's List, on the basis of which the division between Germans and Poles is strictly demarcated . . . The Wartheland [in occupied Poland] is a developing area. More and more Germans are flooding into this new region of the Reich . . . The task for all of them is to turn the Wartheland into a flourishing German territory . . . 136,000 women and girls are today in this community, inspired and imbued with the task of making a German homeland out of alien Polish territory.
(Institut für Zeitgeschichte Archiv, MA 225, Gau Württemberg/ Hohenzollern, 2-408814/5, 29 April 1942)

Hitler's war did, nevertheless, create many hardships for valuable women, especially in its later stages, with increasing enemy bombing and then invasion, as well as material deprivation as rationing grew more stringent and everyday facilities and utilities were closed down or destroyed. The evacuation of women and children from urban bombing targets often led to hostility between them and their rural host families. Above all, during and sometimes also after the war, many women had to assume the role of breadwinner and head of the household, with a husband or father temporarily absent or never to return. With three million German men killed, and many others injured, maimed or taken prisoner, many 'valuable' young women would not find a husband. The long-term decline in the German birth-rate would continue, with Hitler able to suggest only one remedy for the post-war period: bigamy, to ensure that 'valuable' women would not be wasted reproductive assets. Nevertheless, while the 'racially valuable' woman was abused in the Third Reich by being subjected to Nazi control and manipulation, she – unlike the less 'valuable' — had some room for manoeuvre, even if that narrowed considerably under the pressures of war. Above all, a 'valuable' woman could not be forced to have more children, and strenuous attempts to deny her the means of birth control clearly failed. Particularly if she belonged to the middle classes, she was in a position to resist propaganda and direct appeals by Party or state functionaries to have larger families, to take paid employment during the war, to participate more in NSF and DFW activities, and to demand fewer consumer goods. 'Valuable' women who failed to comply with these appeals were certainly pestered with propaganda and pressure; but they were generally not subjected to coercion or brutality, because of their value and because these issues concerned mere policy objectives, not racial ideological imperatives.

Women, Motherhood and the Family

Stefan Bajohr, *Die Hälfte der Fabrik. Geschichte der Frauenarbeit in Deutschland 1914 bis 1945* (Marburg, 1979); Gisela Bock, *Zwangssterilisation im Nationalsozialismus. Studien zur Rassenpolitik und Frauenpolitik* (Opladen, 1986); Renate Bridenthal, Atina Grossman and Marion Kaplan (eds), *When Biology Became Destiny: Women in Weimar and Nazi Germany* (New York, 1984); Michael Burleigh and Wolfgang Wippermann, *The Racial State: Germany 1933–1945* (Cambridge, 1991); Frauengruppe Faschismusforschung (ed.), *Mutterkreuz und Arbeitsbuch*, (Frankfurt am Main, 1981); Ute Frevert, *Women in German History: From Bourgeois Emancipation to Sexual Liberation* (Oxford, Hamburg and New York, 1989); Clifford Kirkpatrick, *Woman in Nazi Germany* (London, 1939); Jacques R. Pauwels, *Women, Nazis, and Universities:*

Female University Students in the Third Reich, 1933–1945 (Westport, Conn., 1984); Jill Stephenson, *Women in Nazi Society* (London, 1975; New York, 1976); Jill Stephenson, *The Nazi Organisation of Women* (London and New York, 1981); Alison Owings, *Frauen. German Women Recall the Third Reich* (London 1993); Dörte Winkler, *Frauenarbeit im Dritten Reich* (Hamburg, 1977).

GLOSSARY

'Barbarossa': The German code-name for the attack on the Soviet Union on 22 June 1941.

Einsatzgruppen: The death squads of the SS and SD charged with killing Jews and Communists during the invasion of the Soviet Union.

'Final Solution': The Nazi euphemism for the mass murder of the Jews.

Führer: Leader, the title assumed by Hitler, first as leader of the Nazi party and later as leader of the Third Reich.

Gulags: The Soviet camps in which Stalin imprisoned alleged enemies of his regime along with criminals.

Herrenvolk: Master Race, the Nazi term used to describe the German, or Aryan race and its destiny as a ruler of humanity.

Historikerstreit: The name given to the German historians' controversy over the interpretation of the Nazi past which began in 1986.

Kampfgemeinschaft: Community of Struggle, the Nazi term which idealised the comradeship of soldiers in battle, as well as the `political fighters' of the Nazi Party before it came to power in Germany.

Lebensraum: Living Space, the Nazi term for the areas to be conquered in the East and to be colonised by the Germans.

Mein Kampf: My Struggle, the title of Hitler's book, in which he combined an autobiographical account of his early years with his ideas about history as an eternal struggle between races and his programme for German expansion and domination in Europe.

SS: *Schutzstaffel*, or Protection Squads, originally bodyguard units of the Nazi Party, later a vast organisation comprising military units, concentration and death camp administration, secret police (SD), and huge economic enterprises.

Untermenschen: Subhumans, the Nazi term for inferior races, of whom the Jews and the Slavs constituted the lowest species.

Vergangenheitsbewältigung: Overcoming the past, a term introduced in the postwar Federal Republic of Germany to describe the need to confront, or come to terms with, the Nazi past.

Vernichtungskrieg: War of extermination or destruction, the Nazi term for the war planned in the East.

Volksgemeinschaft: National Community, a Nazi term describing the ideal society of the future based on racial homogeneity and devoid of class tensions.

Weltanschauungskrieg: War of ideologies, the Nazi term for the war in the East as one conducted between two radically opposed world views, one of which would have to be totally annihilated before victory is achieved.

Organisations mentioned in the text (initial in brackets are those of author)

Abwehr, Military Intelligence (JN)
Aktion T-4 (MB)
AZR, Forced Labour Reich (WW)
Catholic Centre Party (PW, HGS)
Community Patients' Transport Service (MB)
Department for Twin and Hereditary Research (PW)
Deutsches Frauenwerk, DFW, German Women's Enterprise (JS)
Fascist Confederation of Industrial Labour (KJS)
Four Year Plan (UH, GA)
Free Corps (JN)
Generalgouvernement (GA, WW, MB)
Generalplan Ost (GA)
German Council of the Four Year Plan (GA)
German Labour Front, DAF (UH, AB, KJS)
German National Peoples' Party (HGS)
German Research Council (GA)
German Womanhood Association
German Women's Association
German Workers' Party (AB)
Gobineau Society (PW)
Hereditary Health Centre (MB)
Hitler Youth (AB, JS, OB)
Honour Cross of the German Mother (JS)
Hygiene Institute of the *Waffen*-SS (PW)
Institute for Deutsch Ostarbeit (GA)
Jewish Winter Aid (AB)
Kaiser Wilhelm Institute for Anthropology, Human Heredity and Eugenics (PW)
Law for the Combating of Gypsies, Travellers and the Workshy, 1926 (WW)

Law for the Confiscation of the Property of Enemies of the State and
   Nation (WW)
Law for the Protection of German Blood and Honour (AB)
Law for the Prevention of Hereditarily Diseased Progeny (MB)
Law for the Restoration of the Professional Civil Service (WW)
League of German Maidens
League for the Protection of Motherhood and Social Reform (PW)
Lebensraum (AB)
Main Trustees for the East (GA)
Marriage Health Law (WW)
Marriage Law, 1938 (JS)
Munich Racial Hygiene Society (PW)
National People's Party (JN)
National Socialist People's Welfare, NSV (AB)
National Socialist Workers' Party, NSDAP (UH, AB, WW)
NS-Frauenschaft, NSF, Nazi Women's Group (JS)
NSV (JN)
NS-Womanhood
Nuremberg Doctors' Trial (PW)
Nuremberg Laws, 1935 (PW, AB, WW, HGS)
Racial Hygiene Society (PW)
Racial Hygienic Research Bureau (WW)
Racial Political Office (*Rassepolitisches Amt*) (PW, WW)
Reich Central Office for the Combating of Gypsy Nuisance
Reich Central Office for the Combating of Homosexuality and Abortion
   (HGS)
Reich Commissariat for the Strengthening of Ethnic Germandom (GA)
Reich Committee for Economic Affairs (GA)
Reich Committee for the Scientific Registration of Serious Hereditary
   and Congenital Illnesses (MB)
Reich Labour Service (OB)
Reich Crystal Night (GA)
Reich Mother Service
Reich Office for Area Planning (GA)
Reichslandbund (JN)
Reichswehr (AB)
SA (UH, PW)
SAKK (JN)
Scientific-Humanitarian Committee, WhK (HGS)

SD, Nazi Security Service (JN)
socialist labour movement (UH)
`Sopade' (UH)
SPD (UH, HGS)
SS Marriage Order (JN)
SS Race and Settlement Main Office
Strength through Joy (UH, AB)
Travellers' Department of the Bavarian Regional Criminal Police (VW)
Vaterlandpartei (PW)
Vitalrasse
völkisch (UH)
Volksgemeinschaft (AB)
Wannsee Conference (OB)
Wehrmacht (UH, OB)
Well of Life association
Winter Aid Programme (JN)
Young Plan (JN)

LIST OF CONTRIBUTORS

Götz Aly is a freelance journalist and historian living in Berlin. He is the author of several studies of the Nazi 'euthanasia' programme and the 'Final Solution', published in the series that he also edits, *Beiträge zur nationalsozialistische Sozial- und Gesundheitspolitik*. His books include (with Karl-Heinz Roth) *Die restlose Erfassung. Volkszählen, Identifizieren, Aussondern im Nationalsozialismus* (Berlin, 1984), *Aktion T-4, 1939–1945* (Berlin, 1987) (with Susanne Heim) *Vordenker der Vernichtung* (Berlin, 1991); (with Peter Chroustand Christian Pross) *Cleansing the Fatherland. Nazi Medicine and Racial Hygiene* (Baltimore and London (1994); *'Endlösung', Volkerverschie bung und der mord an den Europäischen Juden* (Frankfurt, 1995).

Avraham Barkai is a Research Fellow with the Institute for German History, University of Tel Aviv. His books include *Das Wirtschaftssystem des Nationalsozialismus* (Frankfurt, 1988), which has recently appeared in English as *Nazi Economics: Ideology, Theory, and Policy* (Oxford, 1990), and *From Boycott to Annihilation: The Economic Struggle of German Jews, 1933–1943* (Hanover, 1990).

Omer Bartov is Professor of History at Rutgers University and author of *The Eastern Front, 1941–1945: German Troops and the Barbarisation of Warfare* (London and New York, 1986) *Hitler's Army: Soldiers, Nazis, and War in the Third Reich* (Oxford and New York, 1991); and of *Murder in our Midst* (Oxford and New York, 1996).

Michael Burleigh is Distinguished Research Professor in Modern History at the University of Wales, Cardiff. His books include *Germany Turns Eastwards: A Study of 'Ostforschung' in the Third Reich* (Cambridge, 1988); (with Wolfgang Wippermann), *The Racial State: Germany 1933–1945* (Cambridge, 1991); and *Death and Deliverance: 'Euthanasia' in Germany, 1900–1945* (Cambridge, 1994). He wrote and researched 'Selling Murder' (Domino Films/Channel 4) on Nazi propaganda for the 'euthanasia' programme which has been shown in twenty countries and for which he won the 1991 British Film Institute Award for Archival Achievement. He was Programme Consultant to 'Master Race' in the BBC People's Century series.

Ulrich Herbert is Professor of History at the University of Freiburg. His books include *Fremdarbeiter. Politik und Praxis des 'Ausländer-Einsatzes' in der Kriegswirtschaft des Dritten Reiches* (Berlin and Bonn, 1985) which will shortly be published by Cambridge University Press; *A History of Foreign Labour in Germany* (London, 1990); *Arbeit, Volkstum, Weltanschauung* (Frankfurt, 1995) and *Best. Biographische Studien über Radikalismus, Weltanschauung und Vernunft* (Bonn, 1966).

Jeremy Noakes is Professor of History at the University of Exeter. He is the author of numerous articles on the Third Reich and of *The Nazi Party in Lower Saxony* (Oxford, 1971), *Government, Party and People in Nazi Germany* (Exeter, 1980), and (with G. Pridham) of *Nazism, 1919–1945. A Documentary Reader*, 3 vols (Exeter, 1986–9).

Klaus-Jörg Siegfried is an historian and head of the town archives in Wolfsburg. His books include *Universalismus und Faschismus. Das Gesellschaftsbild Othmar Spanns* (Vienna, 1974), *Rustungsproduktion und Zwangsarbeit im Volkswagenwerk, 1939–1945* (Frankfurt am Main, 1986) and *Das Leben der Zwangsarbeiter im Volkswagenwerk, 1939–1945* (Frankfurt am Main, 1988).

Jill Stephenson is a Reader in History at the University of Edinburgh. Her publications on women in twentieth-century Germany include *Women in Nazi Society* (London and New York, 1975) and *The Nazi Organisation of Women* (London and New York, 1981), and numerous essays and articles published between 1971–1992. Since 1985 she has also published essays and articles on her current research interest, society in Wurttemberg during the Second World War. She is joint editor of *German History: The Journal of the German History Society*.

Hans-Georg Stümke is a freelance writer and historian living in Hamburg. His books include (with Rudi Finkler), *Rosa Winkel, Rosa Listen. Homosexuelle und 'Gesundes Volksempfinden' von Auschwitz bis Heute* (Hamburg, 1981) and *Homosexuelle in Deutschland. Eine politische Geschichte* (Munich, 1989).

Paul Weindling is a Senior Research Officer at the Wellcome Unit for the

History of Medicine, University of Oxford. His books include *Darwinism and Social Darwinism in Imperial Germany* (Stuttgart, 1989), *Health, Race and German Politics Between National Unification and Nazism, 1870–1945* (Cambridge, 1989). He has edited *The Social History of Occupational Health* (London, 1985) and *International Health Organisations and Movements 1918–1939* (Cambridge, 1995). He is joint editor of *Social History of Medicine. The Journal of the Society for the Social History of Medicine.*

Wolfgang Wippermann is a Professor of Modern History at the Freie Universität Berlin. His books include *Europaische Faschismus im Vergleich, 1922–1988* (Frankfurt am Main, 1983), *Faschismustheorien* (5th edn, Darmstadt, 1988), *Das Leben in Frankfurt in der NS Zeit* (Frankfurt am Main, 1986), vols 1–4, *Der Deutsche 'Drang nach Osten'* (Darmstadt, 1981) and (with Michael Burleigh) *The Racial State: Germany, 1933–1945* (Cambridge, 1991).

INDEX

ILLUSTRATION ACKNOWLEDGEMENTS

The illustrations in the plate section have been supplied or reproduced by kind permission of the following: Bayerische Staatsbibliothek, München 24; Berlin Document Center 9; Collection Bouqueret 23; Hessisches Hauptstaatsarchiv 2, 12, 13, 14, 15, 16, 17; Public Record Office, Kew 5; Stadt Archiv, Wolfsburg 4; Transit Buchverlag, Berlin 25; Ullstein Bilderdienst 6, 8, 19, 20, 21; US Army Centre of Military History 18.

The publishers have made every effort to clear all permissions, but in certain cases this has not been possible and the publishers would like to apologise for any inconvenience this may cause.

LEONARDO'S
LEGACY

LEONARDO'S LEGACY

HOW
DA VINCI
REIMAGINED
THE WORLD

STEFAN KLEIN

TRANSLATED BY SHELLEY FRISCH

DA CAPO PRESS
A Member of the Perseus Books Group

Designed by Pauline Brown
Set in 12.5 point Arno Pro by The Perseus Books Group

Library of Congress Cataloging-in-Publication Data
Klein, Stefan, 1965–
  [Vermächtnis, oder, Wie Leonardo die Welt neu erfand. English]
  Leonardo's legacy : how Da Vinci reimagined the world / Stefan Klein ; translated by Shelley Frisch.
     p. cm.
  Originally published: Frankfurt am Main : S. Fischer Verlag GmbH, 2008.
  Includes bibliographical references and index.
  ISBN 978-0-306-81825-7 (alk. paper)
  1. Leonardo, da Vinci, 1452–1519. 2. Artists—Italy—Biography. 3. Inventors—Italy—Biography.
4. Renaissance—Italy—Biography. I. Title. II. Title: How Da Vinci reimagined the world.
  N6923.L33K5413 2010
  709.2—dc22
  [B]
                                                                                    2010000130

Published by Da Capo Press
A Member of the Perseus Books Group
www.dacapopress.com

First Da Capo Press edition 2010
First Da Capo Press paperback edition 2011
First published in Germany in 2008 by S. Fischer Verlag GmbH, Frankfurt am Main

PB ISBN: 978-0-306-82008-3
E-Book ISBN: 978-0-306-81903-2

Da Capo Press books are available at special discounts for bulk purchases in the U.S. by corporations, institutions, and other organizations. For more information, please contact the Special Markets Department at the Perseus Books Group, 2300 Chestnut Street, Suite 200, Philadelphia, PA 19103, or call (800) 810-4145, ext. 5000, or e-mail special.markets@perseusbooks.com.

10 9 8 7 6 5 4 3 2

For Irene

CONTENTS

LEONARDO'S
LEGACY

Portrait of Leonardo

INTRODUCTION:
The Mystery of
the Ten Thousand Pages

THE YEAR WAS 1520, A young nobleman and his entourage were leaving the castle of the French king in Amboise. They crossed over the Loire, rode along the river, then headed into forests in the south. The nobleman, Francesco Melzi, had with him a piece of luggage that was not especially large, but so heavy that two men were needed to move it. Even so, Melzi did not let this chest out of his sight for a single moment during the week it took him to travel back to Italy. Once in Milan, the group headed east. After an additional day of travel, the travelers reached a plateau over the town of Vapio d'Adda at the foot of the Alps, where the young man dismounted at his family's majestic country estate. The chest was brought to an upper floor, and Melzi watched over it there for the next fifty years.

He was often visited by envoys from the ruling houses of Italy, who had heard about the unique treasure Melzi had in his possession. He sent them away. Had he served his master faithfully for more than a decade only to sell his work to the highest bidder? Leonardo da Vinci had died on May 2, 1519, at the court of François I of France, but

Melzi's affection for him was stronger than ever. "He was like the best of fathers to me," he had written from Amboise to Leonardo's half brothers, and vowed that "as long as I have breath in my body I will grieve for him. . . . Each of us must mourn the death of this man, because nature will never have the power to create another like him."[1]

Melzi began to sift through his inheritance. Leonardo had bequeathed him about ten thousand pages—his entire vast oeuvre apart from the paintings. The young nobleman's fortune afforded him the leisure to dedicate himself wholly to his mentor's bequest, though he soon realized that one lifetime would not be enough to put this estate in order. He hired two secretaries and tried to dictate at least some of Leonardo's ideas to them. He also painted the way the master had taught him. For guests who wanted to look rather than buy, he was happy to grant access to the inner sanctum of the villa—the room in which Leonardo had once lived and to which his creations had now returned.

Huge sheets of paper were piled up there, along with notepads smaller than the palm of the hand, notebooks bound in leather by Leonardo himself, and an immense quantity of loose papers of all sizes. These were far more than mere jottings by an extraordinary artist; they encapsulated his entire life—the unparalleled ascent of an illegitimate day laborer's son to a man courted by the rulers of Italy, who in his final years chose the friendship of the king of France, the path of a boy who had no higher education but would go down in history as the most famous painter of all time, and at the same time as a trailblazer in science. We cannot tell whether any visitor studied Melzi's collection the way it deserved to be studied; reading Leonardo's mirror writing is no easy task. But anyone who went to the effort of reading the lines from right to left, and the notebooks from back to front, could learn about Leonardo's military expeditions with the dreaded Cesare Borgia, captain general of the papal army, his adventurous escapes, and his trouble with the pope. Leonardo da Vinci had experienced successes and failures, fear for his livelihood, and boundless luxury; he had been both despised and worshiped.

His sketches offered a vision of a distant future in which people would understand the forces of nature and work with machines. There were flying machines, formidable catapults, automatons in human form, and tunneled-through mountains. Turning a single page would transport visitors to this collection to a very different, though no less fantastic, world. Leonardo used chalk and pen to draw the inside of a human heart and a fetus growing in a womb. Other drawings showed aerial views of Italian landscapes and cities—the way we might see them from an airplane today.

Melzi's collection afforded unique insights into the workings of Leonardo's mind. Ideas and dreams were laid out on paper; prophecies and a philosophy of life, theories about the origin of the world, plans for books; Leonardo had even written out shopping lists. He seems to have carried his notebooks fastened to his belt. In any case, he must have always had them with him to make sure that no idea would go unrecorded. It is rare indeed for an individual to keep such a detailed account of the dictates of his mind. Whoever understood Leonardo's notes could follow his train of thought on his flights of fancy and was privy to his doubts and contradictions. The notes document the interior monologue of a lonely man, his fear of not living up to his own expectations, and his awareness of the price of fame: "When the fig-tree stood without fruit no one looked at it. Wishing by producing this fruit to be praised by men, it was bent and broken by them."[2] The chest Melzi had brought from France offered nothing less than a glimpse inside Leonardo's brain.

But Melzi's prized possession is no longer intact. When Leonardo's star pupil died of old age in 1570, his son Orazio proved indifferent

One of the 10,000 pages: Reflections on the flight of birds to his father's passion. He let the plunderers have at the collection. The family's private tutor sent thirteen stolen volumes to the grand duke of Tuscany. A huge bundle went to a sculptor named Pompeo Leoni, who in turn tried to bring order to the chaos by attacking Leonardo's work with scissors and paste. If Leoni failed to see a connection between individual sketches on a given page, he simply cut them apart. He pasted the fragments onto sheets of paper, then bound and sold them. Leonardo's tattered and torn legacy began to sprinkle across the libraries of Europe like confetti. A large part of the legacy is gone. About half of Melzi's roughly ten thousand pages went missing. Studying the rest affords ample opportunity to admire the master's spectacular drawings, but the connections have been severed, and the spirit of Leonardo is no longer evident.

Even the plunderers did not diminish Leonardo's posthumous fame; if anything, the gaps in Leonardo's story created openings for myths. There are countless artists whose works have been preserved perfectly and are accessible to all, yet their names live on for no more than a few specialists. Leonardo, by contrast, whose works on public display number fewer than two dozen, continues to fascinate millions, half a millennium after his death.

The public is drawn to his works of art, of course, but even more to the man who created them. How could one individual fuse within himself what appeared to be knowledge of the entire world—and translate this knowledge into an unparalleled oeuvre? How was he able to create epoch-making paintings—and at the same time immerse himself in designing flying machines, robots, and all kinds of other devices and in contemplating a broad range of scientific questions? It seems miraculous that any one person could make his mark in so many areas in the course of a lifetime.

In 1550, his first biographer, the Tuscan painter and architect Giorgio Vasari, called Leonardo "divinely inspired."[3] The more time went by, the harder it was to understand how a man of the fifteenth century could have produced all these works. When the first facsimiles of Leonardo's scattered sketches were made available to the public toward the end of the nineteenth century, Leonardo's stature grew immensely, and he became the epitome of the "universal genius." Even Sigmund Freud, the father of psychoanalysis, shared the romantic sentiment that Leonardo was a man far ahead of his time: The artist, he declared, was like a man who awoke too early in the darkness, while all others were still asleep. Few admirers of the *Mona Lisa, The Last Supper*, and the rarely displayed drawings would disagree.

Additional documents by and about Leonardo, the son of Ser Piero from Vinci, bolstered his legendary status. His notes and the statements of contemporaries portrayed him as a highly contradictory and extravagant character. He proudly noted that in contrast to sculptors, he did not have to dirty his hands when he painted—yet he dissected dozens of decaying corpses. He upheld high moral values as a vegetarian and a pacifist—while designing weapons of mass destruction for bloodthirsty tyrants. He adopted a critical stance in matters of religion and was even called a heretic, yet his paintings suggest profound devoutness, and near the end of his life, he even joined a religious order.

While the artists of his era wore simple craftsman's garb, he dressed in a knee-length pink cloak and had jewel-studded rings on his fingers. A contemporary, Anonimo Gaddiano, reported that "his beard came down to the middle of his breast and was well-combed and curled."[4] A portrait (probably by Melzi) shows Leonardo as a man in the prime of life, with perfectly proportioned features and laugh lines at the corners of his eyes (see image at the beginning of this chapter). He was said to be extremely attractive and sophisticated, have a lovely singing voice, and play the lute. But some passages in his notes suggest that he was terribly lonely.

The fact that Leonardo made it difficult for us to understand him only heightens his allure. The more enigmatic an individual, the greater the temptation to fill in the blanks with fantasies. Leonardo leads us to indulge in dreams. Just as people who have recently fallen in love tend to see their own ideals in the object of their affections, Leonardo functions as a mirror of our own desires. We revere his greatness of mind, his success—and his immortality. In describing the lasting lure of Leonardo da Vinci, the French poet Paul Valéry wrote in 1894 that what remains of a person are the dreams we associate with his name.

But Leonardo has much more to offer us today than just a dream. The true significance of his achievements has become more fully apparent to us in recent years, now that researchers have devoted several decades to reviewing the pages and folios from Melzi's villa and reassembling the fragments of Leonardo's notebooks that were scattered throughout Europe and America. The spectacular discovery of a long-lost codex also shed new light on Leonardo's oeuvre. Leonardo is now finally taken seriously not just as an artist, but also as an explorer of our world. In recent years, experts in every conceivable field have begun to focus their interest on his sketches and writings. In the past, scholars who studied Leonardo were primarily art historians, who typically found many of his designs and ideas difficult to fathom. When heart surgeons, physicists, and engineers now look at these same projects from the perspectives of their respective fields, they are amazed at what they find.

Perspectives of these kinds form the basis for this book. It is not intended as a standard biography of a masterful artist as much as an attempt to get inside the mind of one of the most extraordinary individuals who ever lived—and to see the world through his eyes. The unique documentation provided by his notebooks enables us to track the development of his ideas. Nearly five hundred years after his death, we are able for the first time to read and understand these notes as they were conceived—and to learn from Leonardo.

His most precious legacy turns out to be neither the twenty-one paintings nor the approximately one hundred thousand drawings and sketches he left behind, but rather his creation of a new way of thinking, which can serve as a source of inspiration today more than ever.

His approach enabled him to find answers in an era in which old certainties had been thrown into question and people had to cope with unforeseen new problems—just as we do today. Leonardo was far more than an outstanding artist. In exploring the world around him, he invented it anew.

I

THE GAZE

DARSHAN IS THE NAME INDIAN philosophy gives to visions of the divine on earth. Meeting a guru can be *darshan*, but generally it entails an encounter with an idol. Devout Hindus undertake long journeys to experience *darshan*. When they reach their destination, they wend their way through often labyrinthine temples and push past thousands of other pilgrims into a cramped, gloomy inner sanctum, where they finally see the idol with their own eyes.

I couldn't help but think of *darshan*, the destination of all pilgrimages, when I visited the Louvre to do research for this book. The trail to the *Mona Lisa* also leads through winding corridors, through the underworld. In the pyramids of the Louvre, throngs of museum visitors descend into a gigantic hall, where escalators suck in the masses and convey them back up past all manner of mezzanines and colonnades. Then they have to walk through a long gallery, past dozens of masterpieces of Italian art, each of which would merit careful examination. Even so, nearly all visitors make a beeline for their goal, guided by signs in fifteen languages.

The visage of the Mona Lisa

I had come to Paris because the Louvre has more paintings by Leonardo on display than anywhere else in the world. The *Mona Lisa* tempted me least of all. I felt as though I'd seen her face far too often already—on prints, posters, coffee cups, with and without a mustache. But I couldn't tear myself away from it. Out of the corner of my eye I noticed that I could have had *The Virgin of the Rocks*, *The Virgin and Child with St. Anne*, and *St. John the Baptist* virtually all to myself. Hardly anyone stopped to look at these important works by Leonardo.

Without giving the matter much more thought, I joined the stream of people in the center of the gallery heading into one of the largest halls of this former royal palace. It was here that Napoleon III once held his state meetings. Today a gigantic wall divides the back third of the hall; anyone who has visited a Greek Orthodox cathedral will be reminded of the ikonostasis, the flower-bedecked partition that separates the common worshipers from the sanctuary. The wall in the Louvre, though, tall and wide enough to accommodate a small apartment building, features a single display case made of bulletproof glass and an oak table about the size of an altar.

No one gets close. Upon entering the hall, people have to squeeze into a funnel-shaped cordoned area with hundreds of other visitors and hope for some of the fortunate few way up front to leave the enclosed area so that others can move up. Even when you finally make it all the way up, you are still about thirty feet from the display case, held back by two more insurmountable cordons and a row of security guards, but you can still pick out a smiling, rather full woman's face behind the glass. The second striking feature is those brightly lit hands, which the woman in the portrait holds crossed in front of her black dress. Many tourists want to capture this image with their cameras, but the guards will not hear of it. When they see flashbulbs go off, they pounce on the offenders with a cry of "No photo!" and order them to leave.

In front of the Mona Lisa

For the most part, though, the hall is absolutely silent, aside from hushed assertions in every imaginable European and Asian language that Mona Lisa is looking right at *them*, that her smile grows more intense as they stare at it. Behind me, I heard a German visitor murmur in a broad Franconian dialect that this museum was very well organized. Audio guides explain the masterpiece to tourists wearing earphones.

Awestruck visitors stand riveted in front of the display case. I suddenly had the feeling that I was experiencing something quite special as well. But why? Under normal lighting, the onlookers tend to see themselves reflected in the mirroring bulletproof glass. Only when the sun in the Parisian sky is at just the right angle over the glass ceiling can they recognize the finer points in Mona Lisa's features. A careful look reveals how painstakingly Leonardo must have calculated each individual effect in this painting. The shadow play around the eyes, for instance, is easy to discern even from a great distance, and makes the gaze of the young woman look deeply penetrating. But the elusive portrait does not yield much more even under optimal lighting conditions. The face on the painting, which is just under thirty inches high, is not even life-size, and the splendors of the landscape in the background cannot even begin to be appreciated from this distance. Even so, the *Mona Lisa* is a commanding presence in her glass case.

What makes this picture so extraordinary that it attracts more than five million visitors every year? Why did this painting, catalogued with Louvre inventory number 779, the portrait of a Florentine housewife of no more than average beauty, become the most famous artwork in the world?

The hordes in the Louvre cannot really study Leonardo's artwork; with all the pushing and shoving, they can barely catch an unhurried glimpse of it. Perhaps the effect of the pilgrimage to the *Mona Lisa* is far more direct. Anyone who has made the trip to the French capital and dealt with the escalators and the lines in the museum and finally comes face-to-face with the *Mona Lisa*, the best-known painting in the world, is witness to the fact that an original of all the *Mona Lisa*s on advertisements, postcards, and screensavers really does exist. Right there is the poplar panel that Leonardo held in his own hands. He worked on it for more than four years, then chose not to part with it for the remaining ten years of his life. The visitor to the Louvre is up close to an object that Leonardo took along on his travels from Florence to Rome, from Rome to Milan, and then to the French court. It seems beside the point that it is easier to make out the fine details of Leonardo's painting on any halfway decent print.

Darshan is not an aesthetic treat: the holy statues, which devout Hindus endure days of train travel to see, are often little more than roughly hewn stones. The Greek Orthodox never gain a full view of their miracle-working icons; a covering of hammered silver conceals the bodies of Jesus and Mary. But precisely because the devout cannot describe why the image is so compelling, it seems infinitely worthy of reverence. *Darshan* is an encounter with mystery.

The *Mona Lisa* is an attraction *because* it is the *Mona Lisa*. We are incapable of viewing this painting as just a picture. Everyone in the Louvre has heard about this lady's inscrutable smile. She sometimes looks as though she is peering down at the whole business somewhat mockingly. And the longer you gaze at her, the more you wonder why she is smiling—if she is—where she is sitting, and, above all, who she is. So many myths have sprung up around each individual enigma that the legends about the *Mona Lisa* have come to seem even more remarkable than the painting itself.

But how did the *Mona Lisa* become *the Mona Lisa?* Immersing yourself in the literature about this painting feels like roaming through a world of fantasy. One of the first—and still most impressive—of the many testaments to its magic was written by the British art critic Walter Pater in 1869, who regarded the *Mona Lisa* as the archetype of femininity, a force that preceded creation and would live well beyond it. Mona Lisa's eyelids may look "a little weary," but it is no wonder:

> *She is older than the rocks among which she sits;*
> *Like the vampire,*
> *She has been dead many times,*
> *And learned the secrets of the grave;*
> *And has been a diver in the deep seas,*
> *And keeps their fallen day about her*
> *And trafficked for strange webs with Eastern merchants;*
> *And, as Leda, was the mother of Helen of Troy,*
> *And, as St. Anne,*
> *Was the mother of Mary;*
> *And all this has been to her but as the sound of lyres and flutes,*
> *And lives*
> *Only in the delicacy*
> *With which it has moulded the changing lineaments,*
> *And tinged the eyelids and the hands*[1]

Less lofty commentators have focused on finding out whose face was on the picture. There is still disagreement on this issue today. Most experts now concur with Leonardo's first biographer, Giorgio Vasari, that a Florentine woman named Lisa Gherardini posed for it. Gherardini's husband, a silk merchant named Francesco del Giocondo, probably commissioned the work to celebrate the imminent birth of their son Andrea. If that is the case, the *Mona Lisa* is the portrait of a pregnant woman.

But Leonardo never parted with this painting. And no one knows how the painting was transformed during the years Leonardo spent reworking it. Some researchers think that Leonardo kept the painting for himself because after all the changes he made, Lisa Gherardini was barely recognizable on it. The Italian literary scholar Carlo Vecce claims that the Mona Lisa we see today was a courtesan, namely Isabella Gualanda, whose clientele was drawn from the upper echelons of society while Leonardo was living in Rome. When a rich patron commissioned a portrait of this woman, the story goes, Leonardo simply recycled the unfinished painting of Lisa Gherardini. While it is certainly possible, the idea that this much-admired painting actually portrays a high-class prostitute has not been substantiated.[2] To his credit, Vecce sticks quite close to the historical sources; he is the author of the most detailed Leonardo biography to date.[3]

Lillian Schwartz, a New York artist, came up with an even bolder theory, which became the subject of a cover story in *Scientific American* in 1995.[4] Using image editing software, she concluded that Leonardo and Mona Lisa were one and the same person. As the Tuscans were fond of saying in Leonardo's era: "Every painter paints himself." And this, in Schwartz's view, is precisely what Leonardo did. When he worked on the unfinished painting for years without a sitter, he used his own face as a model.

Turin self-portrait

Schwartz conducted a computer analysis of the most famous of all of Leonardo's self-portraits, the original of which is a red chalk drawing now housed in Turin. The artist is an old man. Flowing hair and beard frame his face, which appears deeply skeptical and even a bit mocking. The corners of his mouth are turned down, and he has prominent cheekbones. His face is lined with wrinkles across his forehead, at the corners of his eyes, and the area extending from his nostrils to the outer edges of his lips. The upper lip is thin, little more than a line, as though there were no incisors beneath it. The deep-set eyes are piercing, but the barely visible pupils are not trained on the viewer; they are fixed on a point somewhere in the distance.

The expressions on these two pictures could hardly be more different. Moreover, Mona Lisa is looking to the left, and the old man to the right. But when Schwartz flipped the self-portrait and superimposed the two images, they fit exactly. The distance between the eyes, the size of the mouth, even the cheekbones of the old man and the young woman are identical. The deviations amount to less than 2 percent. And the two pictures feature the exact same prominent brow, which protrudes in a manner that is typically male. Schwartz claims that Leonardo even encrypted a clue that he was portraying himself: Along the upper edge of Mona Lisa's black bodice, the artist drew countless knotted cloverleaf patterns in a wickerwork design. The Italian word for wickerwork—*vinco*—is nearly identical to the name of Leonardo's birthplace.

Leonardo was a master of concealment; that much is certain. He loved entertaining people with fanciful tales and puzzles, and there are dozens of clever wordplays and picture puzzles tucked away in his manuscripts. Now and then he also encoded notes about his inventions and plans for the future to shield them from prying eyes. But first and foremost he sought to conceal *himself* from his fellow man. On the rare occasions that he made reference to his feelings and desires on the six thousand extant pages of his diaries, he obscured his identity by substituting animals for people, for instance, and assuming the role of a mythical figure.

Even so, art historians consider Lillian Schwartz's theory implausible. They dismiss the idea that the portrait of the *Mona Lisa* is that of Leonardo himself, and point out the lack of historical evidence for this theory. The wordplay with the knots proves nothing, they contend, and the fact that the faces fit together so well simply reflects a similarity of artistic technique.

Perhaps Schwartz was just concocting an amusing game involving a painter and his most famous model—two larger-than-life figures who make it difficult for us to distinguish reality from invention. But neither Schwartz nor her critics can explain why it is that in surveys today more than 85 percent of people, when asked to name a famous work of art, respond with the *Mona Lisa*.[5] (In second place is Van Gogh's *Sunflowers* series, named by a mere 4 percent of respondents.) In religious portraits, a story of a miracle invariably precedes veneration of a subject's artistic representation. But no one has claimed that Mona Lisa, the subject of the portrait to end all portraits, performed miracles. So it must be Leonardo's special way of painting that is responsible for the extraordinary fascination that this work of art holds for us.

THE ARTIST AS NEUROSCIENTIST

One of the first to marvel at the *Mona Lisa* was Raphael. This painter, whom we today associate primarily with lovely pictures of the Virgin Mary, must have had access to Leonardo's workshop in Florence. In any case, the Louvre has a document the size of a sheet of paper on which Raphael drew the unfinished *Mona Lisa* with quick strokes of the pen. The woman portrayed here displays the features as we know them today, but she is unsmiling. Her face seems narrower, more feminine, and younger, and there is no background landscape. This was evidently how Leonardo's painting looked in about 1504.

Raphael's impressions from Leonardo's studio were fresh in his mind when he painted the *Lady with a Unicorn* and the *Portrait of Maddalena Doni*. Both subjects are seated on a balcony in front of an open landscape. Their left shoulders are rotated toward their viewers, and

Raphael, Lady with a Unicorn

their overall pose is strikingly similar to the *Mona Lisa*, right down to the positions of their hands. (This unique pose was Leonardo's invention and is found nowhere else in the art of the period.[6]) Raphael's technique is flawless; although he was barely over twenty at the time, he was already regarded as a great master. In contrast to Mona Lisa, the fair-haired lady with the unicorn is a beauty by today's standards. If she were to step out of the picture frame and walk down the street, she would be sure to collect admiring glances.

Nonetheless, the woman with the mythical beast on her lap has never achieved worldwide fame. If you stand in front of Raphael's picture, you soon notice that this painting is far less compelling than its model. The difference goes beyond the magic of the names *Mona Lisa* and Leonardo. The lady with the unicorn is certainly beautiful and the skill of her creator estimable, but the painting fails to move us.

The effect of the *Mona Lisa* can be summed up in two words: She lives. The British art historian Martin Kemp, a Leonardo expert, has provided this apt description of how her face engages her spectators: "She reacts to us, and we cannot but react to her. Leonardo is playing upon one of our most basic human instincts—our irresistible tendency to read the facial signs of character and expression in everyone we meet. We are all intuitive physiognomists at heart. No matter how many times our expectation of character on the basis of facial signs may be proved false, we cannot stop ourselves doing it."[7]

Leonardo himself considered it his chief goal to arouse feelings in spectators. Artists, he said, are "the grandsons unto God," because they could "dismay folk by hellish fictions" if they so desired.[8] But how can a dead piece of canvas stir emotions? Leonardo contended that spectators unconsciously project themselves onto the figures on the picture, not as a mere mental exercise—or even consciously—but in a direct fashion that allows them to experience the emotions of the people on the canvas within their own bodies. Smiling and yawning are known to be contagious because we unintentionally imitate the movements of others; we can also suffer inner torment just by seeing someone wracked with pain.

Leon Battista Alberti, a guiding intellectual force in Renaissance art, had written an influential book on painting back in 1435 that urged artists to make the most of this effect. Leonardo concurred: "The painter's most important consideration is for the movement of each figure to express its state of mind—desire, disdain, anger, sympathy, and so forth. . . . Otherwise art is not good."[9] And if the work is successful, it triggers physical manifestations in the spectator: "If the picture depicts horror, fear, flight, sorrow, weeping and lament, or enjoyment, pleasure, laughter, or similar conditions, the minds of those who regard it should make their limbs move in such a way as to make the spectator feel that he is in the same situations as the figures on the picture."[10]

In the past few years, brain research has proved that this seemingly implausible idea really does hold true. Neurophysiologists have even isolated specific brain cells that enable us to empathize with other people while we observe them. Because these neurons mirror the motions of others within our own bodies, they are called mirror neurons. These neurons make our facial muscles break into a smile when we see a happy person. The brain then interprets these muscle movements as an expression of our own pleasure—and actually makes us experience good feelings.[11]

Leonardo structured his pictures accordingly nearly half a millennium ago without the benefit of these modern neuropsychological insights. "Most painters are also neurologists," explains London scientist Semir Zeki, an expert in the neurobiology of vision. "They are those who have experimented upon and, without ever realizing it, understood something about the organization of the visual brain."[12]

NOSES FROM THE CONSTRUCTION KIT

How are facial expressions and human emotions connected? Leonardo spent a great deal of time pondering this question. Only a painter who knows the subtlest variations in facial expressions can portray them convincingly enough to effect an emotional impact on the viewer.

Leonardo's notebooks feature the full spectrum of faces, in virtually every shape and expression. Vasari reports that Leonardo often followed a person around for an entire day on the street if he had a striking appearance. Thus the study of the notebooks becomes a journey through the gamut of the human countenance. There are young women and old men, with faces ranging from the aristocratic to the uncouth. We see joy, devotion, pride, and bitterness. Some heads are fully realized, with light and shadow; others are hastily sketched with just a few strokes of the pen. Still others have extremely distorted features, like caricatures, as though Leonardo was aiming to grasp certain facial expressions by exaggerating them.

Elsewhere we find a whole catalogue of human noses. Leonardo created a system to classify the many shapes of noses, from the aquiline to the bulbous: First they were sorted by basic types, such as straight or rounded, second by how they are curved, both above and below the center, and whether these curves were convex or concave—or neither. Using variables of these kinds, he explained, the painter could not only form a mental image of an unknown face, but also create new faces from a set of component parts.[13]

Above all, Leonardo wanted to know how facial expressions are formed. He dissected the heads of cadavers to expose the facial muscles and found that the lips were actually muscles that compress the mouth, while lateral muscles draw back to widen it when we laugh. He identified the cranial bones where these muscles begin and how the skin of the face alters its shape as they move. He even went so far as to ascertain the interplay of these muscles with the brain, discovering nerves that guide muscle movements and thus bring about the expression of feelings.[14]

No other artist of his era came close to penetrating this deeply into the mysteries of human nature. The knowledge Leonardo gained enabled him to juggle the features of Mona Lisa and the feelings of her viewers so masterfully. For example, the features of the young woman are not symmetrical: the left corner of her mouth is higher than the

Grotesque heads

right, and the shadow above her left eye is more pronounced. Each side conveys a different mood. If you cover the left half of Mona Lisa's face, she seems serious, but the other side displays a distinct smile.

Facial expressions often contain subtle asymmetries of this kind because the brain is divided into two hemispheres that target the two sides of the body in mirror image. The left side of the brain controls the muscles of the right side of the face, while the right side of the brain is in charge of facial expressions on the left. And because the right hemisphere is more directly responsible than its counterpart for processing emotions, feelings are usually expressed more prominently on the left side of the face. We normally fail to register this difference because we look at faces as a whole. Experiments conducted during the past few years have clearly established these connections.[15]

But Leonardo was keenly aware of these subtle effects, and he employed them to make Mona Lisa's face appear inscrutable by exaggerating the natural differences between the two sides of the face, thus making the viewer wonder what the young woman might be thinking or feeling. As Paul Ekman and J. C. Hager have demonstrated, facial asymmetry becomes more pronounced when a person masks annoyance with a smile or otherwise feigns feelings. What does Mona Lisa wish to hide from us?[16]

Leonardo did all he could to heighten the mystery. Even if each side of the face is considered independently, the lack of sharp outlines makes it difficult to figure out what it expresses, and the transitions between the various parts of the face and between light and shadow are blurred. Where we expect the skin of Mona Lisa to be, we are actually seeing only unbounded patches of color; from the red on her cheeks to the olive-green on her chin, the shades blend without our being aware of it. This effect, known as *sfumato*, makes us think that the face is moving in relation to us; actually, though, it is our own gaze that does not linger in any one place, because Leonardo does not offer it anywhere to alight.[17]

Leonardo evidently knew which subtle deviations would convey a very different impression. A slight modification of the area around the mouth is enough to make a happy face look sad—and vice versa. The Russian-American visual neuroscientist Leonid Kontsevich produced metamorphoses of this kind by placing a blurring filter of "random visual noise" over Mona Lisa's mouth on a computer monitor to make her lips and the adjacent areas of the cheek and chin look as though they are on a snowy television screen. Sure enough, some of the resultant images suggest such torment that we might think Lisa

"What makes Mona Lisa smile?"

Gherardini had just spent weeks coping with devastating news.[18] That is how strongly we react to the slightest of variations when reading faces. Of course, Leonardo had already worked this blurring effect into the original painting; Kontsevich had merely to enhance it. The expression on Mona Lisa's face remains an unfathomable enigma. And because the look on another person's face automatically triggers emotions in the viewer, every encounter with this picture becomes an emotional roller coaster.

PYRAMIDAL LAW

Leonardo was able to manipulate our perceptions so brilliantly because of his unique ability to track his own. He noticed that a burning piece of wood flying through the air leaves a trail of light in the eye. His notes describe the movements of a dragonfly: "The dragonfly flies with four wings, and when the anterior are raised, the posterior are dropped."[19] Pictures taken on today's high-speed cameras prove that he was essentially correct, apart from the fact that during a dragonfly's descent, the front pair of wings is ahead of the back pair by an eightieth of a second, while the upward movement is synchronized. But who could blame Leonardo for this minor inaccuracy? It is amazing that he was able to detect the phases of wing movement with the naked eye at all. Normally we do not perceive even movements that are eight times slower—it takes humans an average of about a tenth of a second to register images.

Was Leonardo really blessed with an "inhumanly sharp eye," as British art historian Kenneth Clark claimed? Perhaps he was simply able to draw the correct inferences from minuscule distinctions. Leonardo may have noticed a tiny imbalance in the flight of the dragonfly—which in itself would be quite astonishing—and figured out its implications. His notebooks are full of reflections inspired by details other people would likely deem insignificant and ignore. Leonardo, however, refused to take anything for granted. His mind worked like that of a child seeing everything for the first time and always wondering why things are the way they are and whether it might be possible for them to be some altogether different way.

For Leonardo, seeing something with his own eyes was the starting point of all knowledge, but he did not put blind faith in his vision. Precisely because he examined everything so scrupulously, he knew how tricky human perception could be. In countless passages in his notebooks he remarked that some objects simply cannot be the way they appear. The subtlest irregularities caught his eye: that we regard buildings as bigger in the fog, that we have crisp vision in only one small area of our field of vision,[20] and that the colors at the edge of a surface are brighter and more sharply defined than in the center.[21]

An artist who understands how to portray these effects artistically can create amazingly realistic paintings. However, in order to apply the rules of optics, you first have to grasp them.[22] In Leonardo's view, "the painter who draws by practice and judgment of the eye without the use of reason is like a mirror that copies everything placed in front of it without knowledge of the same."[23]

Leonardo began experimenting with optical instruments in the very early years of his career, perhaps even during his apprenticeship to the painter Verrocchio. He designed concave mirrors and machines to polish them, as well as a floodlight with a lens that clustered candlelight.[24] He spent years refining the rules of perspective, which were quite imprecise at the time; his subsequent study of spatial representation led him to the laws of optics. Using a perspectograph, Leonardo was able to establish that objects appear only half as large when they are twice as far from the viewer—which leading authorities of antiquity and even many of Leonardo's contemporaries disputed.[25]

Leonardo used the term "pyramidal law" to designate the manner in which objects appear to grow or shrink in relation to our distance from them. Light rays drawn from the eye of the viewer to the corners of an object form a pyramid. Although Leon Battista Alberti had established this fact back in 1435, he failed to recognize its broader implications. Leonardo realized that an immutable geometric law was at work here, namely that the apparent size of an object increases or decreases according to its distance from the viewer. Later he applied this

Perspectograph

principle to many other problems. Numerical relations that could be sketched with a few quick strokes of the pen must have been quite an eye-opener for Leonardo, whose limited education had never allowed him to master even the basics of arithmetic, for they provided him a point of access to science that built on his extraordinary visual talent.

We find the *Mona Lisa* so riveting because it incorporated many of the optical rules Leonardo had discovered and enabled him to bring enormous depth to the picture, which can make the young woman seem like an almost incorporeal being. Viewers who focus on the background find that Lisa Gherardini is like a spectral vision floating somewhere in the ether between themselves and the infinitely distant landscape.

In the notebook now known as the Codex Leicester, Leonardo recorded not only his observations about how proportions change in relation to distance, but also how light is transformed as it passes through the atmosphere as "minute and insensible atoms" scatter it.[26] He was mistaken only in his belief that the atoms of the air itself scatter sunbeams and not only, as he thought, those of steam. To reach this conclusion, he spent years studying light diffraction during periods of haze and with various types of clouds, and even the origins of weather itself. We see the result of this research in the blue and hazy mountains behind Mona Lisa, which fade into a boundless depth.[27] Leonardo explained this effect in terms similar to the proportions described in his pyramidal law: "If one is to be five times as distant, make it five times bluer."[28] And the peaks are lighter than the valleys, because Leonardo knew that the atmosphere grows "thinner and more transparent" at higher altitudes.[29]

Still more remarkable is how the light pours over Mona Lisa's body and plays with her fingers, each of which is finely shaded like a miniature sculpture. The hands project far forward to counterbalance the landscape in the distance, which augments the painting's sense of depth. The folds of the sleeves sparkle like sunbeams on the waves of the sea. Most importantly, the illumination makes Mona Lisa appear both animated and mysterious; the distribution of light and shadow foils any attempt to construe her frame of mind. Obviously Leonardo calculated the brightness of each and every square inch of his painting to achieve a particular effect. Nevertheless, no detail seems contrived or calculated; the light that falls on the young woman appears quite natural.

In the Library of Her Majesty

The *Mona Lisa* displays the culmination of Leonardo's optical ideas and experiments, but his sketches allow us to follow the master step by step on his path of discovery. Seventeenth-century merchants sold many of these items in Melzi's valuable collection to the British royal family; today they are in Windsor Castle. A staff member there led me into a quiet room high above the Thames, the ceiling of which was elaborately ornamented with rosettes. A frame had been set up to hold the drawings while I examined them, and I was supplied a magnifying glass and white cotton gloves (visitors are not allowed to touch the originals with bare fingers). Without further ado, the woman opened a glass case and took the first pages and a mount out of a cardboard box.

Landscapes, studies of anatomy, architecture and rocks, portraits, maps, and visions of the end of the world—the librarian had prepared a cross section of Leonardo's oeuvre, and whenever I wanted to view the next page, I gave her a sign and she placed it on the frame. Some drawings were in pen and ink, others in red chalk, coal, chalk, or a combination of media, and on nearly all of them I saw details that are not captured on even the best reproductions. These works were at my exclusive disposal for an entire day, and sometimes I got the feeling I could commune with their creator, which was a pleasant contrast to my experience with the Louvre crowds.

One of the pages, half the size of a standard sheet of paper, shows the profile of an elderly man.[30] His wrinkled face, hooked nose, jutting chin, and protruding lower lip do not lend him a handsome appearance. The old man is facing a set of light rays, which Leonardo drew as a series of straight lines. All the rays merge at one point, which is evidently the sun. The uppermost ray meets the top of the man's scalp, and the lowest touches his chin. The remaining rays illuminate his forehead, nose, and mouth, and Leonardo marked all the spots where a ray makes contact with his face with a letter in mirror writing. There was no way I could read the extensive commentary on the page, which was also in mirror image; still, I had a good idea of what Leonardo was hoping to accomplish in this drawing, namely to figure out how the brightness of each spot on the face depends on the angle at which the sunlight meets the skin. The top of the head and the chin, which the light merely grazes, have to appear darker than the base of the nose and the forehead, where the rays come straight down.

Sure enough, the comments in mirror writing describe these very connections, as I learned while reading a transcript that I came across

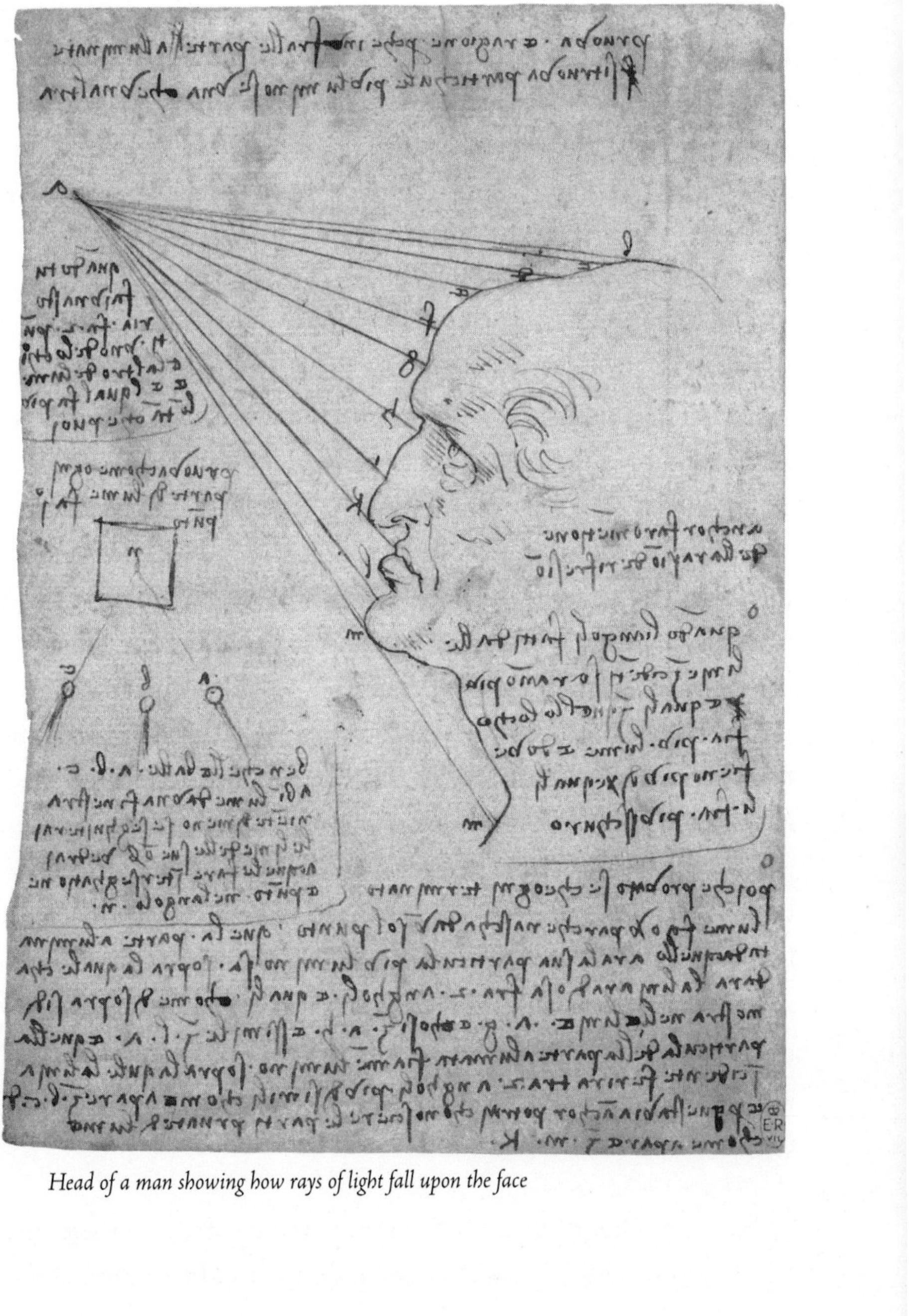

Head of a man showing how rays of light fall upon the face

later in the Berlin State Library, and the facsimiles of other notebooks housed there reveal that Leonardo spent years trying to gain a precise understanding of light and shadow and calculating degrees of brightness. One sketch in the Codex Arundel even analyzes the sun's reflection of light on waves in the water—a problem that remains one of the most challenging in computer graphics today. The *Mona Lisa* has more in common with current attempts to construct images synthetically than with the traditional painting that was standard in Leonardo's era.

We nearly always recognize computer-generated images for what they are when we encounter them in films, video games, and even in museums; by contrast, the light on Mona Lisa seems quite natural. But a closer look reveals that something is not quite right: The woman is sitting on a loggia, as the bases of the columns still visible at the corners of the picture indicate. Therefore the illumination would have to come primarily from the open side of the balcony toward the landscape, so we ought to be seeing Mona Lisa against the light. But in Leonardo's painting, she is illuminated from the front upper left corner, a direction from which a vaulted soffit ought to have cast its shadow. Leonardo, however, used the laws of optics to such perfect effect that the illusion is not conspicuous. And we are not bothered in the least by the fact that light would never really make the subtlest curves of Mona Lisa's body stand out so prominently. We simply accept that the young woman looks more real than reality itself. Leonardo did not paint this picture in accordance with reality; he created a new one—a virtual reality.

"HOW THE SCINTILLATION OF EACH STAR ORIGINATES IN THE EYE"

Leonardo himself provided the key to the mystery of his painting with a tiny picture, smaller than a passport photo, on the margin of the

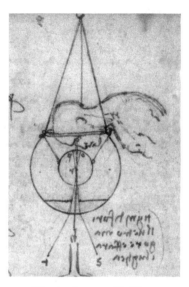

*Glass bowl as a model of the
human eye*

third page of the collection known as Notebook D, which is housed
in the Institut de France in Paris. In this picture, a man with a bare
torso is bending forward and immersing his face in a round glass bowl.
The bowl, containing a small amount of water at its base, is suspended
from two ropes. Its light rays travel across the glass of the bowl, are
refracted in the water, and then reach the man's eyes.[31]

Leonardo used this somewhat odd sketch to figure out how vision
works by scrutinizing the manner in which images enter the eye. The
candle is an example of an object that emits light. The round bowl
represents the eyeball. The light comes through the outermost layer
of the eyeball, the cornea, which in Leonardo's sketch corresponds to
the side of the glass bowl. Then the rays make a sharp bend, and just
as the lens of the eye refracts light in reality, the water on the curved
base of the bowl refracts the light. When the rays leave the lens again
in bundled form, they travel to the back of the eyeball and produce an

image on the retina. When the man holds his head into the bowl, he can observe precisely what happens in the retina of a real eye.

Now Leonardo could use this setup to conduct all kinds of experiments. What would happen, for instance, if the candle were moved farther from the bowl? How would the path of the rays change if more water were added? We do not know whether Leonardo actually carried out these experiments or whether he was using the sketch as a model to puzzle out these issues.

His earlier experiments were aimed at determining how the incidence of light alters the appearances of things—flat lighting reduces brightness, the light on remote summits is blue, and so forth. Now his investigations took an important step forward by exploring the process of seeing itself. Leonardo was on his way to understanding how our own perception determines our experience. The images we see are not simply there; they arise within the individual, in the interplay between ourselves and the world. Only someone who knows how the eye functions can understand what is seen: "The order of proving that the earth is a star. First explain the mechanism of the eye, then show how the scintillation of each star originates in the eye."[32]

Leonardo wrote these lines in 1508, the year he devised the experimental setup with the glass bowl. The *Mona Lisa* was still a work in progress, and Leonardo was now sixty-three years old. His discoveries about sight came to represent both the pinnacle and the legacy of his life as a painter and researcher. Had he not realized that a work of art is ultimately created not on the canvas, but in the eye of the viewer, he would have been incapable of producing the magical effect on viewers of the *Mona Lisa*. But to get to that point, Leonardo had spent decades studying the laws of optics. Step by step, he had to free himself from the biases of his era, conduct experiments, and make missteps, until he finally arrived at a rough idea of how images come into the head.[33]

He conducted major experiments with the camera obscura, a device that was well known to the painters of his era. Leonardo describes how he cast light on the opposite wall in dark rooms through a little hole and there saw the outside world standing on its head. These experiments brought him to the realization that the eye functions like a camera obscura. The pupil corresponds to the hole through which the light falls; the image originates on the retina. Later on, he drew a camera obscura and an eye directly on top of each other.[34] The sketch illustrates one of Leonardo's strengths—drawing parallels between the known and the unknown—to which he owed many of his most original achievements.

And the lens? Leonardo knew that glass lenses were capable of focusing light rays and concluded that the lens of the eye has no other purpose. And since he was also aware that a curved water surface refracts light, he drew water on the base of the glass bowl. Even though he did not know the laws of refraction, he was still the first to understand this principle of vision.

Almost, that is. Throughout his life, he could never get over his astonishment that man sees everything right side up even though the images in the eye ought to be upside down the way they are in the camera obscura.[35] He never realized that the inverted image later reverts in the brain.

The originality with which Leonardo applied the laws of optics and perceptive psychology explains why his *Mona Lisa* appeals to people far more than its copy, Raphael's *Lady with a Unicorn*, as a simple comparison of how the two artists painted the faces reveals. Raphael portrayed what he saw. He may have idealized the features of his model somewhat, but he did not go beyond what is immediately visible. His artistic awareness of the young woman essentially ended at the level of her skin. What might be going on behind it, let alone in the mind of a viewer, was of little interest to Raphael. Thus his painting is what it appears to be—lifeless.

Leonardo, the visionary, dug deeper. He exposed the layers beneath the facial features to understand where facial expressions originate. He wondered how an image takes shape on the retina and what feelings it arouses in the person gazing at it. And he knew how to put the knowledge he gained to artistic use. Raphael was an exceptionally gifted painter, but Leonardo probed beneath the surface.

And his intellectual curiosity did not stop at the questions that pertained directly to painting. That, too, is reflected in the *Mona Lisa*— not so much in the figure of Lisa Gherardini, but rather in the landscape behind her back, which in its way holds at least as many secrets as the disconcerting smile on the woman in the foreground.

It would appear that Walter Pater's effusive claim that the painting portrays epochs long before living memory was not so far off the mark. Still, Leonardo's prehistorical vision is reflected not in the face of the young woman, as Pater thought, but rather in "the rocks among which she sits." While painting the *Mona Lisa*, Leonardo was deeply engaged in geological studies of how mountains, rivers, and living beings originated. He regarded the constantly changing earth as a kind of organism. The extensive river landscape behind Mona Lisa appears to incorporate his theories, and perhaps we respond so powerfully to this picture because it seems to herald a very distant past. This setting would surely have looked less imposing if Leonardo had not sought to fathom the formation and fading of the earth.

The noblest aspiration of Renaissance art was to reproduce nature to perfection—to paint things precisely as they are. Leonardo broke with this endeavor. His quest to understand nature and people aimed at *recasting* reality. Accordingly, he did not adhere to a traditional sense of realism in his art, or, for that matter, in his designs of turbines,

robots, and flying machines. His desire to investigate nature had originated in a pursuit of artistic perfection, but as the years went by, his
intellectual quest increasingly broke away from its practical application
to art and took on a life of its own. Once Leonardo started asking questions, he could not stop.

Waterfall

II

WATER

FOR MANY YEARS I KEPT a postcard-size pen-and-ink drawing over my desk. From a distance all I could make out was a whirling something that held a strange fascination for nearly everyone who came to visit me. Only up close could they see that this odd image was actually a torrent of water breaking through a rectangular opening in a wall and pouring down into a pool. The stream of water is no more than a set of curved lines that resemble a well-coiffed ponytail. Spume forms where these lines strike the surface of the sketched water in the pool. Little waves shoot up, break, and tumble. Around the periphery, the water streams in large spirals. The whole pool is in a state of upheaval.

The bubbles on the water, which have combined to form rings, look like blossoms with a funnel-shaped vortex opening out in the center— like a chasm heading into the depths. And the surface of the water curves to form a valley where the torrent enters the pool.

Viewers can even look right through the maelstrom, X-ray-vision-style, and see that the current on the surface amounts to a minute portion of the movement in the pool. The air bubbles and funnel are only the external indications of a much greater turbulence below. The farther down you look, the mightier the flow becomes and the more the water spirals. A modern viewer may be reminded of the spectacular images of solar protuberances or collisions of two galaxies that astronomers are sometimes able to capture on film.

This is how Leonardo da Vinci portrayed the impact of water on water in about 1506. I had discovered the picture in a folder with cheap prints that circulated in my high school art class. The reproduction was so poor that it did not even hint at the brownish color of Leonardo's ink. The lines appeared blurred, and the explanations in mirror writing that Leonardo had inserted under his drawing were missing.

Even so, the picture held my attention. I tried to imagine where I might re-create this drama for myself. Wouldn't the same thing happen in the bathtub as the water pours in, or even in a teacup when you add milk? So many mysteries are revealed in the most mundane activities if you look carefully enough. Leonardo's drawing seemed to me the very symbol of how tiny a sliver of reality we tend to register. Standing at the edge of a basin, we may notice the waves at the surface, but we don't ponder what lies beneath.

When I was finally able to examine the original in the Royal Library at Windsor Castle, I realized that my reproduction conveyed only a rough idea of the intensity with which Leonardo saw and depicted the world. The longer I studied Leonardo's pen strokes, the more they drew me in. The lines stood out so sharply that they radiated a peculiar dynamism, as though the artist had just finished drawing them. I saw some of the very fine lines merge into what seemed like a three-dimensional image—almost like a hologram. Some currents receded into the background, while others pressed forward, forming curlicues that spiraled out toward the viewer. It seemed more and more incredible that I was looking at a flat object, a somewhat graying piece of paper mounted behind a thin pane of acrylic glass.

The drawing is a snapshot of shapes that disappear in the very next moment, never to recur in the same way. Leonardo succeeded in capturing the liveliness of inanimate nature. And yet the current is not a reflection of reality, but a fiction. Just as the *Mona Lisa* played with the laws of perception to animate the woman's face, here, too, the artist aimed higher than merely depicting the visible world; he sought to explain it.[1]

Leonardo highlighted what he considered the essential elements, emphasizing some elements and omitting others. Air bubbles on the water, for instance, never appear as perfectly round and crowded together as in this picture. Leonardo apparently believed that the raging of the water, no matter how chaotic it might appear, adheres to a mysterious order. Under the sketch of the torrent, he noted, in mirror writing, "Water entering a pool moves in three ways, and the air pushing into the water creates a fourth movement."

But how does order arise in the whirling water? Today this question would go straight to scientists, and the discipline of hydrodynamics would be there to provide an answer. In Leonardo's era, this field did not exist. No one thought of focusing on the way water flows, let alone of drawing pictures of turbulences or describing these kinds of phenomena in words. And that was only one of Leonardo's many pioneering ventures. In fields as far-flung as optics, geology, and anatomy, he was the first to describe problems that generations of researchers after him would tackle. Even more than his virtuosity with the paintbrush, it is this versatility that we admire today in Leonardo, the universal genius, the man who apparently knew, and could do, anything and everything.

His mythic status notwithstanding, experts continue to debate whether Leonardo merits the status of a scientist, let alone of the first scientist. For some, he is a true pioneer of the modern study of the world, while others consider him an outstanding artist who only dabbled in science. However, the drawing of the torrent of water reveals that art and science are far more interrelated than many believe. Both explore an unknown reality, and both attempt to make it comprehensible to man. If there is one central theme linking Leonardo's wide-ranging interests, it is water. *The Annunciation*, *The Virgin of the Rocks*, the *Madonna of the Yarnwinder*, the *Mona Lisa*—again and again Leonardo painted his figures in front of rivers and lakes. As an engineer he planned to redesign the major watercourses in Italy. As a naturalist he studied fossils and discovered that his homeland must once have been the bottom of a gigantic sea. In the final years of his life, he used deeply moving words and images to portray the Flood as the end of the world. The range of Leonardo's disposition and his unique way of thinking are revealed not in the *Mona Lisa* or in the *Last Supper*, but in his studies, sketches, and descriptions of water.

REMAINS OF A LOCK

During a visit to Milan, I traveled out to the elegant Brera district. My hosts had told me that a lock built by Leonardo near the San Marco Church was on display there. I spent quite a while wandering through streets lined with boutiques and bars. It was late in the afternoon, and the cars were so tightly wedged together, motors running, that I often had to squeeze sideways between the bumpers.

I tried to console myself with the thought that even Leonardo had complained about the cramped conditions in Milan (a "huge gathering of people who herd together like goats on top of one another and fill every part with their stench"). The Church of Santa Maria delle Grazie, which Leonardo was commissioned to embellish with his *Last Supper*, and the lock I was looking for were still way before the walls of the city at the beginning of the modern age. Even so, Milan was then one

Ideal city

of the most densely populated metropolises of Europe, with nearly 200,000 people crowded into a tiny area.[2] To alleviate these conditions, and presumably also to cope with the plague epidemic he experienced here in 1485, Leonardo proposed an "ideal city" with dual-level streets. The houses would have two entrances, one atop the other. The lower level would be reserved for deliveries and servants. Leonardo pictured covered carriage routes and canals on this lower tier, with a drainage system for sewage. In his vision, the bourgeoisie would go about its business in loggias and gardens on the pedestrian boulevards above this level, undisturbed by noise and stench.

I finally entered a passageway that looked quite promising, and emerged at a long plaza. It was quieter here; the sound of cars at a multi-lane intersection could be heard only at a distance. A street led down the narrow end of the square, then ended abruptly. I walked for a few feet and peered into a ditch full of brambles and willows. Here were the remains of a canal, with two rotted wooden lock gates on a brick foundation separated by exactly the length of a barge. Atop the gates, two cats were basking in the sun. Down below I saw large open wooden hatches with bolts. The bolts, hatches, and gates formed a complicated linkage system up to the banks of the canals. Evidently this device was once used to open and close the hatches. I tried it out, but the hinges were rusted solid.

According to a plaque, the canal was still navigable in 1960, then the water was rerouted to subterranean pipes. It has not been used for transportation since then—and does not begin to resemble Leonardo's vision of covered carriage routes in his ideal city. In 1497, Ludovico Sforza, the Duke of Milan, had commissioned the construction of the lock where I was standing to connect a higher Alpine canal with the waterways in the city.

A painting in the Gallery of Modern Art in Milan by a now-forgotten nineteenth-century artist named Cherubino Cornienti portrays the fictitious scene of a proud Leonardo explaining the canal to the ruler, who is standing at the edge of the lock. But not all experts are convinced that this idyll is historically accurate, and some even doubt that Leonardo designed it.

Be that as it may, there is evidence that this structure was Leonardo's only invention to have survived·into our era. His notebooks contain several pages of sketches of the exact wooden hatches, bolts, and posts that the lock gate still has today. You can even make out the brick foundation and a recess in the wall of the canal into which the gate folds when open.[3] The hatches and their sophisticated mechanism were not used in any other structure during this early era of technology. Fifteenth-century locks nearly always had primitive lifting doors that needed to be pulled upward like the blade of a guillotine—there was no evidence of swinging gates, let alone recessed hatches.

The skeptics argue that the famous architectural theorist Leon Battista Alberti had described locks with swinging gates twenty years earlier,[4] and that not a single document proves that Leonardo actually directed the construction of the locks of San Marco. Perhaps, they say, he was simply copying what others had devised.[5]

Lock near the San Marco Church in Milan

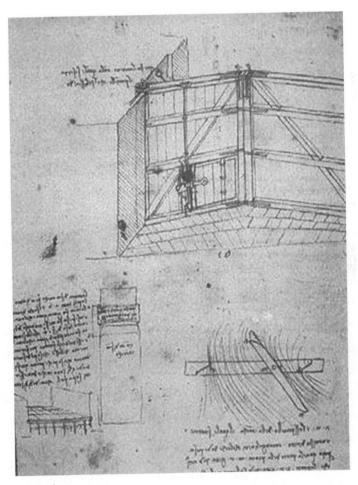

Lock gate

Most likely the dispute will never be resolved, primarily because Renaissance engineers tended to transmit their technical knowledge orally. No one knows how many ideas for the lock at San Marco were adopted from others and how many improvements Leonardo himself added. Still, Alberti provided only explanations of how to mount gates that are easy to use under hydraulic pressure, but he mentioned neither double lock gates of the kind that are standard today nor recessed hatches to equalize the pressure. And he did not describe a complete closing mechanism. All three principles, however—double doors, hatches, and closing mechanism—were used in San Marco, and it is hard to imagine that Leonardo would have drawn this lock in such detail if it had not been his own design.[6]

Whether or not he personally designed the lock at San Marco, he fully grasped the principle behind it, as the notebooks also reveal. Under a particularly exquisite drawing of the closing mechanism, Leonardo sketched the flow lines along which the water passes through the hatches into the lock chamber.[7]

Leonardo was also well aware of the challenges inherent in this construction. To avoid undercurrents, he recommended mounting the hatch not in the exact center of the lock gates, but a couple of inches away, so that the difference in pressure could interact with the closing mechanism to make the door gently swing open automatically and let in water as soon as the gate opened.[8] If, on the other hand, the water were to stream into the lock chamber too quickly, a dangerous swell of water could build up, which "would spill into the ship, fill it instantly, and sink it."[9] He also advised recessing the open gates in the wall, as was done in San Marco, to prevent eddies from forming at their edges and eroding the bank reinforcements over time.

Leonardo's extraordinary *Mona Lisa* put his years of research on the laws governing perception to optimal use. The drawings of the lock at San Marco reveal his similarly intense devotion to studying the mechanics of currents. In both cases Leonardo sought solutions to practical problems—how to create a startlingly lifelike portrait in the one instance, and how best to hoist ships in the other. Thus his studies of vortices and locks had more in common with the *Mona Lisa* than with the learned treatises of his university counterparts, who studied these issues on a purely theoretical level.

SEEKING EMPLOYMENT FROM THE TYRANT

Unlike the scholars of his era, Leonardo earned a living by promising his employers spectacular works of art and technology. His studies of hydraulic engineering were especially valuable for Milan, because the city owed its prosperity to water. The canal at San Marco, which is choked with weeds today, was then only one of many waterways in this metropolis, which bore a strong resemblance to Amsterdam or Venice. On canals that stretched across the Po Valley, ships made their way to the lakes at the foothills of the Alps or into the Mediterranean. On their return from the north, the barges transported marble for the construction of the immense cathedral.

Business in Milan textiles and weapons boomed. The success of the metalworks and textile industries was made possible by the rivers in Lombardy, because water power was the only reliable energy source. Animals and wind were too undependable, and steam engines and motors lay so far beyond the capabilities of technology that even a Leonardo could not picture them. Gristmills, saws, hydraulic presses, bellows, forge hammers—wherever there was a machine, a course of a river was sure to be nearby.[10] According to the French historian Jean Gimpel, water power was just as important to that era as oil was to the twentieth century. And the farmers in the vicinity of Milan benefited from Alpine water making the land fertile and enabling them to grow mulberry trees, which provided food for silkworms, and thus making possible a highly profitable industry.[11]

Leonardo was well aware of this when he applied for a position at the court in Milan in about 1482. We do not know exactly what made him decide, at the age of thirty, to give up his career as a freelance artist in Florence, which had begun so promisingly, and to try his luck in Milan. Perhaps he feared that his unhurried style of working would make it difficult for him to maintain his position in the highly competitive art market. In the transition period between the late medieval and the modern ages, artists were still regarded as craftsmen; just as a metalworker received money for making a railing, a painter was paid for furnishing a portrait or an altarpiece according to specified guidelines and deadlines. Leonardo often took years to complete his paintings, which made it difficult for him to live from the sale of his works.

In contrast to the situation in Florence, Milan offered Leonardo a realistic chance of finding support from a patron, namely Ludovico Sforza, one of the most elusive and unscrupulous rulers of the Renaissance. An unknown painter portrayed his face with fleshy but severe features that radiate resoluteness and self-confidence.[12] His fur hood features a golden *M*, the initial of Ludovico's epithet, *il Moro*, which can mean both "mulberry tree" and "Moor"—a reference to his dark complexion. Ludovico was the son of a mercenary leader who had staged a coup and made himself ruler. Now, Ludovico ruled Milan successfully with an iron fist. The economy flourished, and the city became a leading Italian power. A steady job at the court of il Moro would enable Leonardo to pursue his interests without having to worry about selling his artwork.

A detailed and remarkably self-assured application to il Moro spelled out in ten points what he was willing to provide in exchange for a

*Ludovico Sforza, known as
il Moro—The Moor*

position at the court. The first nine provided specifics of the horrific weapons and other military equipment he would construct. He wrote that he would be good at building armored cars, catapults, and bombs that would instill great fear in the enemies of his new employer and would inflict even greater damage. In the tenth point, finally, Leonardo claimed that "in time of peace" he would prove a first-rate architect and "conduct water from one place to another." Almost as an afterthought, he then offered to build a colossal bronze horse, an equestrian statue, "which shall endue with immortal glory and eternal honor the auspicious memory of the Prince your father and of the illustrious house of Sforza."[13]

Ludovico, the ragamuffin among Italian rulers, was in sore need of glorification. Although he had no right to call himself "duke," he used the title anyway. He was from a family of parvenus and had usurped his nephew's throne. Ludovico's incompetent brother, Galeazzo, was assassinated in 1476, and there is considerable evidence that il Moro had helped engineer the conspiracy from his exile in France. He proceeded to wrest control of the government from his sister-in-law, guardian of Galeazzo's underage son Gian Galeazzo, while she acted as regent, and he held them both in confinement for nearly two decades. In 1494, Gian Galeazzo, like his father, fell victim to an attempt on his life. This time there was no doubt that Ludovico was the person responsible.

To win over the powerful families of Milan for himself, il Moro organized splendid galas; to confer legitimacy on his rule, he sought to make Lombardy a center of intellectual life. He appointed prominent scholars, such as Dimitrios Castrenos of Greece, to his court, and the first Greek book—a grammar book—was printed in Milan. A court poet named Bellincioni hailed Milan as the rebirth of ancient Greece: "Come, I say, to today's Athens in Milan, for here is the Ludovican Parnassus."[14]

Humanists such as Francesco Filelfo also contributed to il Moro's intellectual propaganda. The poet wrote a *Sforziade* in the style of Homer—an epic poem in hexameters telling the story of Ludovico's ancestors. And the duke commissioned the preeminent architects Donato Bramante and Francesco di Giorgio to design cathedrals in Milan and Pavia.

Leonardo served as a kind of technical adviser to Sforza. A document written in the 1490s refers to him as *Ingeniarius Ducalis* ("ducal engineer"). His duties ranged from supervising shipping routes and military equipment to tending to the water pipes in the duchess's bathroom. (Several of Leonardo's sketches illustrate these plumbing tasks.) He set to work on the promised 23-foot-tall equestrian statue and organized pageants for il Moro. He was given a workshop at the palace in Milan, the Corte Vecchia, but he was not a part of the royal household. Hierarchically speaking, an engineer was above a painter, but still a craftsman. He most likely ate his meals at the table for the household staff, with the masons and gardeners, but at least he did not suffer the same indignity as his Florentine colleague Domenico Ghirlandaio ten years earlier, whose meals consisted of his patrons' leftovers. Times were changing.

LOVE NEST IN THE MILL

The duke's pet project was a model farm named La Sforzesca (derived from his family name, Sforza) in the plain eighteen miles outside of Milan, where Ludovico installed a broad network of main and subsidiary canals to enhance rice cultivation. An inscription in Vigevano, the nearby town where Ludovico was born, hails his achievement here: "The desert waste became a green and fertile meadow; the wilderness blossomed like a rose." The ruler had built a small country palace for himself and his wife, and he enjoyed falconry. A visitor from France even wrote that life on the country estate felt like paradise.

Even so, the trip to La Sforzesca is monotonous. From the lock at San Marco you cross through Milan on streets that were once canals until you get to the spot where the water, which was routed through pipes under a fish market, reemerges from below. You then follow a waterway called the Naviglio Grande, which takes you west for an hour by car. I passed by fields and buildings that might be factories, warehouses, or shopping centers.

The model farm is now in ruins. An enormous courtyard filled with debris surrounds four towers with ramshackle stables between them. Small stone houses adjoin one of the stables, and a construction fence runs along them. During my visit, smoke was rising from one of the chimneys. I crossed a road with clattering trucks and came to a Renaissance church. It was locked. Next to it I saw another courtyard, which was part of the palace. An alarm went off as I approached the passageway, so I slipped into a bar in one of the stables, where several

La Sforzesca

men were drinking espresso laced with grappa and talking in a dialect I couldn't follow. Some of them also held liqueur glasses, and all had bad teeth. I wondered whether these people were surprised to see me, and what sort of impression the flamboyant stranger Leonardo must have made on the local farmworkers back in his day.

The barkeeper told me that people say Leonardo had spent quite a long time here and lived in the ducal palace, but he did not know many specific details.

Leonardo made several references to the model farm in his notebooks. In describing a canal construction project, he wrote: "On the second day of February, 1494, at the Sforzesca, I have drawn twenty-five steps, each of two thirds of a braccio high and eight braccia wide."[15] We are not told whether Leonardo was designing a new set of steps or merely drawing an existing one.

A later note explains how steps were used to obtain fertile land beneath the Sforzesca: "One hundred and thirty steps . . . down which the water falls . . . dried up a swamp."[16] The trick was to slow down a torrential stream by directing it over the steps. Once the water moved slowly, it no longer carried away the soil. Instead, the mud settled, and new fields formed over time. The duke's engineers, perhaps even Leonardo himself, had put nature to good use.

Leonardo also examined the gristmills in the vicinity, calculating their daily output and estimating the costs of new mills that could use water power more efficiently. He even reported the discovery of a prehistoric ship ten arm's lengths under the earth.[17]

From La Sforzesca I headed over to the Mill of Mora Bassa, which Duke Ludovico once gave to his wife, Beatrice, as a wedding present (although the barkeeper informed me that Ludovico used the mill, which was still surrounded by woods at the time, for secret trysts with his mistress, Cecilia Gallerani). The duke also commissioned Leonardo to paint Cecilia's portrait. The painting in question is the famous *Lady with an Ermine*, which now hangs in Krakow. Cecilia, who was just seventeen years old at the time, may have been the most beautiful woman Leonardo ever painted. The artist included the upper part of her body in frontal pose. She is clad in a simple but elegant velvet dress; in the center of the painting, Cecilia's slender fingers are petting a furry white animal. But the young woman is not looking at the viewer; her head is turned toward her shoulder, and her rather girlish, yet flawless, features appear in three-quarter profile.

A golden net covers her forehead. Her light brown hair comes down over her cheeks and enhances her finely etched appearance. A smile plays around Cecilia's thin mouth, and her alert gaze suggests a high level of intelligence. She spoke fluent Latin, composed sonnets, and earned praise as a singer. It is said that Cecilia liked Leonardo.

Cecilia Gallerani

In any case, he was later a regular guest in her apartment at the ducal palace in Milan, and she had a major role in helping the Tuscan painter become one of Europe's preeminent naturalists and writers. Leonardo made the acquaintance of the country's top scholars in her salon.

Leonardo had great difficulty accepting his status as craftsman. He considered painters far superior to men who dirtied their hands to earn their pay. His notebooks rattle off arguments about the superiority of painting over the other arts: Music does not last, while paintings do; poems cannot be touched, but paintings can. The painter, we are told, is more elegant than his major rival, the sculptor: "The painter sits in front of his work at perfect ease. He is well dressed and moves a very light brush dipped in delicate color. He adorns himself with the clothes he fancies; his home is clean and filled with delightful pictures and he often is accompanied by music or by the reading of various beautiful works to which he can listen with great pleasure."[18]

LEONARDO BECOMES A WRITER

While a regular visitor to Cecilia's salon, Leonardo developed in yet another area that would henceforth set him apart from his fellow artists: He began to write. His notebooks now included stories in addition to sketches, projects, and observations. The duke's engineer invented fables and riddles suitable for entertainment at the court. He also tried his hand at so-called prophecies, gloomy images that ostensibly predicted the future but actually described the current state of affairs. Since he was not especially skilled at language—Leonardo had had a limited formal education and spoke the dialect of his Tuscan homeland—he decided to enlarge his vocabulary systematically. Now more than thirty-five years old, he began studying up on standard Italian. In Codex Trivulzianus, a collection of his notes from the years he spent in Milan, the reader suddenly comes across endless word lists. And because a more varied vocabulary would be helpful for his scientific work, Leonardo compiled lists of technical terms, including a set of sixty-seven words describing the movement of water. Another manuscript, which Leonardo composed during the same period, made reference to waters intersecting, surging, upwelling, and swelling, with careful distinctions drawn between water that was eddying and pushing away, and between the meeting and merging of two flow paths.[19] He later studied Latin, although he did not get beyond the basics. He also acquired a small reference library. By the end of the 1490s, he owned more than forty books, as we know from a list in his notebooks.

Knowing full well that university scholars would not regard him as an equal anyway, he decided to mount a counterattack:

I am fully aware that the fact of my not being a man of letters may cause certain presumptuous persons to think that they may with reason blame me, alleging that I am a man without learning. Foolish folk! Do they not know that I might retort by saying, as did Marius to the Roman Patricians: "They who adorn themselves in the labors of others will not permit me my own." They will say that because I have no book learning, I cannot properly express what I desire to treat of—but they do not know that my subjects require for their exposition experience rather than the words of others.[20]

Leonardo aimed to develop a whole new approach that relied not on traditional knowledge, but on his own perceptions. And he knew that he had at least one important authority to back him up. Hadn't the philosopher Aristotle defined sensory perception as the basis of all true knowledge? When Constantinople fell in 1453, the Greek original texts by this ancient thinker came to the West, and reliable translations were now available. Leonardo owned several books by and about Aristotle.

As an author, he sought to put into practice what the philosopher had proposed more than eighteen hundred years earlier. For his first work, Leonardo was planning a book about water. Even his early notes invoked the poetic hold of this element on man.[21] They are punctuated with sublime and pithy formulations, such as this: "Sea, universal lowness and sole resting-place of the roaming waters of the rivers."[22]

Leonardo hoped that his writings would inspire other researchers and artists "to study the many beautiful motions that arise when one element permeates another."[23] While most of his other notes were brief and to the point, Leonardo waxed eloquent when writing about water: "It goes round and round in continuous rotation, hither and thither from above and from below, it never rests in quiet, either in its course or in its own nature. . . . So it changes continually, now as regards place, now as regards color, now it absorbs new smells or tastes . . . now it brings death, now health."[24] It would be impossible to overstate the significance of this element, he contended, because "water is the driving force behind all of nature."[25]

WATER MUSIC

On my way to the Mill of Mora Bassa, I tried to appreciate Leonardo's special connection to water so that I would find it easier to see the world through his eyes. It is nearly impossible to picture this area as it once was, so densely wooded that Duke Ludovico was able to use the mill as a hidden love nest. Today the area is wide open. The only relatively tall plants are the mulberry trees that Ludovico planted along the canals to make Lombardy a center of silk manufacturing.

It was a clear day in February when I strode through the Lomellina, as this plain is called, and saw the snowcapped peaks of Monte Rosa illuminated on the northern horizon. Leonardo, a pioneer in mountaineering as well, probably climbed up to a height of nearly 10,000 feet.[26] In any case, his notebooks mention in passing that he climbed up the "Monboso" to explore the origin of all the waterways of Europe. The base of this mountain, he wrote, is the point of origin of the four rivers that flow over the entire continent in the direction of the four compass points. By the "four rivers," Leonardo was referring to the Rhône, the Danube, the Rhine, and the Po. We do not know the origins of this odd theory, although Leonardo may have taken it from the historian Flavio Biondo's atlas of Italy, which is the first recorded use of the name "Monboso" for the Monte Rosa.[27]

He wrote that when the air rises on the mountain slopes, humidity builds up. Of course the Monte Rosa is so high that precipitation rarely falls as snow, but rather as hail that piles up to form an immense mass of ice. Leonardo evidently reached the glacial region. The sun, he wrote, shone far more brightly than in the plain. And the air up here had a strange deep blue color, which Leonardo correctly attributed to its low humidity.

The sight of the Monte Rosa reconciled me somewhat to the plain, if only from afar. People like me, who have grown up in the mountains, can easily feel lost in a landscape devoid of hills. Everything seems to look identical. The eye seeks and fails to find a focal point (there is not even a forest) and winds up looking off into the distance. What could an artist from the pleasantly undulating landscape of Tuscany find appealing in this monotony? Leonardo spent twenty-three years in the plain in Lombardy, more time than he had in Florence. And these years utterly transformed his art and his research.

After about an hour, I began to get a sense of the richness of the Lomellina. Its rice fields were interesting after all—just very different from the ones I'm used to. You can take in a landscape not only with your eyes, but also with your ears. In the canals and drainage channels along the fields, the water gurgled, roared, whispered, and trickled in constantly changing patterns. A variety of obstacles in the channels produced still other sounds. Here a waterfall cascaded over a little weir, there a rivulet crossed under the path in a pipe and rippled out into a rice field. In another spot, groundwater bubbled up out of the ground, then collected in a basin. And at nearly every junction there were weirs of various designs—orchestras among the hydraulic engineering works into which a river splashed down, then settled in, only to resurface in the underflow with a gush, a gurgle, or a roar. Leonardo regarded the sounds of water as music, and even pondered how they could be created systematically. His later project for a hydraulic organ has been preserved.[28]

Peering into the water was even more riveting than listening to it. The water cascaded down in white stripes, waves swirling into braids behind bridge piers and intersecting like the sides of a triangle when approaching a constriction. Currents of water rose up above the flow, pushed underneath it, and formed hilly landscapes of foam in the whirlpool basin of a dam. All the shapes from Leonardo's manuscripts, and more, were in evidence. You could see them from many angles and watch one shape glide into another. Leonardo faced the challenge of capturing the waves, eddies, and currents on a two-dimensional sheet of paper.

The idea of studying nature for its own sake was alien to Leonardo's contemporaries. It would not have occurred to people in the Middle Ages to call a landscape or even a plant "beautiful." A cornstalk was useful, a poppy a mere weed, and a lily nothing more than a symbol of the purity of the Virgin Mary.[29] When Petrarch, the Tuscan poet, described the rapture he experienced during his famous ascent of Mont Ventoux in southern France in 1336, he did not devote a single word to the view he enjoyed at the summit; instead, the reader learns how nature whetted his appetite to open a book he had brought along about St. Augustine, whereupon the mountain hiker began to contemplate all the foolish mistakes in his life and the insignificance of mankind as a whole. Even when Leonardo's fellow artists began to move away from the tradition of painting their figures of saints in front of a gold background and instead situated them in front of mountains, rivers, and gardens, the landscape was nothing more than a template.[30] Every object had a meaning, like a prop on a stage. A mountain stood for the crucifixion, a river for the baptism of Christ, a garden for the fertility of the Blessed Virgin.

Leonardo broke away from this kind of symbolism when he was still a young man. His first known and dated drawing (August 5, 1473)

Arno Valley drawing

features a river landscape as its central image. Just twenty-one years old at the time, he created the first landscape drawing in the history of European art. Beyond that, however, he also portrayed water in a manner unusual in painting: as a force that shaped the earth.[31] In the foreground of the picture a stream gushes down out of a cave. The cascade has made deep carvings into the rock, and in the valley below the water has eroded a gorge.

The *Baptism of Christ* (Plate III), which Leonardo painted a few years later together with his mentor Verrocchio, also features a waterfall, which flows into the Jordan between John the Baptist and Jesus. Leonardo was still feeling his way toward this new type of motif, and the torrent is portrayed somewhat awkwardly.[32] Foam spraying into the air anticipates his later pen-and-ink drawings. Through the surface of the water, John and Jesus can be seen seeking firm footing on the stones of the riverbed. Eddies have formed around the ankles of the two men. Viewers feel as though they are themselves standing in water, because the Jordan occupies nearly the entire front edge of the picture, then flows out to the horizon.

Evidently Leonardo was already enthralled by nature's inexhaustible abundance of shapes and creatures, which emerge, evolve, and fade away in some mysterious way. The things that were unfolding before his eyes—light shimmering in the leaves of a tree, intersecting ripples from skipping stones, marvelous life inside the human eye—so riveted him that he had no time for

Waterfall (Detail from The Baptism of Christ)

otherworldly matters. Aren't discoveries of this sort far more exciting and poetic than the lives of the saints?

This was the unexplored treasure he set out to mine in his art—a whole world that no one had ever captured on paper or canvas. But would he have been able to grasp the dynamics of water as successfully back home in Tuscany? The steep streambeds full of curves and stones cascading down from the mountains into the Arno Valley make it difficult to study the currents, and the chaotic swirling of water does not allow for a good overview. Lombardy, where nature is tamed, offered Leonardo the opportunity to grasp its laws. The absolutely straight lines and vertical banks of the watercourses here enabled him to study flow patterns, current formations, and the emergence of waves. An environment that offered few distractions allowed him to focus his attention on the essentials.

Single File Through an Alley

Leonardo's insatiable thirst for knowledge gained new momentum during his stay at the La Sforzesca model farm. It was here that he realized that conventional technological methods would fall short in designing mills and canals for the duke.[33] In drawing up his plans for the lock, he was guided by the principle that working *with* the forces of nature—not *against* them—would be the only way to design optimal hydraulic plants. First, however, he had to figure out the laws that governed these forces.

At the outset, Leonardo followed the typical path of those who come up against the limits of their knowledge, namely looking things up in books or seeking expert advice. But Leonardo quickly realized how fragmented and incomplete the standard wisdom was. The science of liquids, for instance, had barely moved ahead since Archimedes supposedly ran naked through the streets of Syracuse in Sicily yelling "Eureka!" after discovering in his bathtub why some bodies sink and others swim.

So Leonardo embarked on his own quest for the laws of nature, using very simple means. A dewdrop helped him fathom the mystery of surface tension: "If first you take a cube of lead of the size of a grain of millet, and by means of a very fine thread attached to it you submerge it in this drop, you will perceive that the drop will not lose any of its first roundness, although it has been increased by an amount equal to the size of the cube which has been shut within it."[34] And he explored the laws of pressure with a wine cask: "If a cask is filled four braccia high with wine and throws the wine a distance of four braccia away, when the wine has become so lowered that it has dropped to a height of two braccia in the cask, will it also throw the wine through the same pipe a distance of two braccia, that is whether the fall, and the range

Loss of pressure in a water cask

that the pipe can throw, diminish in equal proportion or no."[35] If we substitute the modern term "energy" for "range," Leonardo was right on target: The force of the water decreases along with the water level (though this does not hold true for the range of the jet). And by capturing on paper the current and waves in the canals, he gained insight into hydrodynamics.

Leonardo understood that all physics can be explained by laws of motion; that is, by mechanics, and he sought the simplest examples to highlight general problems. The jet pouring from the wine cask stands for water that powers a mill; the straightened canal for a winding river. The only way to understand nature is by asking the right questions. It is crucial to select the right detail from the overall picture of the universe.

Leonardo was thus one of the first to use a simplified experiment to grasp the rules of a complex reality, which remains the most important method today.[36] A good scientist approaches nature the way a caricaturist approaches the features of a politician: Both simplify and overdraw their objects until the essence clearly emerges. The drawing over my desk is also a caricature of a waterfall, albeit of a highly artistic nature.

Some of Leonardo's discoveries are still considered valid, and two of them even inspired American historian of science Clifford Truesdell to regard Leonardo as a forefather of fluid mechanics.[37] Leonardo may have come across the first of these while observing water in a narrowing canal and noticing that the river flowed more rapidly there. After the constriction ended, the speed slowed down again. The speed therefore depended on the breadth and depth of the riverbed—and more generally on the surface the current crosses.

Leonardo explained why this was so with an innovative thought experiment: The reader is asked to picture a group of men sidling through an alley as though they were dancing the Polonaise.[38] The rule is that the men can never lose physical contact. Now the alley expands out into a street that is four times as wide. At all times the street has to accommodate all the men who enter it from the alley; the flow cannot break off. That is Leonardo's key insight. Even today, all of hydrodynamics is based on this principle, the "principle of continuity." Without the principle of continuity, weather forecasts and airplanes would be unthinkable.

His second principle similarly reveals Leonardo's powers of observation and his refusal to take anything for granted. He wondered why the water in the center of a vortex rotated much more quickly than at the outer edges. It seemed strange to him, because a wheel worked the opposite way. A nail on a tire moved much faster than one on the hub. Evidently the movement of fluids proceeded according to different laws. Leonardo was able to guess the correct correlation: The speed of the water depends on the path on which it moves around the center of the vortex.[39] The shorter the path, the faster the speed—a correlation anyone can verify by watching a bathtub drain.

Liquids swirl in a drain, and water particles squeeze through a canal just like men through an alley. Leonardo thought in pictures. He owed his highly significant discoveries to this pictorial approach, though it also led him astray at times, because looks can be deceiving. A sheet from the year 1500, for instance, has drawings of the arm of a scale, the trajectory of a stone cast upward, a jet of water that tapers toward the bottom, and a device to measure the water pressure. At the top is this remark, in mirror writing: "All forces are pyramidal."[40] Throughout nature, he sought the ratios he had come across while studying perspective and called his findings "pyramidal law." Just as objects twice as far away seem to dwindle to half their size, he noted, other sizes change proportionately to each other. Balance scales confirm this idea: If you double the weight of an object, the counterweight on the other arm of the scale has to be moved twice as far away from the suspension, in accordance with lever law. Also, the pressure of a jet of water doubles with the water level in the container. Matters are not quite so simple when considering the speed of a stone cast upward and the diameter of a jet of water flowing downward. These decrease with the square root and with the fourth root of the height, respectively. And the range of a jet of water pouring from a cask changes with the square root of the water level in the container. But Leonardo did not know how to perform these arithmetic operations.

Because many of his theories are incorrect, some art historians tend to discount his significance as a researcher. However, this dismissive attitude does not do him justice—and betrays a lack of information as well. In natural science, errors are not only admissible, but invaluable. Only when a theory proves contradictory does it give rise to new experiments and thus to progress. In all eras, the greatest minds have also claimed quite a bit of nonsense along the way. That Isaac Newton believed in the alchemy of gold production does nothing to diminish his achievement of having founded modern physics.

While Leonardo's experiments paved the way for modern research, he was not a scientist in today's sense of the term—not because he was often wrong, but because his working method was too different from the standard method in modern laboratories. Instead of relying on visual perception, today's scientists strive wherever possible to count and to measure. Leonardo appreciated the value of mathematics, but his notebooks contain unsuccessful attempts at even simple division. His pencil remained the major instrument of his thought processes.

Natural scientists today seek to establish connections. They are not satisfied with a theory until its hypotheses can be confirmed—or refuted—in experiments. Leonardo, by contrast, described, and based his conclusions on, what he saw, but he did not try to fashion a coherent theory from his findings. He did not even carry out systematic series of experiments. Instead, his interest leaped from one topic to the next.

But Leonardo's noncoordinated and comprehensive approach is precisely what enabled him to lay the foundations for a new, broader scope for science, and it provided a way out of the dead end in which science was caught as a result of its overdependence on book learning. Ultimately, this approach grew out of Leonardo's background in craftsmanship, where results took precedence over reading. Even later, when he acquired a literary education, he shied away from launching into extended theoretical discussions; none of the ideas in the notebooks fills more than a single page.

Ever the consummate craftsman, he preferred to explore every new insight with an eye to how it could be implemented. And if he found he was getting carried away with his ideas, he would caution himself to stick to practical applications: "When you write about the movements of water, think about specifying its practical uses for each project."[41]

At the Mill of Mora Bassa, where Cecilia Gallerani (the lady with the ermine) seems to have enjoyed the company of the duke, visitors today can see how Leonardo envisioned the fruits of his research. Enterprising residents have turned the ruins into a museum, and the giant water wheel still turns out front. A cabinetmaker from Leonardo's hometown of Florence provided two dozen wooden models of machines Leonardo once designed in the service of Duke Ludovico, including pumping stations powered by water, clock mechanisms, construction cranes, flying machines, a spring-driven automobile, and huge catapults—the enormous engines of war that Leonardo had promised his ruler.

Most visitors react with a combination of fascination and disbelief to the fact that the same man who painted *The Last Supper* and the portrait of the beautiful Cecilia designed all this equipment as well. Leonardo would never have described himself as a universal genius, because he regarded art, technology, and science, which we now consider such dissimilar endeavors, as a single pursuit of the human mind.

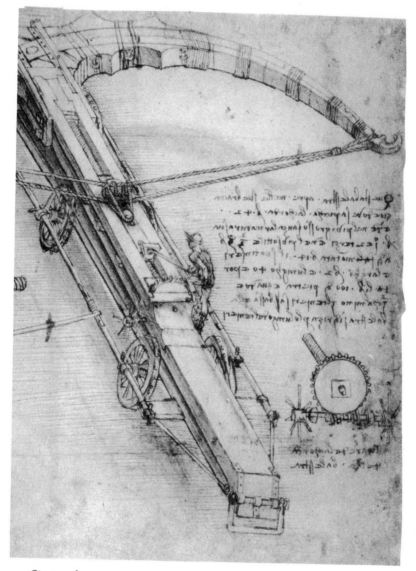

Giant crossbow

III

WAR

ONE OF VASARI'S LOVELIEST ANECDOTES about Leonardo concerns the artist's love of animals: "Often when he was walking past the places where birds were sold, he would pay the price asked, take them from their cages, and let them fly off into the air, giving them back their lost freedom."[1] Did Leonardo, who had an exceptional desire for freedom and himself tried to fly, feel a special rapport with birds?

A letter from the west coast of India addressed to the Florentine regent Giuliano de' Medici in 1515 is revealing. A seafarer named Andrea Corsali reported that he had discovered gentle people clad in long robes who lived on milk and rice, refused any food that contained blood, and would not harm any living creature—"just like our Leonardo da Vinci."[2] Corsali was describing the Jains, known for their extreme nonviolence; in the twentieth century they would have a profound influence on Mahatma Gandhi.

Of course Corsali would not have been reminded of the artist far away if Leonardo's attitude had not seemed so remarkable. That a person would display empathy at all was quite unusual in this era, which had been devastated by violence. But the idea of actually forswearing the consumption of meat out of simple consideration for other creatures was unheard of in the West.

Vasari, who later wrote a biography of Leonardo, may have known these and other reports about customs in the Orient. In the Buddhist countries of Southeast Asia birds are offered for sale in front of some temples even today so that people who want to ensure good karma can buy their freedom and send them soaring into the air. Vasari's account of Leonardo's bird liberation may have been no more than an appealing embellishment to his text.

Still, there is no doubt that Leonardo had a deep-seated aversion to all violence, as several passages in his notebooks confirm. His attitude certainly had more in common with the ethos of Eastern nonviolence than with the harsh customs then prevalent in the Christian West. Precisely because he respected the value of every creature, he was firmly convinced of the sanctity of human life. In reference to his anatomical studies, he wrote: "And thou, man, who by these my labours dost look upon the marvelous works of nature, if thou judgest it to be an atrocious act to destroy the same, reflect that it is an infinitely atrocious act to take away the life of man."[3]

Leonardo's words make it difficult to grasp the gruesome fantasies his mind was capable of in designing his engines of war. On hundreds of pages, Leonardo sketched giant crossbows, automatic rifles, and equipment to bombard strongholds with maximal destructiveness. The sole function of these devices was to kill and destroy. He did not just record the technology, but provided graphic descriptions of the devastating impact of his inventions. In one sketch, archers are running away from an exploding grenade, which Leonardo referred to as "the deadliest of all machines."[4] In another, a war chariot with rotating scythes as large as men is mowing down soldiers and leaving behind

Scythed chariot

a trail of severed legs and dismembered bodies.[5] The battle plans Leonardo drew up are equally chilling. On Sheet 69 of Manuscript B, housed in Paris, we read about his preparations for chemical warfare:

> Chalk, fine sulphide of arsenic, and powdered verdigris may be thrown among the enemy ships by means of small mangonels. And all those who, as they breathe, inhale the said powder with their breath will become asphyxiated. But take care to have the wind so that it does not blow the powder back upon you, or to have your nose and mouth covered over with a fine cloth dipped in water so that the powder may not enter.[6]

His involvement in the wars of his era extended well beyond the design of weapons and began even before he signed on with the infamous, bloodthirsty Cesare Borgia in 1502. How could a man whose sense of empathy is said to have inspired him to free birds from their cages come up with ideas of this sort?

On one occasion, Leonardo justified his military activities with a statement that a modern-day reader could easily picture coming straight from the Pentagon: "When besieged by ambitious tyrants, I find a means of offense and defense in order to preserve the chief gift of nature, which is liberty."[7]

Doubts are certainly warranted here; after all, his first employer, Ludovico Sforza, was not exactly a champion of freedom. The historian Paolo Giovio, a contemporary of il Moro, called him "a man born for the ruin of Italy." That might sound harsh, but without a doubt, "the Moor" was a major reason that Italy lost its freedom for centuries and became a battlefield for foreign powers.

Ludovico, an inveterate risk-taker, sized up his position on his very first day in power and realized that he was surrounded by enemies. In his own empire his right to rule was in dispute, since he owed his power to the violent murder of his brother, for which no one had been charged, and the arrest of the sister-in-law. Moreover, Venice and the Vatican tried to exploit Ludovico's insecure position, and they armed for war. In March 1482, the Venetians attacked Ferrara, which was an ally of il Moro. At this time, Leonardo arrived in Milan and in his famous ten-point letter of application promised il Moro a whole new arsenal of weapons. Two years later, Ludovico was able to defeat the Venetians.

But il Moro, who was focusing all his efforts on legitimating his rule once and for all, needed a seemingly endless supply of weapons. Over the next few years, his dodges would determine not only the further course of Leonardo's unsettled life but also result in the so-called Italian Wars, which lasted sixty-five years and brought about the political collapse of the country.

The disaster ran its course when Ludovico sought a strong ally against Naples. The king of Naples, Ferdinand I, had meanwhile given his daughter's hand in marriage to the legitimate heir to the throne in Milan, Gian Galeazzo, and was quite indignant when he realized that Ludovico had no intention of ceding power to his son-in-law. Ludovico encouraged Charles VIII of France to invade Italy to overthrow Ferdinand. What followed was a bloody farce: Charles was asked to invade Lombardy with forty thousand soldiers, whereupon Gian Galeazzo was murdered. Two days later, Charles declared il Moro the legitimate duke of Milan. But the latter showed no gratitude. When the Neapolitans rebelled against the French occupation in the following year, the opportunist switched sides and entered into an alliance with Venice and the pope. The French were expelled and suffered great losses.

Just a few decades earlier, wars had been highly ritualized battles with relatively few casualties, but now they were developing into horrific bloodbaths. The handgun had been widely adopted; a few years later, Leonardo would contribute a wheel lock, which was one of the handgun's first effective firing mechanisms.[8] And there were growing numbers of portable cannons on battlefields. Since the earlier stone balls had been replaced by metal projectiles, the firearms shot more effectively than ever before, as Charles VIII's soldiers proved when they demolished the ramparts of the mighty castle of Monte San Giovanni Campano with small cannons within hours, before attacking Naples. Until then the battle was won by the side that had more and better soldiers. From this point on, technology was key.

Leonardo had promised marvelous weapons to il Moro and was granted a tremendous degree of freedom in return. As the engineer of the duke, he received a fixed salary and no longer had to rely on selling his art on the market. This was the only way he could pursue his research interests and continue to perfect his paintings without any pressure to meet deadlines. We owe the magnificence of the Milan *Last Supper*, the studies of water, and his explorations of the human body to Leonardo's clever move of offering himself up to one of the most unscrupulous warlords of his era. During his first seventeen years in Milan, serving Ludovico, he sketched the great majority of his weapons, among them his most dreadful ones.

All the same, Leonardo's interest in weapons went far beyond the steady job they brought him. His drawings reveal an unmistakable fascination with technology. In the end, his inventions were the product of his inexhaustible fantasy, which gave rise to paintings, stories, projects to transform entire regions, tools—and weapons. One of these weapons, which he designed in Milan, looks like a water mill, but is actually a gigantic automatic revolver. Leonardo arranged four crossbows in a compass formation, with one pointing upward, one downward, one to the left, and one to the right. The wheel was powered by four men running along its exterior to turn it at breakneck speed. An ingenious mechanism with winches and ropes caused the bows to tighten automatically with each turn. The marksman crouched in the middle of the mechanism and activated the release. In one version, the wheel was equipped with sixteen rather than four crossbows. Leonardo devoted himself to refining the driving mechanism as well.[9]

Even so, in comparison with the truly revolutionary firearms of the era, this contraption looks charmingly old-fashioned. At least for the years until 1500, Kenneth Clark was probably right in claiming that Leonardo's knowledge of military matters was not ahead of his time.[10] Even Leonardo's most spectacular weapon, the giant crossbow he invented in 1485, was not really pioneering. With a 98-foot bow span, this monster was intended to stand up to cannons, to fire more accurately, and to save the soldiers from often fatal accidents with exploding gunpowder. There is no evidence, however, that anyone attempted to construct this giant crossbow during Leonardo's lifetime. More than five hundred years later, when a British television production undertook this project, the results were pitiful. Specialized technicians were brought in to build a functionally efficient weapon using twentieth-century tools, guided by Paolo Galluzzi, one of the leading experts on Renaissance engineering. Since they were required to restrict their materials to those that were available in the Renaissance, they opted to build a bow with blades made of walnut and ash that would be five times larger than any before. A worm drive designed by Leonardo himself had to muster a force equivalent to the weight of ten tons to tighten this enormous spring, thus making it possible to catapult a stone ball over 650 feet. But when British artillerymen tried out the construction on one of their military training areas, the balls barely left the weapon. After a mere 16 feet in the air, they plopped to the ground. Video recordings showed that they could not detach properly from the bowstring. When the technicians added a stopping device to the string (not drawn by Leonardo), the range increased to 65 feet—

still hardly sufficient to produce anything but guffaws on a Renaissance battlefield. And the fact that the replicators had made the bow thinner than in Leonardo's design came back to haunt them—the wood broke.

When you look at many of Leonardo's drawings from his years in Milan, it is hard to shake the feeling that Leonardo had no intention of supplying serviceable weapons. It seems to have been far more important to him to impress his patron—especially when he emphasized the enormous dimensions and the impact of his weapons. As the most talented draftsman of his generation, he knew how to create a dazzling effect. Leonardo enjoyed an outstanding reputation as a technician of war because he was a great artist. He portrayed the details of his designs so meticulously, using the effects of perspective, light, and shadow so skillfully, that it was easy to mistake reality for wish. The drawing of the giant crossbow features not only the knot of the string and the details of the trigger mechanism, but also the soldier handling the weapon. Like the face on the *Mona Lisa*, Leonardo's war machines seem alive.

THE PHYSICS OF DESTRUCTION

While Leonardo proved a master of illusion in designing weapons, he also made concrete contributions to military development. Military commanders needed to figure out how to put the latest firearms— mobile cannons—into action. How should they shoot? With bows and crossbows, the shooter simply aimed straight ahead; the range of the new firearms, by contrast, meant that the trajectory curve had to be determined to make the cannonball hit its target. But no one had a clear idea about the laws governing the paths of cannonballs. Progress on this matter could determine the outcomes of wars.

Traditional physics offered little help, because this discipline still adhered to the ancient view that a body moves only while a force acts on it. But if that were so, a cannonball would come to a standstill just after leaving the barrel of the cannon. The seemingly plausible concept of "impetus" was introduced: The cannon gives the ball its impetus, and only when the impetus is completely used up as it flies through the air does it fall to the ground. The cannoneers of the time were well aware that the impetus theory could not be correct; anyone who relied on it was off the mark. The error is that gravity sets in immediately to begin pulling down on the cannonball.

Leonardo's interest in this question went far beyond its military implications. He was determined to figure out the laws of motion. He kept going around in circles because he could not relinquish the idea of impetus and because the crucial concept of the earth's gravity was still unknown at the time. His notebooks document how bedeviled he was by the laws of motion. His explanations of mechanics were riddled with inconsistencies; at times he argued both for and against impetus within the space of a single paragraph.[11]

But then he had a brilliant idea of how to determine the trajectory of projectiles not by conceptualizing, but by observing: "Test in order to make a rule of these motions. You must make it with a leather bag full of water with many small pipes of the same inside diameter, disposed on one line."[12] One sketch shows the small pipes in the bag pointing upward at various angles, like cannons that aim higher at some points and more level at others. The arcs formed by the spurting water correspond to the trajectories of the cannonballs. Leonardo's trajectories were accurate in both this sketch and others.[13] By means of a clever experiment—not involving mathematics—he had discovered the ballistic trajectory that Isaac Newton finally worked out mathematically some two hundred years later.

This little sketch offers a glimpse inside Leonardo's mind. He was able to link together fields of knowledge that appeared utterly unrelated.

From the laws of hydraulics, which he had investigated so exhaustively, he gained insights into ballistics. His thoughts ran counter to the conventional means of solving problems. Instead of attacking the matter head on, formulating the question neatly, and penetrating more and more deeply below the surface, Leonardo approached the problem obliquely—like a cat burglar who has climbed up one building and from there breaks into another across the balconies. Leonardo was unsurpassed in what is sometimes called "lateral thinking," which enabled him to explain the sound waves in the air by way of waves in the water, the statics of a skeleton by those of a construction crane, and the lens of the eye by means of a submerged glass ball.

Leonardo's experiments with models also represented a new approach. Since he neither understood how to use a cannon nor was able to observe the trajectory of an actual cannonball up close, he used a bag filled with water as a substitute. Of course an approach of that sort is unlikely to yield a coherent theoretical construct, because similarities between different problems are always limited to individual points, and Leonardo was far too restless to pursue every last detail of a question. Still, his models yielded astonishing insights. The French art historian Daniel Arasse has aptly called him a "thinker without a system of thought."

In an impressive ink drawing, Leonardo illustrated the damage that could be inflicted by applying his insights into ballistics.[14] A large sheet in the possession of the Queen of England shows four mortars in front of a fortification wall firing off a virtual storm of projectiles. Not a single square foot of the besieged position is spared from the hundreds of projectiles whizzing through the air. For each individual one, Leonardo marked the precise parabolic trajectory, and the lines of fire fan out into curves like fountains. Ever the aesthete, Leonardo found elegance even in total destruction.

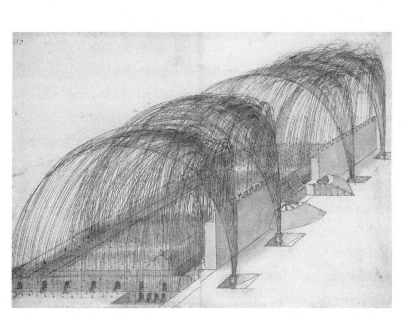

Saturation bombing of a castle

It is difficult to establish to what extent Leonardo's knowledge of artillery was implemented on an actual battlefield. When Ludovico had Novara bombarded in February 1500, the mortars were so cleverly positioned that the northern Italian city quickly fell. In the opinion of the British expert Kenneth Keele, il Moro was using Leonardo's plans for a systematic saturation bombing.[15]

Leonardo's close ties to the tyrants of his day offer a case study of the early symbiosis of science and the military. Now as then, war not only provides steady jobs and money to pursue scholarly interests, but also prompts interesting theoretical questions. Even a man as principled as Leonardo was unable to resist temptations of this sort. He was not the first pioneer of modern science and technology to employ his knowledge for destructive aims. Half a century earlier, Filippo Brunelleschi, the inspired builder of the dome of the Florence Cathedral, had diverted the Serchio River with dams to inundate the enemy city of Lucca. (This operation came to a disastrous end; instead of putting Lucca under water, the Serchio River flooded the Florentine camp.) Leonardo's struggle to strike a balance between conscience, personal gain, and intellectual fascination seems remarkably modern, and brings to mind the physicists in Los Alamos who devoted themselves heart and soul to nuclear research until the atomic bomb was dropped on Hiroshima.

Of course we cannot measure Leonardo's values by today's standards. We have come to consider peace among the world's major powers a normal state of affairs now that more than six decades have passed since the end of World War II, but we need to bear in mind that there has never been such a sustained phase of freedom from strife since the fall of the Roman Empire. In Italy, the Renaissance was one of the bloodiest epochs. The influence of the Holy Roman Empire had broken down, mercenary leaders had wrested power from royal dynasties, and a desire for conquest seemed natural. War was the norm, and a prolonged period of peace inconceivable.

Leonardo's refusal to regard death and destruction as inescapable realities is a testament to his intellectual independence from his era. As far back as 1490 he was calling war a "most bestial madness."[16] And one of his last notebooks even contains a statement about research ethics. While describing a "method of remaining under water for as long a time as I can remain without food," he chose to withhold the details of his invention (a submarine?), fearing "the evil nature of men who would practice assassinations at the bottom of the seas by breaking the ships in their lowest parts and sinking them together with the crew who are in them."[17] The only specifics he revealed involved a harmless diver's suit in which the mouth of a tube above the surface of the water, buoyed by wineskins or pieces of cork, allows the diver to breathe while remaining out of sight.

Leonardo must have had his reasons for withholding particulars about the dangerous underwater vehicle. Perhaps his ideas were still quite vague, or he was afraid that imitators might thwart his chances for a promising business. But the key passage here is Leonardo's statement about the responsibility of a scientist. He was the first to assert that researchers have to assume responsibility for the harm others cause in using their discoveries. Insights like these, and his high regard for each and every life, were quite extraordinary at the time. It is amazing that he embraced these ethical principles—but not surprising that he repeatedly failed to live up to them, at least by today's standards.

AMORRA, ILOPANNA

War would continue to chart the course of Leonardo's career. When King Louis XII ascended to the throne in Paris and formed an alliance with the pope against il Moro, a new invasion by the French was just a matter of time. On April 1, 1499, Leonardo paid up the employees in his workshop in Milan, and on September 6, French and papal troops occupied the city. The cover of Leonardo's Notebook L, which is housed in Paris today, features this bitter comment: "The duke has lost his state, his property, and his freedom, and none of his projects was finished." This last clause seems to refer in part to the projects the duke had commissioned Leonardo to build, in particular the giant equestrian statue. More painful still was the loss of his position at the court, which had offered him high status and a steady salary. Ludovico himself had departed for Austria.

At this time, Leonardo wrote a strange note to himself: "Find Ingil and tell him you will wait Amorra, and will go with him Ilopanna."[18] He evidently wrote this message in code to ensure that it could not be made out if it fell into the wrong hands. Leonardo does not appear to have considered his adversaries very clever; decoding this text is simply a matter of reading it backwards:

Ingil= Ligny
Amorra= a Roma (to Rome)
Ilopanna= *a Napoli* (to Naples)

So Leonardo wanted to join Ligny, the mercenary leader, on his way from Rome to Naples. Louis of Luxembourg, Count of Ligny, was an influential cousin of the king of France. Leonardo figured he had found himself a new patron. Perhaps as a small favor to Ligny, Leonardo sketched a map of Lombardy.[19] But his hopes were dashed when Ligny left for France empty-handed in the wake of political disputes. Moreover, rumors started circulating that il Moro, equipped with new troops by Maximilian I, head of the Holy Roman Empire, was returning to Milan and intended to punish collaborators harshly.

Leonardo decided to flee. On the page with the Ligny note, he jotted down a few items he would need to prepare: "Have two trunks covered ready for the muleteer. . . . Buy some tablecloths and towels, hats, shoes, four pairs of hose, a great coat of chamois hide, and leather to make new one. The turning-lathe of Alessandro. Sell what you cannot carry."[20]

On December 14, he deposited six hundred florins in a bank in Milan with instructions to transfer it to his account in Florence, and left the city in the nick of time. A few weeks later, Milan was back in Ludovico's hands. Those who had cooperated with the French feared for their lives.

Leonardo made it safely to Venice. He was quite welcome there, because this maritime power on the Adriatic Sea feared an attack by the Turks. The senate dispatched him to the border area of Friuli to take measures to prevent an onslaught of Ottoman troops from the northeast. Leonardo returned with a report that suggested inundating the valley of the Isonzo River to block an invasion. He was an expert on the subject of water, and most likely he knew the details of Brunelleschi's attempt to force Lucca to its knees by means of an artificial flood. It is not clear what specific measures Leonardo recommended to the Venetians, because only fragments remain of a draft of a letter to the "illustrious Lords," as he customarily called his patrons.[21] The basic idea was to build a giant dam in the riverbed with gates that could be used to raise and lower the water level quickly. Later references to construction at the Isonzo indicate that his plan was carried out at least in part.[22]

Even so, Leonardo's stay in Venice was no more than an episode. He could not gain a foothold in this city, where policies were determined by a few influential merchant families and benefices were already assigned, so Leonardo decided to return to Florence, where he knew the customs. By Easter, he was back in his hometown. Now that he was nearly fifty years old, he would have to build a new life for himself. But competition among artists was stiff, and Leonardo, who had attained so much independence in Milan, had little desire to paint pictures according to the wishes of patrons, as his colleagues did. Instead, his next employer was Cesare Borgia—a man feared throughout Italy.

PACT WITH THE DEVIL

Cesare was the commander of the Vatican troops and an illegitimate son of the reigning pope, Alexander VI, alias Rodrigo Borgia, who had bought his way into office by bribing the electors, as was customary at the time. He aimed to start a dynasty.

It was common knowledge that Alexander and Cesare had no moral scruples. Beginning on July 19, 1497, when Cesare's older brother Juan

Bartolomeo Veneto, a portrait said to be of
Lucrezia Borgia

was found stabbed to death and floating in the Tiber, the Borgias, who were originally from Spain, did everything in their power to stand up against the long-established Roman clans. Anyone who got in their way was simply done away with. "Every night four or five murdered men are discovered—bishops, prelates, and others—so that all Rome is trembling for fear of being destroyed by the Duke [Cesare]," the Venetian ambassador reported just as Leonardo was planning naval wars in Venice.[23]

The third member of this grim family enterprise was Cesare's sister Lucrezia. Her role was to marry the right men. Her contemporaries called her a bewitching beauty. (The Städel Museum in Frankfurt houses the enchanting *Ideal Portrait of a Woman*, by Bartolomeo Veneto, which may be a portrait of Lucrezia Borgia.) As soon as the marriages had served their political purpose, the pope would annul them. At the age of 13, he married off his daughter for the second time, to a cousin of Ludovico Sforza, in order to secure an alliance between the Vatican and Milan. Four years later, when the power of il Moro began to dwindle, the pope proclaimed that the marriage had never been consummated, and that the husband, Giovanni Sforza, was impotent. That claim could not be leveled against the next husband, who was from the royal dynasty of Naples, because Lucrezia had borne him a son, so Cesare had his brother-in-law strangled before his eyes.

It fell to Cesare to use the money and the soldiers of the church to conquer a territory to rule in central Italy. His adversaries feared the undeniably talented Cesare, although he was a mere twenty-five years old. Envoys reported that he was consumed with ambition, but he was also quite eloquent and engaging. Soldiers praised his horsemanship, his strength, and his courage. A contemporary painting in the Uffizi Gallery in Florence shows him in profile with well-proportioned features; his mouth, framed by a well-groomed full beard, is half open, as though he is engaged in conversation. The most compelling feature is Cesare's piercing gaze.

The portrait must be highly idealized, because Cesare was suffering from syphilis, which had disfigured his face and given him a repulsive look. A series of three drawings by Leonardo that appear to be of Cesare Borgia seem more realistic. They, too, highlight the full beard and the expression in the eyes, but they convey a totally different impression. His beard is so wild and his glance so shifty-eyed that his portrait instills not fascination, but fear.

After a blitzkrieg that lasted less than eighteen months, this man controlled nearly all of central Italy. On June 4, 1502, Arezzo, spurred on by Borgia, rose up against its neighbor Florence, which until then

Cesare Borgia

had been superior in strength. In Leonardo's hometown, there was widespread panic of becoming Cesare's next victim.

Leonardo signed on with Borgia at this very time. Perhaps he used the turmoil surrounding the rebellion to switch unnoticed to the side of the enemy. We do not know what enticed him to do so. A single note making reference to Cesare's promises is all we have to go on: "Borges [Borgia] will get the Archimedes of the bishop of Padua for you."[24] The reference is to a manuscript with texts by the famous Greek mathematician and physicist, which the pope's son had probably stolen from the library in Urbino not long before.

The prospect of receiving a rare manuscript can hardly have sufficed to entice him to work for a tyrant who was notorious as the most brutal mercenary leader of the time and was even threatening Leonardo's hometown. According to political scientist Roger Masters, Leonardo seems to have switched sides with the full knowledge of the Florentine government, and possibly even on its behalf.[25] A note by Leonardo suggests that the enemy camp had approached him for information. We know that he swiftly produced a map of Arezzo and the surrounding areas that specified the distances between the locales and fortifications. But it is unclear whether he did so on behalf of Borgia or for the Florentines.[26] Florence had now paid an exorbitant thirty thousand gold ducats in protection money to buy off Borgia. Leonardo's employment in enemy headquarters would thus have served as a supporting measure to learn of Borgia's intentions ahead of time, and Leonardo was traveling through Italy on a double assignment—working for Borgia *and* spying for Florence.

It is difficult to picture Leonardo, who was introverted and always out for his own interests, as a secret agent. It is more likely that personal motives drove him to accept his new post as Borgia's "architect and general engineer," in the words of a pompous letter of appointment dated August 18, 1502. His financial situation in Florence was dire, and his bank statements make it abundantly clear that he was living from the money he had saved in Milan. Now the opportunity arose to gain the patronage of the son of the pope, a man with an apparently brilliant future ahead of him.

Was Leonardo also attracted to Cesare's commanding personality? The two men had almost certainly known each other from when Borgia had occupied Milan as the leader of the papal troops in collaboration with the French.[27] Cesare was an affable young conqueror, open to excesses of all kinds, besotted with power and eager for quick victories; Leonardo, an aging artist and researcher who was withdrawn, unruffled, and intent on fathoming the mysteries of the world, who abhorred violence and spent years on each of his great works. It would be hard to imagine a greater contrast between two characters, aside from the fact that each was considered the undisputed genius of his era in his respective arena. Neither bothered about taboos, and both had lightning-quick minds. Leonardo clearly preferred the intelligence of a Borgia (as he had the shrewdness of il Moro) to the mediocrity of the patrician families and clergymen who had been his business partners in Florence. And a capable tyrant, who did not have to answer to anyone, could more easily be persuaded to sponsor bold projects than bourgeois committees looking to shield their own interests.

The new position was certainly alluring. Leonardo was in charge of the entire network of fortifications in Borgia's sphere of control. Not even il Moro had given him this much responsibility. He galloped through central Italy and checked the positions. Within just a few weeks, he had inspected Piombino, Urbino, Pesaro, Rimini, Cesena, and Porto Cesenatico.

The town of Imola, located in a plain southeast of Bologna, is the best place to view the results of Leonardo's activities. Today Imola has become synonymous with the Formula One San Mariono Grand Prix, but it is so unchanged from the way it was in Leonardo's day that if you take a walk in the center of town and picture it without all those bicycles, you feel as though you have been transported back in time. In the arcades, which cast shade along the paved main streets, you hear the echoing voices of people going about their business or stopping to chat. No one is in a hurry. Cars are not allowed in the downtown area, there are no modern buildings, and even the town gates and sections of the ramparts are still standing. For centuries, this place was of paramount strategic significance, because this was the key control point for the routes leading into Romagna, which was fiercely contested, and the Adriatic ports.

The Rocca Sforzesca, Borgia's winter quarters

Heading west from the center of town, I arrive at a large open square that must have been used as a field of fire. At the end of it, ramparts rise out of a ditch, with smooth and uniform reddish walls that extend for more than three hundred feet until they come to an end in a circular tower at each of the four corners of the fortress known as the Rocca, the fortifiable stronghold in a town, its "rock" of refuge. The whole structure is so out of place here that it might as well be a spaceship from another galaxy. In the past, the ramparts must have looked even more disconcerting, because as Leonardo's drawings show, even the openings over the parapet walks, a good 65 feet above the ground, were covered by wooden lids.

Cesare Borgia set up his headquarters behind these walls in the winter of 1502 after seizing the Rocca.[28] He owed his success in large part to a betrayal, because the fortress was considered impregnable. It is still easy to see why today. The only way inside leads over a stone bridge first on a man-made island, where the intruder, in full view and shooting range of the defenders, steps onto a second bridge, at the end of which the entrance gate finally looms up. Inside, a corridor leads along 40-foot-thick ramparts. When I reemerge into the light, I find myself in a courtyard surrounded by parapet walks and casemates. Leonardo must have spent the cold months of 1502 in these vaults among Borgia's entourage. The general, who, according to chroniclers, threw wild parties at night, planned to restructure the Rocca as a permanent military base and possibly make Imola the capital of his future empire.[29] As Borgia's general engineer, Leonardo must have been chiefly responsible for this project. Several detailed drawings of the Rocca confirm that this was the case. Evidently Borgia hoped to remodel the fortress to make it truly impregnable and to transform it into a magnificent noble residence.[30]

Leonardo's precise survey of the area has ensured that his name will forever be associated with Imola. Weeks of hard work resulted in nothing less than the first city map the world has ever seen. It is a masterpiece of graphic design (Plate II). Portrayed as a circular vignette with very fine strokes indicating the compass points, Imola resembles the pupil of the eye. The roofs of the houses, each individually painted in water colors, have a reddish hue; the main streets, in white, contrast with the yellowish-green municipal gardens and the wheat-colored fields outside the fortification walls. A moat, which varies in color from bright blue to silver, divides the city from the country, and the Santerno River flows past the minutely detailed gravel banks in such dynamic flow lines that you can almost hear the crunch of the pebbles when the waves hit. "It is far from being a lifeless object, a blandly flat record of measured features. It perceptibly stirs with life," writes the Oxford art historian Martin Kemp. "Under the touch of Leonardo's pen and the scrutiny of his eyes, nothing remained inert, not even a flat map."[31]

Leonardo's map of Imola opened up a new perspective on the world. Until then, pictures were largely restricted to images that the eye could see. Leonardo's depiction of Imola, by contrast, while oriented to reality, abandoned the realm of natural sensory perception. His abstract rendition was so revolutionary that it would take more than 450 years until people would next view their world from a similarly alien perspective—when they saw our blue planet rise from the moon.

Today we are so accustomed to using maps to find our way around—and now we even have satellite images of the surface of the earth—that the magnitude of Leonardo's achievement can be appreciated only by those who compare it to one of the standard city maps of that era. The old illustrations nearly always pictured the areas they were mapping at a diagonally downward angle, as though the draftsman were looking at the streets and houses from a high mountain. Even though walls and roofs—and often trees—could be made out in those pictures, they had a strangely distorted perspective. Finding your way around with a map like that would be just about impossible, because the setting looks different at varying angles. Moreover, distances can never be accurate in a picture of this kind.

Leonardo chose to forgo any obvious similarity with what he saw, and he depicted Imola as though he were aloft above the town. Because Leonardo was not able to assume this position in reality, he applied mathematical methods (still used today) to derive a true-to-scale layout of the houses and streets on the basis of surveying data. To get these data, Leonardo and his assistant must have paced off every street and every house. A drawing in the notebooks displays two different wheelbarrow-like carts with gear mechanisms on the axles to count the wheel revolutions and thus record the distances.[32] Sketches attest to this surveying work.

Reproductions of the maps give us no more than a hint of the extreme precision Leonardo must have employed. The original, which is housed in Windsor, conveys a more accurate impression; to recognize the true value of this masterpiece, you need to examine it with

Cyclometer

a magnifying glass. Every courtyard, and even the entrances to the houses, can be made out.

Leonardo's map of the town is accurate to within a few feet, and because Imola's town center has changed so little since Borgia's age, I was able to use a copy of it to find my way around without any difficulty, though the river banks, so stunningly portrayed on this map, are gone today, having been replaced by the race track. It was also odd to see that the main street in town, the Via Emilia, which is elegantly curved on the map and takes up the bends of the river so harmoniously, actually runs straight as an arrow. Did the artist distort the direction of this street for aesthetic effect?

Leonardo's talents as a cartographer were unquestionably invaluable for Borgia. Art historian Martin Kemp has established a link between the map of Imola and sketches of lines of fire that Leonardo drew during the same period of time: "Presented with a map of the Imola kind, Cesare could have literally grasped matters in his own hands, formulating plans of action, ordering the dispositions of forces and weapons even more accurately than was possible on the spot. For good measure, Leonardo has added the compass bearings and distances of neighboring towns."[33] He must have produced similar maps of at least two additional cities, Cesena and Urbino; the preparatory sketches in his notebooks have been preserved.[34] And the maps of entire regions and of the area surrounding Arezzo, which Leonardo also drew, made it possible to organize military campaigns with record precision. Leonardo may not have provided his employer any sophisticated killing machines, but he did give him a far more effective weapon: information.

STRANGLED AT DAWN

Leonardo must have met Niccolò Machiavelli in the fortress in Imola as well. Evidently the two men became friends; at any rate, they worked together on at least three later projects.[35] Leonardo and Machiavelli, who had to spend time with Borgia as a Florentine envoy, were certainly kindred spirits. Both were loners, and both struggled mightily to grasp the nature of reality. Leonardo and Machiavelli were prepared to defy

traditional wisdom and taboos. When in doubt, they relied on observation. Neither engaged in metaphysical speculations about the ultimately inexplicable facets of life. Leonardo focused on nature and art,
and Machiavelli on people and their life in the community, namely the
state. Leonardo forever transformed art, and Machiavelli man's notions
of power and politics.

The very mention of Machiavelli's name was chilling during his lifetime and still is today, since it is associated with utter ruthlessness,
particularly because of his most famous book, *The Prince*. In reality,
however, Machiavelli was merely being blunt in describing what he
observed while serving as secretary of the Florentine government and
as a diplomat. Suspiciously often, accusations against Machiavelli were
leveled from the Church and from the aristocracy. While others
sounded off about the meaning and lofty aims of their rule, he straightforwardly laid out techniques for retaining power.

Machiavelli so admired Cesare Borgia's skill that he made him the
hero of *The Prince*. He considered the events of December 1502 (which
Leonardo in all probability witnessed) a stroke of genius.[36] To gain
complete control over occupied Romagna, Borgia granted complete
authority to his deputy, a cruel man named Ramiro de Lorqua. As
soon as calm and order were restored, Borgia no longer considered
such a harsh regime necessary. On the morning of December 26, he
had Ramiro arrested, brought to the main square in Cesena, and cut
in two. He then ordered the corpse and the bloody executioner's sword
to be placed on display. "The brutality of this spectacle left the people
both stunned and appeased."[37]

Borgia needed to win over the civilians because he was in deep trouble. Some of his mercenary soldier leaders had formed a covert alliance
against him, and the rebels were about to topple him. (Possibly Borgia
had doubts about Ramiro's loyalty by this point as well.) Cesare sum-

moned the renegades to Senigallia for a reconciliation meeting and demanded that all troops be withdrawn in advance from this newly conquered small town. On the morning of New Year's Day, he appeared before his mercenary soldier leaders, accompanied by a single mounted escort, and greeted them cordially. But during the banquet, his small group barricaded the town gates and surrounded the palace in which the party was feasting. On New Year's night, two of the leading renegades were strangled with a garotte, and the others were arrested (and later killed). Meanwhile Borgia's soldiers were looting the town, as Machiavelli reported to Florence. The ever-audacious Cesare was at the height of his power.

The sources show that it is likely (though not certain) that Leonardo was still with Borgia at this time. We do know that he resigned no later than the first weeks of the new year, but the reason is unclear. Had Borgia's machinations become unbearable to him during these final days of December? Was he afraid of falling victim to this unscrupulous man himself? He had had a good relationship with Vitellozzo Vitelli, one of the two mercenary soldier leaders executed on New Year's night. (When Leonardo signed on with Cesare, Vitellozzo Vitelli was leading the rebellion of Arezzo.) Or Leonardo may have sensed that the era of the Borgias would soon come to an end. When Cesare's father, Pope Alexander VI, died in August 1503, his successor, Julius II, relieved the son of his post as commander of the Church state. Borgia fled to Spain and was killed in a melee. He was only thirty years old.

By March 4, 1503, Leonardo was back in Florence. A bank statement documents his withdrawal of fifty gold ducats from his account on that day—evidently he had not received his pay from Cesare. Ultimately, the military campaigns yielded no income for him. Everything he designed for the son and military commander of the pope progressed no further than the planning stage.

Even so, his military adventure was a formative experience in his life. In 1504, the Florentine government sent Leonardo to Piombino, which had reverted to its previous ruler, so that he could design a better way to fortify the seaport. The sketch he drew about a year later reveals his intense dedication to the problems of static warfare. The trip was almost certainly initiated by Machiavelli. Going far beyond his actual assignment, Leonardo drew a ring-shaped citadel quite unlike its Renaissance counterparts; it has more in common with twentieth-century defensive structures used in the two world wars.

A model is on view at the National Museum of Science and Technology in Milan. It was part of the very first major Leonardo exhibit in 1939. The Mussolini regime laid claim to the master from Vinci with a grand spectacle, using his genius to confirm the superiority of the Italian mind to the world once and for all.

The fascist organizers of this exhibit had thousands of drawings to choose from, but it was no accident that they picked this design for a fortification, because the model they produced conveys one key point to anyone who looks at it: This fortress has to be impregnable. Even Leonardo's most gruesome engines of war are not as spine-chilling as his vision of defense in a modern war. It looks especially menacing if you kneel down a little and look at the vast installations from the perspective of an attacker. The entrenchment is like a streamlined bulge, protruding from the ground so minimally that even a hurricane would not damage it. Furthermore, all the walls are curved, and there are no edges. Where could enemy forces attack? Viewers see nothing but a monotonous series of tiny square openings, each of which appears to contain artillery aimed straight at them.

Once you return to a standing position and view the model from above, you see that the fortification forms three concentric rings, each in the shape of an inflated bicycle inner tube. While conducting his ballistic studies, Leonardo had noticed that a cannonball causes far less damage on a crenallated surface than on a flat one.[38] A straight wall, in contrast to a curved one, is easy to bombard frontally. Geometry was Leonardo's response to the destructive force of cannons. But even if attackers had been able to blow up the outer wall of the fortification, they would not have accomplished very much—the defenders would simply retreat into the inner rings, and the battle would go on.

THE BEAST WITHIN MAN

The grim determination and the violence and cruelty that Leonardo must have experienced in the war were reflected in his painting. In the same year that he returned from the expeditions with Borgia, Machiavelli, on behalf of the municipal administration, commissioned a monumental fresco of the Battle of Anghiari, which had ended in victory for Florence, to decorate the council hall—a colossal hall in the Palazzo Vecchio, the building on the city's main square, which is topped by a high tower, and now displays a copy of Michelangelo's David at its entrance. Never had Leonardo been offered such a glorious assignment.

The Florentines were hoping for a fresco that glorified their ability to defend themselves. Instead, Leonardo created the first painting in the history of art that deliberately and drastically highlighted the horrors of war. His fresco, along with Goya's Execution of the Rebels, his etchings about the Napoleonic War, and Picasso's Guernica, represents one of the most stirring images of all time.

There is particular irony in the fact that this painting, which portrayed destruction so graphically, was itself destroyed. The decomposition of the work began while Leonardo was still working on it. To avoid the fate of the Last Supper fresco in Milan, which had already started peeling, Leonardo had mixed new types of primers and colors to add to linseed oil, but they proved utterly useless for mural painting. The colors did not dry in the council hall, and when Leonardo tried to heat the room using iron tubs filled with glowing coals, the colors simply ran and merged. Leonardo lost his patience with the project. He broke his contract with the city fathers and abandoned his artwork, which, though unfinished, was already crumbling. In the end, the city council settled on Giorgio Vasari, Leonardo's first biographer, to paint over the remainder.

These unfortunate circumstances notwithstanding, we still have a good idea of how the fresco might have looked. For one thing, we have Leonardo's own sketches of details of his painting. For another, the Louvre has on display a copy of *The Battle of Anghiari* by Peter Paul Rubens, which is based on an older engraving. Although Rubens's drawing is not in full color and reproduces only a detail of the destroyed painting, it conveys a good sense of the fresco as a whole (Plate V). Instead of portraying a traditional battle scene, Leonardo directed our attention right to the focal point of the battle, to the cavalrymen fighting for what appears to be the standard of Milan, and brought the viewer up so close that the soldiers no longer appear as men in uniform representing a state power, but as creatures in the throes of death.

Here is the description by Vasari, who painted over Leonardo's masterpiece in 1563:

> Rage, fury, and vindictiveness are displayed both by the men and by the horses, two of which with their forelegs interlocked are battling with their teeth no less fiercely than their riders are struggling for the standard. . . . An old soldier . . . grips the staff with one hand and with the other raises a scimitar and aims a furious blow to cut off both the hands of those who are gnashing their teeth and ferociously defending their standard. Besides this, on the ground between the legs of the horses there are two figures,

foreshortened, shown fighting together; the one on the ground has over him a soldier who has raised his arm as high as possible to plunge his dagger with greater force into the throat of his enemy, who struggles frantically with his arms and legs to escape death.[39]

Even Rubens's cartoon conveys how this battle erases all differences between friend and foe, and even between man and animal. The horses have human-like faces, while the features of the combatants are so contorted that they do not appear human. They are filled with the raw emotions of fear and belligerence. The horseman on the far left is even fused with his steed to suggest a centaur-like creature. He is leaning so far forward that the upper part of his body covers up the horse's head. On his back there is a shock of hair—precisely where a horse's mane would be—and the head and arms of the man emanate from a mass of flesh that could be man or monster.

War brings out the beast in man. In one of Leonardo's short stories, which he collectively called *Prophecies*, Leonardo predicted that man would see creatures on the earth who were forever locked in battle and who "set no bounds to their malice."[40] They would tear the trees in the forests from the ground and spread death, affliction, suffering, and terror among all living beings. "There shall be nothing remaining on the earth or under the earth or in the waters that shall not be pursued and molested or destroyed, and that which is in one country taken away to another."[41]

The title of this piece is "Of the Cruelty of Man." It is tempting today to construe these lines as a foreshadowing of the all-out wars in the twentieth century—or even as a vision of a nuclear end to the world. But Leonardo did not intend his *Prophecies* as a glimpse into a distant future. He was straightforwardly depicting his own era as a period in which people lost no time implementing scientific innovations

Soldiers' heads, a preliminary drawing for the Battle of
Anghiari *fresco*

to wage war. Leonardo was playing a unique double role at this turning
point in history: As one of the first modern researchers, he resolutely
served the military—and as an artist he unsparingly described the
business of destruction.

THE DREAM
OF FLYING

To GET TO THE TOP of Monte Ceceri, you walk steadily uphill from Fiesole through a dense and unvarying forest of pines, cypresses, and holm oaks until you suddenly find yourself standing in front of a quarry wall gaping open between the trees. This is where the master builders of the Renaissance in Florence acquired sandstone for their palaces. You climb the final few feet along bare rockfaces to get to the summit, which is crowned by an iron stele in commemoration of Leonardo, who is said to have tried out his flying machines on this spot.

I made my way here on a hot evening in June. Although the sun was already going down, it was still stiflingly hot in the valley. There was not a hint of a breeze, and the air was so milky that it absorbed the fading light like murky water. Even so, I was able to look out over the landscape dozens of miles beyond the quarry. Monte Ceceri rises over Florence like a pulpit. It is the highest peak of a range of hills on the northern boundary of the Arno Valley. Where would a paraglider take you from here? Circling over the Arno Valley and the roofs of Florence, a flier could gain height, glide into the hills of Chianti, which

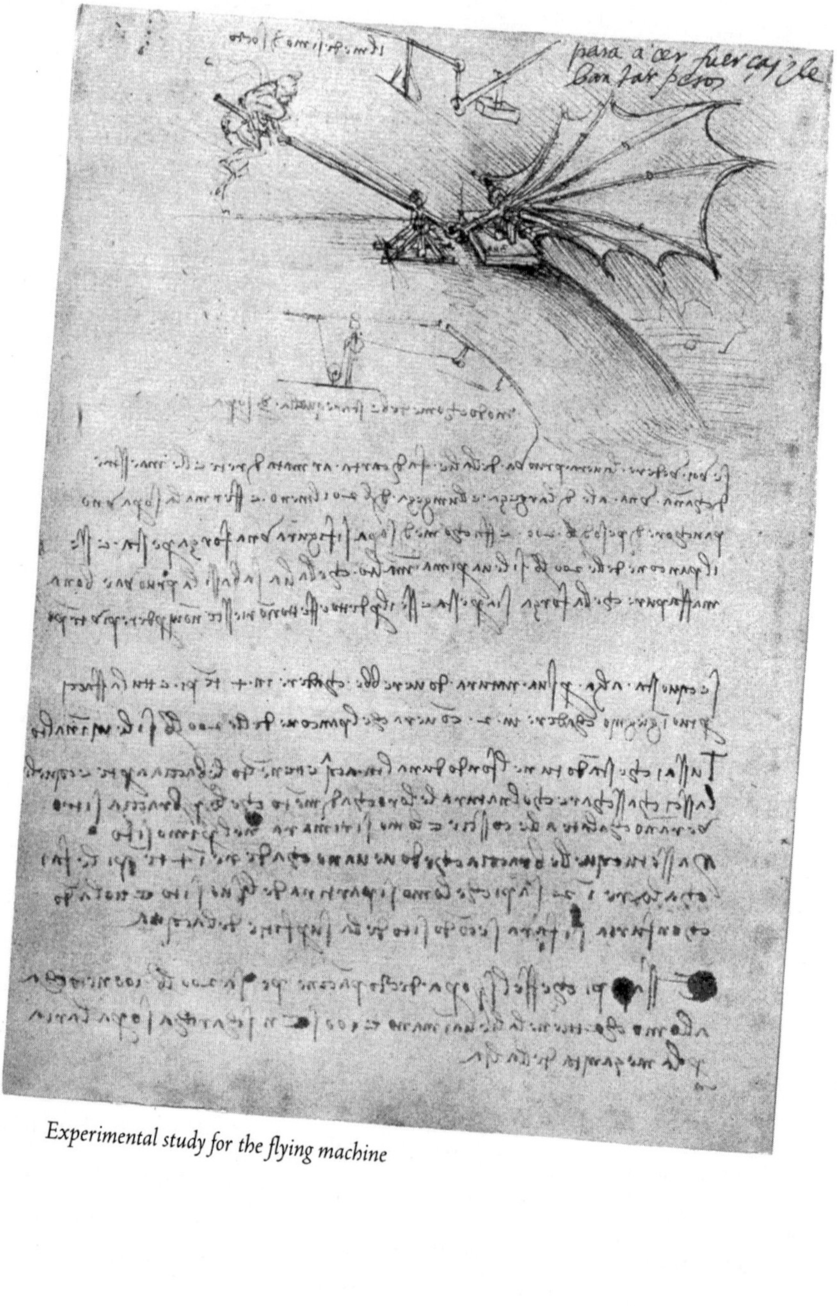

Experimental study for the flying machine

View of Florence from Monte Ceceri

appeared in a bluish blur in the distance, and perhaps soar over to the Monte Albano Ridge, where the small town of Vinci is situated. Eventually the milky sky would simply envelop the flier.

But a flier who went into a tailspin right at the start would likely plunge over the edge of the quarry and crash onto sharp rock ledges at the base of the hillside. The architect and mathematician Giovanni Battista Danti had the good fortune of landing on the roof of the Church of Santa Maria Nuova when he donned feathered wooden wings in 1498 and plummeted from a tower in Perugia. Several sources indicate that he suffered no more than a broken leg.[1]

The Arno River and the lights of Florence glistened a quarter of a mile below me. Between them the cathedral dome loomed up like one lone, enormous molehill, three times as high as any of the houses in the city. Leonardo's contemporaries must have found this view breathtaking. For over a millennium, the concrete dome of the Pantheon in Rome had remained unsurpassed; then, in about 1430, Filippo Brunelleschi succeeded in building a dome that stood some 350 feet

Daedalus on the Florence Cathedral

in the air, more than double the height of the Pantheon. (In Verrocchio's workshop, the young Leonardo would later work as an apprentice on the gilt ball to be placed atop the lantern of the dome.)

Brunelleschi's achievement was mankind's greatest triumph over gravity to date, and his creation made him one of the most famous men of his era. When he died in 1446, he was buried under his dome, and the chancellor of the republic of Florence contributed an epitaph that compared the deceased to Daedalus—the great architect of antiquity who is said to have learned how to fly, although it cost him the life of his son. The high-spirited Icarus came too close to the sun with the wings his father had fashioned for him, and plunged to his death.

The notion that people could fly was no more than a dream for the builders of the cathedral in Florence. Daedalus's deeds were considered a symbol of what the bold human mind can achieve. The Greek hero was commemorated on the church tower on a relief of a bearded man gazing upward and clutching giant birds' wings, his feet lifted off the ground.

Leonardo regarded the legend of the ancient birdman not as a dream, but as a promise. To realize it, all that was needed was a machine that would enable man to imitate the incomparable elegance of the flight of birds. Form and function, art and technology would merge in an invention of this kind. Could there be any greater challenge for the re-searcher and artist Leonardo? It was a matter of approaching flight with scientific curiosity, observing the way birds of prey glide so carefully that the underlying mechanism becomes apparent, counting how many times falcons beat their wings as they begin their nosedive, figuring out how swifts attain their amazing speed, drawing clouds to discover indications for upwinds and downdrafts, and, finally, being guided by the wings of the eagles and buzzards in constructing wings. The results portended euphoria and immense freedom as well as extraordinary sources of inspiration for art. The eyes of the painter, no longer fixed on the earth, would see the world from a near-divine perspective.

This pioneering adventure would take place on Monte Ceceri: "The first flight of the great bird from the summit of Monte Cecero will fill the universe with wonder; all writing will be full of his fame, bringing eternal glory to the place of its origin."[2] To understand this dramatic pronouncement on the cover of Leonardo's codex on the flight of birds, you have to read on. On page 18 of this volume, where Leonardo jotted down his notes about flying, we find the explanation: "From the moun-tain that bears the name of the great bird, the famous bird will take its flight and fill the world with its great fame."[3] Only one mountain in this entire area bears the name of a "great bird," namely *Cecero*, an old Florentine word for "swan."

Leonardo wrote these lines in about 1505, the year he returned from the war and tackled the disastrous *Battle of Anghiari* fresco. His effusive tone may stem from his great longing to leave behind the atrocities he experienced in his military campaigns with Borgia and the humiliating failure of what was probably the most prestigious commission of his career. It is as though he was dreaming of soaring up into another world.

Was he merely contemplating this spot for his initial flight—or did the "bird" actually take wing? Leonardo certainly spent time at Monte Ceceri and the surrounding areas on several occasions and made a detailed study of the wind conditions there. His notebooks provide information on this subject: On March 14, 1505, for instance, he observed the flight of a large bird of prey near Fiesole, but his notebooks make no mention of attempts at flight. Even today, though, people around here say that once a giant bird rose into the air on Monte Ceceri and vanished in the distance, never to be seen again.[4] Did the legend originate in the fate of a man who flew over the quarry into the depths, suspended from enormous wings? Girolamo Cardano, the preeminent physician and natural philosopher of the Renaissance, featured a description of Leonardo's attempts at flying; Cardano's text even implies that Leonardo crashed.[5] Cardano had apparently learned of these events from his father, Fazio, who was friends with Leonardo.

At any rate, the time was ripe for experiments of this kind. Drawings made by engineers in Siena in the mid-fifteenth century show men sailing through the sky with primitive wings, suspended from pointed parachutes.[6] By 1500, tales of aerial acrobats began to proliferate. There was talk of leaps with man-made wings in Nuremberg and Scotland, and mocking tales poked fun at both the audacity of the intrepid fliers and the public's hankering for sensations. In the now-classic stories about Till Eulenspiegel recorded during this era, the legendary trickster decides to entertain the people of Magdeburg by preparing to fly: "There at once arose such a clamor in the city that young and old gathered at the market place, hoping to see him do it. Well, Eulenspiegel took up his position on the roof of the town hall, flapping his arms, and acting as if he really meant to take off."[7]

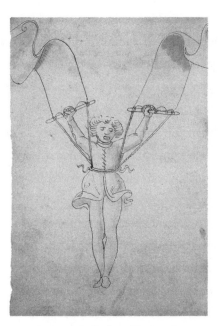

Drawing of a "birdman" by an unknown draftsman from Siena

Just a few decades earlier, it would have been unthinkable for people to place such fervent hopes in soaring up into the skies. In antiquity, conquering gravity was left to the gods, in the Christian West to the angels, a few saints, and of course Jesus and Mary. All others had to be content with the view, represented by Saint Augustine in his *City of God*, that a particular element was intended for each creature to inhabit—the earth for humans, the sky for birds. The utmost ecstasy possible for man's soul would be to float through the spheres of paradise after death, as described in Dante's *Divine Comedy*. But anyone trying to emulate Christ's Ascension was clearly in league with demons and thus guilty of heresy, deserving of the kind of punishment purportedly meted out to the early Christian sorcerer Simon Magus when he levitated up into the sky. Peter prayed to God to make Simon fall, and

Simon came crashing down to earth and broke his legs. He was stoned to death by bystanders.[8]

But once the intellectual revolution gained steam in the first half of the fifteenth century, this kind of reasoning was no longer a deterrent. The fall of Constantinople had resulted in the relocation not only of entire libraries of ancient manuscripts to Italy, but also of scholars who understood them; suddenly there were alternatives to Church doctrine. Technology was developing rapidly, surpassed only by the pace at which artists invented ever-new forms of expression. Wealth abounded, cities had become independent of the central power, and there seemed no good reason to endure limitations. Trade with the non-Christian new rulers of the eastern Mediterranean was blossoming, and the news from Spain was that Christopher Columbus had discovered the sea route to India. Nearly anything seemed possible—even flying.

The Church had preached humility for over a millennium, but now the Florentine philosopher Marsilio Ficino was contending that man's dignity arose from his ability to transform himself and his world according to the dictates of his will and that the highest good was creative power. Ficino, with whom the young Leonardo spent a good deal of time, even maintained that the human soul should strive to return to its natural state of perfection.[9]

Leonardo's contemporaries recognized that he had come further down this road than anyone else. Who better to be the first human being to challenge the supremacy of gods in the sky? Conquering the force of gravity with knowledge and resourcefulness meant coming that much closer to perfection. The dream of the Renaissance was crystallized in man's yearning to fly.

Leonardo made it his mission to realize this dream, and in 1505 he recorded the following vision, just as he was planning to launch his "great bird" at Monte Ceceri: "To write thus clearly of the kite would seem to be my destiny, because in the earliest recollections of my infancy, it seemed to me when I was in my cradle that a kite came and opened my mouth with its tail, and struck me within upon the lips with its tail many times."[10] That Sigmund Freud chose to interpret these words as a statement of Leonardo's intensely erotic attachment to his mother and of his nascent homosexuality (mistranslating the Italian *nibbio* (kite) as "vulture" in the process) reveals more about Freud than it does about Leonardo. It is highly unlikely that this story reflected an actual childhood memory; as far as we know, Leonardo told it for the first and only time when he was a fifty-three-year-old man. The point was probably to emphasize that he was one of the chosen few, striving for eternal fame as the builder of the "great bird," as we learn on the cover of his notebook about the flight of birds.

Leonardo's ambition was also an outgrowth of an epoch in which people strove for esteem as never before. As the British historian Peter Burke has pointed out, the literature of the Renaissance brimmed with words like "competition" (*concertazione*), "emulation" (*emulazione*), and "glory" (*gloria*).[11] Just two generations earlier, the ill-fated Icarus had been considered guilty of hubris, but the tide turned by the sixteenth century, as evidenced in this sympathetic statement by the Neopolitan poet Luigi Tansillo: "This one aspired to the stars, and if he did not reach them, his life faded, but not his daring."[12] And Leonardo made a note of Dante's cautionary words in the *Inferno*: "He who goes through life without achieving fame leaves no more vestige of himself on earth than smoke in the air or foam on the waves."[13]

The folk legend about Monte Ceceri fits so perfectly with Leonardo's vision of flying that we might well share the art historian Ludwig Heydenreich's hunch that Leonardo, the consummate storyteller, concocted the glorious legend of the swan himself. Another possibility is that he knew the story from his childhood and chose this spot for his experiments to make it seem like the fulfillment of an old myth. In either case, the coupling of this story with Leonardo's attempts at flight would have enhanced his own fame.

While I was coming down from Monte Ceceri, I asked a woodsman who was gasping for breath as he made his way upward about this story, and he told me that Michelangelo—Leonardo's archrival—is said to have broken his legs here while flying.

Alone Against Gravity

Would anyone spend half a lifetime drawing flying machines without the slightest intention of putting them to the test? For over three decades, Leonardo threw himself headlong into filling his notebooks with hundreds of sketches of man-made wings, propulsion mechanisms, and birds' wings. He jotted down notes about the flight of birds, pondered airstreams and the forces on a flying body, and wondered how a human could survive a crash.

All the same, many biographers and art historians have declared Leonardo's flying machines "technical utopias," by which they mean that he merely dreamed of flying but did not actually believe that his ideas could be realized, and that he did not attempt to execute his designs. Arguments of this sort emphasize that no extant document substantiates any attempt at flight, but they tend to disregard the numerous references in his notebooks to preparations for this kind of experiment. It is hard to imagine that a mind as curious as his would leave things at a merely theoretical level. We have to assume that Leonardo tried out some of his designs.

The doubts are certainly understandable, though. Leonardo's drawings of flying machines seem so far removed from anything people had previously produced that it is easy to come away thinking that Leonardo was merely daydreaming. But once we realize how intensively he grappled with the problem of flying, we get a sense of just how seriously Leonardo really took it—and how bold his fixation was. In the decades he spent working on flying machines, aerodynamics, and the physical structure of birds, he was all on his own. The science of his era was not in a position to contribute virtually anything of value on these subjects.

How far can a gifted individual go alone? Leonardo's attempts to conquer the sky were a test of the boundaries of the human mind.

"BOARD UP THE LARGE ROOM ABOVE . . ."

Leonardo had his first documented encounter with the dream of flying as a young man in Florence. In 1471, his mentor Verrocchio was involved in the preparations for a spectacle honoring the visiting duke of Milan. In three churches in the city, angels with flapping wings, pulled by invisible cables, floated over the heads of the faithful, and a Christ soared up to the heavens.[14] Soon afterward, Leonardo began to draw machines for the stage; the graphic arts collection in the Uffizi Gallery still has his first sketches on red paper. The aerial screw he designed appears to have been intended for the theater as well; its unique construction gave some later historians of technology the idea of hailing Leonardo as the inventor of the helicopter, although there is no evidence that he believed his contraption would ever rise into the air on its own.

These early sketches of flying machines seem especially alluring because they blend realistic ideas with absurd fantasies. The young Leonardo drew the most implausible designs—feathered wings that spread out as they opened up, and a kind of treadmill in which a standing man would use cranks and pedals to operate paddles over his head, working so vigorously that he would effectively row his way into the air.

Aerial screw

Yet Leonardo soon went beyond mere special effects. In about 1487, he designed a skeletal structure for wings on which the pilot's outstretched fingers were separated by webbing,[15] and complex steering mechanisms enabled the pilot to engage each finger joint of the wings individually.

Clearly he was planning to construct wings even at this time. He noted down every last detail of the materials he would need. The skeletons would be made of "fir, and reinforced with limewood"[16] and covered with the "skin of the sea hen" (a flying fish), or, if that were not available, with normal skin.[17] Leonardo also built an entire arsenal of measuring instruments for his experiments. The notebooks feature anemometers to gauge the wind force, inclinometers to measure slopes, and a giant device resembling bellows used to test whether individual wings produced enough lift to raise a 200-pound man into the air (see illustration at the beginning of this chapter).

But the more research he did, the more questionable these designs began to seem. Leonardo started to wonder whether the human mind was capable of creating a workable flying machine without relying on a model. He reasoned that it would be safer to let nature be his guide:

"Although human subtlety makes a variety of inventions . . . it will never devise an invention more beautiful, more simple, or more direct than does nature, because in her inventions nothing is lacking, and nothing is superfluous."[18]

Leonardo studied birds and bats (he even made himself a note to "dissect the bat"[19]) and examined the movements of butterflies and flies. Birds, he wrote, *are* flying machines.[20] In doing so, incidentally, he anticipated the fundamental insight of Otto Lilienthal—the first successful aviator—who collected extensive data on sparrows and storks and wrote an entire book on their art of flight before attempting his own first takeoff from the Mühlenberg mountain near the village of Derwitz, outside of Potsdam.

Leonardo's designs reflect the way their inventor increasingly modeled his creations on the workings of nature. With his unique powers of observation, he had figured out that birds make headway by flexing their wings.[21] As photographs with high-speed cameras reveal, the tips of the wings work like little propellers: When they are lowered, their leading edges are pulled downward, and when they are raised, the edges rise, which is how the wings, like the rotor blades of a helicopter, produce lift and forward thrust at the same time. Although Leonardo did not know the principle of the propeller, he sensed that his flying machines would have to imitate the flexing of birds' wings, so he planned for a large number of joints in the wings.

But how does a bird soar up into the air? The answer—by beating its wings—seems so obvious at first that any further thought on the subject appears pointless. Leonardo was never able to move beyond this plausible but incorrect explanation. The air, he reasoned, is compressed under the bird, and as its body escapes the resistance, it is pushed aloft.[22] He therefore equipped nearly all his constructions with wings that could be raised and lowered using muscle power.

Study of the flight of birds

When Leonardo began his systematic study of the anatomy of humans and birds in about 1490, he realized that, by body weight, humans are much weaker than birds. More than half of a bird's body mass is concentrated in its pectoral muscles, as compared to a tiny fraction in humans. Leonardo set out to compensate for this disadvantage by making the most of the pilot's arm and leg strength with slings, stirrups, and foot spars. On several sketches we see prone figures positioned in a frame, their legs drawn up and their limbs anchored to the machine. Even the head is used for steering within an enclosure. The would-be pilot is thus strapped to an instrument of torture and equipped with wings that are clearly far too small. The drawings he made during his early years in Milan look heroic, yet somewhat desperate.

The shortcomings of the construction and of human anatomy did nothing to stop Leonardo from coming up with concrete ideas for a test flight. Above the somewhat unclear drawing of a flying device with giant wings, placed on a ladder, we read his thoughts about secret locations for his experiments in the Corte Vecchia in Milan: "Board up the large room above, and . . . you will have space upon the roof above. . . . And if you stand upon the roof at the side of the tower the men at work upon the cupola will not see you."[23] At one point he was considering launching the artificial bird's first long flights over a body of water and equipping the pilot with an inflated wineskin to use as a life preserver.[24] Later he designed leather bags "tied after the fashion of the beads of a rosary" and fastened to the pilot to cushion his landing. "If you should fall with the double chain of leather bags which you have tied underneath you so manage that these are what first strike the ground."[25]

What finally made him question whether it was possible to fly using muscle power: failed attempts at flight, theoretical insights, or both? Whatever the case, Leonardo started to realize, during his final years in Milan, that beating wings were insufficient for flight. Humans were simply too weak to rise into the sky on their own power. Once, in about 1495, he broke away from the model of the birds with two designs, at least one of which would have had a good chance of success.[26] The first is a sphere with circular sails, the pilot floating through the air in its middle as though suspended within a bubble. The second drawing features a rigid wing that bears a striking resemblance to a modern stunt kite. Unfortunately Leonardo did not pursue this promising idea.

Instead, he returned to studying nature. He noticed that the larger the bird, the less frequently it flapped its wings. Now he saw a solution that made it possible to remain aloft for hours, and even to rise, with far less use of force: An eagle draws on the force of the wind, and uses its wing movements almost exclusively for the purpose of steering. Leonardo must have observed birds executing their maneuvers on countless solitary hikes, his notebook attached to his belt. Sketches show vultures in various wind conditions circling in the sky and eagles beginning their nosedive by adjusting their wings. Still other birds glide down in wave movements or use thermal activity to spiral upward.

In the flying machines Leonardo was now constructing, there was less emphasis on thrust, but movable, adjustable wings continued to be of paramount importance. Still, the ropes and guide pulleys would now serve primarily to steer the "bird" by flexing its wings. The flying machine would soar through the air, elegant as a swallow, with an occasional beating of wings by the pilot to help it along. Leonardo had understood that in gliding the critical element is achieving the optimal shape of the wing. Only then can the wings transform the force of the headwinds into lift. The book about the flight of birds and other sheets reveal the most astonishing plans: Leonardo designed wings with an aerodynamic profile and thought about the airstream at the outermost edges of the wings, where modern engineers attach upwardly curving pieces on top of their jets, called "winglets," to conserve fuel. Later he even made a sketch of how the air swirls under the curved interior surface of a bird's wing.[27]

The drawings give us a good indication of how the "great bird" lifting off from Monte Ceceri might have looked.[28] With its curved, partially movable wings and a smaller steering wing at the tail it would have resembled a giant kite or eagle from afar. Under the wings, at the precise center of gravity of the construction, the pilot would be attached to a gondola in a standing position and would steer the device by flexing his upper body. One of Leonardo's most profound insights was that birds steer the direction of their flight by shifting their body weight and flexing their wings. An entire section of the codex about the flight of birds treats these delicate problems of equilibrium.

"LEONARDO COMPLICATED MATTERS"

To see the kind of glider Leonardo might have built, I traveled to Bedfordshire, England. It took me a good hour of driving through villages

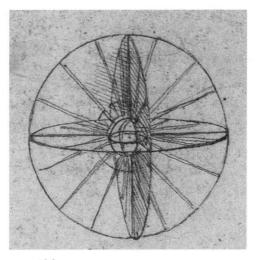

Glider

to get to the abandoned Rotary Farm. There, seven men who enjoy tinkering with aviation devices are spending their days assembling historical flying machines using original parts. Steve Roberts, a precision mechanic, who until several years ago serviced the printing presses for the *Times of London*, accompanied me into a big barn with so many biplanes that I felt as though I were standing in a World War I hangar. Roberts explained to me that these vintage planes were always ready for takeoff, and even the machine guns could still shoot. I saw one of his colleagues fiddling with a strange vehicle that had a spluttering motor on its loading area. It was a machine to start up old propellers, the man said. Did I know what it took to get your hands on an original set of coil springs in good condition for a 1915 carburetor control cable? He finally struck gold at a scrap dealer in Australia.

Producers from the London television station that had arranged for the construction of the giant crossbow had come here back in the summer of 2002 to see the design engineers, bringing with them Martin Kemp, the Leonardo expert from Oxford. The scholar produced several

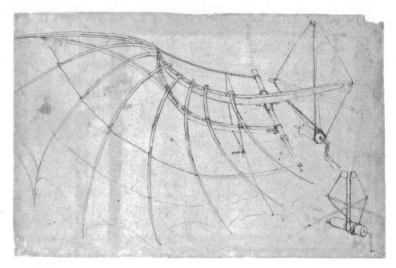

Wing construction

drawings from the notebooks and asked Roberts if he thought that something constructed on the basis of these designs could fly.

"I felt like saying 'never,' because the drawings seemed far too absurd," Roberts told me, "but I decided to hold back a bit, and we embarked on the project of building a flying machine according to Leonardo's designs." The hobbyists had three months to complete the machine. The greatest challenge was trying to forget everything they knew about airplanes and to consider only how Leonardo would have proceeded. "Since we were restricted to the materials he had available to him as well, we opted to construct a frame out of poplar, hemp ropes, and a linen wing cover. We made glue from a component of rabbit skins. Leonardo almost never provides measurements on his drawings, so we made the flying machine the size a man would just about be able to carry."

The wing designs that Roberts and his colleagues studied generated too little propulsion, and the project began to seem hopeless. "But then, Kemp showed us a sketch with a covering around the leading edge of the wing that allowed a good airstream to form. Leonardo quite clearly intended this. We just had to simplify his plan: Instead of two movable wings on the right and left we built one single rigid piece. Leonardo complicated matters." The mechanic thus changed the historical design in a small but significant way by departing once and for all from the concept that birds fly by flapping their wings, which Leonardo had found so difficult to relinquish.

Under the ceiling of Roberts's barn was a brownish wing more than 30 feet wide, with a pyramid-like frame dangling from the middle, where the pilot would be suspended. The whole thing resembled one of today's hang gliders, but the sweeping S-shaped wing made it far more elegant.

When Roberts tested the construction on the roof of a special-purpose automobile that was traveling against the wind, nothing happened at first, but when the headwind reached nearly gale force, the wing moved upward, instilling new hope in the television crew, which had begun to have its doubts about Leonardo and the broadcast after the fiasco with the crossbow. Now they needed to find a pilot who was lightweight, but strong enough to take a run-up with this heavy structure. But who would be willing to face a storm with Leonardo's wings?

THE INTREPID JUDY LEDEN

Judy Leden had not only won the world championship in hang gliding three times, but she had also paraglided from the highest active volcanoes in the world. She had sailed over the valleys of the Himalayas with flocks of vultures, and in Patagonia she took to the air with giant condors. The forty-seven-year-old described the experience of flying as though she were realizing Leonardo's dream of making man fly like a bird. "For me, it is like entering into another state of mind. I am aware of the sun, the wind, and the pressures on the wing. I stop *thinking* about how the interaction of the elements affects my flight—I *feel* it physically. Over the years I've actually developed a kind of bird brain. When I leave the ground, I'm not just floating through the air; I'm feeling and thinking the way a bird does."

She tells me that she did not hesitate for a second when she got the offer to make the maiden voyage with the glider: "I considered it a great privilege to learn for myself whether Leonardo would have been able to fly." Even though the TV documentary clearly shows that Leden gasped when Roberts's first model fell to the ground like a ripe apple during a test flight, she held to her promise.

One stormy October morning, the team at the hills of the southern English coast was ready for takeoff. "I had a silly discussion with my husband, who wanted me not to go into the sky in this storm," Leden recalled. "We have two small children. But the glider was only able to fly with strong headwinds." Assistants used long ropes to hold onto both ends of the wings, because Roberts was afraid that the glider might otherwise rise at breakneck speed, topple over, and crash. "I ran up, took off right away, and climbed above the treetops, until the ropes slowed me down and I sailed down the hill. It was scary when the wing began to swing around in the air—but I landed safely on my feet at the edge of the hillside. It was fantastic."

All the same, the experienced pilot struggled mightily to handle this contraption: "Of all the devices I have ever flown, this was the hardest to control. Since the wing was stiff, you couldn't steer. I felt as though I were in a car traveling at a hundred miles an hour with the steering wheel unbolted. I literally had to learn how to fly all over again." While Leden was learning to maneuver it, there were dramatic landings. The glider was thrown off course and its nose or wing wound up buried

Judy Leden's maiden voyage with the Leonardo glider

in the ground. "But after my best start, I flew thirty feet high and more than six hundred fifty feet in length, which beat the records of pioneers Lilienthal and Wright. Leonardo was an incredible genius."

Does this mean that Leonardo would have been able to build a functional airplane nearly five hundred years before Lilienthal? Leden hesitated before replying, "Well, if he succeeded in building a plane, he surely paid for this success with the life of his test pilot." Now it was my turn to gasp. The fact that the British experiments turned out so successfully and exceeded expectations was thus due solely to the skill of both Leden and design engineer Roberts. An inexperienced pilot would have plunged to his death even without a crisis. The shock of feeling the earth disappear under his feet would have been enough to make him lose control.

Still, it seems highly doubtful that one of Leonardo's gliders of this kind ever soared into the air. For one thing, Leonardo—in contrast to the British hobbyists—had not taken the crucial step of fusing the two movable wings into a single one. But even if he had combined the rigid hang glider he had designed in 1495 with aerodynamically ingenious wings, a test flight would most likely have been doomed to failure. Leonardo had not grasped the fact that the pull upward can develop only if the pilot gets a running start. Instead, he pictured his flying machines taking off the way small birds do. A sparrow can generate enough flux by beating its wings to lift its slight weight up, but a bird as large as a swan has to run to create sufficient air movement on its wings to lift off. And a human being needs a good deal more lift.

Thus, a daredevil taking off from the slope of Monte Ceceri would certainly have plunged into the quarry. There is no doubt that Leonardo was aware of dangers of this kind. Is that why he kept his attempts secret? Or did he ultimately shrink back from this hazardous enterprise?

After 1506, Leonardo made just one more sketch of a device for human flight (which he definitely did not build). Apart from this single sketch, however, he did not pursue the matter again, but he redoubled his efforts to study the mechanics of the flight of birds and wind flow. He had evidently come to terms with the fact that he understood far too little about the basics to fly himself. We would love to know what caused his change of heart, but there are no notes on this subject. What had Leonardo attempted before 1506—and how many times? Was there even a tragedy on Monte Ceceri that made him give up?

FLYING DOES NOT MEAN FLAPPING WINGS

Leonardo had everything he needed to build a functional glider, as the trials in England prove. He went to incredible lengths to achieve this goal. For the crucial question—the wing profile—he had even found solutions that come astonishingly close to those used today, yet in all likelihood, he never flew.

Why was he bound to fail? Leonardo himself provided the answer: "Those who are enamored of practice without science are like a pilot who goes into a ship without rudder or compass and never has any certainty where he is going."[29] Leonardo wrote this comment a few years after his confident proclamations about a big swan soaring into the sky over Florence.

He had ventured into areas of physics in which his visual way of thinking no longer sufficed. Leonardo was able to provide brilliant descriptions of what he saw, but he could not join all his observations together into a comprehensive theory that would provide practical solutions.

He continued to pursue the seemingly obvious solution—that humans could fly like birds—even though his own research had long since indicated otherwise. Although he came to recognize the significance of gliding, he never stopped reflecting on the wing movements of birds. Again and again he designed contraptions with movable wings that were too unstable to work. He never seriously considered the possibility that the solution might lie in a rigid wing, since every bird was able to raise and lower its wings.

Unlike most of his contemporaries, Leonardo knew that he needed to question what he saw, but, being the extremely visual person that he was, he neither could nor would forgo this type of perception altogether. But science is the business of disengaging yourself from the obvious: The world is not flat, and birds do not remain in the air because they flap their wings, but only because their wings are shaped like an aerofoil, to take full advantage of updrafts. A bird is both pushed and lifted upwards.

Because the wings face against the direction of flight, the air passing above the wings moves more quickly on its upper surface than the air on its underside.[30] This creates a subpressure above the wing, forcing the body to rise. Faster-moving air has a lower pressure and results in lift. That is the secret of flight.

Although Leonardo understood so much else about airstreams and water flow, he never made this connection, but he took an important step in the right direction when his research about water made him realize that a current gets faster when constricted. He even had all the tools to measure the undertow of the more rapid current, yet it took two hundred years after his death for the Swiss physicist Daniel Bernoulli to come up with this idea. Leonardo's mind was unprepared to look for the proper physical quantities. His ideas about the pressure of fluids and gases were far too vague; he was in sore need of a theory—not that he could fathom what such a theory might have conveyed. Compared with later researchers, Leonardo was lacking less in technology and knowledge than in a method of organizing his knowledge.

It is thus all the more astonishing that he got as far as he did—single-handedly and without knowing the rules of the game his successors used to tease out the secrets of the world. After its beginnings in the sixteenth century, science quickly developed into a giant parlor game. From the outset, hundreds of scholars in Europe took part in it, and today there are millions of men and women throughout the world whose discoveries follow a set procedure: reconcile a new idea with others' observations and corroborate it with experiments and measurements. If the idea turns out to be sound, it is published and others can test it and develop it further. The system is so successful precisely because it works even when the players are no better than average. No individual researcher need be a genius—it requires only the addition of a few more pieces to the big puzzle while relying on previously published findings.

As a result, an ample foundation of well-organized knowledge was in place by the seventeenth century. Even the father of modern physics, Isaac Newton, who was ordinarily not given to modesty (and was anything but an average scholar) explained his success by claiming he was able to see farther than others because he was standing on the shoulders of giants.

Leonardo was larger than life, but his feet were planted firmly on the ground. While later researchers were able to enjoy a productive exchange of ideas, his communications were restricted largely to jottings in his notebooks. And instead of conducting systematic experiments to test his ideas, he kept up a kind of interior monologue. It is fascinating, and often touching, to trace the way he kept questioning his ideas and discovering contradictions—and often arriving at better insights. But just as often, as with his imperfect understanding of the flight of birds, he lacked the interaction with others that might have helped him get past an intellectual impasse.

His attempts at flight did not go beyond the technical capabilities of his era, but his approach was quite novel. Still, nothing would be more unfair than to call him a "utopian," as people often do. Only researchers who know how to dream advance the progress of mankind.

Leonardo's quest for the truth was arduous and solitary. By the time of his final visit to Monte Ceceri, he must have known that it would be left to later eras to fulfill his greatest dream. He himself would never enjoy the fame of being the first human to fly. The only reward for his efforts was his increasingly profound understanding of the mysteries of nature. But this prospect was enough to keep him exploring the flight of birds for another dozen years. He was extraordinarily tenacious. His notes contain only a single remark that appeared to cast doubt on the advisability of forging ahead with his work: *O Leonardo, perché tanto penate?*[31] Oh, Leonardo—why do you torture yourself so?

Toward the end of his life, he found an easier means of approaching the object of his greatest yearning. His first biographer, Giorgio Vasari, noted in amazement that Leonardo began to construct artificial birds, little toys that flew over the heads of his visitors, as if to poke fun at

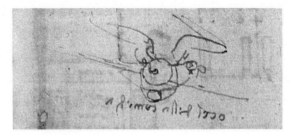

Small mechanical bird

his own dream of flying: "He experimented with a paste made out of a certain kind of wax and made some light and billowy figures in the form of animals which he inflated with his mouth as he walked along and which flew above the ground until all the air escaped."[32]

In 1506, the year of the apparent failure on Monte Ceceri, Leonardo left Florence, the place where he had experienced so many disappointments, and, after considerable wavering, took up residence in Milan again. Two years later, he made a sketch of a small mechanical bird consisting of a cylindrical trunk and two essentially useless wings. It looks like one of those Chinese plastic toys you see everywhere these days. The bird is mounted on a slanted cord, and as it slides down, its wings are set in motion. But the flight is mere illusion. After thirty years of tireless work, Leonardo's dream of flying had reverted to what it was in the first days of his research—a flight of the imagination.

ROBOTS

MARK ROSHEIM LIVES IN A bright green, wood-framed house near the Minneapolis airport. A tin-can robot greeting visitors at the front stoop is the only distinguishing feature of Rosheim's home in a sea of single-family dwellings with gable roofs and carports. Rosheim is a lean man in his late forties who bears the traces of his Scandinavian heritage. The tidy living room is furnished with upholstered armchairs and a smoked glass coffee table. A reproduction of Leonardo's Turin self-portrait hangs next to the fireplace. Rosheim lives alone.

On the coffee table I saw a column-like object about as long as my forearm, with dozens of intertwined pieces of steel. I assumed this object was a work of art, but my host informed me that it was a humanoid robotic joint. This construction gives an artificial claw the mobility of a human hand. Rosheim has a patent for it and for countless other components to make human-like machines. Mechanics construct the mechanical shoulders, wrists, and arms, as well as complete robots, in the rear wing of the house—but Rosheim felt that the workshops were too messy to be shown to visitors. He told me that he has been

Spring

*Mark Rosheim with his reconstruction of
a spring-driven car*

able to sell some of his inventions to NASA and that he has received some funding from the Pentagon.

Rosheim taught himself the art of engineering after a few short months in a mechanical engineering program at the University of Minnesota. He applied for his first patent at the age of eighteen. When he was trying to figure out the right proportions for a robotic shoulder joint, he found a phenomenally precise model in Leonardo's *Vitruvian Man*, the famous drawing of a man inscribed in a circle and a square, and Rosheim became a confirmed Leonardo fan and bibliophile. He opened a cabinet in his living room that held facsimiles of all six thousand extant drawings by Leonardo, stored in leather-bound cases. Rosheim proudly announced that he had several copies of a group of rare reprints and that his collection was unsurpassed in the entire Midwest.

Then he rolled in a black wooden frame on three wheels from the next room. The machine was flat, about the size of a stove top, with a jumble of wooden gears, springs, cams, and levers, and bore a resemblance to a giant clock mechanism. Rosheim turned a wheel to wind up a spring, placed the little car back on the floor, and let go. The vehicle began to move straight ahead, then turned and executed a bold but precise slalom between the couch, the floor lamp, and the fireplace.

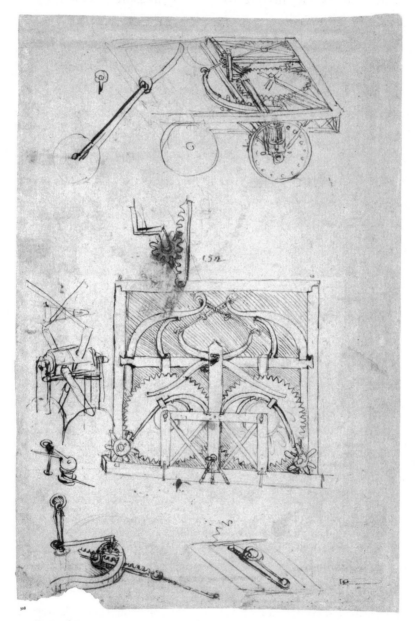

Spring-driven car

Rosheim stopped it, tinkered with the mechanism, and exchanged a couple of cams. After he wound it up again, the car charted a different course over the rug. "You are seeing what is likely the oldest programmable automaton in the world," Rosheim explained, adding that he built it according to plans by the young Leonardo.

As if this were not startling enough, Rosheim went on to say that Leonardo had made still more inroads into twenty-first-century-style technology. Leonardo had designed a mechanical man driven by cables and even digital components of the kind found in computers today. All it takes to recognize this is a careful reading of Leonardo's notebooks. "Leonardo," Rosheim explained, "was a pioneer of robots and computers."

Had this man from Minneapolis gotten too caught up in his studies? He would not be the first to be carried away with notions of genius and to make untenable claims when contemplating the notebooks. There are few technological achievements that have not been attributed to Leonardo at one time or another. He is said to have come up with the ideas for bicycles, helicopters, submarines, and paddle steamers— even automatic rotisseries.

Nowadays, people who regard Leonardo as a futurist of the early modern period are viewed with suspicion. Just as we can no longer look at the *Mona Lisa* without preconceptions, we find it difficult to take Leonardo's inventions at face value once inundated with marvelous stories about them. Enthusiasm for Leonardo, who seems so far ahead of his time, has a long history. The initial wave of euphoria crested in about 1880, when the first scholars studied Leonardo's technical drawings and were startled to discover cutting-edge innovations of their own era in Leonardo's jottings. A couple of decades later, though, it became apparent that many of Leonardo's designs could not function in practice.

A search for evidence that anyone had built machines according to the practicable sketches ensued, and when nothing turned up, Leonardo was dismissed as a dreamer. His star as an inventor sank still further in the second half of the twentieth century, when historians of technology came across more and more construction plans from the early modern period and compared them to Leonardo's ideas. They discovered that much of what the master had sketched was also found in the work of his contemporaries. Now experts cast doubt not only on his scientific achievements, but on his aptitude as an engineer.

Was Leonardo da Vinci a revolutionary, a dreamer, or someone who just copied the ideas of clever contemporaries? Even today, each of these views has its proponents, and many scholars find elements of all three in his designs. Leonardo Olschki describes his namesake as follows: "His scientific and technological work is little more than a mass of eloquent literary fragments and realistic drawings, of ingenious projects that would hardly have withstood a practical test."[1]

But Rosheim is confident he has proved that Leonardo was far more than a mere Jules Verne of the Renaissance.

HANDBAGS AND WATER HEATERS

One of Leonardo's most spectacular extant plans, a machine to shear cloth, was conceived in about 1490.[2] The idea was to have an automaton perform the laborious task of trimming the nap off woolen cloth by carrying out three simultaneous tasks on four pieces of fabric stretched across a frame in parallel rows: The scissors would open and close, then move across the cloth after every cut, whereupon the device would bring in more fabric from the reel. A mechanical control system for such a complex sequence would pose quite a challenge even to a mechanical engineer today. Leonardo's plans for this device were metic-

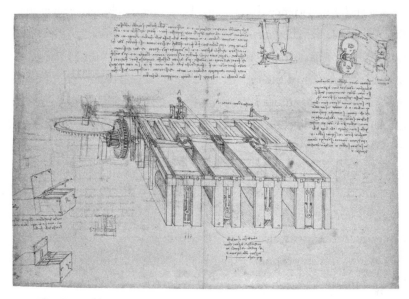

Shearing machine

ulously executed. Even Bertrand Gille, a French historian who was otherwise quick to disparage Leonardo's technical achievements, was full of admiration for these sketches: "There is no doubt, as a single glance will be enough to show, that these sketches are, from the technical point of view of course, the best drawings of Leonardo da Vinci which have come down to us."[3]

Leonardo developed dozens of appliances of this kind, from a file-cutter (one of his first machines) to a device for grinding concave mirrors (one of his last). He found the notion that machines could perform highly complex tasks nearly as exhilarating as the idea of flying. In this respect, Leonardo was pursuing the same goals as engineers in the industrial age. Even his aim of cutting costs sounds modern. When designing a machine to produce needles, he made careful calculations to find out how much money the implementation of his invention would yield annually if it were used for twenty working days a month: 60,000 ducats.[4]

He was one of the first engineers to advance the process of automation. The astonishing brilliance of his technical achievements is often played down by art historians, who reduce this aspect of his creativity to a mere outgrowth of his artistic prowess, and skeptics like to point out that there is no documentation to confirm that any of Leonardo's designs were implemented. The latter claim is true only up to a point: In a codex that was discovered in the Biblioteca Nazionale Marciana in Venice in 1953, a clockmaker named della Golpaja described a water wheel that Leonardo made for the wealthy Bernardo Rucellai. The description matches one of Leonardo's sketches.[5]

In addition, there are statements by contemporaries, such as the painter Lomazzo, who noted after the death of Leonardo that "all Europe [was] full" of his inventions.[6] Toward the end of the sixteenth century, Don Ambrogio Mazenta reported that workmen in Lombardy were using Leonardo's machines to polish crystal, iron, and stone and that "there is one [machine] much used in the cellars of Milan, for grinding large amounts of meat to make *cervellato* [sausage made with pork meat and brain] with the help of a wheel turned by a boy."[7] Both statements are of questionable value, however: Lomazzo's wording is vague, and Mazenta, who himself owned Leonardo's notebooks, is not considered a reliable source.

However, the manuscripts leave no doubt that Leonardo was a highly practical draftsman who was much in demand. Water heaters, locks, ladies' handbags, hydraulic lifts, looms, and hundreds of other items that appear in his notebooks are anything but technical utopias; they were clearly made to be used in the workplace and elsewhere. Historian of science Bern Dibner wrote, "Leonardo's notebooks often read like a modern mail-order catalogue that offers an ingenious tool or gadget for every conceivable purpose."[8]

And there is no reason to believe that the devices depicted on Leonardo's sketches were never built. While flying machines might be the stuff of dreams, the only reason to draw practical items such as hydraulic lifts and water pipes would be if commissioned to construct them. It is not surprising that Leonardo was much sought after: His reputation as an outstanding engineer was sure to have preceded him.

The question of which parts he invented and which he took over from others will likely never be answered. This uncertainty was already evident in the discussion about the San Marco lock in Milan. There was no orderly system of publication in the Renaissance to use in reconstructing the development of technology. Although the Republic of Venice had enacted the world's first patent law in 1474, it was universally ignored. Plagiarism was the order of the day. In any case, the success of an engineer depended far less on his wealth of ideas than on his ability to produce a needed piece of equipment. The employers wanted solutions, not strokes of genius. They did not care whether an engineer had thought up a particular mechanism by himself or adopted someone else's idea. We wonder about Leonardo's significance as an inventor today because of our interest in learning about him as an individual. Back then, the question was of little consequence.

When historians of technology, such as Paolo Galluzzi in Florence, began a systematic comparison of Leonardo's manuscripts with the notes of other Renaissance engineers, the result was as expected. The master had openly helped himself to the work of his peers. Many of his designs bore a strong resemblance to older notations by Francesco di Giorgio Martini and Taccola. Both men worked in Siena, where engineering had thrived even in the century before Leonardo's birth. Manuscripts from this city featured diving bells, parachutes, and paddle steamers.[9] These ideas were subsequently often falsely ascribed to Leonardo because his manuscripts were known, while the designs of others had been consigned to oblivion. In praising Leonardo, people were effectively praising the inventiveness of an entire century.

Findings of this sort tend to dishearten those with a romantic bent who embrace the notion that a genius of the stature of Leonardo was of his era in body, but centuries ahead of his time in mind. But of course Leonardo was a child of the fifteenth century. His writings and drawings are not merely the legacy of an extraordinary individual, but a unique testament to the capabilities of the era in which he lived. This realization should not detract from our admiration for Leonardo, but rather help us recognize the supposed dreamer for what he was: a realist who took a practical approach to testing the limits of what could be achieved. And Leonardo's very reliance on established knowledge enhanced his chances for success—whereas his attempts at flight were doomed to failure because they lacked a scientific foundation.

Even more than in his innovative designs, Leonardo was pioneering in his grasp of technology. His precursors, who were still under the sway of the Middle Ages, regarded engineering as a craft. They put their faith in tradition, and new inventions came about by trial and error. An engineer did not set down his knowledge for posterity—he just passed it on by guiding his pupils. Whole cathedrals were built by relying on past experience in placing more and more weight on a supporting structure until at some point it collapsed. The brilliant architect Brunelleschi departed from this practice, using a new type of shuttering process—which he had tested out systematically on a model—to construct the immense dome for the Cathedral of Florence. It was a sensation.

Leonardo similarly rejected the haphazard approach of his colleagues. He did not want simply to turn out machines without investigating why one construction worked and another did not. Just as Leonardo studied nature and the laws of vision to enhance his artistic skills, he devoted himself to physics to find optimal technical solutions. In doing so, Leonardo was the first to lay a scientific foundation for engineering.

Leonardo showed the absurdity of the many attempts then under way to build a perpetual motion machine. In systematic thought experiments he devised various pieces of equipment that supposedly functioned without an energy supply and realized that they all had to come to a standstill at some point. The dream of a machine that performed a job without expending energy, he found, would never be fulfilled—just as it would be hopeless to try to turn dross into gold. "O speculators about perpetual motion, how many vain chimeras have you created in the like quest? Go and take your place with the seekers after gold."[10]

A sensational discovery in 1965 shows how sketchy our understanding of Leonardo's thinking remains to this day. Scientists in the National Library of Madrid happened upon two long-lost manuscript collections. The two notebooks, bound in red kid leather, had been in this spot all along, but had been assigned an incorrect catalogue number, and no one noticed that they contained original texts by Leonardo. This discovery revived the hope that additional works by Leonardo were tucked away in archives and would resurface one day, and it also shed new light on other extant writings.

The first of the two manuscripts, now referred to as Codex Madrid I, is a virtual anatomical atlas of technology. The author chronicled the machines of his era, reduced to their component parts. He filled page after page with views of couplings, flywheels, connecting rods, valves, and cams. The codex contains the first known drawings of ball bearings and worm drives. (The Italian historian of science Ladislao Reti was exaggerating only slightly when he claimed that of all the

138

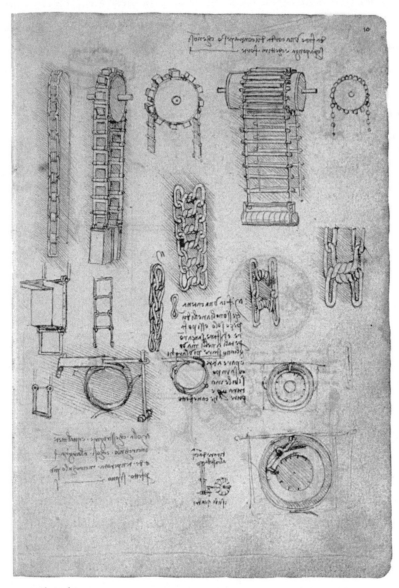

Chain drives

elements of machines now in use, the only one missing was the rivet.) Evidently Leonardo was planning to publish these as a book. In contrast to the hastily drawn sketches in most of his other manuscripts, these drawings seem so meticulous that they could easily pass as a printer's copy.

The manuscript from Madrid confirms the modern nature of Leonardo's ideas about engineering. His way of thinking about machines differed quite significantly from that of his contemporaries, the way a biologist's perspective on an ear of corn differs from that of a farmer. The farmer sees the plant as a whole entity, knows from experience how to handle it, and tends to stick to tried-and-true methods of cultivation. The biologist, by contrast, breaks down the plant into its component parts, analyzes the inflorescences, places them under the microscope, isolates individual cells, and perhaps gets as far as the genetic makeup in the cell nucleus, thus determining species and subspecies, clarifying the relationship to other plants, and using this information to develop better methods of cultivation and new varieties.

In the same way, a screw was not just a screw. Leonardo regarded its thread as an inclined plane wrapped around a cylinder and the screw as a kind of wedge, and proceeded to determine how for both parts the angle of inclination had to be set to lift weight most effectively. Compared with the sketches of the aerial screw, diving bell, or giant crossbow, these studies may not seem very spectacular, but they—not his fanciful designs—are what made Leonardo the first engineer of the modern era.

Leonardo was also a pioneer in the field of technical drawing. He had realized that the current language no longer sufficed to describe these increasingly sophisticated machines and to draw up construction manuals for them. Using elevation, exploded views, and isometry, he formulated an entire vocabulary of technical drawing, which is still in

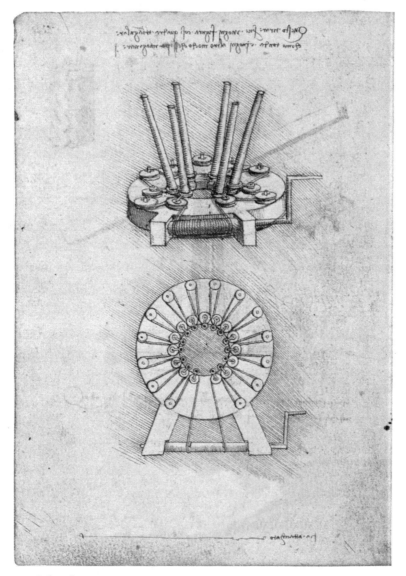

Lifting device

use today and remains the most important tool for engineers even in our era of computerized design.

His sketches attest to his extraordinary ability to think three-dimensionally. Leonardo seems to have had no difficulty turning three-dimensional shapes every which way in his mind. Early studies of the automatic car, the successor of which now winds about on Rosheim's carpet, show how brilliantly Leonardo met this challenge.[11] Gears, worm threads, levers, and bearings on these sheets can be viewed from the front, then from the side at an upward angle, then from behind. Some of the sketches seem like quick jottings, as though Leonardo had drawn them while lost in thought—the way we doodle while talking on the telephone.

Leonardo probably drew on older models for this vehicle as well. Francesco di Giorgio Martini from Siena, one of the most prominent engineers of the Renaissance, had drawn several cars for passengers to operate with a crank. But his designs are of clumsy vehicles—rolling cabins in which he planned to install man-size cogs and gears. In the interior, di Giorgio Martini wasted quite a bit of space between the various mechanisms. Leonardo, by contrast, was able not only to replace the cranking passengers by a spring drive and to provide for an automatic steering device—he also fit the entire device, which was now far more complex, into a flat frame. Leonardo had aspired to and achieved a goal pursued vigorously by today's engineers: reducing the size of technology.

Of all his many talents, his ability to work with the concept of space may have had the most significant effect on his creations. The powerful impact of his paintings derives from the way he makes viewers experience space in ever-changing fashion. To a person standing in the refectory of the Convent of Santa Maria delle Grazie in Milan, *The Last Supper* seems like a natural extension of the walls out to the horizon;

Mona Lisa, by contrast, seems to be hovering in front of the water in the background.

Since Leonardo drew no distinctions among art, science, and technology, his technical designs are more than mere construction guides—they overwhelm and enthrall the viewer. The French art historian Daniel Arasse wrote that at some point, Leonardo fell victim to his own rhetoric, and regarded his visions as reality—which would also explain why he spent decades designing one flying machine after another.[12]

THE PERFORMANCE OF THE MECHANICAL LION

Let us not forget that Leonardo earned his living by conjuring up dreams and illusions. After all, his primary task at the court was to entertain his patrons. Thus it was quite logical that his extended efforts at flying eventually resulted in a little mechanical bird, which was evidently designed to delight the guests of the French governor of Milan. During the period that Ludovico Sforza was still ruler of Milan, Leonardo had already proved a success as an entertainer. When il Moro arranged a brilliant political match between Isabella of Aragon and his nephew Gian Galeazzo in 1490, Leonardo was asked to devise a spectacle with the theme of "paradise on earth." He had seven actors costumed as planet deities float from the sky to greet the bride. The spectacle was such a success that the guests referred to the wedding reception as the Paradise Festival. From then on, Leonardo enjoyed the monarch's highest regard.

His mechanical lion was a sensation as well, as we learn from several documents. Michelangelo Buonarroti the Younger, a nephew of the famous artist, describes the appearance of this automaton at a banquet honoring the king of France's entry into Lyons in 1515. The lion is

Face of an animal; possibly a sketch of the mechanical lion

said to have walked a few steps, then risen on its hind legs and opened its breast, revealing a bouquet of lilies, the coat of arms of the French royal family.[13]

A performance of this kind in an era when the laws of mechanics and biology were unknown must have amazed spectators. They surely felt a combination of fear, bafflement, and admiration when the lion performed his tricks all on his own—just like a trained circus cat, but with oddly stiff movements that would never be found in nature. The thought that only God can make animals that move, live, and procreate must have been swirling through their heads. Hadn't the builder of this mechanism tread suspiciously close to the realm of the Almighty? In any case, he seemed to have deciphered some of His secrets. People wondered whether the engineer had breathed a soul into his creation.

These feelings of shock and awe were exactly what Leonardo's employers were hoping to generate. Impressing people with marvels was proof positive of their power.[14] And Leonardo truly seemed to enjoy shocking people—even his notes on painting had called artists "grand-sons unto God" because artists could exercise power over the feelings of others and "dismay folk by hellish fictions."[15] As Vasari tells us, Leonardo's ability to "frighten the life" out of his friends delighted him to no end.[16]

But Leonardo was not just trying to get a rise out of his audience. His pleasure in bizarre games and his enthusiasm for automatons was also fueled by his aversion to charlatans and superstitions of all kinds. His notebooks inveighed against greedy "inveterate fools and magicians" and scoffed at the "simple souls" who believed in pied pipers.[17] Leonardo's spectacles cast the cold light of reason on white and black magic, because they did not require the invocation of higher powers, but instead relied solely on the laws and nature and the resourcefulness of the human mind.

A Life for Leonardo

The drawing of the wind-up car, the reconstruction of which I saw in Minneapolis, is part of the Codex Atlanticus in Milan, the most ex-tensive collection of Leonardo's technical sketches. Experts had known about this sketch for quite some time, but no one had understood it properly. Art historians and historians of technology interpreted the jumble of ink as a plan for a nonfunctional, self-propelled vehicle. Carlo Pedretti was the first to realize that Leonardo might have had an au-tomaton rather than an automobile in mind.

In the world of research on Leonardo, Pedretti is a living legend. He attained this status the first time he entered the public eye, just after World War II. Pedretti, who had been fascinated by Leonardo from the days of his childhood, distinguished himself by his enthu-siasm, eloquence, and extraordinary visual facility. At the age of thirteen, he could both read and write Leonardo's mirror writing; when he was sixteen, he published a newspaper article about Leonardo's friendship with Machiavelli. Soon afterward he was himself the subject of a news item. In 1951, *Corriere della Sera*, the most highly regarded daily newspaper in Italy, featured a portrait of the astonishing young scholar, with the heading: "At the age of twenty-three, he knows everything about Leonardo."

Pedretti later moved to Los Angeles and became a professor of art history at UCLA, to which a wealthy urologist had bequeathed a unique collection of Leonardo facsimiles. Pedretti, now over eighty and retired, has purchased an old villa in the hills over Vinci, where he gathers together scholars in the summer. The terrace affords a view of olive groves and the house where Leonardo was born.

A darkened upstairs room, nearly as large as a banquet hall and furnished with antiques, serves as his study. Behind the shutters at the back wall I was barely able to make out the June sun. Hefty tomes are piled up on an oak table in the middle of the room. Once my eyes had adjusted to the dim light, I saw that books, most of which were old, surrounded us on every wall. This was just a small part of his library, Pedretti explained to me while sitting down at his desk. Since he was still spending his winters in California, he had brought only his most important materials to Italy.

What fascinated Carlo Pedretti to the point of devoting his entire life to the pursuit of understanding Leonardo? "It is a heady experience to have a connection with one of the greatest minds of all time," Pedretti told me. "I quickly realized that there is a great deal more to be said about Leonardo." All the clichés about his genius, the flawed interpretations of his art, his character, and his ostensible views about sexuality and religion stemmed from the fact that we knew so little about what Leonardo actually wrote, drew, and thought.

Pedretti decided to begin right at the beginning and to understand Leonardo within the context of his era by focusing on what the manuscripts revealed. "Over the years, I learned how to recall every little detail of the many thousands of pages. My photographic memory was a big help. My brain was really like a computer scanning the pages for patterns and similarities to find out what might fit where."

He went to great lengths to introduce order into Leonardo's doubly muddled legacy. Although the looters and dealers who had torn apart his precious possession and scattered it throughout Europe were primarily to blame for the disarray, the notes were extremely jumbled even in their original condition, when Melzi received them from the hands of the dying Leonardo. Pedretti displayed a few pages of his facsimile volumes to show how much must have been buzzing around in Leonardo's head. Some pages have caricatures, technical plans, landscapes, studies of the flight of birds, and flow lines of water sketched adjacent to—or even on top of—one another.

To establish a basis for dating these pages, Pedretti and his colleagues examined how Leonardo's handwriting and drawing style evolved over the years. They compared paper qualities, watermarks, and the strokes made by various pens, inks, and even tears. This work took decades to complete, and by the end, the chronology of a large part of the drawings had been rearranged. Now it was finally possible to trace the path of Leonardo's thought from beginning to end.

In his search for evidence, Pedretti came across sheets that no one had ever studied because they were so difficult to interpret. Some of them show cable systems running over complicated pulleys and images of partial suits of armor and shoulder and elbow joints.[18] On one sketch, the structure of the cables suggests a man with outstretched arms, with pulleys where we might expect hands, elbows, and shoulders.

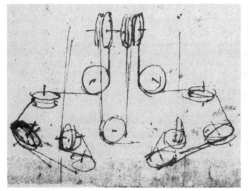

Cable system in the shape of outstretched arms

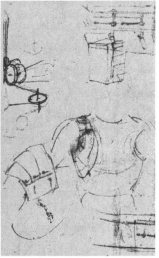

Knight and cable system

Did Leonardo have a mechanical man in mind? The contours of the armor suggest that he might have reconstructed a warrior in full uniform and made it appear to come alive with a system of cables. Pedretti does not know whether Leonardo ever built this robot, but the sketches prove how seriously he took the idea of automatons.

Pedretti concluded that the ominous wind-up car was also equipped with an automatic steering device, although as an art historian, he could not explain how it might function. The answer to this puzzle, Pedretti said, did not become apparent to him until the winter of 1994, when a young engineer, Mark Rosheim, appeared at his door in Los Angeles.

Rosheim had just finished writing a book about the history of robots, and since Leonardo's mechanical warrior was featured in it, the author hoped to interest Pedretti in his work. From the fragments in the notebooks, Rosheim had put together a rough blueprint for a robot, which meant that Leonardo really could have built an artificial knight—not that Rosheim could prove that he had had this exact machine in mind or that he might have actually built it. The fragmentary sketches fell short of providing this information.

The engineer had also studied the wind-up car that had consumed Pedretti's attention for so long. He surmised that this automaton was none other than the mechanism of the artificial lion that had pulled lilies from its breast to honor the French king. The artificial animal, he concluded, only appeared to walk, but actually rode, and the little car served as both steering device and propulsion. The figure of the lion was perched on the flat wooden car, which held the gearwheels, springs, and camshafts. Impressed by the young American's bold ideas, Pedretti arranged for Rosheim to give the keynote speech at a traditional ceremony commemorating Leonardo's birthday in Vinci. Never had this honor been bestowed on an individual without a doctorate. In this venue, exactly 547 years after the birth of Leonardo, Rosheim explained the mystery of the mechanical lion.

THE BELL RINGER

Pedretti gave Rosheim another puzzle to work on. For years, Leonardo experts had been perplexed by a mysterious set of sketches in the possession of the Queen of England. Leonardo had made a series of about ten sketches showing a figure holding a hammer way above his head, poised to ring a bell. The figure resembles the two bronze statues on the clock town of Piazza San Marco in Venice that revolve every hour and strike the hour with mallets. Pedretti is convinced that Leonardo knew this mechanism.

However, Leonardo must have had something other than a standard clock in mind. An especially striking picture shows the bell ringer

Bell ringer and water cylinder to operate the device

bending his knee and resting his foot on the edge of a *bottino* (little barrel), with the bell hanging over the barrel on a pole. Under the sketch there are geometric diagrams and some text in mirror writing. According to Pedretti, this sheet was once joined to a second one on which the *bottino* is subdivided into twenty-four smaller containers. The fold lines on both sheets fit together perfectly.[19] The explanation is found on an additional sheet with a similar drawing, which shows that Leonardo was actually planning a timekeeper: "In 24 containers there are the 24 hours, and the one of these 24 containers that opens the first then opens all of them. Now you can make a drum-like well (*bottino*) that keeps all the 24 containers."[20] Leonardo was clearly working on a water clock. Whenever a container fills up at the top of the hour, the bell ringer is set in motion. After twenty-four hours, all the containers are emptied, and the process begins anew.

I had trouble imagining that such a sophisticated hydraulic operation could have been possible in the early sixteenth century, even if the engineer was Leonardo da Vinci, but Pedretti drew my attention to the astonishing machines in the Ancient Near East, in which the legacy of antiquity lives on. Later I came across *The Book of Knowledge of Ingenious Mechanical Devices* by Ibn al-Razzaz al-Jazari, a twelfth-century Mesopotamian engineer. It contains automata of the sort Leonardo might have planned. Al-Jazari's color drawings are so magnificent that they seem less like pages from a technical handbook than illuminations to accompany fables from the East. There are elephants with water clocks in their bellies playing with balls and beating drums at the top of the hour, jolly lads using a pump to measure out equal quantities of wine in a series of glasses, and a boat with mechanical dolls that play music when set in motion.[21]

Leonardo is likely to have known about these inventions; copies of Arabic manuscripts were in circulation. In any case, it is not all that far from al-Jazari's figures to Leonardo's own bell ringer and the mechanical lion. *The Book of Knowledge of Ingenious Mechanical Devices* started me thinking about what we hope to achieve with technical progress. Is human inventiveness truly impelled by a desire to lighten our workload and to wage war effectively? There is no trace of these motives in al-Jazari's brilliant constructions, which seem more playful than practical, as do Leonardo's designs for the bell ringer and the mechanical lion. Wouldn't the two most creative technicians of their respective eras have been better off spending their time on more useful pursuits? They were well aware that the reigning monarchs were more concerned with their palaces than with the houses of their subjects and were more inclined to invest in an intricate entertainment machine than a better loom. After all, part of the reason manufacturers today keep coming out with faster computers is to satisfy the desire of game players for better and better animation. But just as increasingly sophisticated computers spur on the development of office software, the technology of Leonardo's entertainment devices might have been used to enhance human productivity. If you can program a mechanical lion, you can also make machines to cut cloth. Leonardo was uniquely able to carry over solutions from one field to another.

Leonardo's Computer

But what is so special about the strange bell ringer mechanism? "You are about to see the boldest invention that Leonardo ever came up with," Rosheim promised. For a minute I was hoping that I would finally get to peek into his workshop full of secret robots, but my host brought me to his kitchen instead. Then he disappeared into a storeroom and returned with a length of garden hose. I must have looked somewhat aghast; for the life of me, I could not make out anything remarkable about it. "There it is," Rosheim laughed. In the sink I saw a cylinder about as long as my arm, which looked like an oversized drain stopper. It had two parts: The upper half was black, and the lower half was made of clear Plexiglas, with a gray vertical tube and two red plastic rings inside. Copper tubing and three horizontal ports were attached to the area between the upper and lower halves. Rosheim stuck the garden hose into one of them, and attached the other end of the hose to the faucet with some insulating tape. When he turned on the faucet, the water sprayed in all directions, because, as might be expected, the insulating tape did not provide a tight seal. Rosheim had to hold his finger on the hose, and the hem of his shirt started dripping. The engineer did not seem to notice how wet he was. He kept his eyes trained

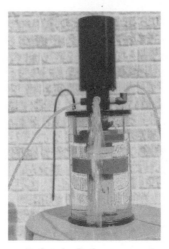

Rosheim's cylinder reconstruction

on his prized cylinder, where the water was splashing in the lower section. When the cylinder was nearly full, there was a sudden click, and a fountain gushed out of one of the other ports. This stream soon stopped and the water now poured out of the third port. "You are looking at man's oldest digital computer in action," Rosheim said.

I didn't know whether to question his sanity or mine, and I held my tongue. My host was unfazed. He leaned forward to suck at the siphon with his mouth. The cylinder emptied out. While the container was filling up again, Rosheim, who was soaked to the skin by this point, explained patiently how this spitting and spraying device could be used to measure time. The water supply just had to be set to make the containers fill in exactly sixty minutes. An array of twenty-four containers would yield a clock, with each cylinder representing an hour and serving as a timer for the bell ringer.

When an hour goes by and the cylinder is full, a rotary valve starts up in the gray vertical tube, blocking off the cylinder and diverting the water to the container for the next hour. At the same time, it opens

Rotary valve

up a reservoir in the black upper half—producing the fountain I had seen earlier. This surge, in turn, can be directed onto a waterwheel and set the bell ringer in motion. Since each cylinder has a larger reservoir than the one before, more water shoots out from one hour to the next. The amount in the first cylinder is just enough to make the figure strike the bell once, the water in the second reservoir generates two strikes, and so forth.

With this principle, which was clearly described in the notebooks, Leonardo had invented something altogether original. Although there were clock mechanisms and planetariums before him, notably the *astrarium* (astronomical clock) built by Giovanni de Dondi in Padua and hailed as a wonder of ingenuity, the passage of time was always marked by the gradual advancement of a hand, a cog, or a planet, using analogue technology. Leonardo may have learned how to use water for sensitive mechanisms from al-Jazari, but al-Jazari's clock repeated the same process hourly, as had earlier clocks, in contrast to Leonardo's design for a timepiece with an ability that no machine had ever had: It could count. If the water cylinders were connected in a different way, a calculator would result.

"Our computers today are made up of billions of identical electronic circuits," Rosheim said, "and each circuit operates with only two options: current or no current. Leonardo did the very same thing with his hydraulic clock." For the water cylinder, the only thing that matters is whether it is full or empty—it functions digitally. And by engaging a series of cylinders, Rosheim explained to me, Leonardo taught his machine how to count: "The only essential difference between this and the principle of a modern computer is that Leonardo worked with water and not with electric current."

How much of this hydraulic computer is Leonardo's work, and how much is Rosheim's? Most likely Leonardo never built a digital water clock. His sketches are too inexact, and too many details are left open. As was so often the case with Leonardo, who was busy with many projects at once, he appeared to lack interest in struggling with the countless tricky aspects that invariably arise in any attempt to translate a flight of fancy into practice. Rosheim tackled these difficulties, filling in the blanks in Leonardo's sketches with his own knowledge of engineering. The cylinder spouting water in his sink in Minneapolis is therefore just as much his creation as it is Leonardo's.

The fate of the digital water clock is quite typical for Leonardo's engineering ideas. His most remarkable projects generally came to a halt somewhere along the developmental stage and were not completed, apart from a few noteworthy exceptions, such as the spectacular performances by the mechanical lion. But often he saw no need to prove that his designs would actually work. So was he a daydreamer, and his inventions mere pie in the sky?

"Leonardo was a rebel," historian of science George Sarton once wrote. "He was anxious to obtain not money, or power, or comfort, but beauty and truth."[22] He was after not the pragmatic solution, but the ideal one. As an artist who often spent years on a painting, he chose to use experimental color mixtures, which resulted in two of his most important works disintegrating before they were complete. And as an engineer, he had to face the fact that he would never be able to realize many of his bold projects.

But perhaps it is wrong to judge inventors by how many of their ideas come to fruition. Ultimately, the implementation of an idea is only a minor element in intellectual achievement. The crucial part is what precedes it. Behind every significant milestone is a new perspective on a problem. Coming up with this concept—a digital clock, for example—is arguably the actual task of an inventor. Leonardo was brilliant at unearthing new approaches of this kind.

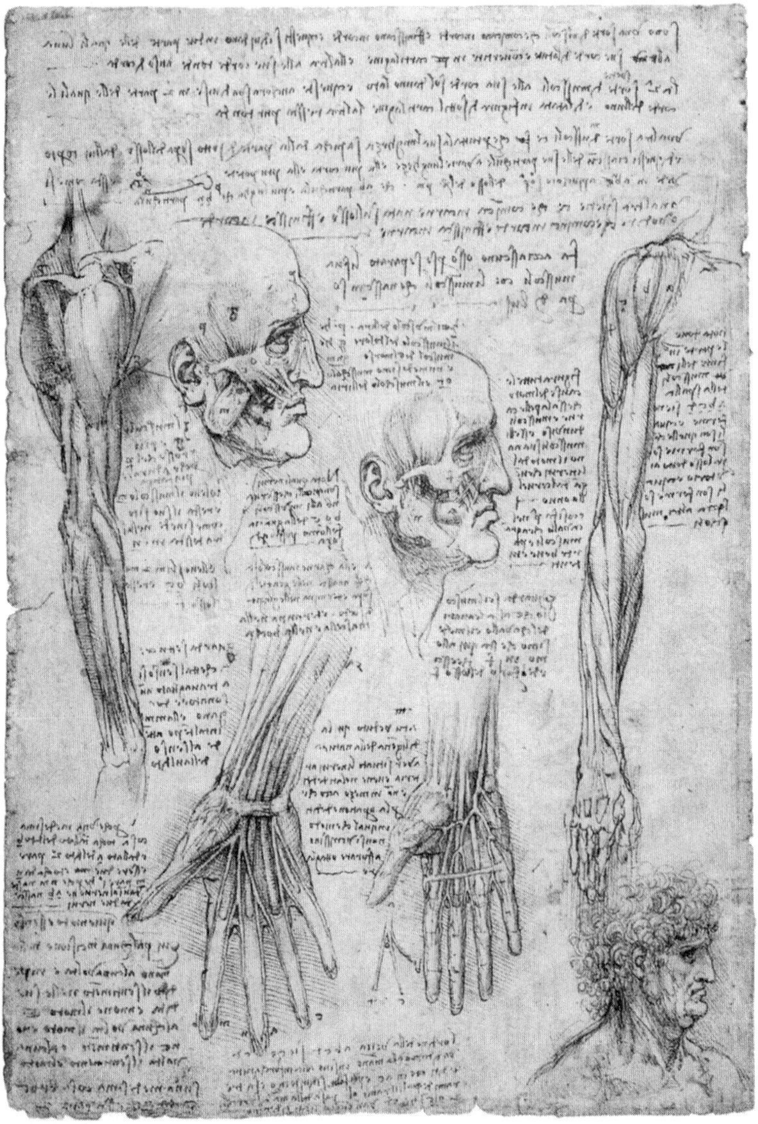

Anatomy of face, arm, and hand

VI

UNDER THE SKIN

ON A SHEET FILLED WITH writing in the British Library, which is located near the St. Pancras International train station, Leonardo recounts his exploration of a cavern. He does not reveal where this excursion might have taken place, but simply describes a horrific landscape: "[Not even] the tempestuous sea make[s] so loud a roaring when the northern blast beats it back in foaming waves between Scylla and Charybdis, nor Stromboli nor Mount Etna when the pent up, sulphurous fires, bursting open and rending asunder the mighty mountain by their force are hurling through the air rocks and earth mingled together in the issuing belching flames." But these horrors did not deter him from forging ahead:

> Drawn on by my eager desire, anxious to behold the great abundance of the varied and strange forms created by the artificer Nature, I came to the mouth of a huge cavern . . . my back bent to an arch, my left hand clutching my knee, while with the right I made a shade for my lowered and contracted eyebrows; and I was bending continually first one way and then another

in order to see whether I could discern anything inside, though this was
rendered impossible by the intense darkness within. And after remaining
there for a time, suddenly there were awakened within me two emotions,
fear and desire, fear of the dark threatening cavern, desire to see whether
there might be any marvelous thing therein.[1]

It is highly unlikely that Leonardo was recalling one of his solitary
hikes through the landscapes of Italy in this passage. When describing
his discoveries in nature, he tended to adopt a terse, sober tone, and
he nearly always named the setting. This big cavern, portrayed so haunt-
ingly with references to ancient legends, seems to have existed only in
his imagination. His venture into the underworld gives us a glimpse
into his own inner world. These few lines transport the reader into a
realm that Leonardo usually took pains to conceal: the realm of his
emotions.

The Russian historian of science V. P. Zubov called the cavern story
a literary self-portrait—the only one we have of Leonardo.[2] He succumbs to feelings that are not directed at another human being, as one
might expect, but at the exhilarating, yet unsettling conflict he faces
in his yearning to enter into uncharted territory while fearing the consequences of pursuing this desire. Leonardo situates these wrenching
emotions at the fateful moment he first peers into the cavern. Exploring
terra incognita can be frightening, even if the pioneer does not have
to fear for life and limb. It is deeply disconcerting to come face-to-face
with something never seen before. Every new discovery entails the loss
of an old certainty, which is replaced by uncertainty, stumbling and
fumbling while attempting cautiously to resolve discrepancies between
old and new realities. The French geneticist François Jacob has called
this phase "night science." Announcing a revolutionary discovery is
sure to trigger attacks from contemporaries who defend the traditional

Raphael, portrait of Pope Leo X with two cardinals

view. Socrates paid for expounding his philosophy in public with a cup of hemlock, Galileo for his declaration "And yet it moves!" with years of house arrest. Conservatives are riled by Charles Darwin even today.

Research is about extending boundaries, and Leonardo was not willing to bow to the taboos of his day. He must have figured that one day his thirst for knowledge would land him in serious trouble. His long history of strong connections to the high and mighty allowed him to skirt such difficulties for decades. But in the final years of his life, luck turned against him. "The Pope has found out that I have skinned three corpses," he wrote anxiously in a draft of a letter to his patron Giuliano de' Medici in about 1515.[3] Now more than sixty years old,

Leonardo was trying to make yet another new start, this time in Rome. But the commissions he was hoping for did not materialize, because the new pope, Leo X, who was Giuliano's brother, did not appreciate Leonardo's art. He even made fun of Leonardo in public, claiming that the artist was spending his time distilling oils and plants to prepare the varnish instead of getting down to the work itself.[4] We also learn from Leonardo's letter that an employee in his own workshop was responsible for having maligned Leonardo to the Vatican as a desecrator of corpses, evidently as revenge for Leonardo's having accused this craftsman, whom he called Giovanni of the Mirrors, of divulging trade secrets. Leonardo wrote that Giovanni, who was originally from Germany, had spread this slander not only to the pope, but also to the hospital at which Leonardo was obtaining his cadavers.

If Leonardo's examinations of corpses had stopped short of full dissections, his actions would most likely have been overlooked. Clergymen were well aware why the artworks displayed in their churches were so astonishingly true-to-life. Many prominent artists of this era—from Domenico Veneziano to Luca Signorelli to Michelangelo—secretly studied the skeletons and the muscles of cadavers. But Leonardo went far beyond his colleagues. He was not content just to examine the visible surface of human limbs. He wanted to know how the body functioned deep inside, and he dissected hearts, brains, and reproductive organs. This invasive level violated the Church's time-honored view that the body was a microcosm of the universe as a whole, and its organs were ruled by the planets. And hadn't the blood of Christ been chosen to redeem the whole world? Anyone who undertook a voyage of discovery inside a human being was committing an offense against all of God's creation.

Not even doctors had the right to investigate the workings of the internal organs. Long gone was the enlightened era of the thirteenth century, when Friedrich Barbarossa required surgeons in his empire to have studied anatomy for at least one year before entering the medical profession. The Church ensured that dissections, even at universities, took place only under exceptional circumstances, and then solely on the bodies of people whom the clergy considered fallen individuals, namely executed criminals and executioners.[5] The resulting paucity of visual aids forced the medical students of Leonardo's day to rely on memorizing the writings of the ancient doctor Galen, who most likely never actually saw the internal organs of a human being. Disregarding the ban could result in the most severe punishment the Church could impose: excommunication. The unauthorized opening of cadavers thus held out the dismal prospect of ostracism on earth and rotting in hell for all eternity.

We do not know how Leonardo's conflict with the pope turned out, but he seems to have gotten off lightly. His letter to his patron, Giuliano de' Medici, the brother of the pope, states simply that he was "hampered" in his anatomical research. A few months later, Leonardo left Rome for good, and moved to France.

IN THE MORTUARIES OF SANTA MARIA NUOVA

He had been drawing interior views of the body for more than a quarter of a century before the big trouble began brewing in Rome. While in Milan, he had focused on the human skull, hoping to discover the location of the soul.[6] Like many artists of his time, Leonardo studied anatomy in order to hone his artistic skills. He sketched bones in the skeletal system, attempted to learn as much as he could from surface muscle movements, and pored through the imprecise (and generally inaccurate) depictions in medical books, but he did not dare to dissect bodies. In 1507 and 1508, during his second stay in Milan, he had to

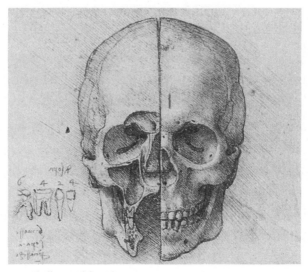

Skull, partial frontal section

spend several months in Florence to resolve a dispute over his uncle's inheritance. The major hospital here, Santa Maria Nuova, granted him access to cadavers.

Leonardo had been acquainted with some of the people whose bodies he opened in this facility. He was even at the side of one elderly man as he died: "And this old man, a few hours before his death, told me that he had lived a hundred years, and that he did not feel any bodily ailment other than weakness, and thus while sitting upon a bed in the hospital of Santa Maria Nuova without any movement or sign of anything amiss, he passed away from this life," Leonardo wrote. "And I made an autopsy in order to ascertain the cause of so peaceful a death."[7] This was one of his first autopsies.

The encounter with the old man must have taken place in the gigantic men's ward in Santa Maria Nuova, which is still used as a hospital today. The ward once encompassed a cruciform building, with corridors as long as the naves of a cathedral. It has been subdivided

Santa Maria Nuova, Florence

into a huge number of examination rooms, but a walk through the endless corridors that connect all the rooms now used for diagnoses, X rays, and various forms of therapy conveys a sense of how overwhelming this ward must once have felt. I was told by my guide, Esther Diana, an architectural historian who has been studying Santa Maria Nuova for many years, that in the nineteenth century there were still 450 beds here. Most of the patients lay head to toe, with two or even four to a bed. In the words of a late eighteenth-century visitor, "the odor of decomposition may be described as a mixture of the acidic, the sickly, and the fetid," which resulted in a nauseating stench, even though the ceiling in this ward was 40 feet high to promote better ventilation.[8]

By the time Leonardo began frequenting this building, Santa Maria Nuova had been in existence for over two centuries but was still considered the most modern hospital in Europe. In contrast to other hospitals, the physicians here tried not only to care for their patients, but to cure them. Over 80 percent of the men and women who were admitted to Santa Maria Nuova left alive, except during outbreaks of the plague. As the fame of the hospital spread, it prospered, and all around the central men's ward countless other buildings were constructed. A wall enclosed the entire site, and Santa Maria Nuova seemed like a small town within the city. Additional properties throughout Florence yielded such a large income that the hospital even opened its own bank and made funding available to Leonardo.

Santa Maria Nuova was a secular foundation, and its affluence gave the hospital an unusual degree of autonomy, even from the Church. Esther Diana explained to me that with this autonomy, the hospital could be more permissive about dissections than was the case elsewhere. Although the doctors were officially required to restrict their autopsies to the cadavers of criminals, and hospital regulations stipulated that these procedures could take place no more than once a year, pioneers such as Dr. Antonio Benivieni were able to conduct numerous autopsies on ordinary bodies as long as doctors kept quiet about these activities. Artists who were associated with the hospital were also permitted to work with the dead bodies. In many cases, they paid for this privilege with their artworks.

The cadavers were easily accessible anyway. After a brief chapel service, the dead were transported directly to the adjacent Chiostro delle Ossa (cloisters of the bones). Part of this area is now overgrown with ivy and rhododendrons, and another part has been turned into the hospital's entry wing. But back then, there were skeletons in the four corners to remind the visitor of the evanescence of earthly life. Of course, it is just as likely that the cemetery was named for the bones that washed out of the ground when it rained; even in Leonardo's day, the Chiostro delle Ossa was far too small to give a proper burial to the more than three hundred patients who died in this giant hospital every

Tub for washing corpses

year. People complained about the deplorable state of affairs here. On an area that measured no more than 30 by 30 feet, so many dead bodies were decaying "that there was no soil left to cover them."⁹ New arrivals were often simply laid out on the ground, and if no family members claimed them, they were fair game for anyone who wanted to use them.

From the Chiostro delle Ossa, there is a walkway leading to a steep staircase and down into the vault under the hospital chapel. "This is where Leonardo is said to have washed his corpses," Esther Diana explained. Along the walls of the room, which had several bulky pillars, there were three stone tubs carved out of a single piece of rock and marked with Roman numerals. The tubs were large enough to hold horses, and my guide wondered whether they were really used to wash the dead. Perhaps they were actually granaries, as the Roman numerals would appear to indicate.

We walked past shelves full of dust-covered files into another vault, where in all likelihood the dissections once took place. Two bulbs were the only source of light in this low-ceilinged, windowless room. The light was so dim that I could picture Leonardo struggling to see as he labored by torchlight. This place was far from prying eyes. To make himself even less conspicuous, Leonardo worked after hours and wrote about his "fear of passing the night hours in the company of these cadavers, quartered and flayed and horrible to behold."[10]

Leonardo cautioned: "Though possessed of an interest in the subject, you may perhaps be deterred by natural repugnance."[11] Anyone who has ever witnessed an autopsy knows what he meant. At least cadavers are chilled these days, often preserved with chemicals, and opened up under a powerful ventilation hood. That observers are profoundly repulsed even under these conditions makes it disturbing to contemplate what an anatomist of the Renaissance must have experienced, with the decay of the body setting in after just a few hours in the abdominal cavity and spreading throughout the body. The cool temperature in the vault slowed down the decomposition process, but the putrefactive gases were surely overpowering in this windowless room.

Leonardo had no chance of winning the race against time and disintegration. Exposing the veins, nerves, and tendons in a manner that enables an artist to draw them is a laborious business, because they are embedded in fat and connective tissue, which the dissector has to scrape away slowly and carefully. The long fingernails of Leonardo's bare hands must have served as an important tool. It is not surprising that he needed access to many cadavers to get anything accomplished under these trying circumstances: "I have dissected more than ten human bodies [because] one single body did not suffice for so long a time [and] it was necessary to proceed by stages with so many bodies as would render my knowledge complete."[12] Working with decaying cadavers would have been difficult for anyone, but Leonardo's problematic relationship to physicality made the situation even worse, as is evident in his remarks about the genitalia: "The act of procreation and the members employed therein are so repulsive, that if it were not for the beauty of the faces and the adornments of the actors and the pent-up impulse, nature would lose the human species."[13]

Still, Leonardo was rewarded for his efforts with astonishing insights into the workings of the body. His autopsy of the old man whose death he had witnessed while sitting at the edge of his sickbed in Santa Maria Nouva was so thorough that he was able to establish that deterioration of the coronary vessels was the cause of death: "I found that it proceeded from weakness through failure of blood and of the artery that feeds the heart and the other lower members, which I found to be very parched and shrunk and withered. . . . Another autopsy was on a child of two years, and here I found everything the contrary to what it was in the case of the old man."[14] Leonardo had discovered arteriosclerosis—more than three centuries before this term was coined by Jean Lobstein, a surgeon in Strasbourg. He even correctly surmised why death ensues from what is often referred to as "hardening of the arteries," although he mistook these arteries for veins: "The old who enjoy good health die through lack of sustenance. And this is brought about by the passage to the mesaraic veins becoming continually restricted by the thickening of the skin of these veins; and the process continues until it affects the capillary veins, which are the first to close up altogether. . . . And this network of veins acts in man as in oranges, in which the peel becomes thicker . . . the more they become old."[15]

AN X-RAY VIEW OF SEX

Leonardo must have had more in mind than painterly ambition when he examined corpse after corpse over the following decade. He drew hundreds of views of human organs while living in Florence, Milan, and Rome. His knowledge of surface musculature and the skeleton was certainly valuable for his portraits, but the facts he amassed about the digestive system and the anatomy of heart valves were of no practical use in this regard. His initial desire to learn more about the human body in order to enhance his painting had long since become an end in itself. Leonardo conducted this research to enhance his understanding. He had peered into the cavern, and his burning desire to know won out over fear and revulsion.

At the same time, he could not escape the beliefs of his era. Like his contemporaries, Leonardo accepted the idea that the body was a microcosm of the world, but in contrast to his orthodox peers, Leonardo's acceptance of this idea did not impose any limits on his scientific inquiry. In fact, the idea of man as microcosm seemed to pique his interest in researching the body:

> So then we may say that the earth has a spirit of growth, and that its flesh is the soil; its bones are the successive strata of the rocks which form the mountains; its cartilage is the tufa stone; its blood the springs of its waters. The lake of blood that lies about the heart is the ocean. Its breathing is by the increase and decrease of the blood in its pulses, and even so in the earth is the ebb and flow of the sea.[16]

As abstruse as we may find these comparisons today, they made perfect sense to any educated person in the fifteenth century. Concepts of cause and effect were just beginning to take hold; people were far more accustomed to thinking in analogies. And Leonardo was the champion of the similarity game: If a mirror bounces back light according to the same laws that a wall bounces back a ball (he was correct on this point), if birds use the same principle to fly that fish use to swim (this was incorrect)—then why not regard the innermost layers of rock as the innards of the earth? To Leonardo, cutting open an abdominal wall and entering the darkness of a mountain cavern were one and the same thing.

His philosophy of nature, however, went well beyond the equation of "human body = planet earth" that prevailed in his day. In Leonardo's view, everything in the universe was part of a larger harmony that could be captured in simple geometric rules: "Proportion is found not only in numbers and measurements, but also in sounds, weights, times, positions, and in whatsoever power there may be."[17] Leonardo even saw harmonic laws at play in smells "just as in music."[18] He also believed that there was a single force (which he described in glowing terms) that set all things in motion and induced change. His most powerful portrayal of an all-encompassing mathematical order was his best-known drawing, the *Proportions of the Human Body According to Vitruvius*. The navel of the man with outstretched arms and legs appears at the exact center of a square, and the man's fingertips and the tips of his toes lie along the circumference of a circle. The length of each side of the square and the radius of the circle—and even the ratio of the individual parts of the body to one another—correspond precisely to what is known as the "golden section."

But in his basic assumptions, Leonardo was too much a product of his era to make a complete break with traditional biases. He was also mistaken about certain anatomical features, particularly in regard to male genitalia, which seems odd in light of his attraction to men. He made a spectacular drawing of the act of sexual intercourse, with the united bodies of a man and a woman in a longitudinal section, as though using X-ray vision to see right through them. Still, he situated the base of the male sperm canal not in the testicles, but in the spinal column. This error can be explained in part by the early date of origin of this print. In 1492, Leonardo had yet to see the inside of a human

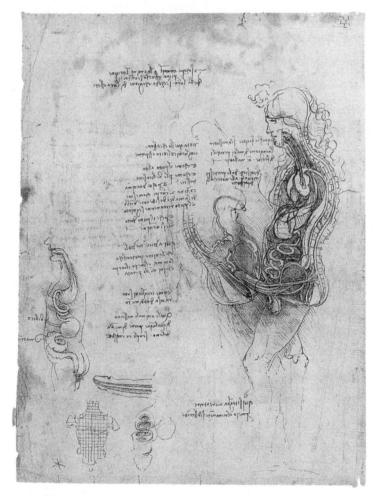

Coitus

body—which makes this depiction even more astonishing, since he needed to rely on ancient writings asserting that man's reproductive capacity was a function of his mental capacity, with the spine as the point of connection. The Church later embraced this notion because of its implication that too much sex sapped the lifeblood from the brain.[19]

Twenty years later, when Leonardo had long since opened up and studied internal organs, he continued to make errors of this magnitude. For example, he drew a septum of an ox heart perforated with pores and noted under it: "This is how it needs to be drawn." By then, Leonardo had already dissected dozens of hearts and certainly never saw perforations in the septum between the two ventricles of the heart—because there are none. The idea that the blood passes from the left ventricle to the right one through pores was nothing but a figment of the ancient Greek physician Galen's imagination.

Can we blame Leonardo, who normally paid such attention to detail, for his occasional tendency to attach more importance to the prejudices of others than to what lay before his own eyes? Scientists whose work results in revolutionary breakthroughs are famous for mistrusting what they see in front of them. Even the most self-assured spirits can hesitate to wage a solitary battle against the universally accepted dogmas promoted by the renowned scholars of their era. It is often easier to doubt one's own findings. And even those who come up with entirely new ideas rarely make a complete break with tradition. Leonardo's conservative bent put him in the best of company; some of the greatest innovators in science were conservative to a fault, in the view of their successors, who often wondered at their pigheadedness and sometimes even considered them downright insane. Galileo, who ought to have known better, rejected the notion of elliptical planetary orbits as described by Kepler with the argument that "God did not wish it so." In a respectable universe, celestial bodies would orbit on circular paths—just the way astronomers had been drawing them since antiquity. Einstein, whose ideas formed the basis of modern quantum physics, refused to accept the notion of randomness in the realm of atoms: "God does not play dice." Letting go of the errors of the past once and for all and completing an intellectual revolution is generally left to researchers of the following generation. In Leonardo's case it was a Flemish physician, Andreas Vesalius, whose 1543 edition of his anatomical textbook praised God for the wonderful creation of pores so small that the eye could not detect them, but amended his view in the revised edition and explained that no such pores existed.[20] Vesalius, who knew some of Leonardo's work, no longer regarded humans as a microcosm of the universe. For him, the body was just a body.

Man Is a Machine

In 1509, the anatomist Marcantonio della Torre joined the faculty in Pavia. His presence gave new impetus to Leonardo's research on the human body. We know little about this young man, who enjoyed great fame as a medical researcher but who succumbed to the plague at Lake Garda in 1511, at the age of twenty-nine. Leonardo and he were definitely friends. When Leonardo, who was living in Milan at the time, visited della Torre in Pavia (only a day's journey away) to observe his dissections, both profited from the encounters: Leonardo soaked up medical knowledge, and della Torre came away with anatomical drawings of unparalleled quality.[21]

Spurred on by the young professor, Leonardo worked so feverishly on his anatomical studies that he now felt capable of completing a book on this subject, as he had been planning for more than two decades: "I hope to finish the whole of this anatomy in the winter of 1510."

Leonardo even developed special dissection methods for organs that are notoriously difficult to sketch, such as the eyes, which lose their shape when the gelatinous vitreous body is pierced. He came up with the idea of boiling eyes in the white of an egg to solidify them so that he would be able to cut them transversely after they cooled down

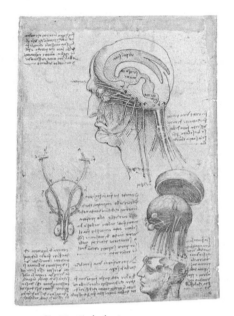

Cavities in the brain

and draw a sectional view.[22] He created air holes in the cavities of the brain and injected them with molten wax to make a cast, after inserting "narrow tubes into the holes so that the air in these ventricles can escape and make room for the wax entering the ventricles."[23]

Here, too, Leonardo derived great benefit from his powers of imagination. The soft tissues, the organs, the tendons, and the fibers under the skin, which we are used to seeing in clearly defined forms in anatomical illustrations, are in reality utterly shapeless. A heart without blood is nothing but a bulky lump of flesh, a dead man's lung is like a rag, and to the untrained eye, the various glands in the abdominal cavity are hard to tell apart. When medical students today take anatomy classes and dissect their first cadavers, they have a textbook and a mentor to guide them; Leonardo, by contrast, was in uncharted territory. Even so, he created vivid images of shapes he was never able to make

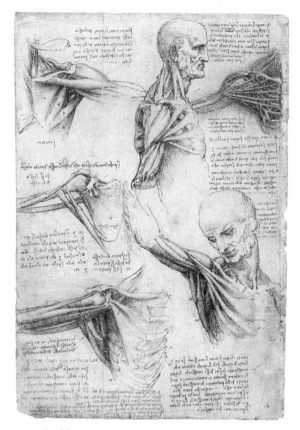

Shoulder joint

out clearly. He portrayed our soft tissue so graphically that it feels tempting to stick a finger into the aorta of the heart he drew.

Another impressive example of his anatomical artistry is found in his studies of the shoulder joint. The upper part of the body and the arm are juxtaposed in a series of perspectives, and subtle light and shadow effects highlight the interplay of the muscles.[24] In some places on the sketches the surface of the skin is included, and in others layers of the musculoskeletal system are exposed, so a single drawing takes the viewer from the familiar exterior to deeper and deeper interior realms of the body. Parts of a given drawing show lifelike tendons, and others nothing more than schematic lines to highlight a functional principle, with the humerus peeping out from between the muscle fibers.

On other pages he renders the organs translucent in spots, making them look somewhat like frosted glass, which keeps their shape visible while offering an unobstructed view of what lies behind them. And Leonardo's analysis of the blood vessels leads the viewer through all the stages of abstraction—from the amazingly lifelike pen-and-ink drawing of a body part with a network of tiny capillaries down to a mathematical scheme showing blood vessels branching off.

Leonardo was a consummate explainer, and he was convinced that pictures can offer a better overview than language. He noted on one illustration of the heart: "With what words O writer can you with a like perfection describe the whole arrangement of that of which the design is here? . . . I counsel you not to cumber yourself with words unless you are speaking to the blind."[25]

In an era ruled by laborious descriptions, with few explanatory images, Leonardo employed the very modern approach of emphasizing visual imagery. Even today, medical students learn from pictures, and it is no accident that Leonardo's anatomical drawings resemble visual aids of the kind found in today's magazines and the stylistic techniques we see on interactive computer images. His interior views of the body look as though they were drawn in the twenty-first century.

How had he developed this unusual way of depicting man? In the lower right corner of one sheet, we see only the bones of a foot. The long bones of the lower leg seem to fly up and away from the tarsus, and we recognize how perfectly the tibia, fibula, and anklebone combine to form the ankle joint. Leonardo had invented this technique, known as an exploded view, to explain his machines. In this illustration, the foot seems like part of a machine.

Leonardo employed many other optical strategies to bring out the complex dimensions of the body—light and shadow, transparency, views from various angles—that he had tried out on his earlier structural plans. And the idea of breaking something down to its component parts was not new to him, either. During the years he spent in Florence and Milan, he went to great lengths to understand the mechanics of machines by analyzing their elements piece by piece. Consequently, when he began to dissect cadavers in 1507, he merely had to switch the object of his investigations rather than devising a new approach. Instead of screws and gears, he now turned his attention to bones, muscles, and nerves.

The laws of mechanics had become second nature to him during his years as an engineer. He now scrutinized the human body with the eyes of a technician: Arms and legs, even the bite force of individual teeth, were consistent with the lever law. Tumescent muscles worked like gussets. Tendons, he wrote, hold thighs in joints the way shrouds hold up the mast of a ship. And hadn't he even designed a robot in human form, whose limbs moved by means of a complex system of ropes inside the body? Now he was drawing tendons as ropes.

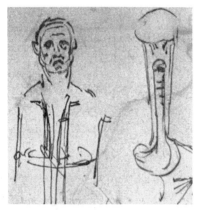

Engulfed valve

In one of the sketches for the bell ringer mechanism that Mark Rosheim reconstructed, man and machine actually merge: A man and the inner workings of the water cylinder to measure time are superimposed to make it look as though the man has engulfed the technology of the cylinder. His neck turns into a water pipe, and on the level of the diaphragm the rubber ring activates the striking of the hour. Next to it Leonardo drew two incisions through the stomach and esophagus. Evidently he was looking for analogies between his construction and the mechanics of swallowing—and wondering whether he could learn something from nature.[26]

Man is a machine. This view enabled Leonardo to break away little by little from traditional dogmas, although he never quite succeeded in liberating himself from superstitions. He recognized that the earth follows rules unlike those of the human body. The veins of the old man he autopsied in Florence had narrowed in old age, whereas the rivers, "the veins of the earth," "are enlarged by the prolonged and continuous passage of water."[27] Notions of the body as a mirror of the earth lost their persuasiveness and were replaced by the matter-of-fact laws of cause and effect, by verifiable rules of mechanics.

But although Leonardo described the body as a machine, he did not lose his sense of awe—quite the contrary. The longer he conducted his research, and the more cadavers he dissected, the more his amazement grew at the complexity and perfection of the human body. At an earlier point in his life, he had been optimistic that a clever engineer would be able to reconstruct nature and create an artificial bird or something of that sort. He now realized how presumptuous this wish had been. "[Humans] will never devise an invention more beautiful, more simple, or more direct than does nature," he wrote in reference to a drawing in which he tried to establish the origins of sounds in the movements of the lips and tongue.[28] An examination of the shoulder joint inspired him to praise nature for its "marvelous works."[29]

Precisely because he recognized the complexity of nature, Leonardo sought to fathom every single detail—and to render everything exactly, "as though the actual person were standing before you."[30] His goal was to understand every single mechanism in the body. It was here that medicine began to follow its current path. Only the focus has shifted; modern researchers are less interested in the rotations of the shoulder joint than in what occurs in the cell nucleus to cause cancer.

The years Leonardo spent at the dissection table transformed his view of the world. Up to the time Santa Maria Nuova opened its mortuaries to him, he was searching for a general principle behind the functioning of the cosmos. Once he had examined the body exhaustively, Leonardo abandoned his quest to find a totality of the world—and adopted the much humbler approach to nature on which modern science is based. To understand the world, you have to describe its phenomena one by one. There can be no shortcut. The leap of imagination that carries armchair scholars from the organism of man to that of the earth, from theology to physics, can lead them astray. The only way to advance a bold new theory is to make meticulous studies and conduct the requisite experiments. Truncating this laborious process "does injury to knowledge and to love, for love of anything is the offspring of knowledge, love being more fervent in proportion as knowledge is more certain."[31]

Expeditions into the Beating Heart

Leonardo's last major inquiry in Rome was also his most astonishing one. Just five years before his death, he explored the mysteries of the human heart. His discoveries are recorded in a series of ten bluish sheets now in the collection of the Queen of England. One of them contains his diatribe against "abbreviators."[32] The sketches are not easy to read, because they depict what no eye has ever seen: blood flowing through the ventricles of the heart.

Incisions through the aorta reveal the three crescent-shaped pockets of the aortic valve. This tripartite division is found again in an abstract

Interior views of the heart

sketch that bears a striking resemblance to the Mercedes logo. It looks as though Leonardo had wanted to explore the diversity of shapes in an artery. There are also helical swirls to indicate blood forced from the left ventricle into a protrusion of the aorta. Between the sketches, Leonardo squeezed in explanatory notes in mirror writing. When the heart muscle contracts and presses the blood out of the ventricle, swirls form in the aortic valve. As soon as the muscle relaxes at the end of the heartbeat, these swirls in some miraculous way press against the valve and shut it, thus blocking the blood from flowing back into the heart and sending it on its way through the body.

How could Leonardo know this? It is not possible to view blood flowing, because we cannot see into the beating heart. The sound of the valve shutting is all we can detect. Even centuries after Leonardo, scientists did not have a clear idea of how the human heart valve worked. In 1999, speculation came to an end when researchers in London, Boston, and California, using magnetic resonance velocity mapping, were finally able to obtain images of blood flow in the living heart. They found exactly what Leonardo had described.[33]

Morteza Gharib, a professor of bioengineering at Caltech, is one of the foremost specialists on heart function today. He holds more than a dozen patents for artificial hearts, improved heart valves, and other related devices. Gharib says that his own heart skipped a beat when he first saw Leonardo's drawings of the blood flow at the aortic valve. "Since I am an experimenter myself, I realized immediately that Leonardo must have conducted experiments. That is the only way he could have made these discoveries." Gharib scrutinized Leonardo's drawings for evidence to substantiate his assumption—and struck gold. Sure enough, Leonardo described a method of constructing an artificial heart. "Blow thin glass into a plaster mold and then break it. But first pour wax into this valve of a bull's heart so that you may see the true shape of this valve," he wrote on one of the blue pages.[34] Around these words, Leonardo drew the shape he had just described, which looks exactly like the curvatures of the aorta. His goal was "to see in the glass what the blood does in the heart when it closes the little doors of the heart."[35] Gharib interprets the odd Mercedes logos as plans for mechanical heart valves. Elsewhere Leonardo explains how flow patterns can be traced in the glass heart by adding particles to the fluid: "Do this test in the glass and stir in water and millet seeds."[36]

To prove that Leonardo really conducted these experiments, Gharib built a mechanical heart valve in his laboratory using Leonardo's sketches. A flask whose shape Leonardo had outlined with a few quick strokes of his pen on a blue sheet of paper sits atop a Plexiglas plate, with a pump pressing water from below into a container at regular intervals. With each pulse beat, a valve composed of three leaflets at the base of the flask opens like a swinging door. Its soft synthetic material makes the components seem like delicate flaps of skin. Whenever the supply of water from below stops, the opening shuts again, then the whole process begins anew, and the contents of the flask pulse to the beat of the pump.

Modern scientists observe flow patterns just as Leonardo had recommended—by placing particles in the liquid, except for the fact that Gharib did not pick up millet at the health food store, but instead used tiny, silver-coated glass spheres, in accordance with the now-standard practice. And instead of relying on the naked eye to follow their movements, he used a complex laser measuring device. But Gharib's computer screen showed him exactly the same flow lines that Leonardo had sketched more than five hundred years earlier. Gharib reports a feeling of profound humility while conducting these experiments: "Leonardo's eye was so sharp that he grasped connections using nothing more than his pencil that it took other scientists many generations later to formulate in equations."

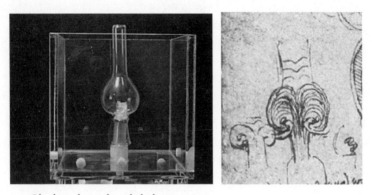

Blood circulation through the heart

But Leonardo's sharp eye would have been useless without his ability to synthesize knowledge from different arenas. Decades earlier, he had worked on flow patterns and lock gates. Now he understood what to look for in the heart, assuming that blood acted like water in a canal. After a constriction, a backwater builds up and eddies form, which can shut the lock gate from the outside. A hydraulic engineer had to prevent this from happening—but nature used this process to good effect in the heart.

But why does the aortic valve need to have three cusps? Here Leonardo benefited from his earlier obsession with squaring the circle. One could easily regard the countless pages he filled with similar geometric figures as the jottings of a madman, but they helped him understand the workings of the three triangular sections of the aortic valve.[37] If the valve had only two cusps, it would be harder to open, and with four it would be unstable.

Leonardo's glass heart proved that he was a true prophet. He anticipated scientific methods of the modern age. While his contemporaries continued to discuss how planets control the human heartbeat, Leonardo constructed a model based on nature to study it. The *Mona*

Lisa is the reconception of a face, and the artificial heart is the reconstruction of an internal organ according to the rules of nature.

"A PHILOSOPHER MORE THAN A CHRISTIAN . . ."

To announce his discoveries, Leonardo could have made use of the most significant invention of his era: Gutenberg's printing press. Why didn't he? Instead of going down in history as the creator of the first serious anatomical atlas, Leonardo never advanced his plan to publish an anatomy book beyond a set of loose manuscript pages. Quite a few biographers have puzzled over what made him falter, particularly because a note on those pages indicates that he had every intention of having his pictures of the insides of the body printed as a book: "I am marking how these drawings should be reprinted in order and I ask you, the successors, not to let stinginess cause you to print them in—"[38] Here the sentence breaks off.

The solution to this mystery is straightforward, and Leonardo himself provided it. This project, like so many others, was never realized because it would have required an endless amount of work to transform private jottings into a publishable text. At the close of a curious passage, in which Leonardo justifies himself to an imaginary reader of his unwritten books, he puts his finger on the problem: "Concerning which things, whether or no they have all been found in me, the hundred and twenty books which I have composed will give their verdict 'yes' or 'no.' In these I have not been hindered either by avarice or negligence, but only by want of time. Farewell."[39]

Leonardo was pursuing so many interests that he could rarely take full advantage of his chance to solve any particular problem; he simply lacked the time to do so. In cases where an additional experiment would have given him more precise information, he was already moving on to the next unknown territory. And because he was working for himself, rather than for others, he did not devote much time to the issue of publishing his findings. In contrast to modern researchers, Leonardo simply did not care whether others would be able to build on his work. Does a man who makes significant discoveries but keeps them to himself deserve the glory of a discoverer?

All the same, his reports about his expeditions inside of the body, unlike other manuscripts, were never forgotten altogether. When Leonardo left Italy, small bundles remained at the hospital in Santa Maria Nuova, where he had dissected his first cadavers. But the vast majority of the anatomical sketches were inherited by Melzi, who was happy to grant access to researchers and artists who had heard about this valuable collection.[40] They studied and copied Leonardo's pages, and some of his pictures of the human body were disseminated along strange byways. One depiction of the finger muscles, which is strikingly similar to a sketch by Leonardo, adorned the title page of the first anatomical atlas by Andreas Vesalius in 1543. Rembrandt, in turn, used this image as a model for the focal point of his *Anatomy Lesson of Dr. Nicolaes Tulp*, a painting of doctors observing the dissection of a forearm.[41]

Nevertheless, only a small group was aware of Leonardo's pioneering accomplishments, and it is fair to assume that no one in this select group fully grasped the breadth and depth of his research. Thus Leonardo's work, which could have marked the beginning of modern medicine, did not gain the recognition it deserved in the centuries to come. Today, Vesalius is considered the father of modern anatomy.

Judging by the merits of Leonardo's achievements, we would have to conclude that he would have been equally worthy of this honor. But apart from the muddled state of the manuscripts, it is, paradoxically, Leonardo's extraordinary talent as a draftsman that stood in the way of his fame as a scientist, because his anatomical depictions were re-garded as the magnificent legacy of an artist. Drawing the mechanics of the shoulder, the muscle strands of the tongue, or the blood vessels of the forearm with such refinement represented an enormous artistic advance. Just as Columbus was discovering new territories beyond the ocean for the Spanish queen, Leonardo, at virtually the same time, was revealing a realm previously unknown to Western art. Until then, artists had portrayed the world as people were used to seeing it; even paintings of biblical miracles made the saints look pretty much like people on the street. Leonardo, by contrast, introduced objects beyond the realm of everyday experience. His anatomical drawings and his sketches of eddies and rock formations reveal the minutest details of the world in which we live, yet we do not really know.

Even so, Leonardo's anatomical drawings mark more than just the beginning of a new artistic era. They describe the path of a man who gradually cast off his own errors and the illusions of his era. Peeling away human skin altered far more than his vision of the human body; it shook the foundations of his view of life. Leonardo's fear of gazing into the unknown cavern proved all too justified. "In the course of philosophizing on nature . . . Leonardo formed such heretical ideas that no religion could be reconciled with them; evidently he wanted to be a philosopher more than a Christian," Vasari scolded in the first edition of his Leonardo biography. When the book was reprinted, Vasari deleted this passage.

The old man and the water

VII

FINAL QUESTIONS

AN OLD MAN IS SITTING on a rocky ledge, his back hunched, gazing into the distance.[1] He is resting his head on his left hand and knitting his brow as though deep in thought. A couple of wisps of hair stick up at the hairline, but otherwise his head is bald apart from a fringe of hair in the back. Only the full white beard, which comes down to his chest, conveys a sense of what a magnificent head of hair he must have had earlier in life. His right eye, which he turns to us in profile, is wide open and alert, but the crow's feet in the corner of his eye give his face a weary look. And his slumped posture makes him seem melancholy and even resigned. Who is this old man, and what is on his mind?

Several sketches on the reverse side of the page leave no doubt as to when and where Leonardo made this pen-and-ink drawing. They display details of Villa Melzi, the country residence of the family of Leonardo's favorite student, Francesco, where the master spent the better part of 1512. In Milan, a day's journey away, war was imminent: Troops sent by the deposed Sforza ruling family were advancing into the city to reconquer it. The end of French rule seemed to loom just

The old man and the water

a matter of weeks ahead. The French had paid Leonardo generously and given him every freedom as an artist; now the Sforzas would regard him as a collaborator. Here in the country, he was safe.

Leonardo must have sensed that he was running out of time—but he had no idea how he would spend the rest of his life. He did not yet know that he would soon travel to Rome to try his luck as a painter for the Vatican. And could he foresee that he would eventually undertake an odyssey to France and would die there, but that his art would return here, in Melzi's care?

It is revealing to compare the drawing of the old man with the portrait that Francesco Melzi had made of his master years earlier (facing first page of introduction). Leonardo had a luxuriant head of hair in the earlier picture, but the same pointed nose, the same forehead with the characteristic S-curve above the base of the nose, the same shape

Villa Melzi, Vaprio d'Adda

of the eyes as on the drawing of the old man. We can therefore assume that Leonardo's sad old man was a portrait of himself.

The elderly man's gaze is fixed on images of water. This page, which was once folded, consists of two halves. The man is on the left, and to the right of the fold—the direction he is facing—Leonardo made four drawings of the complex shapes that form when a current comes up against a barrier. With powerful strokes of his pen, he drew dams and eddies and waves interwoven like a woman's braid. He made many studies of this kind in those years, including the riveting picture of the torrent I have hanging over my desk.

Perhaps it was this setting that inspired him to return to the subject of water, the element he had begun investigating three decades earlier. The villa is perched on a hill overlooking the Adda River, which has its source in the Alps, crosses Lake Como, and eventually empties into the Po. At every turn, the visitor to this estate hears the gurgling of water. The imposing building is still in the possession of the family, but there is only a single remaining document here of Leonardo's once-rich legacy: his letter of appointment as chief engineer for Cesare Borgia. The rooms in the villa are now vacant. Most of them face east, along the length of the main facade, and the windows look out onto a terrace behind which the steep bank drops off. Down below is the Adda, originating in the mountains and cascading through a gorge into a wide valley. Leonardo drew this scenery repeatedly, and it is clear that he spent many hours on this terrace. Might he have drawn the picture of the old man here as well?

The windows facing north and south, which offer entirely different views, convey a sense of two worlds colliding. The view to the north is of the Alps; to the south is the Po Valley, which was once covered by the sea. On a clear day, the first hills of the Apennines can be made out on the horizon—a landmass that drifted up the unimaginably long time of 135 million years ago and impelled the Alps upwards and continues to move a few inches north every year.

Leonardo must have had a vague notion of the processes that took place here long before the advent of man, because it was in this landscape that he pondered the question of the origins of the world. The degree to which this question haunted him is recorded on the thirty-six pages of the Codex Leicester, which Leonardo probably bound himself and is in the private collection of Bill Gates today. In 1994,

Landscape on the Adda River

Gates bought the manuscript for thirty million dollars at an auction—the highest price ever paid for a book. Most of the Codex Leicester was composed while Leonardo was staying at Villa Melzi, and it recounts his version of the history of creation, based on his examinations of stones, watercourses, and landscapes. This was a scandalous undertaking, which shook at the foundations of biblical revelation.

Leonardo did not stop there. He contemplated not only the beginning of the world, but also its end. Would the mightiest mountain masses simply disappear one day? What is the future of our planet? Later, in Rome, he would try to provide an artistic answer to these questions. On a drawing of the Apocalypse he made at the Vatican, humans appear as tiny creatures at the mercy of an overpowering nature. Hurricanes and floods rage over them, and exploding mountains destroy every last shred of life.

Leonardo, who was now more than sixty years old, contemplated his own finiteness. He pondered the connection between body and soul. Is there really a substance within man that goes into another life after death? Perhaps the Church was right, and the mysteries of the origins of the world and those of immortality were indeed interconnected.

From the terrace of Villa Melzi, a staircase leads down to a wide canal flanked by stone walls, on which ships continued to sail as recently as the post–World War II period. Leonardo was commissioned by the French, who ruled in Lombardy, to design this waterway through the gorge to Lake Como,[2] but it was not built until three centuries after his death.

To work up a suitable design, Leonardo must have spent a good deal of time walking from the villa down to the gorge, just as he had walked along the canals of the plain in Lombardy decades earlier as an engineer in the service of Ludovico Sforza. At that time, he had devoted his attention to the fine points, such as the breaking of the waves in a current and the eddies at a closing lock gate. By studying flow patterns, he gained insights into the microcosm—the laws according to which water moves analogously to the flow of blood in the human heart. The Codex Leicester, by contrast, which he wrote much later in life, branched out to encompass the big picture, and comprised Leonardo's reflections on how water shaped the world. The topic was unchanged, but Leonardo now regarded it more expansively.

This shift in focus was reflected in his landscapes. In the austere plain in Lombardy, eye and ear are receptive to fine points that tend to be overlooked in spectacular surroundings; moreover, the flow lines of the water appear in their purest form along the very straight canal, almost as they would in a laboratory. For his studies of the development of mountain chains and entire continents, on the other hand, Leonardo could hardly have picked a better spot than the gorges of the Adda.

When glaciers still covered the Alps during the Ice Age, they accumulated an enormous amount of glacial debris known as end moraines through which the water flowing down from Lake Como had to carve a path to reach the alluvial land of the Po Valley, giving rise to rugged landscapes that suggest a sculptor at work even today. As we learn from his notes, Leonardo was also fascinated by the great variety of stones and cliffs that surrounded him.

After a good three hours of walking, the walls of the gorge loom so high and become so narrow that I was bathed in a mysterious light that I have never experienced anywhere else. The rays of light cannot take a direct path down onto the ground of the ravine, particularly since the sky is shielded by beech trees, which in some spots have grown almost horizontally out of the rock and span the gorge. The glint of light that fills the gorge is reflected back and forth dozens of times between the ocher, brown, gray, and reddish walls of conglomerate rock, and ultimately takes on these colors itself. Deep down there is neither white nor black, nor are there sharply defined shadows. Often the brightness seems to come from below as much as it does from above when the valley curves and the walls suddenly move apart. There the water turns calm and forms mirrors, bluish green pools with occasional reddish hues from the algae. The rock formations appear to be doubled, and the view of a submarine world opens out of the walls of the gorge descending into boundless depths.

When you come around the next rock ledge, the Adda again becomes a torrential river, although the canal and a power station have now depleted some of its water. In Leonardo's day, it must have been far more powerful. Not only does the water pour down on the bottom of the gorge; it also cascades from countless sources high up in the walls of rock and rushes toward the spume of the river. Waterfalls resembling veils mask the entrances to caves that the Adda has carved out of the stone, when its bed lay even higher. The history of the river over the course of many millennia is revealed in its slopes. Where the gorge widens out again, the ground is often strewn with pieces of rock that in the course of the ongoing metamorphoses have broken out of the solid compound.

The Adda gorge cuts a good 400 feet into the ground; crossing it made Leonardo feel as though he could dissect the earth. He thought of subterranean watercourses as planetary arteries that came to the surface in the depths of the gorge. He described mountain springs as "nosebleeds of the earth," producing liquid when a small blood vessel bursts, the way it does in man and in animals.[3]

SHELLS ON THE MOUNTAIN SLOPE

When Leonardo saw this scenery for the first time, it must have seemed as though his own imagination were coming to life before his very eyes. The background of *The Virgin of the Rocks* bears such a strong resemblance to the Adda gorge, which the painter had not seen so soon after arriving in Milan. This painting, for the altar in the Franciscan church, which was the second-largest church in the city after the Milan Cathedral, was his first major commission in his new home, and he was asked to include rock formations in the background. Leonardo came up with a brilliant solution: In the cave, where Mary sits with the Christ child, John the Baptist, and an angel, there is faint yet colorful light, which also illuminates the bottom of the Adda valley (Plate VII). A windowlike opening in the cave rock offers one a view onto a bluish green river that meanders out to the horizon between the mountains. The rocks are the same ocher color as those rising from the Adda and have a similar shape—a world molded by erosion and underground water.

This similarity is no coincidence. *The Virgin of the Rocks* displays the extent to which Leonardo regarded water as a force that shapes the earth. Some fifteen years later, he painted *The Virgin of the Rocks* a second time, and now the geological formations were even more detailed. He kept returning to this subject. In the view of art historians such as Martin Kemp, the *Mona Lisa* even draws a parallel between two mother figures: While the obviously pregnant Lisa Gherardini is creating a new human being, the water in the background is creating a new landscape. And *The Virgin and Child with St. Anne*, one of his last paintings, has an entire mountain chain rising from the ocean behind the heads of Mary and her mother, Anne.

Leonardo came up with odd theories about how continents might have arisen from the water. He reasoned that over the course of time the rivers washed so much debris into the sea that the bottom of the ocean was lowered and became unbalanced. To restore the balance, the bottom of the ocean rose elsewhere, like a scale, causing mountains to grow out of the water in those places.

These strange ideas notwithstanding, it is remarkable that Leonardo regarded creation in a totally new time perspective. As he saw it, continents did not originate on the day that God separated the water from the land, but were formed during immeasurably long periods of time. Thus he departed from the Christian Creation story and drew on the ancient idea of earth's gradual transformation. He was arguably the first man in the modern age to get a sense of what Stephen Jay Gould would later call "deep time," the billions of years of early history before man appeared on earth. In an age in which no one cast doubt on the story of Genesis, this was an enormous intellectual achievement: After all, Christian fundamentalists continue to dispute Darwin's theory of evolution and the theory of plate tectonics even today.

The Virgin and Child with St. Anne *(detail)*

Rock stratifications

But Leonardo no longer believed that written texts—not even the Bible—could provide information about the events at the beginning of the world: "Since things are far more ancient than letters, it is not to be wondered at if in our days no record exists of how these seas covered so many countries."[4] But, he surmised, a researcher could learn to read the book of nature by studying fossils and the stratifications of stones.

And that is precisely what he did. The Codex Leicester recounts his studies of rocks as a young man during his first stay in Milan: "In the mountains of Parma and Piacenza multitudes of shells and corals filled with worm-holes may be seen still adhering to the rocks, and when I was making the great horse [the equestrian statue for Ludovico Sforza] in Milan, a large sack of those which had been found in these parts was brought to my workshop by some peasants, and among them were many which were still in their original condition."[5] Clearly his

Fossils

visitors were sensing a profitable business—every last mountain village knew about Leonardo's keen interest in fossils.

Nearly two thousand years earlier, the philosopher Xenophanes of Colophon, in Asia Minor, had realized that fossils contained the petrified remains of primeval beings, but after antiquity, interest in this evidence had faded.[6] Leonardo recognized the significance of fossils, so much so that while at Villa Melzi he planned to devote a whole book to them: "In this work of yours you have first to prove how the shells at the height of a thousand braccia were not carried there by the Deluge."[7] Feeling certain that this could not have happened, he reserved a combination of logic and scorn for the author of the biblical depiction and for those who considered it the sole truth:

If you should say that the shells which are visible at the present time within the borders of Italy, far away from the sea and at great heights, are due to the Flood having deposited them there, I reply that, granting this Flood to have risen seven cubits above the highest mountain, as he has written who measured it, these shells which always inhabit near the shores of the sea ought to be found lying on the mountain sides, and not at so short a distance above their bases, and all at the same level, layer upon layer.[8]

He explained in detail why the shellfish could not have descended from the shores on their own, nor could they have ended up as cadavers at the foot of the mountains when the sea ebbed. For one thing, it would have been impossible for the shells to have moved so far during the forty days the Deluge is said to have lasted, and for another, the animals had evidently been embedded alive inside the mud and later fossilized. The "set of ignoramuses" who did not wish to accept that, Leonardo wrote, were simply proving their "stupidity and ignorance."[9]

Leonardo contended that the entire continent was once an ocean floor. Gradually, the land rose out of the water, and the individual layers of shells simply marked the shorelines of various periods.[10] Leonardo regarded the human body as a machine, with fluid circulating throughout, and the planet earth as an enormous version of this same machine, with water ceaselessly winding its way "from the bottoms of the seas . . . to the summits of the mountains."[11]

"HOW ADMIRABLE THY JUSTICE, O THOU FIRST MOVER!"

Where was the Creator in this scheme of things? For Leonardo, nature was full of amazing wonders, but unlike traditional devout Christians, he did not think it held any unfathomable mysteries. When people did not understand a phenomenon, it was only because they had not conducted sufficient research. Everything in the cosmos adheres to invariable laws of nature—rules whose validity can be confirmed in experiments. Thus Leonardo transformed the metaphysical problem of how the world took shape into a matter of physics and did not mention a higher power intervening in the course of the world. If that were the case, a power of that kind would infringe on the unshakable laws of nature. God has to remain aloof from a world in which these rules apply and which man can explore.

The logical conclusion from these arguments is that the only moment for a higher power to have set the course for the cosmos was when the world originated, because the structure of the laws of nature had to come from somewhere. God could have set them in motion before leaving the universe to its own devices. Scientists cannot refute this view because events preceding nature are not their area of concern. Over the next few centuries, this idea proved to be the only way to reconcile faith and science. Today nearly all religious natural scientists envision God as the creator, but not as the guider of the world.[12]

Like most good ideas in philosophy, this one has quite a long history, dating back to Aristotle, who proceeded from the notion that all things change and move. Aristotle considered these two words synonymous, because every change is also a motion, and every motion a change. He saw the world as a giant billiard table with each ball moving the next one forward. Whenever one object changes, another one must have triggered the event. This purely physical explanation shows that all motion is caused by something else already in motion. Still, at some point there has to have been a beginning, a first cause of an altogether different nature. For Aristotle its origin lay outside this world and came from an "unmoved mover," the source of all change that does not take part in the cosmic activity and whose only connection to the world is having set it in motion. Thus the only thing that can be said about the unmoved mover is that this force exists. People cannot grasp this utterly otherworldly being with their senses or with their reason. The divine sphere is forever detached from the world of humans.

Leonardo knew about Aristotle's theories, and they certainly suited his own thinking. The harmonies of the world he was seeking accorded well with the idea of the unmoved mover as a starting place, and Leonardo experienced a rare sense of euphoria in hailing it: "How admirable Thy justice, O Thou First Mover! Thou has not willed that any power should lack the processes or qualities necessary for its results."[13] At the same time, Aristotle offered a view of life in which no higher power needed to—or even could—intervene in the harmonies of nature. Once created, the cosmos developed according to its own laws.

Mountains arise from the oceans, and streams wash their rocks back into the sea. Rivers reroute their beds and hollow out the subsoil; mountains collapse. Animal species die out, leaving behind only traces in rocks. New creatures appear. In this point, too, Leonardo had moved away from the biblical Creation story. According to Genesis, the world remains the way God created it; for Leonardo, however, everything is subject to constant change.

Leonardo was not out to refute (or to substantiate) Church doctrine. He regarded his research task as providing solutions to solvable problems, in contrast to the humanists who demanded that science be of noble rather than of practical use. Jurisprudence was loftier than medicine, they explained, because it can be derived directly from God's wisdom. Medicine, by contrast, concerned itself only with mortal, filthy creatures.[14] Philosophy and theology were considered the noblest of all scholarly pursuits in the view of this intellectual movement. For Leonardo, what mattered was not which subject was under investigation, but only whether it was assessed accurately. The sketch of a non-descript heart valve seemed to him far more valuable—assuming it was accurate—than any learned debate about the Trinity: "Falsehood is so utterly vile that though it should praise the great works of God it offends against His divinity. Truth is of such excellence that if it praises the meanest things they become ennobled."[15] Accordingly, the noblest questions are those that can be answered clearly.

Leonardo railed against all metaphysical speculation. He considered it fruitless to bother with phenomena that "the human mind is incapable of comprehending and that cannot be demonstrated by any natural instance."[16] All philosophical efforts by the ancients to grapple with questions of that kind were a waste of time: "What trust can we place in the ancients who have set out to define the nature of the soul and of life—things incapable of proof—whilst those things which by experience may always be clearly known and proved have for so many centuries either remained unknown or have been wrongly interpreted."[17]

Of course there are problems that do not lend themselves to empirical solutions, and Leonardo saw no reason to speculate about them: "The rest of the definition of the soul I leave to the wisdom of the friars, those fathers of the people who by inspiration know all mysteries." Leonardo wrote these words at the conclusion of a series of remarks about the soul of the fetus in the mother's body.[18] This remark might be seen as an ironic sideswipe at the arrogance of the clergy, but he added: "I speak not against the sacred books, for they are supreme truth." Leonardo knew that research was fundamentally incapable of finding the answers to certain questions, which remained a matter of faith. He thus drew a dividing line between science and religion and concluded that they could coexist as long as their adherents respected the boundaries that separate logic and experiment on the one side, and faith and tradition on the other. The stage was set for future conflicts, and the Church would spend centuries resisting the idea that it was no longer in sole possession of the truth.

THE SOUL OF THE FETUS

If Leonardo had followed his own principles, he would not have had to grapple with the question of the nature of the soul at all. But his curiosity was too great to leave it alone. Even he had difficulty keeping apart the spheres of knowledge and faith.

A drawing housed at the Royal Library in Windsor, in ink and red chalk, shows a tiny human—who is hard to make out at first—crouched inside a capsule. Its face is concealed, its head on its knees, the backs of its hands covering the spot where we might assume its eyes to be. What would it look like if it raised its head? The creature seems so unfinished—and slippery—that we almost shudder at the sight of it. The head is little more than an orb with a tiny ear sprouting from it. Maybe it is a good thing that the front of the creature is hidden from sight.

The right arm is bent and fits right into the space between the upper body and thigh like a puzzle piece. You can almost feel how cramped it is. The little creature has its legs crossed, and holds the sole of its left foot out to the viewer. The umbilical cord is coiled under its heel.[19]

The capsule, which provides a tight fit for the fetus, has a thick three-layered shell and is opened up like the cupule of a chestnut. Huge veins branch out on the exterior, making the skin of the unborn child look even more delicate. Leonardo may well have had a fruit breaking open in mind. Three smaller sketches, containing the word "Afterbirth," show an indefinable something emerging from its spherical shell. Farther down there is a reminder to give "Marco Antonio the book about water."

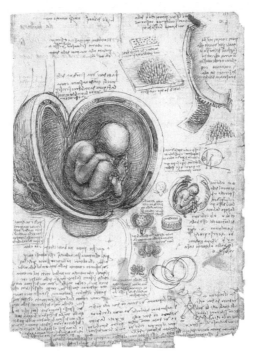

The fetus in the womb

This sheet is part of a series Leonardo drew while studying reproduction in Milan and Pavia with the anatomist Marcantonio della
Torre. In this case he did not have the cadaver of a pregnant woman
to work from, but a cow, as details of the placenta reveal. He drew a
human fetus into the womb of a cow, presumably basing the shape of
the fetus on specimens he had viewed. Thus the unborn baby and its
surroundings are more Leonardo's invention than reality. Even so, the
viewer feels oddly moved, perhaps because the artist's drawings convey,
in Martin Kemp's words, "an extraordinary sense of the wonder and
mystery of the generative process."[20]

Years later, in Rome, Leonardo pulled out the sketch of the crouching
fetus again and added extensive commentary about the symbiosis of

mother and child. He noted that the unborn child is dependent on its mother for life and food,[21] and remarked, "A single soul governs these two bodies, and the desires and fears and pains are common to this creature [and] the mother."[22] In Leonardo's view, the soul is so inextricably linked to the body that two connected bodies share a soul.

This was heresy, pure and simple. The Church held that a human is imbued with a soul at the moment of conception, and although the soul is linked to the body, it is not dependent on it, because the soul is immortal. This topic was a matter of such concern to Leo X that in his very first year as pope he issued a bull condemning the "despicable heretics" who dared to cast doubt on Church doctrine regarding the immortality of the soul.

But Leonardo had seen too much to continue believing in dogmas. In the world as he understood it, every object had its purpose. Nature did not allow for luxuries. What aim would a soul without a body serve? It would be powerless, because without a link to the sense organs it would not be able to perceive anything, and without a body it could not accomplish anything. Aristotle had already advanced this argument. "Every part is designed to unite with its whole, that it may escape from its imperfections. The soul desires to dwell in the body because without the body it can neither act nor feel," Leonardo commented.[23]

He disagreed with the Church's view that the "soul" was a nonmaterial essence in man. He thought it was more along the lines of a cerebral hub where all sensations merge and are transformed into thoughts and feelings. In this respect the soul bore some resemblance to an organ; he imagined that it was located in the ventricles, the four cavities of the brain filled with bodily fluids. Today we know that there is no such single location. What we perceive, think, and feel originates in the interaction of many brain centers with the rest of the body, and so it makes no sense to speak of a seat of personality.

Of course Leonardo's reflections on the soul were pure speculation. And he knew quite well that as a researcher he really had nothing to say on the subject. In a note that extols the amazing nature of the human body and denounces the destruction of life, he confessed his ignorance on matters pertaining to the soul: "Thou shouldst be mindful that though what is thus compounded seem to thee of marvelous subtlety, it is as nothing compared with the soul that dwells within this structure; and in truth, whatever this may be, it is a divine thing."[24]

Here Leonardo was contradicting his own notion of a disembodied soul, and was evidently quite aware of his own ambivalence. But he could not go back to the traditional Church view. Vasari was probably right in claiming that Leonardo's mind, honed by scientific inquiry, had serious doubts from early on about the "highest truth" of Church dogma. In one of the first notebooks he kept in Milan, he wrote a lengthy passage poking fun at the supposed capabilities of spirits who are unable to speak: "There can be no voice where there is no motion or percussion of the air; there can be no percussion of the air where there is no instrument; there can be no instrument without a body; this being so a spirit can have neither voice, nor form, nor force; and if it were to assume a body it could not penetrate nor enter where the doors are closed."[25] Leonardo may have had the twentieth chapter of The Gospel of John in mind, where Jesus speaks to disciples cowering in fear behind their doors.

The metaphysical question of whether death could be surmounted ought to have been of no concern to him as a researcher, but he pondered the issue of mortality. He was evidently not holding out much hope for himself. While not entirely discounting the idea that another world would await him after death, he thought it unlikely: "Every evil leaves a sorrow in the memory except the supreme evil, death, and this destroys memory itself together with life."[26]

In 1515, he joined the order of St. John of the Florentines, evidently to provide for his old age rather than as an expression of religious faith. The men in the Brotherhood of Good Death—this was the actual name of the congregation—had to pledge to take care of one another when they were ill and to arrange for a dignified burial of their deceased fellow members. For Leonardo, who had no living relatives, this arrangement made good sense. But these benefits, like a health insurance plan today, continued only as long as members stayed up-to-date on their premiums. When Leonardo repeatedly fell behind, the Brotherhood ousted him.[27]

While the body perishes, a person can triumph over death by leaving traces in the generation to come. Parents imagine that they can live on in their children, but Leonardo had no heirs. As far as we know, he was not especially interested in sex, and if he was, he seems to have been more partial to men than to women. The only remaining option in triumphing over his own mortality was his fame. And although a dead man has nothing to gain from living on in the minds of others, the prospect of doing so was enough of an incentive for Leonardo and many of his contemporaries to make good use of their time on earth: "O thou that sleepest, what is sleep? Sleep is an image of death, Oh, why not let your work be such that after death you become an image of immortality; as in life you become when sleeping like unto the hapless dead."[28]

In the Middle Ages, life was considered a mere prelude to eternity. Those who, like Leonardo, had a hard time believing in the hereafter in the new age of the Renaissance had to adopt a different perspective on how best to spend their remaining time on earth. Every day, every hour was precious. Leonardo's productivity, which seems immense to us, and his desire for utter perfection, which made him devote years to a single painting in the face of considerable opposition, also signified his rebellion against death.

Religion no longer offered him consolation. His notes include laments about war and ephemerality, as well as gloomy prophecies about creatures whose monstrosity knows no bounds and who are perpetually at war. But there is no mention of redemption, higher justice, or a future Kingdom of God—ideas that had prevailed in Europe for over a millennium. Leonardo was one of the pioneers who used his own body to put the possibility of a successful life in a secular world to the test. He did not reject Church doctrine, but it did not weigh on his mind. He felt that a thirst for knowledge was more commensurate with man than faith, freedom more desirable than humility, and he valued responsibility over obedience. He considered his attempts to shape the world into a better and more beautiful place by his own creative power more promising than hoping for life after death.

Did he believe in a reality beyond what can be perceived by the senses? Clearly he had no intention of invoking God to alter the course of his own destiny. If Leonardo recognized a higher reality, it was in the order of the cosmos rather than in his own individual life.

VISIONS OF THE END OF THE WORLD

By the end of the fifteenth century, it no longer seemed plausible, as it had in the Middle Ages, that the world had been created and then remained just as it was. People had had to cope with too many upheavals. Leonardo lived in a world of turmoil and sweeping change, of war and catastrophe. He saw in nature the same brutality he had observed in society, and commented while contemplating a fossil: "O Time, swift despoiler of created things! How many kings, how many peoples hast thou brought low! How many changes of state and circumstance have followed since the wondrous form of this fish died here in this hollow winding recess? Now, destroyed by Time, patiently it lies."[29]

Deluge (detail)

Leonardo considered water the perfect symbol of the maelstrom of time: "In rivers, the water that you touch is the last of what has passed and the first of that which comes: so with time present."[30] This element, which was so familiar to him, also dominated Leonardo's visions of an unstable world during the final years of his life. In Rome he now explored the artistic implications of a subject he had tackled years earlier as a researcher: the Deluge. All his predecessors depicted man and animal struggling to save themselves from the slowly rising floods; Leonardo's archrival, Michelangelo, portrayed the end of the world in similar terms in the Sistine Chapel. Leonardo, by contrast, no longer referred to the stories in the Bible in his old age. He painted neither a kindhearted Noah nor a vengeful God. Only a single earlier version of the ten drawings of the Flood that are housed in Windsor Castle today has any people on it—and they are tiny.[31]

Instead, Leonardo shows the pure force of the elements. On one of the most impressive sheets, a giant tidal wave is striking the earth (Plate X).[32] Its first offshoots are racing toward a range of hills in the foreground. Evidently they are bringing a wave of pressure, because the first trees are already bowing. The viewer gets the feeling that the whole landscape will have disappeared in a tenth of a second, washed away by the water and demolished. The scenery appears in an eerily pale light; Leonardo later painted over the chalk drawing with ink to add even more detail to the forces of destruction. Every wave is a deadly missile. High in the sky, clouds are brewing. Rain is beating down from them, but the rain never reaches the ground. The center of the wave of pressure between heaven and earth pushes the rain back into the clouds.

We do not learn what unleashed the catastrophe. At the spot where the turbulence seems fiercest, a cliff side collapses, and giant blocks of basalt whirl through the air. Perhaps a hollow space has caved in deep in the earth and has created an explosive shock in the atmosphere. But the collapse might be the effect rather than the cause of the disaster, because the stone blocks whirling through space do not appear to be coming from the earth. It looks as though they originated in the turbulent air itself, in a concentration of enormous energy. A viewer born in the twentieth century cannot help but think of Einstein's $E = mc^2$, a formula in which energy is converted to mass.

For all its drama, the apocalyptic drawing calls to mind Leonardo's scientific studies of hydrodynamics. The eddies in the waterfall drawing, for example, reappear in similar form in the Deluge drawing, albeit on a different scale. The lettering that extends across the clouds demonstrates that Leonardo also had his earlier studies in mind: "Take into consideration the density of the falling rain at various distances and differing degrees of darkness." Even the end of the world had to adhere strictly to the laws of nature and be drawn accordingly.

The idea that nature spun out of control, rather than divine judgment, would bring about the end of all civilization seems plausible to us in the age of climate change. But regarding Leonardo as a cautionary ecologist would mean ascribing prophetic gifts to him that he did not possess. Even though his notebooks repeatedly referred to the destruction of nature by man, his aim in sketching the end of the world was more likely to display the power of natural forces on a grand scale. This explains why humans are virtually absent from these drawings: In a truly cosmic catastrophe, these small creatures are beside the point. Leonardo was moving away from an anthropocentric worldview and looking at man as one creation of nature among many others.

He did not pass judgment on the destruction of the world; he simply portrayed it as a natural process. But he realized that he himself was subject to the same law of creation and destruction that reigned throughout the cosmos. Thus he found the answer to the question of what comes after death by recognizing that man is a part of nature. When the individual dies, his ultimate destination is a simple return to a greater whole.

> Behold now the hope and the desire of going back to one's own country or returning to primal chaos, like that of the moth to the light, of the man who with perpetual longing always looks forward with joy to each new spring and each new summer, and to the new months and the new years, deeming that the things he longs for are too slow in coming; and who does not perceive that he is longing for his own destruction. But this longing is in its quintessence, the spirit of the elements, which finding itself imprisoned within the life of the human body desires continually to return to its source. And I would have you to know that this same longing is in its quintessence inherent in nature, and that man is a type of the world.[33]

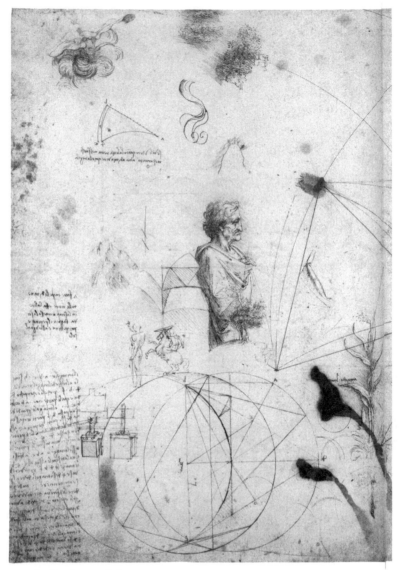

Studies of geometric figures

EPILOGUE:
The Legacy

IN THE SUMMER OF 1516, Leonardo decided to leave Italy for good. He evidently spent months wrestling with the decision whether to accept an offer from the twenty-one-year-old king of France, François I, after meeting the young monarch the previous December. Leonardo's final journey was also his longest, and since he sensed that he was unlikely ever to see his homeland again, he brought his entire oeuvre with him when he headed out over the Alps just before the onset of winter. The ever-loyal Francesco Melzi, his assistant Salai, and the servant Battista came with him.

Leonardo had apparently suffered a stroke in Rome, as we know from a visitor's remark that Leonardo's right hand was paralyzed. The artist himself complained about his maladies in letters without going into details.[1]

The next dated sign of life was a sheet with geometric studies dividing the circle, marked May 21, 1517, which was Ascension Day. A note indicates that the sketches were drawn at Amboise on the Loire,

Clos-Lucé, where Leonardo spent the final years of his life

in the little castle of Cloux, which the king had made available for the exclusive use of Leonardo and his staff.

The manor house is a few minutes downstream from the royal palace, which then served as the main residence of the rulers of France. The palace was later converted into a state prison and ultimately most of it was destroyed, but the manor house seems to have changed little since Leonardo's stay there apart from being renamed Clos-Lucé by later owners. It is the only one of Leonardo's many places of residence that still exists today. The property is on a hill overlooking the Loire, and gables and an octagonal tower top the brick and tufa construction. The battlement parapet and watchtower are reminiscent of the medieval castle that once stood on this spot.

Just inside the entranceway is a hall with a large open hearth adjacent to a tiled kitchen. Above this hall are the rooms Leonardo seems to have used as a studio and bedroom. A canopy bed decorated with elaborate carvings may be the one in which he died. A tablet on the wall bears a remark Leonardo made during the turbulent years following his first flight from Milan: "While I thought I was learning how to live, I was really learning how to die."[2] In the basement of the house, at the entrance to a 6-foot-high tunnel, the current owners have put up a cardboard figure with Leonardo's features. This underground connecting passage once led to the palace and allowed the artist and king to visit each other without being seen by others.

Evidently the ruler made ample use of this setup: "King François, being extremely taken with [Leonardo's] great *virtù*, took so much pleasure in hearing him reason that he was apart from him but a few days a year. . . . He believed there had never been another man born in the world who knew as much as Leonardo [and] that he was a very great philosopher."[3] These words were written by the Florentine sculptor Benvenuto Cellini, who was also employed at the French court and had obtained this information directly from François I. At the manor house in Cloux Leonardo finally had the freedom he had sought. His only duty was to be visible at court. The monarch assured him that he could pursue his interests wholly unconstrained by other obligations, and he paid Leonardo an annual salary of 1,000 ecus—an enormous sum of money. The governor, who received one of the top salaries, earned only 100 ecus. This money enabled Leonardo to devote himself exclusively to the matters that captured his interest.

Leonardo subscribed to the logic that "iron rusts from disuse, stagnant water loses its purity and in cold weather becomes frozen; even so does inaction sap the vigor of the mind."[4] He remained active to the very end of his life. Leonardo traveled fifty miles to the town of Romorantin, where the king was planning to have a new palace built, and furnished designs for a palace with parks, plotting out an extensive system to drain the marshes and render the tributaries of the Loire navigable. He also organized several splendid pageants for which he sketched the costumes. And his mechanical lion took the stage again on October 1, 1517.

Leonardo began sorting out his scattered notes to compile the volumes he had been planning for decades. Melzi transcribed Leonardo's notes, which were nearly impossible for any outsider to decipher, and took dictation for missing passages. The eventual result of Melzi's continued work on these notes was the *Treatise on Painting*, one of the hundreds of volumes Leonardo dreamed of publishing someday. This volume would be Leonardo's only treatise to reach publication in a thematically organized form.

On Midsummer Day, June 24, 1518, Leonardo was in his manor house, puzzling over geometry problems as he had for so much of his life. Then he evidently heard a voice—probably the voice of his housekeeper Maturine—calling him for dinner, and he wrote these words at the bottom of a page filled with triangular diagrams: "etcetera. Because the soup is getting cold."[5] It is Leonardo's last written note to have been preserved.

But it was not until April 23 of the following year that he sent for the notary to dictate his will in the presence of Melzi and other witnesses. The young Francesco would get all his books, writings, and paintings; Salai and the servant Battista were each bequeathed one-half of Leonardo's garden outside Milan. To his half brothers who lived in Florence, he left a sum of money with the treasurer of the hospital of Santa Maria Nuova, where he had once begun his research on cadavers, and he left his housekeeper Maturine a fur-trimmed coat. Leonardo also ordered three high masses and thirty low masses to be celebrated in his memory, in accordance with his status as the king's painter. For the funeral he stipulated that sixty poor men bear sixty candles and "receive money for this." And he commended his soul to God.

Leonardo da Vinci died on May 2, 1519. Melzi remained in Amboise for another year so that he and his father, Girolamo, who came in from Milan to help his son, could sort through the papers. Then he left, Leonardo's legacy in hand.

MELZI LAMENTED IN A LETTER to Leonardo's family, "nature will never have the power to create another like him." He was right in speculating that no one else would create an even remotely comparable oeuvre. But was it really nature's doing? According to the Law of Large Numbers, many similarly gifted children ought to have come into the world by now. More than twenty-five billion people have been born since Leonardo's death, and a good 6½ billion of them are alive today.[6] There should have been men and women with the talents of a Leonardo many times over—and there ought to be more than ever today.

So what was so special about Leonardo? No one can be understood completely, and most certainly not someone as multifaceted and contradictory as Leonardo. The best way of gaining insights into Leonardo is not to focus on the anecdotes and legends that others have circulated about him, but rather to study his own writings.

One sheet of his notes provides a dazzling illustration of the special quality of Leonardo's thought process. It is a large piece of paper, almost the size of a newspaper, which at first glance resembles a puzzle, with nearly two dozen sketches, adjacent to and on top of each other. No two are the same.[7] An exquisitely detailed plant grows into a geometric diagram of circular arcs. An elderly Roman gazes sternly out into the distance, his belly enmeshed with two trees, and his back to a mountain range, making him appear gigantic. Near the bottom, we can make out the axonometrics of a machine, and up top there are curlicues—or are they eddies? Light breaks through the clouds and falls on a church tower. And at the edge of the sheet are instructions in mirror writing for dying hair with nuts boiled in lye.

The sheet, sketched in 1488, shows that Leonardo must have been pondering all these subjects at the same time. The viewer marvels at Leonardo's versatility, then starts to recognize a well-ordered whole in this apparent diversity of themes. Leonardo was juggling shapes, identifying their similarities, and transforming one into another, high-lighting their unexpected connections. Things that seem randomly scribbled at first are actually well thought-out. The hatched arc segments, for example, are equal in size and facing each other. In the plant that juts into this design, nature is transformed into geometry. The curve of a leaf continues in two parallel circles and reappears in abstract crescent-shaped figures. But the little drawing of the Roman is a showpiece of Leonardo's ability to think in images rather than words. The diagram behind the Roman takes up the drapery of his toga, and the mountain chain reflects this geometry as well. And it is no coincidence that the man overlaps with the two trees. As though one could see right through the toga of the old man, the one bare tree seems to merge into the arteries of his body. Was Leonardo exploring the idea that branches and blood vessels open out in the same pattern? Clearly he envisioned the peculiar arrangement even before he began to draw. Leonardo did not even have to put pen to paper to tinker with highly complex shapes. This un-imposing sketch reveals his extraordinary visual talent. Cognitive psy-chologists now associate this aptitude with spatial thinking.[8]

Although his mastery and wealth of ideas in more than a dozen areas gave Leonardo the reputation of a universal genius, he was not universally talented. For example, he tackled mathematics for years without ever getting the hang of long division—not that failings of this kind stood in the way of his enormous productivity. Leonardo de-rived the greatest possible benefit from his extraordinary powers of imagination. A mathematician would describe the similarity between the ramifications of branches and veins using formulas and numbers. Leonardo instead compared the two patterns in an image, and devel-oped a kind of thinking that suited his talent.

The analogies he kept finding everywhere he looked not only helped him to explain the world, but also gave wing to his creative genius. His world was like a set of building blocks, which he used to make ever-new combinations. He let his thoughts roam and alight on ideas. His manuscripts explained "a way to stimulate and arouse the mind to various inventions" by staring at random patterns, such as those found on a discolored rock, and discovering new shapes.[9] Leonardo used this method to hone his creativity.

Anyone can adopt strategies of this kind, and at least some people today ought to be blessed with a gift for spatial thinking on a par with Leonardo's. Perhaps we are not aware of any such amazingly creative individuals because modern Leonardos tend to be invisible: They may be out there, but they work in highly specialized niches in a world that has been thoroughly investigated. It is incomparably more difficult now to delve into every conceivable discipline the way Leonardo did and to make a discovery that would make people sit up and take note.

But how likely is it that young people today would learn to use their talents as Leonardo did? What would become of Leonardo if he went to school today? He would have to pass the standard courses, and the teachers would educate him in a methodology based on language and mathematics. But this system is not designed for aptitudes that deviate from the norm. Leonardo's great visual talents would be of little benefit to a young Leonardo today, as must be the case for countless children with unusual abilities. They do not have much of an opportunity to employ their special gifts to learn about the world in their own way and avoid conforming to a rigid curriculum.

It was probably a good thing that Leonardo's formal schooling was limited and that he entrusted his development to an extraordinary mentor.[10] Andrea del Verrocchio had a remarkable ability to turn talented youngsters into successful artists,[11] and his wide-ranging expertise helped lay the foundation for Leonardo's achievements in a great many fields. Verrocchio was a painter, sculptor, restorer of artworks, goldsmith,

Andrea del Verrocchio

metallurgist, curator of the Medicis' collection of antiques, and mechanical engineer. When he was commissioned to fashion a large gold ball for the dome of the cathedral in Florence, he worked with Paolo dal Pozzo Toscanelli, one of the leading scientists in his city.[12] Verrocchio also used cadavers to teach his apprentices human anatomy.

The versatility of Verrocchio and his pupil Leonardo typified the era in which artists had to master not just their craft, but also a wide range of knowledge. The famous Florentine sculptor Ghiberti compiled an entire catalogue of fields that his colleagues were expected to study, from philosophy and medicine to astrology. When could the "learned artist" have found the time to paint and sculpt in Ghiberti's plan? But Leonardo had the ambition, the stamina, and the intelligence to try his hand at achieving what Ghiberti had outlined—and went well beyond it. Ghiberti thought it necessary to read widely to understand the world, but Leonardo set out to research matters for himself.

His devotion was extraordinary. He could spend decades circling in on the same problem, even if it seemed hopeless. If despite his best efforts he could not arrive at a solution, he blamed his failure on his inability to sharpen his mind sufficiently. In a fable, he compared the mind to a flint that had to "endure its martyrdom" while being struck by a steel so that it could "give birth to the marvelous element of fire."[13] Where does what Leonardo once called the "determined steeliness of will,"[14] a willingness to suffer for a self-assigned task, originate? Most renowned artists and scientists cite a mentor as having played a decisive role in their early years. The key element that a teacher communicates to a student is neither experience nor knowledge—it is enthusiasm. That is where Verrocchio excelled.

Where would the young Leonardo get an incentive of that kind today? What teacher would impress on him that effort is its own reward? In fifteenth-century Florence, being an outsider presented an opportunity. As an illegitimate child, Leonardo da Vinci had no family tradition to pin him down, and he was spurred on by a strong desire to rise above the milieu into which he was born. Would this boy, born on the margins of society today, have the opportunity and the aspiration to rise above his circumstances?

After graduating from high school, he would have to find his way in a highly regulated world. Professors, bosses, and coworkers would reward him for specializing in one field and penalize him for branching out beyond the narrow confines of this field. The intelligent Leonardo would soon learn how to solve problems easily on paths that others had paved long before him. But could he figure out how to define his own tasks, how to pose new questions, how to find answers to questions using unconventional means?

In all probability, the young man would be trained in a working method diametrically opposed to the methods of the historical Leonardo. Today we are guided by our knowledge; Leonardo was open to seeing issues with the eyes of a child even in his old age. We divide up our knowledge according to disciplines and demand logic from them; he regarded the world as a single entity and sought similarities between the most dissimilar phenomena. We try to solve problems as systematically as possible; he did so by employing creative combinations. We want answers; he posed questions. But there is nothing to stop us from learning from Leonardo's approach—not to replace the modern way of thinking, but to supplement it.

Above all, however, Leonardo demonstrated how far a person can take research that has no set goal. Driven by curiosity, he worked for the sheer pleasure of understanding the world. His very lack of objective enabled him to advance to more horizons than anyone before or since and left him free to opt for the most interesting rather than the quickest route. Leonardo da Vinci showed us what man is capable of when liberated from the constraints and apparent certainties of the world. This is his true legacy.

PLATE I: *Portrait of Lisa del Giocondo (Mona Lisa), 1503–1506 and later*

PLATE II: *Map of Imola, 1502*

PLATE III: *Baptism of Christ (together with Andrea del Verrocchio), 1476*

PLATE IV: *John the Baptist, ca. 1508*

PLATE V: *Peter Paul Rubens, Copy based on Leonardo's Battle of Anghiari*

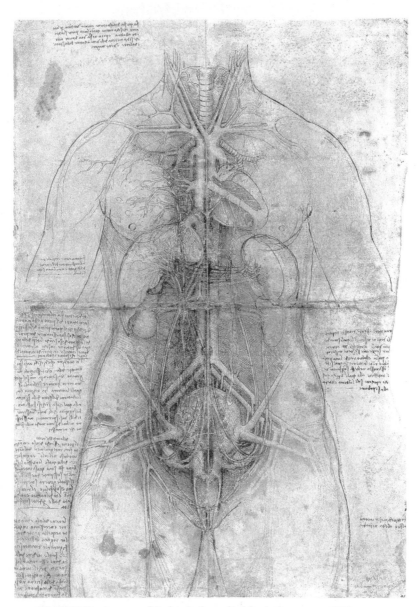

PLATE VI: *Anatomy of the female chest and abdominal organs, ca. 1508*

PLATE VII: *Virgin of the Rocks ("London version"), ca. 1495*

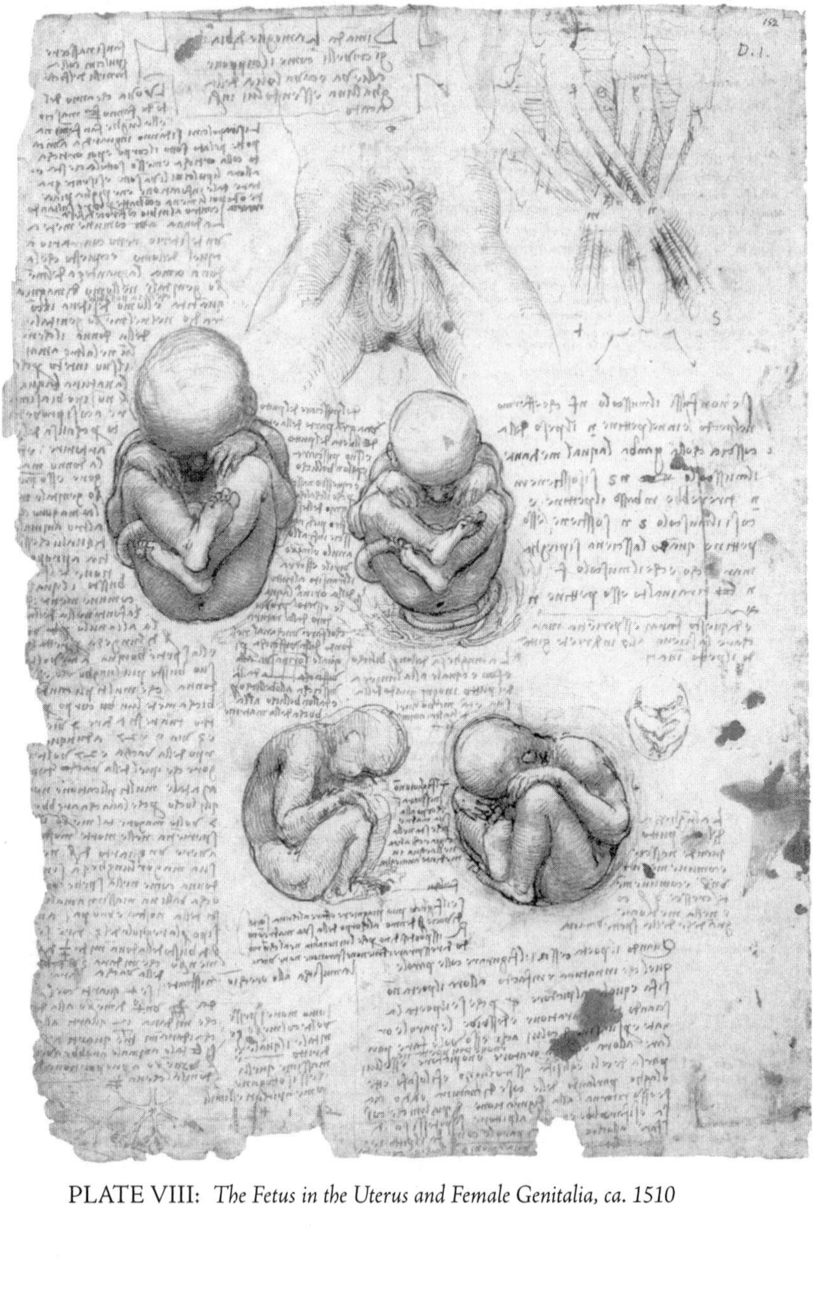

PLATE VIII: *The Fetus in the Uterus and Female Genitalia, ca. 1510*

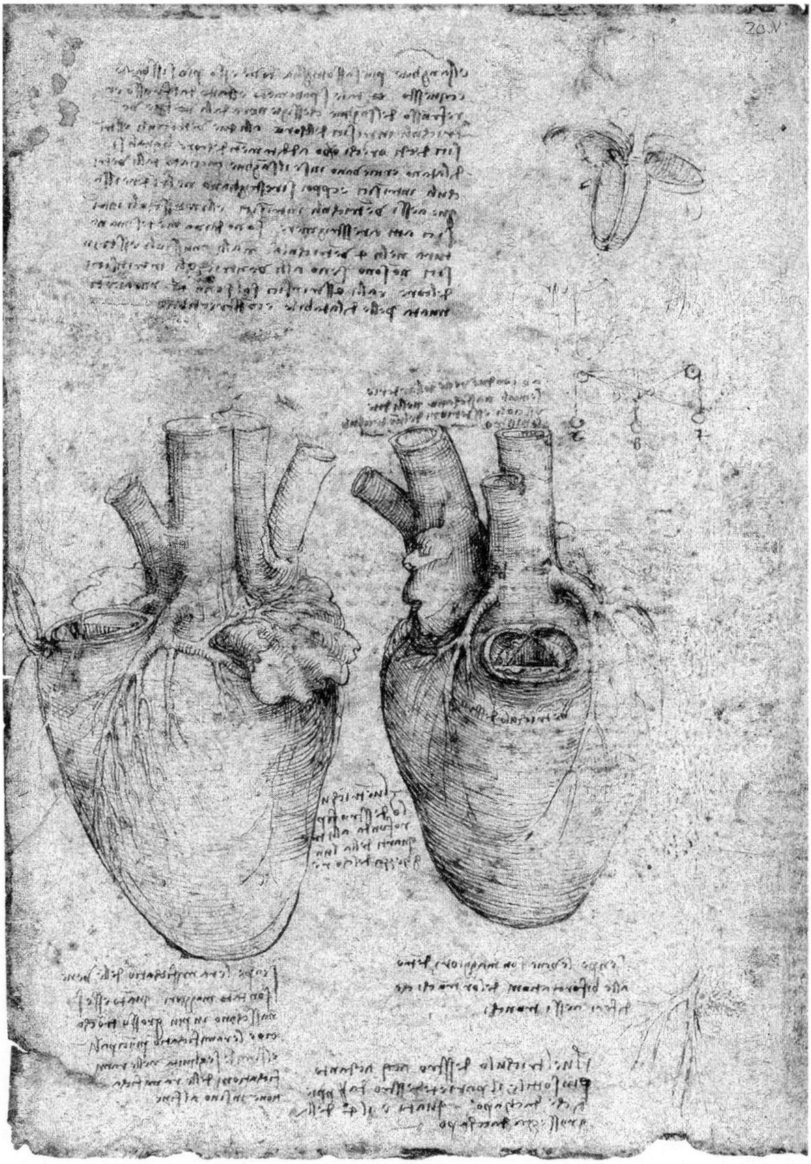

PLATE IX: *Heart and Its Blood Vessels, ca. 1513*

PLATE X: *Deluge, ca. 1515*

CHRONOLOGY

VINCI (1452 TO CA. 1482)

1452

On April 15, Leonardo is born at about 10:30 P.M. in Vinci as the illegitimate child of Ser Piero da Vinci, a notary, and Caterina, a farmer's daughter. Neither his mother nor his father attends his baptism. A few months later, Leonardo's father marries Albiera di Giovanni Amadori, the sixteen-year-old daughter of a rich notary in Florence.

Johannes Gutenberg begins printing the Bible. His printing method using movable metal letters quickly spreads throughout Europe; books become mass-produced goods.

1453

Leonardo's mother, Caterina, marries Accattabriga di Piero del Vacca, a farmer.

Sultan Mehmed II conquers Constantinople. Many intellectuals flee the Byzantine Empire, which has now collapsed, and move to Italy. They bring previously unknown manuscripts by ancient scholars to

Leonardo's birthplace

the West, which reawakens interest in the cultural achievements of antiquity.

1457

According to tax files in the town of Vinci, Leonardo lives with his grandfather Antonio.

FIRST PERIOD IN FLORENCE (CA. **1469** TO **1482**)

1469

Tax files reveal that Leonardo is living with his father in Florence. His father is employed as a notary at the chief public prosecutor's office in what is today the Palazzo del Bargello. Leonardo has probably begun his apprenticeship with Andrea del Verrocchio.

After the death of his father, Piero, Lorenzo I. de' Medici assumes a leading role in the Republic of Florence. He promotes the fine arts and philosophy. Under his rule, Florence becomes the intellectual center of Italy.

1472

Leonardo joins the painters' Guild of St. Luke.

1473

Leonardo completes his first dated pen-and-ink drawing, a view over the Arno Valley, on August 5 (*Our Lady of the Snows*). This is the first pure landscape picture in Western art. (See the section "Water Music" in chapter 2.)

The Portuguese explorer Lopes Gonçalves is the first European to cross the Equator.

1474

Leonardo paints his earliest known painting, *The Annunciation* (Florence, Uffizi Gallery). The commission originally went to Verrocchio.

The Republic of Venice enacts the world's first patent law.

Annunciation, ca. 1473–1475

1476

Leonardo works with his mentor Verrocchio on the *Baptism of Christ* (Florence, Uffizi Gallery). The kneeling angel and the landscape in the background are by Leonardo.

Leonardo is accused of sodomy. He and other pupils of Verrocchio are said to have assaulted a seventeen-year-old apprentice in a goldsmith's workshop. The complaint is dropped for lack of evidence.

After the murder of his brother, Galeazzo, the rightful heir, Ludovico Sforza, denies power to the underage Gian Galeazzo and ascends the throne of Milan himself.

1476–1478

Leonardo, who is still working in Verrocchio's workshop, paints the *Madonna of the Carnation* (Munich, Alte Pinakothek) and the *Portrait of Ginevra de' Benci* (Washington, D.C., National Gallery).

Leonardo drafts his first technical sketches, including a design for a spring-driven car (see page 130). He experiments with optical devices.

Hanging of Bernardo Di Bandino Baroncelli, 1479

1478

The municipal authorities in Florence give Leonardo his first public commission: to create an altarpiece to display in the Capelli di San Bernardo, the chapel of the Palazzo della Signoria. The work is later completed by Filippino Lippi, possibly as a result of political turmoil.

On April 26, Lorenzo de' Medici and his brother Giuliano are stabbed during a high Mass in the cathedral in Florence. Only Lorenzo survives. The assassins are associated with the so-called Pazzi Conspiracy, in which Florentine patrician families try to overthrow the Medicis. The conspirators are hanged. Leonardo draws a hanged man.

1480

Leonardo works on a painting commonly referred to as the *Madonna Benois* (St. Petersburg, Hermitage) and on two others that are never completed: *Adoration of the Magi* (Florence, Uffizi Gallery) and *St. Jerome in the Wilderness* (Vatican).

He evidently moves into his own apartment, as he is no longer mentioned in his father's tax returns.

FIRST PERIOD IN MILAN (1482 TO 1499)

1482

Leonardo arrives in Milan with his assistants Atalante Migliorotti and Tommaso Masini, known as Zoroastro. He submits a written application at the court of Ludovico Sforza.

1483

On April 25, Leonardo signs a contract to paint the *Virgin of the Rocks* (Paris, Louvre) for a high altar in the Franciscan church in Milan.

1484

Sandro Botticelli paints *The Birth of Venus.*

1485

Leonardo witnesses the plague epidemic in Milan and draws sketches for a hygienic "ideal city" (see page 43). He paints *Portrait of a Musician* (Milan, Ambrosiana), which he never completes. Ludovico Sforza commissions him to paint the birth of Christ

Portrait of a Musician, ca. 1485

for the king of Hungary, Matthias Corvinius. On March 16, Leonardo watches a total eclipse of the sun.

1486

Leon Battista Alberti's influential book about architecture is published. It includes a description of then-standard hydraulic engineering designs.

1487

Leonardo draws the grotesque heads (see page 23) and develops his first plans for flying machines. Leonardo designs a model for parts of the dome of the cathedral in Milan.

1489

Leonardo dates a study of the human skull "April 2, 1489" (see page 162). Ludovico Sforza offers him a written commission to make a colossal bronze equestrian statue.

In ca. 1489, Leonardo paints *Lady with an Ermine*, a portrait of Ludovico's mistress, Cecilia Gallerani (Krakow, Czartoryski Museum; see page 154).

1490

Leonardo organizes a "Paradise Festival" for the wedding of the dethroned Gian Galeazzo Sforza to Isabella of Aragon and designs a mechanical stage set.

He accompanies Francesco di Giorgio Martini, one of the preeminent engineers of his day, to Pavia, to redesign the dome there. He draws the first complex automatons and begins the codex on the flight of birds.

On July 22, the ten-year-old Gian Giacomo Caprotti di Oreno joins his workshop as an assistant and remains with him until Leonardo's death. Leonardo calls him Salai ("little devil"). On September 7, Salai steals a silver pen from one of Leonardo's assistants.

Prince Francisco Tasso sets up the first ongoing postal service between the Innsbruck court of the Habsburg king, Maximilian I, and his son Philipp I in the Netherlands.

1491

Leonardo organizes the spectacle for the wedding reception of Ludovico Sforza and Beatrice d'Este. Salai steals another silver pen.

The conquest of Granada by Spanish troops brings an end to seven hundred years of rule by the Moors on the Iberian Peninsula.

1492

Leonardo travels through Lombardy.

He draws the *Vitruvian Man*.

In an undated letter written in 1492, he complains to Ludovico Sforza about insufficient payment for the *Virgin of the Rocks*.

Pope Alexander VI, the father of Cesare Borgia, takes office.

In Florence, Lorenzo I de' Medici dies. His successor as the head of the city-state is his son Piero II the Unfortunate.

Columbus lands in America.

1493

Leonardo has completed the fireclay model for the casting of the equestrian statue. The model is displayed on the occasion of the wedding of Ludovico Sforza's niece Bianca Maria to Maximilian I of Habsburg, who is appointed head of the Holy Roman Empire in the same year.

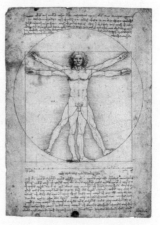

Drawing of proportions according to Vitruvivus

Leonardo begins the Codex Madrid I, an encyclopedic volume on machine parts.

The poet Bernardo Bellincioni praises Leonardo's portrait of Cecilia Gallerani in his ode *Rime* (rhymes).

Pope Alexander VI divides the Americas between Spain and Portugal.

Albrecht Dürer's self-portrait documents a new sense of artistic pride.

1494

Leonardo spends the beginning of the year in La Sforzesca, Ludovico Sforza's model farm in Lombardy.

On November 17, Ludovico sends the bronze that had been selected for Leonardo's equestrian statue to his father-in-law, Ercole d'Este, the Duke of Ferrara, to have a cannon made from it.

In September, the French troops invited by Ludovico to Italy occupy Milan. On October 22, the rightful heir to the throne, Gian Galeazzo Sforza, deprived of power by his uncle Ludovico, is murdered. Ludovico Sforza has himself crowned Duke of Lombardy.

Study for the Sforza monument,
ca. 1488–1489

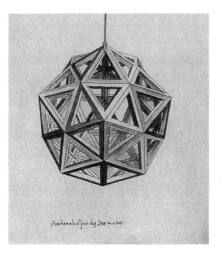

Illustration for Pacioli's De divina proportione

Piero the Unfortunate is driven from Florence; the Dominican monk and mathematician Luca Pacioli, a pupil of the painter Piero della Francesca, publishes his work *Summa de arithmetica*, which explains the principle of double-entry bookkeeping that is still used today.

1495

Leonardo travels to Florence, where he is enlisted as an adviser for the construction of the assembly room in the Palazzo Vecchio.

In this year he apparently begins work on the *Last Supper* fresco in the monastery of Santa Maria delle Grazie in Milan and paints rooms in Sforza's palace in Milan and a second version of the *Virgin of the Rocks* (London, National Gallery; Plate VII).

Charles VIII, king of France, occupies Naples on February 22. His ally Ludovico Sforza switches sides; the bloody Battle of Fornovo on July 6 ends with the French driven out of Italy.

1496

Leonardo paints a portrait of Lucrezia Crivelli, one of the other lovers of Ludovico (*La Belle Ferronnière*; Paris, Louvre).

The project to paint the rooms in the Milan palace is put on hold for the time being. The mathematician Luca Pacioli arrives at the court of the Sforzas and strikes up a friendship with Leonardo, who draws the illustrations for Pacioli's book *De divina proportione* over the next few years.

1497

Ludovico Sforza has his secretary pressure Leonardo to complete the *Last Supper* fresco.

Savonarola has books, paintings, and other "luxury items" collected in Florence and burned in a public "bonfire of the vanities" on February 7. On May 13, Savonarola is excommunicated.

Vasco da Gama rounds the Cape of Good Hope.

1498

On February 9, Leonardo and Pacioli take part in an "honorable and scientific debate" with theologians, philosophers, and physicists, under the auspices of Ludovico Sforza.

On March 17, Leonardo travels to Genoa to examine the harbor, which has been damaged by a storm.

He now works on murals in the so-called Sala delle Asse in the northeast tower of the Sforza palace.

On February 17, Savonarola again orders a painting and book burning in Florence. On May 23, he is hanged and his body burned.

The French king Charles VIII dies; his successor is Louis XII.

1499

On April 26, Ludovico Sforza gives Leonardo a vineyard near Milan.

On September 9 and 10, French troops storm the city, and on October 6, the new king, Louis XII, makes a formal entrance in Milan. Ludovico Sforza flees.

Leonardo meets the French courtier Ligny and plans to accompany him to Rome and Naples; he probably also meets Cesare Borgia.

Switzerland gains independence from the German Empire.

SECOND PERIOD IN FLORENCE (*1500* TO *1505*)

1500

Leonardo and Pacioli flee to Mantua in February. In March, Leonardo arrives in Venice. Commissioned by the city government to design a defense system against a Turkish invasion, he travels through Friuli. On April 24, Leonardo arrives in Florence. He is evidently provided rooms in Santissima Annunziata, the mother church of the Servite order, where he makes preliminary sketches for his later painting of *The Virgin and Child with St. Anne.*

*The Virgin and Child with St. Anne
and St. John the Baptist, 1499–1500*

On January 5, Ludovico Sforza reconquers Milan with the help of troops sent by the Holy Roman Empire, but he is soon repelled again by the French and on April 10 is defeated once and for all at Novara. He is captured by the French.

The Turkish fleet defeats Venice in the naval battle of Lepanto in the eastern Mediterranean.

Cesare Borgia, leader of the Vatican troops, conquers the greater part of central Italy for his father, Pope Alexander VI.

1501

At the beginning of the year, Leonardo takes a brief trip to Rome to study ancient art. Back in Florence, he continues working on the cartoon of *The Virgin and Child with St. Anne* and on the *Madonna of the Yarn-winder* (today in the private collection of the Scottish duke Buccleuch). He devotes himself to studies of geometry and mathematics.

The Signoria (municipal government) of Florence awards Michelangelo the official commission to carve a marble statue of David. Cesare Borgia becomes Duke of Romagna. Louis XII of France conquers Naples. The first slaves are sent by ship to America from Africa.

1502

Leonardo is in the service of Cesare Borgia. In April, he travels to the port of Piombino, whose ruler has been deposed by Borgia, and then returns to Florence. After the rebellion of Arezzo against Florence (June 4) he again travels to the other side of the front and on Borgia's behalf inspects Urbino, Cesena, Porto Cesenatico, Rimini, and Imola. A document dated August 18 appoints him Borgia's "architect and general engineer." Most likely in the fall he draws the map of Imola as well as plans for the reconstruction of the fortification there. Leonardo meets Niccolò Machiavelli, who serves as the Florentine envoy for the Borgia court.

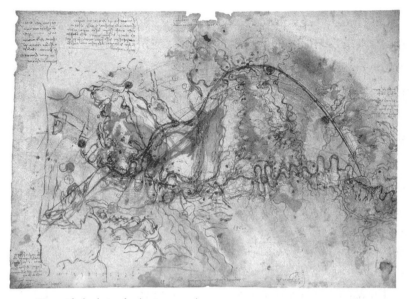

Map with the design for the Arno canal, ca. 1503–1504

Conspiracy of Borgia's officers against their commander. On New Year's Eve, 1502/03, Borgia has his adversaries arrested and murdered in Senigallia. The victims include Vitellozzo Vitelli, with whom Leonardo had a good relationship.

All Jews and unconverted Moors are expelled from Spain.

1503

Leonardo parts company with Borgia, most likely in February, and returns to Florence.

In a letter, he offers to build Sultan Bayezid II a bridge over the Bosporus.

In July, the Signoria of Florence has him draw up plans to divert the Arno River to block enemy Pisa's access to the sea. (The project is later dropped.) In October, the Signoria also commissions him to paint a colossal fresco of the *Battle of Anghiari* in the council hall (Plate V).

Leonardo begins his work on the *Mona Lisa* at about this time (Paris, Louvre; Plate I).

Pope Alexander VI dies on August 18. After just five weeks, his successor, Pius III, succumbs to complications of gout. The next pope, Julius II, dismisses Cesare Borgia from all the offices he holds, and Borgia flees to Spain.

1504

On January 25, Leonardo attends a committee meeting to decide on the best location for Michelangelo's *David*. He receives a regular salary for the preparatory work for the fresco of the *Battle of Anghiari*.

On July 9, his father, Ser Piero, dies; his will leaves nothing to Leonardo.

On November 1, he travels to Piombino, which has reverted to its previous ruler after Borgia's flight, and draws up plans to reinforce the docks.

On November 30, Leonardo notes that he has solved the problem of squaring the circle.

Naples becomes Spanish. The Inquisition begins in Spain.

The painter Raphael Santi relocates to Florence from Perugia and begins producing his *Madonna* paintings. He sees a preliminary sketch of the *Mona Lisa* in Leonardo's workshop.

The painter Matthias Grünewald begins his greatest work, the Isenheim Altarpiece, in the Vosges.

1505

On June 6, Leonardo begins his preparations to apply paint to the fresco of the *Battle of Anghiari* and recounts this inauspicious course of events: "The cartoon tore, the water spilled . . . and just then the weather turned bad, and it started to pour."

He devotes himself to the subject of the flight of birds and the development of flying devices. On Monte Ceceri, he probably conducts a test flight.

Martin Luther is nearly struck by lightning, then joins the Order of St. Augustine. Albrecht Dürer travels to Venice, where he most likely sees Leonardo's anatomical sketches.

SECOND PERIOD IN MILAN (1506 TO 1516)
1506

On April 27, a court of arbitration rules that Leonardo has to finish painting the *Virgin of the Rocks*, which is still incomplete after twenty-three years. In a contract with the Signoria, dated May 30, he agrees to return to Florence after three months in Milan to complete his work on the *Battle of Anghiari*. In August, however, Milan's French governor Charles d'Amboise negotiates with the Signoria to let Leonardo give up the project without financial penalty.

In September, Leonardo sets off to Milan, where he designs a villa and garden for Charles d'Amboise.

The construction of St. Peter's Basilica begins in Rome.

1507

Leonardo travels to Florence in March.

On June 14, he organizes a gala in Milan for Louis XII, the king of France. The French governor insists that the Florentines release Leonardo once and for all from his contract for the *Battle of Anghiari* because "he has to paint a picture for Louis XII."

In Vinci, Leonardo's uncle Francesco dies. To settle an inheritance dispute between Leonardo and his half brothers, he arrives in Florence on September 18 and presumably stays there. In the hospital of Santa Maria Nuova, he performs an autopsy of a man said to be one hundred years old.

Pope Julius II begins selling indulgences to finance St. Peter's Basilica.

Cesare Borgia is caught in an ambush during a battle in Spain and is killed.

A map of the New World signed by the Freiburg cartographer Martin Waldseemüller is the first to use the word "America."

1508

In the spring, Leonardo returns to Milan. He works on the painting *Leda and the Swan* (now lost) and evidently begins work on the paintings *The Virgin and Child with St. Anne* and *John the Baptist* (both Paris, Louvre; see page 243 and Plate IV).

Maximilian I of Habsburg accepts the title of Holy Roman Emperor and starts a war against Venice.

Ludovico Sforza dies in French captivity.

Michelangelo begins painting the Sistine Chapel.

Study for the Kneeling Leda with Swan,
ca. 1505–1510

1509

In Pavia, the twenty-seven-year-old Marcantonio della Torre is appointed professor of anatomy and begins an intensive collaboration with Leonardo.

Copernicus submits his *De hypothesibus motuum caelestium*, which presents his theory of planetary orbits and situates the sun in the center. In Venice, Luca Pacioli's *De divina proportione* is published with illustrations by Leonardo.

1510

Peter Henlein, a locksmith from Nuremberg, makes one of the first portable watches.

1511

Leonardo's patron Charles d'Amboise and the anatomist Marcantonio della Torre die. When rumors circulate that an attack by troops of the Holy League (Vatican, Habsburg, Venice, the Swiss Confederation) is imminent in Milan, Leonardo flees to the family estate of his pupil Francesco Melzi in Vaprio d'Adda and settles there for the time being. On December 10, he witnesses the fires started by Swiss soldiers in the town of Desio in Lombardy.

1512

Leonardo spends the year in Vaprio d'Adda primarily on studies of anatomy and water. In the Codex Leicester he brings together his theories of geology, cosmology, and the origins of the earth. He explains that moonlight is a reflection of solar radiation and that the radiance on the dark portions of the waxing and waning moon comes from the light the earth casts on the moon.

The origin of moonlight

Hurricane over horsemen and trees

The French are defeated in the Battle of Novara; Massimilano Sforza, Ludovico's son, takes the throne in Milan.

The Fifth Council of the Lateran affirms the immortality of the soul as Church dogma.

1513

In October, Leonardo and his pupils and employees leave Lombardy and arrive in Rome on December 1, where Leonardo moves into the Palais Belvedere in the Vatican. His patron is Giuliano II de' Medici, the brother of Leo X, the new pope.

Leonardo completes his final anatomical studies, especially his studies of the heart.

On March 8, Leo X becomes the successor of the deceased pope, Julian II.

Niccolò Machiavelli writes *The Prince*. The model for the main figure is Cesare Borgia.

A woman standing in a landscape,
ca. 1513–1516

1514

Leonardo works on the Deluge drawings and again on the *Mona Lisa*. In September, he makes a brief trip to Parma. In Civitavecchia he explores the harbor and the ancient ruins. He devises a plan to drain the Pontinian swamps south of Rome.

Albrecht Dürer produces his master engraving *Melencolia I*.

1515

Louis XII, king of France, dies on January 1.

On July 12, at a banquet in Lyons to honor his successor to the throne, François I, Leonardo's mechanical lion is presented. The lion is a gift from the Duke of Urbino, Lorenzo di Piero de' Medici.

The new king invades Italy and reconquers Milan. In November Leonardo accompanies the pope to Florence and Bologna, where he probably meets François I.

Leonardo joins the Brotherhood of Good Death. The Curia forbids him to dissect cadavers.

1516

Leonardo's patron Giuliano de' Medici dies on March 17. In August, Leonardo measures the early Christian basilica San Paolo fuori le Mura in Rome.

In the late fall, he goes to France as "painter of the king" François I. Melzi and Salai accompany him.

FRENCH PERIOD (*1517* TO *1519*)

1517

Leonardo moves into the manor house in Cloux near the royal residence in Amboise on the Loire. In his final drawings, the figures seem to merge with the light that surrounds them.

On October 1, the mechanical lion is again presented in honor of François I in Argentan.

On October 10, Cardinal Louis d'Aragon visits Leonardo. The cardinal's secretary, Antonio de Beatis, writes in his diary that he has viewed manuscripts and three paintings by Leonardo, including the *Mona Lisa*, and notes that the artist is paralyzed on the right side of his body, "apparently as the result of a stroke."

The humanist Erasmus of Rotterdam publishes his book *The Complaint of Peace*, which condemns war as an instrument of politics.

1518

At the beginning of the year, Leonardo spends time with François I at his castle in Romorantin, where he designs a new royal palace and a drainage system.

The stage set from the 1490 "Paradise Festival" in Milan is rebuilt for the wedding reception of the king's niece.

On June 24, Leonardo writes his final dated notebook entry.

Luther appears before the papal legate in Augsburg.

Adam Ries (now called Riese) publishes his first mathematics book.

1519

On April 23, Leonardo dictates his will.

Leonardo dies on May 2. On June 1, Melzi sends a letter informing Leonardo's family of his death.

Magellan sets sail for the first circumnavigation of the globe.

NOTES

INTRODUCTION

1. Jean Paul Richter, vol. 2, p. 235.
2. CA 76 r-a (ex 280 r-a); MacCurdy, p. 1067.
3. Vasari, p. 255.
4. Quoted in Goldscheider, p. 30.

CHAPTER I

1. Pater, p. 103. The versification of this text is by W. B. Yeats.
2. Vecce 1990.
3. Vecce 1998.
4. Schwartz 1995; Schwartz 1988.
5. See Sassoon.
6. Leonardo may have been inspired by Flemish painting. The subjects portrayed by Jan van Eyck (ca. 1390–1441) faced the viewer in three-quarter turns, but they lacked background landscape and the display of the subjects' hands, which are key elements of the *Mona Lisa*. It is likely that Leonardo knew the Flemish style: The art collection in the court of Mantua included paintings by Rogier van der Weyden and others, and prints were also in circulation.
7. Kemp 1981, p. 266.
8. MacCurdy, pp. 853–854.
9. TP 68 and B N 2038 20 r; see also Kemp 1971. A passage in Alberti's book about the art of painting expresses the same idea: "We painters ... wish to represent emotions through the movement of limbs," Alberti, p. 78.

10. TP 61 v.

11. The neurons first discovered in monkeys by the Italian neurophysiologist Giacomo Rizzolatti and his team in the early 1990s have a double function: First, they control the musculature of the body. Some give impulses to raise an arm, others to curl the corners of the mouth upward to form a smile, and still others produce looks of sorrow. Second, however, the mirror neurons send out the exact same signals when we merely watch *other* people raising an arm or looking happy or sad—and they prepare us to do the same. In this latter case, the movement of our own muscles is delayed for a later phase of response to signals in the brain, but the signal is retained for the corresponding emotion. Rizzolatti, Fogassi, and Gallese.

12. Zeki, pp. 2–3.

13. TP 289, TP 290.

14. B 29 r, B 38 v, B 42 v; see MacCurdy, p. 144f., p. 156f., and p. 158f.

15. See Nicholls et al.

16. See Ekman and Hager.

17. Even if we were able to keep our eye trained on a particular part of the woman's face, we would still be unable to discern the expression of the *Mona Lisa* with any certainty, because the areas around the eyes and the corners of the mouth—the areas we use to draw the key information about a person's mood—are hard to make out. Shadows over these areas make it impossible to read Mona Lisa's expression. This painting seems perfectly lifelike precisely because Leonardo deliberately kept it so unclear.

18. Kontsevich and Tyler.

19. Quoted in Zubov, p. 190.

20. CA 1002 r-1004 r (ex 360 r).

21. CA 527 v (ex 195 v).

22. Leonardo's contemporaries were aware of optical illusions, and libraries had copies of a seven-volume *Book of Optics* by Abu Ali al-Hasan Ibn al-Haitham, a vizier at the court in Cairo in the eleventh century who was known in the West as Alhazen. But apparently Leonardo was one of the very few to be taken with Alhazen's ideas. The only extensive writings on the foundations of optics in the fifteenth century of which we are aware are his. Alhazen was interested in understanding the laws of light propagation and perception; Leonardo sought to apply them to create a perfect work of art. On Leonardo's reception of Alhazen, see Arasse; Ackerman.

23. CA 207 r (ex 76 r); Irma Richter, p. 225.

24. CA 34 r-b (ex 9 v-b) 1480–1482, CA 17 v (ex 4 v-a) 1478–80, CA 5 r (ex 1 to r-a). According to Keele, these sketches date from the years 1480–1482.

25. A 8 v (1492); Veltman, p. 91f.

26. Leic 10 v.

27. Leonardo invented neither color perspective (distant objects appear bluish) nor aerial perspective (these objects appear blurry), but he was the first to understand the reasons for these phenomena and apply them to his artworks with unparalleled virtuosity.

28. TP 262.

29. BN 2038 18 r.

30. RL 12604 r.

31. D 3 v.

32. F 25 v; MacCurdy, p. 280.

33. It took Leonardo quite a few missteps to make his way to a realistic notion of the act of seeing. As a young man, he embraced the ancient belief that rays of light did not strike the eye from without, but actually emanated from within the eye as it scanned its surroundings. After years of doubt, he was finally persuaded by Alhazen's argument that rays of light take a period of time to travel from the eye to the objects, but if you open your eyes under the night sky, you see the stars right away, so the light must come from outside the eye, and the eye merely registers it. On the sketch Leonardo made in 1508, the candle is the source of the rays (CA 545 r [ex 204 r]; see also Ackerman).

His contemporaries also clung to the medieval image of the lens of the eye as a mirror. From each thing we see, exactly one ray returns to the lens, and images are composed. (In this construal, all parts of the eye behind the lens serve only to pass along a fully realized image to the brain.) But Leonardo devised an ingenious experiment, which anyone can reenact at home, to prove that the matter was not quite this simple. He closed one eye, held a needle close to his face, and fixed on a point in the distance. A mirror would now show the needle, which covers up one part of the background. The eye, by contrast, sees the complete background, while the needle appears pale and hazy, nearly transparent.

Leonardo contended that there could be only one explanation. Many rays—not just a single one—strike the eye from each object. If the needle masks just a few of these rays, it makes no difference, because the remaining rays allow the background to be made out. So the lens is more than just a mirror. This is how Leonardo later came upon the idea of comparing the lens of the eye to the side of a glass bowl.

Just after making this discovery, however, he faced the next puzzle: Why don't we see things as bigger when the pupil dilates? (In his early writings, however, Leonardo uses the word *popilla* for the lens of the eye; only later does he use it in its current meaning.) Leonardo, who was now forty years old, had grasped the fact that the lens of the eye is not a mirror, but he still thought that the image somehow originated on it. If this were the case, the image would be able to occupy a larger surface when the iris constricts and opens up a greater part of the lens (F 32 v). Wouldn't the object being viewed have to appear larger as well?

It took Leonardo until 1495 to realize the true function of the pupil: "At night . . . the diameter of the pupil of the horned owl or the long-eared owl is increased to ten times what it is by day, which amounts to saying that the pupil is a hundred times as large as it is by day" (CA 704 c [ex 262 r-d]; MacCurdy, p. 222). Thus, the pupil does not regulate the size of the image, but rather the amount of light in the eye.

34. D 10 v.

35. This is why the man holding his face inside the bowl is not looking directly at the water at the base, but instead at a glass ball suspended from ropes at the edge of the bowl, in which the light rays refract yet again, making the image revert. Leonardo was

of course unable to locate an organ of this kind during his dissections of animal and human eyes, because it does not exist.

CHAPTER II

1. See Gombrich 1999.
2. Kemp 1981, p. 100.
3. CA 656 r-a (ex 240 r-c), CA 80 r (ex 28 r-b).
4. Lombardini 1872.
5. Beltrame 1987.
6. William Barclay Parsons (1976), a renowned American hydraulic engineer and historian of technology, was one of those who advanced this argument. Dozens of other sketches verify how intensely Leonardo worked on the technology of locks.
7. CA 656 r-a (ex 240 r-c).
8. Lücke, p. 610.
9. CA 127 (ex 46 v-b); Lücke, p. 610.
10. Maschat, p. 25.
11. Later in his life, Leonardo's own income depended on water, when the French ruler in Milan allowed him to sell water to farmers.
12. See Della Peruta.
13. CA 1082 r-a (ex 391 r-a); MacCurdy, p. 1153.
14. Quoted in Garin, p. 201.
15. MacCurdy, p. 779.
16. Leic 32 a; MacCurdy, p. 1051.
17. Leic 9 v. See also Vaccari, Solmi, and Panazza, p. 70.
18. Irma Richter, pp. 330–331.
19. I 71 v, 72 r.
20. CA 327 v (ex 119 v-a); Irma Richter, p. 2.
21. He pictured a temple of Venus, the goddess of love, as an idyll surrounded by water: "You should make steps on four sides by which to ascend to a plateau formed by nature on the summit of a rock; and let this rock be hollowed out, and supported with pillars in front, and pierced beneath by a great portico, wherein water should be falling into various basins of granite and porphyry and serpentine, within recesses shaped like a half-circle; and let the water in these be continually flowing over; and facing this portico towards the north let there be a lake with a small island in the center, and on this have a thick and shady wood." RL 12591 r; MacCurdy, p. 370.
22. CA 302 r (ex 108 v-b); quoted in Marinoni, p. 115.
23. Quoted in Arasse, p. 107.
24. CA 468 r (ex 171 r-a); Irma Richter, p. 47.
25. CA 417 r (ex 154 r).
26. See Oberhummer.
27. See Alberti de Mazzeri.
28. See Pedretti 2003.

29. See Büttner.

30. See Kecks, p. 297.

31. See Perrig, p. 52.

32. New studies, so-called infrared reflectography, prove that this part of the landscape is definitely by Leonardo (and not by Verrocchio). The picture was painted over in this spot. An earlier version featured a more conventional landscape. See Zöllner, p. 215; Galluzzi 2006, p. 66.

33. See Galluzzi 1996, p. 65.

34. F 62 v, MacCurdy, p. 786.

35. I 73 r, MacCurdy, p. 788.

36. One of Leonardo's predecessors was Roger Bacon, a thirteenth-century British Franciscan monk who experimented with the refraction of light and the production of gunpowder. Paolo dal Pozzo Toscanelli, an Italian doctor and mathematician who had also predicted the possibility of a sea route to India, succeeded in determining that the obliquity of the ecliptic was 23°30'. ("Ecliptic" refers to the angle between the plane of the earth's equator and the plane in which the earth orbits the sun. The obliquity of the ecliptic is responsible for the change of seasons.) He was only 14 angular minutes off the correct value. Toscanelli accomplished this with an astronomical instrument that he had attached to the dome of the cathedral in Florence. But these men were exceptional figures. (For an overview, see Walzer.)

37. See Clagett, p. 13.

38. CA 160 a/160 b (ex 57 v-a/57 v-b); see also Macagno.

39. CA 812 (ex 296 v); see also Clagett, p. 13.

40. CA 407 r (ex 151 r-a).

41. F 2.

CHAPTER III

1. Vasari, p. 257.

2. Jean Paul Richter, vol. 2, p. 104.

3. MacCurdy, p. 80.

4. This sketch is preserved in the École Nationale des Beaux-Arts in Paris (Zöllner, no. 578); the statement is found in Manuscript B, and quoted in Dibner, p. 122.

5. Turin, Biblioteca Reale, Inv. 15583 r.

6. MacCurdy, p. 846.

7. BN 2037 100 r; MacCurdy, p. 806.

8. CA 158 r (ex 56 v-b), CA 518 v (ex 217 v-a), CA 979 ii (ex 353 r-c). It is unclear, however, whether the first wheel lock was developed by Leonardo or by clockmakers in Nuremberg. See Dibner, pp. 110–112.

9. CA 1070 r/1071 r (ex 387 r-a/b) and CA 498 r (ex 182 r-b) / CA 182 v-b (ex 64 v-b).

10. See Gille, p. 144.

11. VU 13 r.; MacCurdy, p. 413.

12. C 7 r; quoted in Dibner, p. 109.

13. See also Ma I 147 r. Both sheets were drawn in ca. 1490.

14. RL 12275 r.

15. See Keele, pp. 27–28.

16. TP 177; MacCurdy, p. 22.

17. Leic 22 v; MacCurdy, p. 746.

18. CA 669 r (ex 247).

19. CA 608 v (ex 224 v-b). For the interpretation of the coded note, called the Promemoria Ligny, see Vecce 1998 and the literature cited there.

20. MacCurdy, p. 1123.

21. CA 638 ii (ex CA 234 r-b); MacCurdy, p. 1154.

22. Vecce 1998.

23. Paolo Capello; quoted in Burckhardt, p. 89.

24. MacCurdy, p. 1170.

25. See Masters.

26. CA 628 e (ex 230 v-c); RL 12277.

27. Vecce 1998.

28. See Cloulas.

29. See Montanari, p. 22.

30. See Pedretti 1985.

31. Kemp 1981, p. 221.

32. CA 1 br (ex 1 r-b); see also Pinto, p. 393.

33. Kemp 1981, p. 230.

34. L 80 v.

35. These are their plan to divert the course of the Arno River, the fresco of the *Battle of Anghiari*, and the mission in Piombino.

36. It is likely that Leonardo was staying in Imola at this time. His personal contact with Borgia cannot be substantiated after October 1502, but there are no documents to confirm his stay in Florence until March 1503. See Kemp 1981.

37. Machiavelli, p. 29.

38. L 43 v; see also Marani.

39. Vasari, pp. 267–268.

40. MacCurdy, p. 1112.

41. CA 1033 v (ex 370 v-a); MacCurdy, p. 1113.

CHAPTER IV

1. See Boffito.

2. Quoted in Keele, p. 34.

3. Quoted in Vallentin, p. 368.

4. See Solmi; cited in Boffito.

5. Cardano, p. 816.

6. Galluzzi 1996.

7. Oppenheimer, p. 26.

8. Simon Magus is considered the first heretic in Christianity. The apocryphal Acts of Peter report how he rose into the air to prove his divinity. See Behringer and Ott-Koptschalijski.

9. For a good overview of the Neoplatonic Renaissance, see Kristeller.

10. CA 186 (ex 66 v-b); MacCurdy, p. 1122.

11. Burke, p. 194.

12. Luigi Tansillo (1510–1568) lived one generation after Leonardo, primarily in Naples. Quoted in Cirigliano, 383.

13. Canto XXIV, lines 49–51. In Leonardo, CA 43 v (ex 12 v-a).

14. Laurenza 2007, pp. 52–53.

15. CA 747 r (ex 276 r-b).

16. CA 201 r (ex 074 r-a).

17. CA 844 r (ex 308 r-a).

18. RL 19115 r.; MacCurdy, p. 179.

19. F 53 v.; MacCurdy, p. 472.

20. Quoted in Kemp 1981; see Manuscript K.

21. See, for example, VU 15 (14) v.

22. CA 434 r (ex 161 r-a).

23. CA 1006 v (ex 361 v-b); MacCurdy, p. 496.

24. B 74 v.

25. VU 17; MacCurdy, p. 418.

26. Ma 64 r.

27. E 23, 45, 46, CA 1098 r-b (ex 395 r-b).

28. Giacomelli, p. 181f.

29. G 8 r; MacCurdy, p. 910.

30. However, the reason is not that the air has to move more quickly above the wing because it has farther to travel. Wind tunnels reveal that this common misperception is incorrect. In reality, circulation arises when the air current under the wing stops at its back end, resulting in a self-contained eddy current around the wing profile. This current moves over the wing in the direction of flight. Its speed is added to the speed of flight, making the air over the wing flow more rapidly than the speed of flight. Underneath the wing, by contrast, the circulation flows against the direction of flight, which is why the total speed of the air is lower here.

31. CA 195 r (ex 71 r). It is not clear whether this line was written by Leonardo himself (see Pedretti 1977, p. 386), but the same page contains a melancholy remark by Leonardo about the passage of time and the futility of his efforts.

32. Vasari, p. 268.

CHAPTER V

1. Olschki 1949, pp. 308–309.

2. CA 1105 r (ex 397 r-a).

3. Gille, p. 166.

4. CA 875 r (ex 318 r).

5. Pedretti 1957.

6. Lomazzo 1973.

7. Reti, p. 135.

8. Dibner, p. 86.

9. Galluzzi 1996.

10. For II 92 v; MacCurdy, p. 803.

11. CA 812 r (ex 296 v), CA 878 v (ex 320 v), GDS 4085 A r, GDS 446 r, CA 926 r (ex 339 r a), CA 656 r (ex 347 r b).

12. See Arasse.

13. Similar though far less sophisticated entertainment machines had been displayed in the courts of Europe on occasion. The Duke of Burgundy's account books, which were recorded in the thirteenth century, make reference to a group of mechanical monkeys and a hydraulic stag. See Daston and Park, p. 95.

14. Daston and Park, esp. pp. 100–108.

15. MacCurdy, p. 854.

16. Vasari, p. 269.

17. RL 19070 v, TP 222 r.

18. CA 579 r (ex 216 v-b).

19. RL 12716 and RL 12688. See also Pedretti 1985.

20. CA 943 r (ex 343 v-a); quoted in Rosheim, pp. 124–125.

21. The fourteenth-century Burgundian court owned much simpler reproductions of hydraulic machines from the East. See Daston and Park.

22. Sarton, p. 233.

Chapter VI

1. Ar 155 r; MacCurdy, pp. 1127–1128.

2. Zubov, p. 278.

3. CA 500 (ex 182 v-c); quoted in Keele, p. 38.

4. Vasari, p. 269.

5. See Turner and the literature cited there; also see Sarton; Roberts 1990.

6. By "soul," Leonardo meant not a metaphysical entity, but an organ in which all sensory impressions converge and are assessed. See the next chapter, "Final Questions."

7. RL 19027 v, RL 19028 v; MacCurdy, p. 116.

8. Henderson 2006, p. 158.

9. Diana, p. 16.

10. MacCurdy, p. 166.

11. RL 19070 v; MacCurdy, p. 166.

12. RL 19070 v.; MacCurdy, p. 166.

13. RL 19009 r.; MacCurdy, p. 97.

14. RL 19028; MacCurdy, p. 116.

15. RL 19027 v.; MacCurdy, p. 116.

16. Leic 34 r; MacCurdy, p. 86.

17. K 49 r.; MacCurdy, p. 622.

18. Ma II, 67r.

19. This theory originated with Hippocrates and Plato.

20. See Zwijnenberg.

21. It is likely that della Torre was the one to acquaint Leonardo with Galen's original writings. Until then, Leonardo, who had never attended college and barely understood Latin, must have known about Galen's theories only from others' interpretations. Under della Torre's guidance, he was finally able to gain inspiration from the findings of this ancient anatomist unhampered by secondhand or thirdhand errors.

22. K 119 r.

23. RL 19127 r.

24. RL 19003 v and RL 19011 v.

25. RL 19071 r; MacCurdy, p. 166–167.

26. RL 12282 v.

27. F 1 r.

28. RL 19115 r; MacCurdy, p. 179.

29. RL 19001 r; MacCurdy, p. 80.

30. RL 19061 r.

31. RL 19084 r; MacCurdy 83.

32. RL 19073 r, RL 19074 v, RL 19076 v, RL 19079 v, RL 19082 r, RL 19083 r, RL 19084 r, RL 19087 r, RL 19088 r. Thematically related (though evidently written earlier) are RL 19116 r, RL 19117 v. The dating is from Kemp 2006.

33. See Kilner et al.

34. RL 19082 r.

35. RL 19076 v.

36. RL 19116–19117 v.

37. Kemp 1981, p. 294.

38. RL 19007; Zubov, p. 71.

39. RL 19070 v; MacCurdy, p. 166.

40. See Roberts 1999.

41. Heydenreich, p. 147.

CHAPTER VII

1. RL 12579.

2. CA 335 r-a; CA 141 v-b.

3. Leic 21 v.

4. Leic 31 r; Irma Richter, p. 27.

5. Leic 9 v.; MacCurdy, p. 337.

6. For a history of paleontology, see Rudwick.

7. Leic 3 r.; MacCurdy, p. 330.

8. Leic 8 v.; MacCurdy, pp. 330–331.

9. Leic 10 r; MacCurdy, p. 338. Leonardo was not claiming that the Old Testament was in error. He did not dare to pass judgment on whether an enormous flood actually occurred. He merely stated that it did not account for the fossils he found.

10. E 4 v and Leic 8 v.

11. Ar 58 v; MacCurdy, p. 345.

12. Leonardo changed his mind on this issue in the course of his life, as he did on so many others. As a young man, he still believed in a God who shaped history: "I obey thee, O Lord, first because of the love which I ought reasonably to bear thee; secondly, because thou knowest how to shorten or prolong the lives of men." (For III 29 r; Mac-Curdy, p. 80). He wrote this in the oldest extant notebook, during his first years in Milan.

13. A 24 r; MacCurdy, p. 519.

14. It is not that humanists thought of science as a purely theoretical pursuit. They certainly considered the practical implications, but they regarded it primarily as intellectual enrichment. The argumentation above is from Coluccio Salutati (1330–1406), who held the key political office of chancellor of Florence for three decades. Cited in Zubov, p. 92.

15. VU 12 r; MacCurdy, p. 87.

16. RL 19084; MacCurdy, p. 83.

17. CA 327 v (ex 119 v); MacCurdy, p. 232.

18. RL 19115 r; MacCurdy, p. 179.

19. RL 19102 r.

20. Kemp 1999, p. 263. On the back of RL 19102 v, he drew an embryo four to six weeks after conception. He distinguished the yolk ("lemon-yellow") from the "crystal clear" liquid of the amniotic fluid and the embryonic sac, known as the allantois. He also wondered why the liver is located in the center of the body of the unborn child at this stage, but later moves to the right side of the body. He was thus describing the development of the embryo in the earliest phase after conception.

On RL 19101 v, he contemplated the act of procreation at its inception: "The woman commonly has a desire quite the opposite of that of man. This is, that the woman likes the size of the genital member of the man to be as large as possible, and the man desires the opposite in the genital member of the woman, so that neither one nor the other ever attains his interest because Nature, who cannot be blamed, has so provided because of parturition." Quoted in O'Malley and Saunders, p. 480.

21. See Laurenza 2004.

22. RL 19102 r; MacCurdy, p. 173.

23. CA 166 r (ex 59 r-b); quoted in Nuland, p. 100.

24. RL 19001 r.; MacCurdy, p. 80.

25. B 4 v.; Irma Richter, p. 51.

26. H 33 v; MacCurdy, p. 71.

27. Frommel 1964.

28. CA 207 v (ex 76 v a); MacCurdy, p. 63.

29. Ar 158 r; MacCurdy, p. 1128.

30. Triv 34 v, p. 68; Irma Richter, p. 274.

31. Clark counts RL 12377 to RL 12386 as the Deluge series. RL 12376, a picture of scattered horsemen, apparently belongs just before it.

32. RL 12380 r.

33. Ar 156 v.; MacCurdy, p. 75.

EPILOGUE

1. CA 671 r (ex 247 v-b); MacCurdy, pp. 1141–1142.

2. CA 680 r (ex 252 r-a); Pedretti 1975.

3. Cellini, pp. 858–860; quoted in Turner, p. 52.

4. CA 785 b-v (ex 289 v-c); MacCurdy, p. 88.

5. The dated sheet is CA 673 r (ex 249 r-a-b). "Etcetera" is on Ar 245 r, but this quite obviously belongs with CA 673 r. The two sheets have the identical black markings, and Leonardo's handwriting, pen strokes, and triangular diagrams are unvarying. We may therefore assume that Leonardo worked on CA 673 r and Ar 245 r on the same day (Pedretti 1975).

6. These data are from the Population Reference Bureau, Washington, D.C.

7. RL 12283 r, which Carlo Pedretti has aptly called a "Theme Sheet."

8. Juggling images and shapes in the mind places high demands on the perceptive faculty. Neuropsychological research has shown that mental imagery and perception are essentially based on the same brain functions. They are almost like two sides of the same coin. Careful perception sharpens the ability to think in images, and vice versa. Experiments by Roger Shepard and Jacqueline Metzler provided the first substantiation for spatial thinking. These two cognitive psychologists showed subjects illustrations of several contraptions that looked like a cross between a Rubik's cube and an IKEA wrench. Some of these shapes were dissimilar, others were identical but in different orientations. The more twisted the shapes, the longer it took the test subjects to figure this out. Evidently the rotation in their mind's eye functioned exactly as though the subjects were actually holding the objects in their hands and watching them rotate. Since then, many experiments have confirmed an extremely close link between perception and mental imagery in other arenas. When it comes to colors, shapes, sounds, or faces, the brain uses the same regions when processing sensations as it does when indulging in flights of fancy. See Shepard and Metzler. For an extensive current overview of the connection between visual perception and visual mental imagery, see Bartolomeo and the literature cited there.

9. "If you look at any walls spotted with various stains or with a mixture of different kinds of stones . . . you will be able to see in it a resemblance to a variety of landscapes adorned with mountains, rivers, rocks, trees, plains, wide valleys and various groups of hills. You will also be able to see diverse combats and figures in quick movement, and strange expressions of faces, and outlandish costumes, and an infinite number of things which you can then reduce into separate and well-conceived forms." BN 2037 22 v;

MacCurdy, p. 873–874. My book *Alles Zufall* (All a Matter of Chance) contains a long discussion on the foundation of this method.

10. Modern longitudinal studies substantiate the importance of an early teacher-student relationship in the lives of people who have made significant contributions to their disciplines. Cognitive psychologist Benjamin Bloom made an exhaustive analysis of this issue in 1985 when interviewing the 120 top young American pianists, sculptors, mathematicians, and brain researchers. There was little in their early childhood to indicate their spectacular gifts and likelihood of future success apart from their dogged determination—and the degree of support they had from adults. Their parents were typically willing to make great sacrifices of time and money for their children's careers; sometimes they even moved to a new town so that their children could have better teachers. Strikingly often, the young people who achieved fame in their fields reported that they had a strong bond with their mentors. Great achievements thrive in a climate of emotional closeness. Bloom summarized his findings with the statement that he had sought out extraordinary *children*, but had found extraordinary *circumstances*.

In any case, great accomplishments cannot be explained solely on the basis of a high degree of giftedness. Longitudinal studies have also shown that the vast majority of the highly gifted do not demonstrate unusual achievements at any point in their lives. (See Terman; also Subotnik et al. The Marburg Giftedness Project in Germany has conducted one of Europe's largest longitudinal studies of the development of the highly gifted and of high achievers; see Rost 2000.)

By the same token, extraordinary success in life does not necessarily imply extraordinary intelligence. The majority of those who stand out in the sciences, as artists, or as chess grandmasters have above-average IQs ranging between 115 and 130 (see Dobbs; Ross), but that is not a very high bar, because 14% of the population falls in that range. In Germany alone, that adds up to more than eleven million men and women.

Surveys of the most gifted artists and scientists and of top-ranked athletes consistently show that they worked much harder to foster their talents from an early age than their less accomplished peers. They consistently take on challenges that lie beyond their current capabilities, and do not give up until they have surmounted any hurdles. Their success ultimately depends on this tenacity. No matter what the field of endeavor, people nearly always overestimate the role of talent and underestimate the extents to which training determines success. Without tireless effort, the best talents never amount to anything. (A 2006 study by Ericsson et al. offers extensive data on this subject. In Ericsson's extreme, but influential and well-founded view, the quantity and quality of practice are the sole crucial factors in determining the standard of performance that people achieve. See Ericsson and Lehman.)

11. Perugino, Lorenzo di Credi, and several others who were able to make names for themselves on the competitive Florentine market did their training in his workshop.

12. Vecce 1998.

13. CA 692 r (ex CA 257 r-b).

14. RL 12701.

BIBLIOGRAPHY

LEONARDO'S MANUSCRIPTS

A-M, BN 2037, BN 2038 Paris Manuscripts, Institut de France (Mss 2172–2185)
Facsimile edition: I manuscritti dell'Institut de France, ed. Augusto Marinoni. 12 vols.
    Florence, 1986–1990.

Ar Codex Arundel, British Museum, London (Arundel MS 263). 283 sheets in a typical
    format of 210 x 50 mm.
Facsimile edition: Il Codice Arundel, 263, ed. Carlo Pedretti and Carlo Vecce, Florence,
    1998, with a chronological rearrangement of the sheets.

CA Codex Atlanticus, Biblioteca Ambrosiana, Milan. Collection of diverse drawings
    and writings that earlier consisted of 401 large-format (645 x 435 mm) sheets com-
    piled by Pompeo Leoni in the sixteenth century and made into an edition of 12
    volumes with a total of 1,119 pages between 1962 and 1970. The marked difference
    in length came about because many pages of the old compilation had smaller pieces
    affixed to them, and these were detached in the new one. Because the old numbering
    system is still often used in the secondary literature, I have provided it alongside
    the new numbering. Thus, CA 52r (ex 191 r-a) refers to the front side (recto) of
    the new page 52, which was formerly designated as part "a" on the front side of
    Sheet 191.
Facsimile edition: Il Codice Atlantico, ed. Augusto Marinoni. 24 vols. Florence, 1973–
    1980.

For Codices Forster, Victoria & Albert Museum, London. 3 vols. with 5 diaries: Fors
1¹, 40 sheets; Fors 1², 14 sheets, 135 x 103 mm; Fors 2¹, 63 sheets; Fors 2², 96 sheets,
95 x 70 mm; Fors 3, 88 sheets, 94 x 65 mm.
Facsimile edition: I Codici Forster, ed. Augusto Marinoni. 3 vols. Florence, 1992.

GDS Gabinetto dei Disegni e delle Stampe, Uffizi, Florence.

Leic Codex Leicester, Bill Gates Collection, Seattle, 88 sheets, 94 x 65 mm. Formerly
known as Codex Hammer.
Facsimile edition: The Codex Hammer, ed. Carlo Pedretti, Florence, 1987.

Ma Codices Madrid, Biblioteca Nacional, Madrid (MSS 8936/8937). Ma I, 184 sheets,
149 x 212 mm; Ma II, 157 sheets, mostly 148 x 212 mm.
Facsimile edition: The Madrid Codices, ed. Ladislao Reti. New York, 1974.

RL Royal Library, Windsor. Collection of 655 drawings and manuscripts, designated
sheet by sheet as nos. 12275–12727 (general) and nos. 19000–19152 (anatomical).
The anatomical sheets were previously compiled in three volumes: Anatomical
mss. A (RL 19000–19017), B (RL 19018–19059), and C, which was divided into
six anatomical diaries "Quaderni di anatomia I-VI" (RL 19060–19152).
Facsimile editions: The Drawings of Leonardo da Vinci in the Collection of Her Majesty
the Queen, ed. Kenneth Clark and Carlo Pedretti. 3 vols. London: Phaidon, 1968.

TP Biblioteca Vaticana, Codex Urbinas Latinus 1270. Selection of diverse diaries and
manuscripts compiled by Francesco Melzi ca. 1530; an abridged version was published as Trattato della pittura. Paris 1651.

Triv Codex Trivulziano, Castello Sforzesca, Milan, Biblioteca Trivulziana MS N2162,
55 sheets, 195 x 135 mm.
Facsimile edition: Il codice nella Biblioteca Trivulziana, ed. A. Brizio. Florence, 1980.

VU Manuscript about the flight of birds, Biblioteca Reale, Turin, 13 sheets, 213 x 153
mm.
Facsimile edition: Il Codice sul volo degli uccelli, ed. Augusto Marinoni. Florence, 1976.

ANTHOLOGIES AND COMMENTARIES
Chastel, André, ed. *Leonardo da Vinci: Sämtliche Gemälde und die Schriften zur Malerei.*
Trans. Marianne Schneider. Munich: Schirmer-Mosel, 1990.
Lücke, Theodor, ed. *Leonardo da Vinci: Tagebücher und Aufzeichnungen.* Leipzig: List Verlag,
1952.
MacCurdy, Edward, ed. *The Notebooks of Leonardo da Vinci.* New York: George Braziller,
1958.

McMahon, A. Philip. *The Treatise on Painting by Leonardo da Vinci.* 2 vols. Princeton, NJ: Princeton University Press, 1956.

Richter, Irma A., ed. *The Notebooks of Leonardo da Vinci.* New York: Oxford University Press, 1952.

Richter, Jean Paul, ed. *The Literary Works of Leonardo da Vinci.* 2 vols. London: Oxford, 1939.

SECONDARY LITERATURE

Ackerman, James S. "Leonardo's Eye." *Journal of the Warburg and Courtauld Institutes* 41 (1978): 108–146.

Alberti, Leon Battista. *On Painting.* Trans. Cecil Grayson. London: Penguin, 1991.

Alberti de Mazzeri, Silvia. *Leonardo: Die moderne Deutung eines Universalgenies.* Munich: Heyne, 1995.

Andenna, Giancarlo, et al. *Storia d'Italia.* Vol. 6: *La Lombardia.* Turin: Einaudi, 1998.

Arasse, Daniel. *Leonardo da Vinci.* Old Saybrook, CT: William S. Konecky Associates, 1998.

Bartolomeo, Paolo. "The Relationship between Visual Perception and Visual Mental Imagery: A Reappraisal of the Neuropsychological Evidence." *Cortex* 38 (2002): 357–378.

Bauer, Joachim. *Warum ich fühle, was du fühlst: Intuitive Kommunikation und das Geheimnis der Spiegelneurone.* Hamburg: Hoffmann & Campe, 2005.

Behringer, Wolfgang, and Constance Ott-Koptschalijski. *Der Traum vom Fliegen.* Frankfurt: S. Fischer, 1991.

Beltrame, Giovanni. "Leonardo, I navigli milanesi e I disegni Windsor RL 12399 e MS H f 80 r." *Raccolta Vinciana* 22 (1987): 271–289.

Beltrami, Luca. *Documenti e memorie riguardanti la vita e le opere di Leonardo da Vinci in ordine cronologico.* Milan: Fratelli Treves, 1919.

Benivieni, Antonio. *De abditis nonnullis ac mirandis morborum et sanationum causis* [1507]. Rpt. Florence: Olschki, 1994.

Bloom, Benjamin. *Developing Talent in Young People.* New York: Ballantine, 1985.

Boffito, Giuseppe. *Il volo in Italia.* Florence: Barbera, 1921.

Brown, David Alan. *Leonardo da Vinci: Origins of a Genius.* New Haven, CT: Yale University Press, 1998.

Burckhardt, Jacob. *The Civilization of the Renaissance in Italy.* Trans. S. G. C. Middlemore. New York: Penguin, 1990.

Burke, Peter. *The Italian Renaissance: Culture and Society in Italy.* Princeton, NJ: Princeton University Press, 1999.

Büttner, Nils. *Geschichte der Landschaftsmalerei.* Munich: Hirmer, 2006.

Calvi, Gerolamo. *I manoscritti di Leonardo da Vinci.* Bologna: Zanichelli, 1925.

Capra, Fritjof. *The Science of Leonardo.* New York: Doubleday, 2007.

Cardano, Girolamo. *De subtilitate libri XXI.* Basel 1554, 1611.

Cellini, Benvenuto. *Opere*. Ed. Bruno Maier. Milan: Rizzoli, 1968.

Chastel, André. *Leonardo da Vinci: Studi e ricerche*. Turin: Einaudi, 1995.

Cirigliano, Marc A. *Melancolia Poetica*. Leicester: Troubador Publishing, 2007.

Clagett, Marshall. "Mechanics, an Excerpt from the Leonardo da Vinci Entry." In Claire Farago, ed. *Leonardo's Science and Technology*. New York: Routledge, 1999, pp. 1–20.

Clark, Kenneth. "Mona Lisa." *The Burlington Magazine* 115, no. 840 (1973): 144–151.

Cloulas, Ivan. *César Borgia: Fils du Pape, Prince et Aventurier*. Paris: Tallendier, 2005.

Daston, Lorraine, and Katharine Park. *Wonders and the Order of Nature, 1150–1750*. New York: Zone Books, 1998.

Della Peruta, Franco, ed. *Storia di Milano*. Milan: Elio Sellino, 1993.

Diana, Esther. "Società 'Corpo Morto,' Anatomia: I luoghi e I personaggi." In Enrico Ghidetti, ed. *Anatomia e storia dell'anatomia a Firenze*. Florence: Edizioni Medicea, 1996, pp. 9–41.

Dibner, Bern. "Machines and Weaponry." In Ludwig Heydenreich, Bern Dibner, and Ladislao Reti. *Leonardo the Inventor*. London: Hutchinson, 1981, pp. 72–123.

Dobbs, David. "How to Be a Genius." *New Scientist*, September 15, 2006, 40–43.

Ekman, Paul, and J. C. Hager. "The Inner and Outer Meanings of Facial Expressions." In John T. Cacioppo and Richard E. Petty, eds. *Social Psychophysiology*. New York: Guilford Press, 1983, pp. 287–306.

Ericsson, K. Anders, and A. C. Lehman. "Expert and Exceptional Performance: Evidence on Maximal Adaptations on Task Constraints." *Annual Review of Psychology* 47 (1996): 273–305.

Ericsson, K. Anders, et al., eds. *The Cambridge Handbook of Expertise and Expert Performance*. Cambridge: Cambridge University Press, 2006.

Fiocca, Alessandra, ed. *Arte e scienza delle acque nel Rinascimento*. Venice: Marsilio, 2003.

Frommel, Christoph Luitpold. "Leonardo fratello della Confraternità della Pietà dei Fiorentini a Roma." *Raccolta Vinciana* 20 (1964): 369–373.

Galluzzi, Paolo. *Renaissance Engineers*. Florence: Giunti Editore, 1996.

Galluzzi, Paolo, ed. *The Mind of Leonardo: The Universal Genius at Work*. Trans. Catherine Frost and Joan M. Reifsnyder. Florence: Giunti Editore, 2006.

Gardner, Howard. *Creating Minds*. New York: Basic Books, 1993.

Garin, Eugenio. "La cultura a Milano alla fine del Quattrocento." In Eugenio Garin, *Umanisti, artisti, scienziati. Studi sul Rinascimento italiano*. Rome: Riuniti, 1989, pp. 189–204.

Ghidetti, Enrico, and Esther Diana, eds. *La bellezza come terapia*. Florence: Edizioni Polistampa, 2005.

Giacomelli, Raffaele. *Gli scritti di Leonardo da Vinci sul volo*. Rome: Dott. G. Bardi, 1936.

Gille, Bertrand. *The Engineers of the Renaissance*. Cambridge, MA: MIT Press, 1966.

Goldscheider, Ludwig. *Leonardo da Vinci*. London: Phaidon, 1948.

Gombrich, Ernst. "Leonardo and the Magicians: Polemics and Rivalry." In Ernst Gombrich, *New Light on Old Masters. Studies in the Art of the Renaissance, no. IV*. Chicago: University of Chicago Press, 1986, pp. 61–88.

————. *The Story of Art*. Englewood Cliffs, NJ: Prentice Hall, 1998.

————. "The Form of Movement in Water and Air." In Claire Farago, ed. *Leonardo's Science and Technology*. New York: Routledge, 1999, pp. 311–344.

Grafton, Anthony. *Leon Battista Alberti: Master Builder of the Italian Renaissance*. Cambridge, MA: Harvard University Press, 2002.

Henderson, John. *The Renaissance Hospital*. New Haven, CT: Yale University Press, 2006.

Henderson, John, and K. P. Park. "'The First Hospital Among Christians': The Ospedale di Santa Maria Nuova in Early Sixteenth-Century Florence." *Medical History* 35 (1991): 164–188.

Heydenreich, Ludwig. *Leonardo da Vinci*. New York: Macmillan, 1954.

Howe, Michael, et al. "Innate Talents: Reality or Myth?" *Behavioral and Brain Sciences* 21 (1998): 399–442.

Kecks, Ronald. "Naturstudium und ikonographische Bildtradition." In Wolfram Prinz and Andreas Beyer, eds. *Die Kunst und das Studium der Natur vom 14 zum 16. Jahrhundert*. Weinheim: Wiley-VCH, 1987, pp. 289–305.

Keele, Kenneth David. *Leonardo da Vinci. Elements of the Science of Man*. New York: Academic Press, 1983.

Kemp, Martin. "'Il Concerto dell'Anima' in Leonardo's Early Skull Studies." *Journal of the Warburg and Courtauld Institutes* 34 (1971): 115–134.

————. *Leonardo da Vinci: The Marvellous Works of Nature and Man*. London: Oxford University Press, 1981.

————. "Dissection and Divinity in Leonardo's Late Anatomies." In Claire Farago, ed. *Leonardo's Science and Technology*. New York: Routledge, 1999, pp. 230–264.

————. *Leonardo da Vinci: Experience, Experiment, and Design*. Princeton, NJ: Princeton University Press, 2006.

Kilner, Philip J., et al. "Asymmetric Redirection of Flow Through the Heart." *Nature* 404 (2000): 759–761.

Klein, Stefan. *Alles Zufall*. Reinbek: Rowohlt, 2004.

————. *The Science of Happiness*. Trans. Stephen Lehmann. New York: Da Capo Press, 2006.

Kontsevich, Leonid L., and Christopher W. Tyler. "What Makes Mona Lisa Smile?" *Vision Research* 44 (2004): 1493–1498.

Kristeller, Paul. *Renaissance Concepts of Man and Other Essays*. New York: Harper & Row, 1972.

Laurenza, Domenico. *Künstler, Forscher, Ingenieur: Leonardo da Vinci*. Heidelberg: Spektrum der Wissenschaft Biografie, 2000.

————. *Leonardo nella Roma di Leone X*. XLIII Lettura Vinciana. Florence: Giunti Editore, 2004.

————. *Leonardo on Flight*. Baltimore: The Johns Hopkins University Press, 2007.

Lomazzo, Gian Paolo. *Idea del tempio della pittura*. Milan: P. G. Ponzio, 1590.

————. *Scritte sulle arti*. Ed. R. P. Ciardi. Florence: Marchi & Bertolli, 1973.

Lombardini, Elia. *Dell'origine e del progresso della scienza idraulica*. Milan: Saldini, 1872.

Losano, Mario G. *Automi d'Oriente*. Milan: Medusa Edizioni, 2003.

Lüdecke, Heinz. *Leonardo da Vinci im Spiegel seiner Zeit*. Berlin: Rütten & Loening, 1952.

Luporini, Cesare. *La mente di Leonardo*. Florence: Le Lettere, 1953.

Lykken, David. "The Genetics of Genius." In Andrew Steptoe, ed. *Genius and the Mind: Studies of Creativity and Temperament in the Historical Record*. New York: Oxford University Press, 1998, pp.15–37.

Macagno, Emmanuel. "Lagrangian and Eulerian Descriptions in the Flow Studies of Leonardo da Vinci." *Raccoalta Vinciana* 24 (1992): 251–276.

Machiavelli, Niccolò. *The Essential Writings of Machiavelli*. Ed. and trans. Peter Constantine. New York: Modern Library, 2007.

Marani, Pietro. *L'architettura fortificata negli studi di Leonardo da Vinci*. Florence: Olschki, 1984.

Marinoni, Augusto. "Leonardo's Writings." In Carlo Zammattio, Augusto Marinoni, and Anna Maria Brazio, *Leonardo the Scientist*. London: Hutchinson, 1981, pp. 68–123.

Marx, Karl Friedrich Heinrich. "Über Marc'Antonio della Torre und Leonardo da Vinci: Die Begründer der bildlichen Anatomie." *Abhandlungen der K. Gesellschaft der Wissenschaften zu Göttingen* 4 (1847): 131–148.

Maschat, Herbert. *Leonardo da Vinci und die Technik der Renaissance*. Munich: Profil, 1989.

Masters, Roger D. *Machiavelli, Leonardo, and the Science of Power*. South Bend, IN: University of Notre Dame Press, 1996.

Mazenta, Ambrogio. *Le memories su Leonardo da Vinci*. Rpt. with illustrations by Don Luigi Gramatica. Milan: Alfieri & Lacroix, 1919.

Montanari, Massimo. *La storia di Imola dai primi insediamenti all'ancien régime*. Imola: La Mandragora Editrice, 2000.

Nicholls, Michael, et al. "Detecting Hemifacial Asymmetries in Emotional Expression with Three-Dimensional Computerized Image Analysis." *Proceedings of the Royal Society*, London, B 271 (2004): 663–668.

Nuland, Sherwin. *Leonardo da Vinci*. New York: Penguin, 2000.

Oberhummer, Eugen. "Leonardo da Vinci and the Art of the Renaissance in Its Relations to Geography." *The Geographical Journal* 33, no. 5 (May 1909): 540–569.

Olschki, Leonardo. *Geschichte der neusprachlichen wissenschaftlichen Literatur*. 3 vols. Heidelberg: Carl Winter, 1919–1927.

———. *The Genius of Italy*. New York: Oxford University Press, 1949.

O'Malley, Charles D., and J. B. de C. M. Saunders. *Leonardo da Vinci on the Human Body: The Anatomical, Physiological, and Embryological Drawings of Leonardo da Vinci*. New York: H. Schuman, 1952.

Oppenheimer, Paul. *Till Eulenspiegel: His Adventures*. Oxford: Routledge, 2001.

Pacioli, Luca. *De divina proportione*. Venice, 1509.

Panksepp, Jaak. *Affective Neuroscience. The Foundations of Human and Animal Emotions*. New York: Oxford University Press, 1998.

Park, Katharine. *Doctors and Medicine in Early Renaissance Florence*. Princeton, NJ: Princeton University Press, 1985.

Park, Katharine, and Lorraine Daston, eds. *The Cambridge History of Science*. Vol. 3: *Early Modern Science*. New York: Cambridge University Press, 2006.

Parsons, William Barclay. *Engineers and Engineering in the Renaissance*. Cambridge, MA: MIT Press, 1976.

Pater, Walter. "Leonardo da Vinci." In Walter Pater, *The Renaissance: Studies in Art and Literature*. Ed. Donald L. Hill. Berkeley: University of California Press, 1980, pp. 77–101.

Pedretti, Carlo. "Il codice di Benvenuto di Lorenzo della Golpaja." In *Studi vinciani: documenti, analisi e inediti leonardeschi*. Geneva: E Droz, 1957, pp. 23–33.

———. *Eccetera: perché la minestra si fredda*. Florence: Biblioteca Leonardiana, 1975.

———. *The Literary Works of Leonardo Da Vinci, Compiled and Edited from the Original Manuscripts by Jean Paul Richter: Commentary by Carlo Pedretti*. 2 vols. Oxford: Phaidon, 1977.

———. *Leonardo, Architect*. Trans. Sue Brill. New York: Rizzoli, 1985.

Pedretti, Carlo, ed. *Leonardo, Machiavelli, Cesare Borgia: arte storia e scienza in Romagna*. Rome: De Luca editori d'arte, 2003.

Perrig, Alexander. "Die theoretischen Landschaftsformen in der italienischen Malerei des 14. und 15. Jahrhunderts." In Wolfram Prinz and Andreas Beyer, eds. *Die Kunst und das Studium der Natur vom 14 zum 16. Jahrhundert*. Weinheim: Wiley-VCH, 1987, pp. 41–53.

Pidcock, M. "The Hang Glider." *Achademia Leonardi Vinci* 6 (1994): 222–225.

Pinto, John A. "Origins and Development of the Ichnographic City Plan." In Claire Farago, ed. *Leonardo's Science and Technology*. New York: Routledge, 1999, pp. 387–394.

Reti, Ladislao. "The Engineer." In Ludwig Heydenreich, Bern Dibner, and Ladislao Reti. *Leonardo the Inventor*. London: Hutchinson, 1981, pp. 124–185.

Rizzolatti, Giacomo, Leonardo Fogassi, and Vittorio Gallese. "Mirrors in the Mind." *Scientific American* 295, no. 5 (November 2006): 30–37.

Roberts, Jane. "The Early History of the Collecting of Drawings by Leonardo da Vinci." In Claire Farago, *An Overview of Leonardo's Career and Projects Until c. 1500*. New York: Taylor & Francis, 1999.

———. "An Introduction to Leonardo's Anatomical Drawings." In Frances Ames-Lewis, ed. *Nine Lectures on Leonardo da Vinci*. London: Birkbeck College, 1990.

Rosheim, Mark. *Leonardo's Lost Robots*. Berlin: Springer, 2006.

Ross, Philip E. "The Expert Mind." *Scientific American* 295, no. 2 (August 2006): 64–71.

Rost, Detlef, ed. *Hochbegabte und hochleistende Jugendliche: Neue Ergebnisse aus dem Marburger Hochbegabtenprojekt*. Münster: Waxmann, 2000.

Rudwick, Martin. *The Meaning of Fossils: Episodes in the History of Palaeontology*. Chicago: University of Chicago Press, 1972.

Sarton, George. *Six Wings: Men of Science in the Renaissance*. Bloomington: Indiana University Press, 1957.

Sassoon, Donald. *Mona Lisa: The History of the World's Most Famous Painting*. London: Harper Collins, 2001.

Schneider, Marianne. *Leonardo da Vinci. Eine Biografie in Zeugnissen, Selbstzeugnissen, Dokumenten und Bildern.* Munich: Schirmer/Mosel, 2002.

Schwartz, Lillian F. "The Mona Lisa Identification: Evidence from a Computer Analysis." *The Visual Computer* 4 (1988): 40–48.

———. "The Art Historian's Computer." *Scientific American* 293, no. 3 (April 1995): 80–85.

Shepard, Roger, and Jacqueline Metzler. "Mental Rotation of Three-Dimensional Objects." *Science* 171 (Feb. 17, 1971): 701–703.

Starnazzi, Carlo. *Leonardo: Water and Lands.* Florence: Grantour, 2002.

———. *Leonardo cartografo.* Florence: IGM, 2003.

Subotnik, Rena, et al. *Genius Revisited: High IQ Children Grown Up.* New York: Ablex Publishing, 1993.

Terman, Lewis, and Melita Oden. *The Gifted Group at Mid-Life: 35 Years' Follow-Up of the Superior Child.* Stanford, CA: Stanford University Press, 1959.

Turner, A. Richard. *Inventing Leonardo.* Berkeley: University of California Press, 1992.

Vaccari, Pietro, Edmondo Solmi, and Gaetano Panazza. *Leonardo da Vinci e Pavia.* Pavia: top. Ticinese di C. Busca, 1952.

Vallentin, Antonina. *Leonardo da Vinci: The Tragic Pursuit of Perfection.* Trans. E. W. Dickes. New York: Viking, 1938.

Vasari, Giorgio. *The Lives of the Artists.* Trans. George Bull. New York: Penguin, 1965.

Vecce, Carlo. "La Guarlanda." *Achademia Leonardi Vinci* 3 (1990): 51–72.

———. *Leonardo da Vinci.* Rome: Salerno Editrice, 1998.

Veltman, Kim. *Linear Perspective and the Visual Dimensions of Science and Art.* Munich: Deutscher Kunstverlag, 1986.

Walzer, W. "Kunst und Wissenschaft komplementär." In Wolfram Prinz and Andreas Beyer, eds. *Die Kunst und das Studium der Natur vom 14 zum 16. Jahrhundert.* Weinheim: Wiley-VCH, 1987, pp. 197–219.

Zeki, Semir. *Inner Vision: An Exploration of Art and the Brain.* New York: Oxford University Press, 2000.

Zöllner, Frank. *Leonardo da Vinci: The Complete Paintings and Drawings.* Cologne: Taschen, 2003.

Zubov, V. P. *Leonardo da Vinci.* Cambridge, MA: Harvard University Press, 1968.

Zwijnenberg, R. "Poren im Septum—Leonardo und die Anatomie." In Frank Fehrenbach, ed. *Leonardo da Vinci: Natur im Übergang.* Munich: Fink, 2002, pp. 57–80.

LIST OF ILLUSTRATIONS

ILLUSTRATIONS PLATES

ACKNOWLEDGMENTS

Several of the people who know Leonardo's work best generously allowed me to pick their brains while I was writing this book: Fabio Frosini, Paolo Galluzzi, Claudio Giorgione, Morteza Gharib, Martin Kemp, Pietro Marani, Carlo Pedretti, Mark Rosheim, and Francis Wells. This book would not have been possible without their extensive research and without their patience in answering my questions.

I owe an equal debt of gratitude to the people who familiarized me with the settings where Leonardo worked. Luisella Cerri guided me through the Mill of Mora Bassa, Giuseppe Petruzzo through the gorges of the Adda River, and Esther Diana through the vaults of the Ospedale Santa Maria Nuova. Steve Roberts and Judy Leden filled me in on their attempts to build and operate a flying machine using Leonardo's designs. Manfred Dietl and Andreas Winkelmann of the Charité Hospital in Berlin gave me a vivid introduction to anatomy.

I am greatly indebted to the obliging staff at the manuscript division of the Berlin State Library, the art library of the National Museums of Berlin, and the Biblioteca Leonardiana in Vinci. Giuseppe Garavaglia made available to me numerous documents in the Ente Raccolta Vinciana at the castle in Milan. Martin Clayton and Jean Cozens kindly granted me access to the private collections of Queen Elizabeth in Windsor Castle. My thanks go to all of them.

The historian Jörg Deventer gave me valuable pointers on the social history of the early modern age and went to the effort of checking through the entire manuscript to ensure its historical accuracy. Any remaining errors in the text are of course mine.

Monika Klein provided invaluable help with the source material. I would like to thank Ingrid and Felix Klein for their hospitality in Milan on several occasions.

Franz Stefan Bauer, Thomas de Padova, Volker Foertsch, and Florian Glässing (who also did an outstanding job in placing the book abroad) read earlier versions of the manuscript, and their thoughtful comments helped me improve the text. Hermann Hülsenberg guided my selection of the artwork.

I have had the pleasure and privilege of working with S. Fischer Verlag in the past, and this new project was equally delightful. I would like to thank everyone who transformed my words into a book, in particular my very dedicated editor, Peter Sillem; Katrin Bury, whose resourceful detective work brought together the book's set of illustrations; and, last but not least, Heidi Borhau, who devoted great energy to the book's publicity. Matthias Landwehr was, as always, the best agent there is.

I am deeply grateful to Shelley Frisch. Once again, it was a pleasure to work with her on this book, and once again, her flair for language and scholarly attention to detail so magnificently transformed my words into an English-language book that I cannot imagine how any author could wish for a better translator.

I am at a loss for words to convey my thanks to my beloved wife, Alexandra Rigos. Her unerring instinct for what makes a book good vastly improves my texts, in ways too numerous to mention. The neuroscientist Antonio Damasio once called his wife a "colleague, worst critic, best critic, and day-to-day source of inspiration and reason." I could not have put it better.

INDEX